Between Public and Private

D0958695

The Educational Innovations Series

The *Educational Innovations* series explores a wide range of current school reform efforts. Individual volumes examine entrepreneurial efforts and unorthodox approaches, highlighting reforms that have met with success and strategies that have attracted widespread attention. The series aims to disrupt the status quo and inject new ideas into contemporary education debates.

Series edited by Frederick M. Hess

Other books in this series:

Bringing School Reform to Scale
by Heather Zavadsky

What Next?
Edited by Mary Cullinane and Frederick M. Hess

Stretching the School Dollar
Edited by Frederick M. Hess and Eric Osberg

Between Public and Private

Politics, Governance, and the New Portfolio Models for Urban School Reform

EDITED BY
KATRINA E. BULKLEY
JEFFREY R. HENIG
HENRY LEVIN

HARVARD EDUCATION PRESS
CAMBRIDGE, MASSACHUSETTS

Copyright © 2010 by the President and Fellows of Harvard College

All rights reserved. No part of this publication may be reproduced or transmitted in any form or by any means, electronic or mechanical, including photocopy, recording, or any information storage and retrieval systems, without permission in writing from the publisher.

Library of Congress Control Number 2010931319

Paperback ISBN 978-1-934742-68-6

Library Edition ISBN 978-1-934742-69-3

Published by Harvard Education Press,
an imprint of the Harvard Education Publishing Group

Harvard Education Press
8 Story Street
Cambridge, MA 02138

Cover Design: Sarah Henderson

The typefaces used in this book are Adobe Garamond Pro and Futura.

Contents

Acknowledgments

The authors would like to acknowledge the support of the Spencer Foundation, and in particular of Paul Goren and Andrea Bueschel, which provided the funding for the conferences and the writing of the papers that led to this book. A conference to discuss the ideas that ultimately led to this volume was held in November of 2008. We appreciate the many contributions of the participants at that meeting, including: Jack Buckley, Patricia Burch, Michele Cahill, Andrea Conklin Bueschel, Joseph Daschbach, Josh Edelman, Eva Gold, Paul Hill, Meredith Honig, Steve Jubb, David Menefee-Libey, Gary Miron, Joseph Oluwole, Stephen Page, Andre Perry, Sarah Reckhow, Dorothy Shipps, Josh Thomases, Adam Tucker, and Constancia Warren.

Jeffrey R. Henig would like to thank the Institute for Advanced Study, where he served as the Roger W. Ferguson, Jr. and Annette L. Nazareth Member of the School of Social Science during the year in which he did much of the writing he contributed to the volume. Chapters 6 and 8 were prepared with support from the Ford Foundation to the Project on Governance of Choice School Districts under a grant to the National Center for the Study of Privatization in Education at Teachers College, Columbia University.

Foreword

Larry Cuban

Were a Rip Van Winkle superintendent of a large urban district to have gone to sleep in 1960 and awakened in 2010, he would have been astounded by the degree of federal and state authority over his district's curriculum, instruction, and testing. After learning of President Lyndon Johnson's signing into law the Elementary and Secondary School Act in 1965, the *Nation At Risk* report (1983), and No Child Left Behind (2002), he would have shaken his head in amazement as he slowly came to understand the profound governance changes that had occurred in the nation's decentralized system of public schools.

As a big city superintendent, our Rip Van Winkle school chief could only imagine what would occur, were he to resume his post in 2010. He would have been called a CEO; he would have had to heed state and federal mandates to test all students and then get smacked with penalties over some of his chronically low-performing schools. In short, his heretofore broad zone of decision making would have shrunk considerably.

Equally stunning to our Rip Van Winkle superintendent—he could easily master cell phones, but laptops and iPods would have taken him longer—was learning that private-sector companies, even for-profit ones, now operated some public schools in U.S. major cities. Moreover, the neighborhood school—the basic unit in his district—was fading, as new structures had arisen to let parents choose schools in other parts of the district for their sons and daughters to attend.

What our long-sleeping superintendent would have come to realize is that in the past half-century of expanding federal and state authority, business and civic leaders, cheered by the triumph of market-driven economies but worried about slow economic growth and fierce competition from Asia and Europe, had turned to public schools and universities to produce the next generation of scientists, engineers, mathematicians, and other skilled graduates. Thus, the growth of private-sector involvement in tying public schools to the economy moved in tandem with expanded federal and state authority for governing schools.

When the awakened superintendent asked why these changes had occurred, he was told that both governmental and business leaders, beginning in the late-1970s, had become deeply concerned about U.S. students doing poorly on international tests, high dropout rates among poor and minority students, and their low rates in attending college. These trends worried policy elites who saw the demographics of a changing America, slow economic growth, and the loss of a competitive edge in global markets as alarm-bell warnings that had to be heeded. So, our Rip Van Winkle superintendent came to see how these policy elites' worries over changing demographics and the economy led to the parallel growth of state and federal authority over local schools and private-sector involvement.

Astonished by these developments, our Rip Van Winkle superintendent might have reasonably asked what a superintendent who faced this altered topography of schools could do in 2010.

That is a fair question not only from a fictitious, sleepy superintendent but also from fully awake contemporary urban superintendents, civic and business leaders, and education researchers across academic disciplines. There are few answers, however, for researchers, reformers, and school leaders involved in turning around failing urban districts. That is why *Between Public and Private: Politics, Governance, and the New Portfolio Models for Urban School Reform* is an important place to begin searching for answers.

Fourteen authors (all researchers but one) document and analyze the significant governance and private-sector changes that have occurred in past decades in the United States and how they have led to current initiatives in four big city districts (New York City, Chicago, Philadelphia, and New Orleans). These four districts (and others in the wings watching) are part of an evolving reform called the portfolio management model that combines local control, parental choice of schools, and responses to expanded state and federal authority.

Urban districts experimenting with portfolios of schools—the word *portfolio* is borrowed from the corporate vocabulary of investment portfolios—include regular public schools, magnets, independent and franchised charters, and other customized choices. Often under mayoral or state control, urban superintendents provide parents with choices among schools including those under district management and ones offered by private organizations and charter management companies. Furthermore, in this model, district leaders are expected to open new schools and close those that fail to improve.

The editors and authors thoughtfully analyze portfolio management. They raise issues about the role of the district office when there are many different and autonomous schools competing for limited district resources. They inquire about the degree of autonomy available to portfolio schools and how to manage, assess, and improve these schools, while holding all of them accountable for gains in students' academic performance and, yes, while also opening new schools and closing failed ones. And they ask serious questions about the penetration of private and for-profit organizations into public schools through bundling of educational services and districts' dependency on a few corporations for these services.

The portfolio management model enters the long, flowing river of urban school reforms in the wake of a decade of standards-based reform, testing and accountability, systemic reform, and comprehensive school reform. Even earlier in the 1970s and 1980s, waves of national reforms such as competency testing, school-based management, and restructuring were offered as solutions to urban districts coping with persistent school failures. And were one to reach back to the early twentieth century, the river of reforms overflowed with ones centralizing authority in superintendents, separating schools from partisan politics, and creating progressive schools that combined academics, social services, medical attention, meals, and recreation. Here, again, a century ago, policy elites were offering urban districts different solutions to similar problems.

So the last century of urban school reform ripples with cycles of highly touted changes and piled-up debris of failed efforts that were once hailed as panaceas. The editors and chapter authors are well aware of this history and wisely avoid the hyped language of promoters.

Instead, what these researchers do is carefully analyze the model for its strengths and weaknesses from the varied perspectives of political scientists, economists, sociologists, and policy analysts. The editors know that the current generation of urban district reforms stems from policy elites' deep reverence for markets, standards-based reform, and growing differentiation in schools flowing from expanded parental choice. They acknowledge the importance of context in shaping portfolio management and how its execution varies from place to place. Moreover, they recognize that the model is evolving and not fixed in amber. As problems arise, such as the role of the district office, the politics of closing and opening schools, and monitoring external providers of schools—the editors identify these issues astutely—what becomes evident is that even the most loyal of port-folio management champions will encounter difficulties. Most important, the editors and authors recreate the market-driven and governmental con-text that accounts, in part, for the portfolio management model, while underscoring how politics renegotiates urban district reforms yet still leav-ing untouched the deep uncertainty over whether student and school out-comes will improve.

Few researchers investigating school reform can resist the lure of slip-ping in promotional language. These editors avoid that siren song. They have produced a research-driven book on an evolving reform that both academics and nonacademics would find both provocative and useful—even to a slumbering superintendent.

Larry Cuban
Professor Emeritus of Education
Stanford University

PART I

Mapping the Landscape of Portfolio Management Models

1

Introduction—
Portfolio Management Models
in Urban School Reform

Katrina E. Bulkley

In recent years, we have seen a flurry of substantial changes in large urban schools districts across the country, but the ideas behind these changes are fuzzy, the forces propelling them ill defined, and the likely consequences debated with vague abstractions rather than evidence-based arguments. Chicago, Philadelphia, New York, and New Orleans are national leaders in the movement to shift from a centralized bureaucracy that directly manages a relatively uniform set of schools toward a model in which a central office oversees a portfolio of schools offering diverse organizational and curricular themes. That portfolio includes traditional public schools, private organizations, and charter schools as service providers. Despite minimal evidence of success, at least to date, politicians from the left and the right (including presidents George W. Bush and Barack Obama) and prominent educational funders have held up these districts as models for district reform. Other cities are moving in this direction (including Washington, D.C.; Baltimore; Los Angeles; Cleveland; and Oakland). While the idea of a portfolio management model (PMM) has been around for fifteen years, such shifts are currently offered, in part, as a way to address one of the central challenges in current educational reform—improving persistently low-performing schools.[1]

In Chicago, Arne Duncan, now U.S. Secretary of Education under Barack Obama, started an initiative called "Renaissance 2010." "Ren 10" has played a role in the development of roughly a hundred new schools, including charter schools, schools operated under contract with nonprofit organizations, and empowered schools with greater autonomy than conventional district-run schools. In post-Katrina New Orleans, the schools are now run under two distinct governing authorities, and almost 60 percent of public school students attend charter schools.[2] New York City has also seen major shifts—first to greater centralization, then to a form of decentralization that includes both new schools and the shifting of responsibility for selecting school supports from the district to the individual school. And in Philadelphia, a much touted diverse provider model brought for-profit and nonprofit organizations into schools as school managers, shifting district norms for who can—and should—provide educational services.

The idea of a PMM is most closely tied to the work of Paul Hill and his colleagues, who have been among the leading advocates of portfolio management models.[3] They define a portfolio model as:

> a district that provides schools in many ways—including traditional direct operation, semi-autonomous schools created by the district, and chartering or contracting to independent parties—but holds all schools, no matter how they are run, accountable for performance. In a portfolio district, schools are not assumed to be permanent but contingent: schools in which students do not learn enough to prepare for higher education and remunerative careers are transformed or replaced. A portfolio district is built for continuous improvement via expansion and imitation of the highest-performing schools, closure and replacement of the lowest-performing, and constant search for new ideas.[4]

In theory, a strong performance-based accountability system underlies a PMM, and the schools are evaluated and, if deemed inadequate, closed or altered in significant ways. In a PMM, the role of the central of-

4

fice changes in important ways, as it moves away from directly managing schools toward a greater focus on the closing and opening of schools based on performance.[5]

The policy roots for PMMs in the cities studied for this book draw heavily on local efforts at educational reform and bring together distinct lines of reform into a centrally managed structure. For example, each reform draws on market mechanisms designed to increase competition within public education (through contracting with outside organizations to manage schools or provide services and/or increased student choice). Each emphasizes the importance of common standards and performance accountability—with the threat of closing underperforming schools or making dramatic transformation in those schools at the core of that accountability. And each focuses on individual schools as the appropriate site for differentiation, stressing the idea that schools should not be one-size-fits-all, but instead offer families and the community a variety of educational paths.

These three distinct strategies for reform—market-based reform, standards-based reform, and the differentiation of schools—originate from different theories of action and have been supported by distinct political coalitions. While other reforms have combined two or more of these distinct strategies, they have not been aimed at revamping the overall system of delivering education in a geographic area, nor have they placed the district in the role of being a strategic manager of change. This last point is important. In an era in which local districts have been excoriated as parochial and unresponsive, and in which markets, competition, and choice have been posed as alternatives to government as institutional mechanisms for pursuing public ends, the PMM puts local government and public capacity and interventionism on center stage.

This book seeks to shed light on critical questions about the PMM movement. It emerges from a pair of small conferences sponsored by the Spencer Foundation in 2008 and in 2009. The conferences brought together a group of scholars and educational practitioners in order to share information and begin to shape a conceptual and empirical framework for addressing the portfolio approach as it is unfolding in different cities. It is too early, most agreed, to declare PMM a failure or a success, but it is not premature to begin deeper reflection on what it entails, how it is shaping up, and what potential consequences should be monitored. Is it, as advocates suggest, going to remake U.S. public education (especially urban education), or is it simply another in a long series of attempts to challenge the bureaucratic, top-down structures of large, urban, central offices? Is it a coherent synthesis or a messy mélange? Will it change basic institutions and create its own sustaining forces of change, or will it, like many other "hot" reform ideas, be sanded down to fit conventional norms and expectations?

WHAT IS A PORTFOLIO MANAGEMENT MODEL?

The idea of a portfolio management model offers some broad contours for district reform, but also allows for considerable variation at the local level (the cases presented in this volume show some of the ranges of possibility). The three core elements found in a PMM are:

- The creation of new schools that operate with increased levels of autonomy (including autonomous district schools, contract schools, and charter schools), usually coupled with an emphasis on school choice that moves away from neighborhood zoned schools and toward choice as a way families can find a school suited to their children's interests and needs and a way to create more competition in the public system.

- The development or use of a clear and rigorous accountability system based on student and school academic performance.

- The closures of schools and/or end of partnerships for the management of schools when they do not meet accountability standards.[6] (See also Honig and DeArmond, chapter 7, this volume.)

What pulls these three distinct elements together and makes portfolio management reforms distinct from other reforms that draw on similar elements (such as charter schools) is the role of the district central office in strategically managing the opening and closing of schools. Thus, district leaders do not simply rely on outside organizations to identify where schools are needed and what kinds of schools to place in those locations; instead, the central office is expected to actively recruit providers for schools in areas of need or directly develop schools for these areas. Thus, the district leaders manage the supply side of the portfolio of schools so that the overall set of schools is both high in quality and serves the diverse needs of the district's children. Akin to an investment portfolio, a central office managing a portfolio of schools seeks diversification in the schools, so as not to put all its eggs into one instructional basket, and tries to add to its portfolio those investments that are producing substantial benefits and shed those that are not. (See Levin, chapter 8, this volume, for a more detailed discussion of the ways in which the metaphor of an investment portfolio does and does not help illuminate the idea of a portfolio management model.)

The idea of a PMM is still developing, and each case study in this book describes a distinct evolution of the idea. In some of these cases, district leaders did not begin their work to create a PMM, but rather took different reform pieces that were already in place (i.e., charter schools, autonomous schools, data systems) and put them together to try to build a more coherent and focused effort to improve schools. In addition to the core elements just described, there are a number of common threads in the reforms underway in cities moving in the direction of a PMM, including the expansion of school choice, the use of external providers to manage schools, increasing attention to alternative ways of providing high-quality human capital, and a focus on differentiating central office support for schools. While it shares these common elements, the portfolio approach is very much a work in progress. Different districts are—largely through trial and error but also through attempts to learn from others' experiences—feeling their way around and adjusting both the constituent elements *and* the language they use to explain what they are doing. The various contributions in this volume both underscore this point and begin to identify the forces that may lead disparate versions to coalesce or diverge. Some insights can be gleaned by considering the origins of the PMM and what has led to it emerging on the contemporary policy agenda.

Often (but not always) connected with PMM-style reforms is the expansion of school choice beyond traditional magnet programs and charter schools. Warren and Hernandez place choice at the center of the portfolio idea, arguing, "A portfolio of schools is much more than a mix of schools among which students choose. It is a strategy for creating an entire system of excellent high schools that uses managed universal choice as a central lever in a district change process."[7]

However, while these and other advocates of PMMs often draw on market logic in their rationale, PMMs move away from a heavy reliance on student choice to drive school improvement, treating underenrollment due to choice as just one among an array of indicators they may use for identifying schools to close. Gold and her colleagues argue that, in the case of Philadelphia, the primary consumer in the market for schools is the district, not the family.[8] However, choice is still an important piece of the design in many cities moving toward a PMM, as advocates argue that students and families need to be able to select schools that fit their particular needs when there is no common educational framework across schools. The city where choice is playing the most significant role is New Orleans, where charter schools (which only enroll students based on choice) dominate the educational landscape.

A second common thread involves the use of outside providers to offer services to or manage schools and, in some cases, other aspects of district operations. The involvement of outside providers is presented by advocates of PMMs as a way to more rapidly expand the supply of schools and to bring onto the local scene different ideas and practices, including some that have been field-tested in other places. The use of diverse providers has varied across the cities discussed in this volume, with Philadelphia and Chicago drawing on outside organizations primarily for whole-school management, and New York City using outside organizations both in school management and in providing school support services. In all four cities—New Orleans, New York, Philadelphia, and Chicago—outside organizations have been intimately involved in school reform efforts.[9]

A third common thread in cities engaged in PMM-style reforms is the increased attention to issues of human capital and experimentation with a variety of methods for improving the availability of high-quality educators (including both teachers and school leaders). Such human capital, including leaders who are prepared to be entrepreneurial in building new schools, is seen as essential to a system of distinct schools that does not receive as much guidance in issues of curriculum and instruction as might be found in a more conventional school system. Manifestations of this effort are found in the frequency of both national organizations that provide alternative training to teachers and schools leaders (such as Teach For America and New Leaders for New Schools), as well as homegrown efforts that are designed to prepare educators for work in a specific school system (such as the Teaching Fellows programs in New York City and Chicago).

Finally, central office staff in districts engaged in portfolio management have increasingly found it important to provide differential support to schools within the portfolio, including more support for schools that are struggling. In some of the original descriptions of districts that might be run solely on a contracting model, the role of the central office in supporting schools was limited or nonexistent; all the responsibilities for school improvement were left in the hands of the contractors.[10] However, few districts have been willing to go this far (with New Orleans closer than most). Instead, argues David Menefee-Libey (in chapter 3, this volume), the central office "must differentiate its handling of schools based on the evaluation outcomes, allowing satisfactory schools to go on doing what they are doing until the next round of evaluations, and intervening in underperforming schools."

WHY PMMS NOW?

The following section examines in greater detail the three strategies for educational change that come together in PMM reforms—market-based reforms, standards-based reform, and the differentiation of schools. Each of these has found the strong support of different constituencies over the past twenty years. What, however, has led to bringing them together to shape systemwide reform in large urban districts at this particular historical moment? The reasons are multifaceted. Separately, each draws some of its momentum from a general and long-simmering mistrust in the ability and willingness of conventional institutions of public education to make significant changes to improve educational quality. Professional educators and the systems they helped create once had broad legitimacy in the public mind as the repositories of nonpartisan expertise. This general sense of legitimacy and confidence began to erode as local districts became larger and more bureaucratized, and as teacher unions increasingly were portrayed as self-interested and highly politicized. This distrust prepared the ground for a range of proposals for sharp institutional change designed to shift decision-making responsibility away from locally elected school boards and toward a disparate range of alternative venues, including private markets, higher levels of government, and mayoral control. The conjoining of these within the portfolio model represents a growing sense of the limitations of each when pursued on its own.

The shift to mayoral control in particular is closely tied to at least the first wave of experimentation with the portfolio model. In what is not simply a response to a loss of legitimacy for large urban school districts, some cities are shifting power from elected boards to the mayor, based on the belief that having a single elected official with broad control of public schools can enable significant educational change and overall urban improvement.[11] Mayoral control appeals to business groups because the model of a chief executive officer is familiar in the corporate world and because local business organizations often enjoy better access to and working relationships with sitting mayors than they do with often fractious boards of education. Some cities have received substantial support from a number of foundations (including the Bill & Melinda Gates Foundation, the Broad Foundation, and NewSchools Venture Fund) that have given considerable funding to public education in recent years; these foundations are engaged in what Janelle Scott calls "venture philanthropy," and they focus on principles for reform that are consistent with the entrepreneurial business activity that led to their founders' success.[12] As Sarah Reckhow discusses, these foundations see cities with mayoral or state control as much more hospitable climates for significant change (see chapter 10, this volume).[13] The fact that local business interests often have established channels of access to mayors and that mayors are often more familiar than elected school boards with contracting arrangements in a variety of the policy areas they oversee may play a role.

The broader context of federal policy, especially the No Child Left Behind Act (NCLB) in 2001, has also contributed to the push toward PMMs (see Patricia Burch, chapter 9, this volume). NCLB creates formal and informal pressures on both states and districts to sharply intervene in schools that fail to make Adequate Yearly Progress (AYP). The original legislation favorably presents contracting, charter schools, and dramatic school turnarounds as the ultimate tools for responding. The Obama administration, during its first years in office, has added the leverage of competitive Race to the Top funds as additional incentive for states and districts to expand reliance on charters, contracting, and turnarounds.

While all these reasons for the interest in PMM-style reforms connect with a move away from traditional structures for delivering education, portfolio models maintain a pivotal (but largely redefined) role for the central office. Advocates of PMMs generally believe in market-based solutions, including contracting out and student choice, but there has also been a gradual recognition among some of these advocates that more consumer market-oriented strategies cannot succeed unless carefully managed.

THE POLICY ROOTS OF PMMS

In 1974, David Tyack described what he argued was the "organizational revolution" led by Progressive Era reformers that had taken place in public education, especially urban education, in the late 1800s and early 1900s.[14] This revolution replaced a focus on a strong connection between schools and communities with what educational professionals and advocates of bureaucracy believed was the "one best system" for public education. This system relied heavily on a clear hierarchy for the operation of schools, fueled by bureaucratic controls and professionally based merit.

Over the past twenty-five years, the overall discourse on educational change has been dominated by two competing schools of thought that challenge in important but distinct ways this idea of one best system in which quality is largely defined through the inputs of the educational system (i.e., hours of instruction, level of teacher training, and class size), rather than the outcomes (i.e., different measures of student learning and educational attainment). The first seeks to utilize the tools of markets as an alternative to bureaucracy as the means for delivering education that is both effective and efficient.[15] In both structure and outcome, market-oriented reforms are a sharp departure from the ideals of administrative progressives.

The second and more dominant school of thought involves ideas of systemic and standards-based reform. This approach diagnoses the problems of public education as issues of alignment among different parts of the educational system, directly addresses questions of what students should *know and be able to do,* and focuses on performance accountability based on standards-based measures of learning.[16] While these reforms rely heavily on the bureaucratic structures put into place by the progressives, the shift toward a focus on the outcomes of the educational process marks a distinct departure from the emphasis on inputs and process that some see as the legacy of the progressive reforms.

The idea of one best system for the delivery of public education also incorporated assumptions about how to deliver efficient education, and such reforms embraced the idea of a common school as a melting pot instrument, valuing large schools that could offer a variety of courses and educational tracks, and a bureaucratic structure that arguably contributed to a same-size-fits-all orientation.[17] Tough issues related to race and desegregation kept potential challenges to differentiation on the political margins, due to fears that such differentiation would lead to separatist schools (whether in their white flight or Afro-centered forms). Even other minority groups (such as handicapped or ESL students), in adopting the language of civil rights, tended to promote a model of inclusion and integration. However, as the legal and political environment has shifted, long-standing notions about disparate learning styles and also different values have resurfaced. Thus, a third trend in public education, especially in the last twenty-five years, has involved a series of efforts to differentiate schools based on theme, structure, and so on, in theory to serve better the individual needs of students. Such efforts move education away from the idea of the common school and toward schools that are distinct in theme, organization, etc. Figure 1.1 shows how these three trends in efforts for educational improvement come together in PMM reforms.

Market-Based Reforms and Privatization

The rhetoric surrounding PMM reforms often includes language connected with market-based solutions for improving educational quality, with frequent use of terms such as *contracting out* and *privatization*. Advocates of market-based reforms argue that educational bureaucracies are inherently inefficient and do not create sufficient incentives for high-quality education.[18] Instead, they propose that markets can address both efficiency and quality by shifting incentives for change. Much of the attention to market-based solutions in education has been given to efforts at creating markets for schools among families through different forms of student choice, including open enrollment (choice within the existing system of public schools) and vouchers (choice including private schools). These reforms rely

FIGURE 1.1 Strategies for educational reform

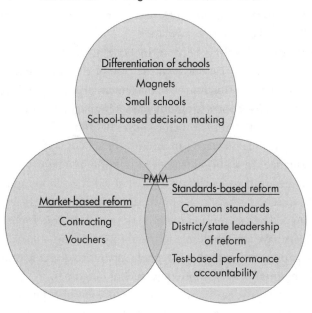

heavily on *demand* for schools to drive school improvement, assuming that low-performing schools either will find ways to improve if faced with the risk of losing students and resources or will close due to underenrollment.

In the case of school choice, the consumer in the educational marketplace is the student and family. Other reforms, however, focus on using other actors to alter the supply of education through mechanisms such as contracting with outside organizations; in these scenarios, the primary consumer is not the student or family, but the district or central governing unit.[19] Increasing attention to managing the supply side of schooling has been fueled by disillusionment with both public and private efforts that rely purely on student-choice–driven demand and a lack of confidence that, for example, parents (consumers) will leave poor-performing schools. Although PMMs often include student choice, the primary means for improvement is by directly intervening in the supply side of the market equation. Specifically, the primary use of markets is via contracts with outside organizations to manage schools or provide services; in theory, since such actors are not a part of government, they can be added and dropped from the portfolio based on their performance.

In recent years, there has been an increase in the use of private organizations to provide services close to the core of the educational process, such as districts contracting for the management of entire public schools.[20] The justifications for contracting out school management focus on both issues of educational quality and efficiency. Hill and his colleagues argue, "Contract schools create strong incentives for school staff to assess their own performance. In addition, the need to build an identity and reputation encourages staff to articulate a mission for the school and to work hard to attain school goals."[21] Rhim focuses more on the efficiency argument, stating, "The assumption underlying school contracting is that private managers have the freedom and the ability to identify slack resources or 'costless gains' and consequently enable schools to decrease or maintain costs while maintaining or improving student outcomes."[22]

While, for several decades, there has been experimentation with performance contracting for schools, the current emphasis on contracts as a means to turn around low-performing schools began in the early 1990s, when Education Alternatives Inc. (EAI) was given contracts to manage schools in Dade County, Florida; Baltimore; and Hartford; the Public Strategies Group and Alternative Public Schools received other contracts in Minnesota and Pennsylvania.[23] While these specific organizations struggled, the idea of private management of public schools came increasingly to the forefront, with Edison Schools (now called *EdisonLearning Inc.*) as the most prominent educational management organization (EMO). As of the 2008–2009 school year, an annual review of EMOs found that for-profit EMOs managed 733 schools nationwide (94 percent were charter schools).[24]

One school-focused reform that has proved to be particularly popular with policy makers from both the left and the right has been charter schools. Started in the early 1990s, charter schools are relatively autonomous schools of choice that receive a contract or charter from an authorizer (usually a public entity such as a local school board, a public university, or a state board of education).[25] This charter allows the school to operate for a specified period and (in theory) requires the school to demonstrate that it is successfully educating children in order to receive a new charter and thus continue to operate. According to the Center for Education Reform, an advocacy organization that promotes charter schools, in the 2009–2010 school year, there were more than 5,000 charter schools serving over 1.5 million students nationwide.[26] While this is a relatively small portion of the students in public schools (a little over 3 percent), charter schools serve a far more substantial portion of students in many of the districts moving toward a PMM. For example, New Orleans; Washington, D.C.; and Dayton, Ohio, have between 27 percent and 57 percent of their public school students in charter schools.[27]

Although advocates of charter schools have maintained their focus on reform, there has been a shift (especially among funders) from pushing simply for more charter schools to pushing for higher-quality charter schools. This has come in the wake of considerable evidence that, while there are individual charter schools that are consistently outperforming regular district schools (including ones that serve low-income minority students), charter schools as a whole do not appear to outperform district schools.[28] This has fueled the charter advocates' increased recognition that choice, in and of itself, doesn't ensure quality.

One common strategy for improving charter school quality is the increased use of charter management organizations (CMOs). CMOs, which advocates hope can help to scale up successful charter schools, include organizations such as KIPP (Knowledge Is Power Program), Aspire Public Schools, and Uncommon Schools, and have received considerable support from foundations including NewSchools Venture Fund, the Gates Foundation, and the Walton Family Foundation.[29] In the 2008–2009 school year, nonprofit EMOs or CMOs managed 609 schools (more than 97 percent were charter schools).[30] Either a for-profit or nonprofit EMO or CMO manages roughly one-quarter of charter schools.

Another strategy is to increase the willingness and capacity of charter authorizers to proactively intervene in order to ensure quality control. While early advocates stressed the importance of charter school autonomy and criticized states whose laws or enforcement policies cramped the opening and operation of new charters, the National Alliance for Public Charter Schools recently put special weight on "quality control" in its 2010 database that compares state charter laws to a "model law" created by the Alliance.[31] Secretary Duncan also called for an increasing focus on quality in a speech at the Alliance's conference: "The charter movement is putting itself at risk by allowing too many second-rate and third-rate schools to exist. Your goal should be quality, not quantity. Charter authorizers need to do a better job of holding schools accountable—and the charter schools need to support them—loudly and sincerely."[32]

Standards-Based Reform

Beginning with the 1983 report *A Nation At Risk*, much of the energy in large-scale change in public education has focused on raising standards and expanding accountability tied to those standards.[33] The 1980s saw attempts to further standards, especially for high schools, and state-level reforms in the late 1980s and early 1990s increasingly combined the development of state-level standards with accountability based on school and student performance on standards-based assessments.[34] This shift occurred along with incorporation of the core elements of standards-based reform (SBR) into federal policy under President Bill Clinton; federal legislation beginning with the Improving America's Schools Act (1994) and through NCLB, which reflected core elements of standards-based reform. The push for alignment of expectations for students and schools, assessments of performance, and other aspects of the educational system are at the center of SBR (sometimes referred to as systemic reform).[35]

While noting that there are important variations across sites, Hamilton and her colleagues identify a number of core elements of SBR: clear academic expectations for students (standards), including high expectations for all students regardless of background; alignment or increased coherence of key elements of the system with the standards—curriculum, instruction, assessment, materials (i.e., textbooks); use of assessments of achievement to monitor performance; decentralization to schools for curriculum and instruction decisions; suppor and technical assistance to foster improvement; and accountability provisions that reward or sanction schools or students based on measured performance.[36]

Over time, SBR has evolved and, in many ways, narrowed. Early arguments for systemic reform focused on challenging curriculum and instruction—tying the structures of performance-based accountability with substance in both curriculum and assessments that were intended to be conceptually rich and complex. While the overall structures of SBR have taken root in much of the current debate about education, this focus on the quality of the thinking required of students to perform successfully has been more uneven.[37]

In addition, some early advocates of systemic reform placed considerable emphasis on granting greater autonomy to schools, allowing them flexibility in how they would meet standards measured by external assessments.[38] However, the added pressure districts face to meet external benchmarks (especially under NCLB) has led many districts to become more prescriptive about school practices, effectively diminishing rather than enhancing school-level autonomy. As Hamilton and her colleagues describe, high-stakes testing influences teacher and administrator behavior, and can reduce the importance of the standards themselves; in such a climate, "alignment and autonomy may become competing goals."[39]

Advocates of portfolio management draw heavily on the linking of external standards, assessments tied to those standards, and high-stakes accountability significantly based on the outcomes of those assessments. They return to the focus somewhat lost over the past years, however, on school autonomy as a potentially necessary condition for improvement in a high-stakes accountability environment. They recognize the potential tension between autonomy and standards-based accountability, but believe the two can be complementary if the accountability system is disciplined in its focus on outcomes—allowing schools to vary in their strategies for meeting these—and if the technical design of incentive systems is properly calibrated to both encourage and reward those who use discretion most effectively.

Differentiation of Schools

A third recurring strategy in educational reform is the shift away from the common school and toward schools that are distinct in some way. Three manifestations of this push toward differentiation of schools are magnet schools; thematic, small schools; and charter schools. Such a shift is purported to serve several different educational purposes, including offering a range of schools within a system of choice, providing schools that incorporate an array of instructional practices and thus serving the varied needs and interests of students, and giving opportunities for educational innovation. While reforms that lead to the differentiation of schools have not always incorporated increased autonomy, advocates of each of these strategies have argued that greater school-level autonomy is critical to allow for meaningful differentiation and development of a strong and shared vision at the school level.

Magnet schools are public, district-run schools that have a particular educational theme, and students choose to attend them. Many magnet schools originated in desegregation efforts, and enticing parents to voluntarily place their children in more integrated settings has often been a focus of these schools.[40] Most magnet schools are located in large districts (those serving more than ten thousand students) and rely either on lotteries or on a first come, first served admissions policy (rather than competitive admissions) for student selection.[41] Expenditures for these schools are often higher than in regular district-run schools, with some receiving additional resources through state desegregation funding and federal grants. Some evidence suggests that magnets can have a positive impact on student achievement.[42] Magnet schools operate in most districts that are engaged in PMM reforms and are one component of a district's portfolio.

A second effort to increase the differentiation of schools has been a push for small schools, especially new, small, autonomous schools; the focus of this effort has been in cities including New York, Chicago, and Boston.[43] One of the most prominent recent pushes toward the differentiation of schools has come from the Gates Foundation, which funded a substantial five-year initiative to create new, small high schools.[44] In theory, such schools are better positioned than larger schools to create a supportive, personalized environment for students and a clear and cohesive vision and culture among school staff.[45] Research on these and other small-school initiatives suggests that smallness can enable, but certainly does not guarantee, improved student performance.[46] Not coincidentally, cities that have actively pursued small-school initiatives are some of the same cities that are profiled in this book, as those initiatives have provided a central component of many districts' portfolios.

Finally, charter schools are based not only on market reform, as discussed earlier, but also on school differentiation. In fact, the charter school idea was first promoted as a means of fostering innovation that teachers, parents, and others would drive.[47] However, the innovativeness of instructional practice in charter schools has been challenged, and some advocates have shifted away from this as a focus for the reform.[48] In each of the cities studied for this volume, and especially in New Orleans, charter schools have become an important part of the portfolio. However, strategically managing charter schools, as opposed to schools controlled by a district, raises distinct challenges.

POLITICAL AND POLICY ISSUES IN THE STUDY OF PMMS

Studying portfolio management reforms is not an easy task, as the model is not fully developed and the actual reforms (and the language used to describe these reforms) are still evolving. As described earlier, PMMs bring together many different strands of reform in the hope of creating a coherent framework for systemwide change, and sometimes even people within parts of those systems do not see their work on one component of the PMM as part of a broader effort for educational improvement. In analyzing these reforms, we focus in this volume on two broad issues—the design and implementation of PMM as a means for school improvement, and the political forces that have promoted and challenged the creation of PMM districts. Ultimately, studying the long-term consequences of PMM in terms of student performance and other social goals will also be important. It is premature to make such summative assessments, although some chapters in the volume offer preliminary information about the impact of PMMs on specific cities, and the concluding chapter outlines ideas for a long-term research agenda.

In a reform that combines local evolution around how schools are governed with broad goals for educational change, both schools and the entity that governs them begin to look quite different. In all three of the strategies for educational change described, there has been an increasing emphasis on the school as the primary unit for change (as opposed to the teacher or the district). In many cities, the most visible aspects of a portfolio model are the presence of schools governed in different ways. In New York City, a widespread shift has empowered schools to select service providers from a list of public and private options. In New Orleans, the rapid proliferation of charter schools has dominated the reform. In many of the cities involved in PMM, schools are operated in a variety of structures—charters, specially empowered schools, and those managed in whole or in part by outside organizations.For example, Philadelphia includes a significant number of charter schools and schools that are partnered with outside providers and is moving toward giving some district-run schools additional autonomy.

The cases in this volume explore the specific configurations of schools in each city and help to explain how these configurations result from both broad policy ideas and specific historical contexts. Among the questions they consider are: What kinds of schools (in addition to district-run schools) are operating in the city and why? What kinds of organizations manage schools or partner with them? What kinds of autonomy do different categories of schools experience, and how does the district support them?

While the focus of the PMM rhetoric is often on schools, the attention to the district role connects with recent research that has highlighted the importance of school districts as potential initiators and leaders in educational reform.[49] Rorrer and her colleagues suggest four roles for districts in improving achievement and advancing equity: "(a) providing instructional leadership, (b) reorienting the organization, (c) establishing policy coherence, and (d) maintaining an equity focus."[50] The PMM idea has offered one direction for advocates of choice-oriented reforms who have become wary of relying on choice as the *only* mechanism to drive quality: instead of relying so heavily on the actions of families, incorporate the district in the reform effort but transform its overall operations.

Two of the chapters in this book focus on the idea of transforming central governing units (most often, districts). In chapter 8, Henry Levin addresses the question of what roles and responsibilities do the governing units that oversee a PMM need to consider and address in order to balance the broad educational goals of freedom to choose, productive efficiency, equity, and social cohesion. Meredith Honig and Michael DeArmond take a different approach, drawing on existing research on districts in order to explore some of the critical demands placed on urban school district central offices as a district moves toward a PMM (see chapter 7).

Along with the details of the model itself are a series of issues around the political forces that have developed (and will be needed to sustain) shifts in institutional roles. One lens for looking at political changes connected with portfolio models is to analyze the nature of the regime that has initiated (and/or sustained or sought to rationalize) these policy changes.[51] Jeffrey Henig explores these ideas in his chapter on contracting regimes; the contracting-regime language allows us to explore how PMMs incorporate outside vendors by contracting in ways that influence power relationships, while still placing district central offices in what Henig calls the role of "consumer supreme" (see chapter 2).

As mentioned, most cities utilizing some form of a PMM have mayors and/or state governments with more direct control over public education than in the conventional district with a directly elected school board. The role of these new actors in school district policy making is important to consider, as is the diminished influence of previously powerful players. Thus, each case explores not only the design of the PMM in a specific city, but also the political context that surrounds it. In addition to looking at the changing role of formal actors such as mayors, school boards, and state government, chapters 3, 4, 5, and 6 examine the changing influence of informal actors such as the business community, civic organizations, foundations, and private providers of educational services.

While the local political context is central for PMM reforms, the broader national environment also needs to be considered. In chapter 9, Patricia Burch discusses the push in NCLB and other federal policies for increased contracting, which has provided fertile ground in which PMMs can grow. The political and financial support of national politicians such as Obama and Duncan, as well as major national foundations, has also aided reforms with the broad contours of a PMM. The role of national foundations, in particular, is important for understanding why common changes are happening in very different cities; in chapter 10, Sarah Reckhow explores the growing influence of foundations as catalysts and sustainers for many of the organizations involved in PMM reforms.

Finally, in chapter 11, Josh Edelman (former executive officer in the Chicago Public Schools Office of New Schools and current director of the Washington, D.C., Office of School Innovation) addresses both politics and policy, drawing on the pieces in this volume and his own experience in order to explore implications for practitioners and policy makers. One of the pitfalls plaguing American school reform has been the sharp disconnection between the abstract theories and models scholars and national leaders are debating and the pragmatic choices practitioners must make while facing particular and localized organizational, fiscal, and political contexts.

CHAPTER OVERVIEWS

In this volume, we combine rich case studies of four districts actively engaged in portfolio management reforms (Chicago, New York City, Philadelphia, and New Orleans) with chapters that bring both conceptual and comparative elements to the discussion. Next, we offer more elaborate descriptions of each chapter.

In chapter 2, Jeffrey Henig discusses what it means to consider portfolio management as an example of a contracting regime. While contracting out for core educational services is a recent development, state and local governments have a long track record of contracting for other social and human services, and Henig argues there are lessons that can be gleaned from this experience. The term *regime*, drawn from the literature on urban politics, emphasizes the fact that contracting arrangements are embedded in a broader formal and informal structure of political power and access. Politicians can use contracting arrangements to weaken groups that stand as obstacles to their reelection or effective governing, to reward allies, and to build supporting coalitions. Although PMM is often presented as technical and apolitical reform, Henig suggests that understanding its role in political maneuvering can be critical in predicting how it will evolve in different local contexts and over time.

In chapter 3, David Menefee-Libey focuses on Renaissance 2010, the Chicago initiative launched by Mayor Richard M. Daley and then-Superintendent Arne Duncan in June 2004. He shows how this initiative evolved as a third wave of reform after state laws mandating decentralization in 1988 and mayoral control in 1995. The main thrust of Ren10 was to close dozens of the district's lowest-performing schools and by 2010 to open a hundred new ones for students who most needed quality education. These new schools take a variety of forms: charters, charterlike "contract schools," and "performance schools" more closely tied to the district. The district takes a neoliberal approach toward improvement, granting these schools conditional autonomies in exchange for high performance on their specialized missions. While the reform has produced mixed educational results, it has brought substantial organizational change to the district.

Using his freshly granted control of the public schools, in 2002 New York City's Mayor Michael Bloomberg launched a series of reforms that were grounded in management theories, articulated in corporate values and metaphors, and fleshed out by teams of external consultants. By 2008, the result appeared to be a highly developed form of PMM, with autonomous schools and empowered principals buying administrative support services from public and private providers and held accountable through a centralized information management system. Along with these reforms, a robust charter-school sector was also established. Yet the current decentralized portfolio approach was by no means a foregone conclusion, particularly when compared to the city's first wave of centralizing policies. In chapter 4, Jonathan Gyurko and Jeffrey Henig investigate the evolution of New York City's current portfolio approach, with special attention to the ways in which rational planning and imported models were frustrated by, layered onto, or grafted onto preexisting norms, institutions, and political processes. They conclude with an analysis of how portfolio management has been influenced by and affected the politics of policy adoption, implementation, and sustainability.

Philadelphia has proved to be a challenging testing ground for PMM ideas, as some radical changes (such as turning to private managers for a significant portion of the city's low-performing schools) have combined with district officials' hesitation to providing noncharter schools with substantial autonomy and a series of reforms that have centralized the instructional program for many city schools. In chapter 5, Katrina Bulkley, Jolley Christman, and Eva Gold analyze the story of the Philadelphia reforms, which began in earnest with a state takeover in 2002, but can be traced further back to the growth of charter schools in the 1990s. The overall shift in the direction of a PMM has been led primarily by two very different leaders—Paul Vallas and Arlene Ackerman—and both intended change and untended evolution have led to a system that now comprises a complex array of schools run by both the district and private actors.

In chapter 6, Henry Levin, Joseph Daschbach, and Andre Perry discuss how the New Orleans public schools were transformed in response to the loss of school facilities from the destruction of Hurricane Katrina and the exodus of people fleeing the flooding and chaos, rather than a planned strategy for school change. The scale of reconstruction needed and the unpredictable flow of returning students shifted the control of the New Orleans schools to the state's Bureau of Elementary and Secondary Education in Baton Rouge, with only minor participation of the local school board. The state—under its Recovery School District (RSD), which had been established in 2003 to take over its failing schools—set about repairing damaged schools and hiring personnel as well as encouraging the expansion of charter schools to accommodate returning students. The result has been the largest system of diverse school sponsorship and management in the United States and declarations to convert the entire system of New Orleans schools to charter schools. What makes this unique is the origin of the new system of schools in a natural disaster as well as the lack of a strong central office to guide and manage the changes. Control is predominantly at the state level, with the vestigial New Orleans School Board having responsibility for only four of the city's eighty-eight public schools and chartering responsibility for an additional twelve. State authorities operate or granted the charter for all the other schools, with no central monitoring by a local school board. No detailed plan has emerged for an overall shift of governance to the local level at this time.

Following the four cases, the book shifts to an examination of the broader influences and themes relevant to analyzing the policies and politics associated with PMMs. As public management scholars outside education have long pointed out, indirect government strategies, such as contracting, are not self-executing; instead they require strong public management and close oversight. With that in mind, in chapter 7, Meredith Honig and Michael DeArmond consider the role that school district central offices play in the implementation of portfolio management reform. They argue that the implementation of such reforms hinges not only on the creation of new formal structures in the central office (e.g., a new portfolio management office) but also on the day-to-day work practices and activities of central office administrators. In particular, they argue for the importance of bridge-building and boundary-spanning skills in the central office. These skills matter because of the complex, networked relationships envisioned by portfolio management, and yet they represent a significant departure for district central offices that have traditionally emphasized hierarchy and control through authority. Honig and DeArmond argue that portfolio management reforms are likely to struggle with implementation absent a system of formal and informal supports for these new skills and activities—supports that crucially operate throughout the central office rather than in an isolated subunit or division.

As school districts managed in ways consistent with a PMM place more and more schools of choice in their portfolios, there is a need to consider the responsibilities that schools and the central office must discharge and carry out. In chapter 8, Henry Levin sets out a range of functions to undertake and develops a strategy for determining whether those functions should be centralized or relegated to schools and other decentralized entities. To undertake this task, Levin borrows three economic concepts: economies of scale, transaction costs, and externalities. Economies of scale refer to those functions associated with declining costs per unit of service as more units are delivered; they call for greater centralization rather than duplication of delivery by individual schools. Transaction costs refer to the costs associated with the search for information on alternatives, contracting for alternatives, and monitoring services, and also suggest the interplay of central office and schools to minimize such costs. Externalities refer to benefits (or costs) that spill beyond the decision-making entity, such as the benefits conferred on families without children when the schools are successful in improving a community's economic vitality or its students' civic mindedness. These must be taken into account through some regulation and coordination of decentralized units. The author analyzes each function within this framework and suggests implications for centralized versus decentralized responsibilities as well as the balance between the two.

Chapter 9 considers federal education policy, in particular, NCLB as a prelude to and influence on the phenomenon of the PMMs described in other chapters as they unfold in Chicago, New York, Philadelphia, and New Orleans. Patricia Burch identifies five pathways of influence of current federal policy on local efforts. She then analyzes some of the complications in privatization schemes that pair the goal of more choices for parents with the theory and language of managerialism—using the case of NCLB to illustrate these complications and examples from portfolio districts as points of comparison and contrast to the NCLB approach. She concludes by presenting the challenges of designing *public* policy that holds the private and public sectors accountable for equity and results in education and the urgency for informed debate and action on the role of national and local policy in market and quasi-market education reforms.

In chapter 10, Sarah Reckhow empirically assesses foundation grant making to show how major foundations have helped to disseminate and legitimize the field of diverse provider organizations (a core element of PMMs). The chapter uses an original data set of major foundation grants from 2000 and 2005 and applies social network analysis to determine how foundations have helped develop an organizational field of diverse providers. Reckhow focuses on three major findings. First, foundations aim their grant making for diverse providers toward a select group of urban school districts with specific political characteristics, including mayoral or state control. Second, foundations target grants toward specific types of organizations within these districts, including nonprofits and charter schools. Third, major foundations have increasingly converged toward similar grant-making strategies, and they are working to strengthen ties among diverse providers and promote a shared national agenda.

Much of this book was written from the perspective of research. In chapter 11, Josh Edelman, a well-respected practitioner who has worked in senior positions related to PMMs in both Chicago and Washington, D.C., brings his own lens to the issues raised throughout the book. Edelman's chapter provides a voice for the perspective of those who must wrestle with the challenges of turning ideas into workable practice, and focuses on what he argues are core issues for PMMs, including district leaders' clear and guiding vision, autonomy, transparency, and the thoughtful support of entrepreneurialism in public education.

In the last chapter, we return to some of the issues raised in this chapter and throughout the book to draw some general and more informed conclusions about where the portfolio model may be heading and whether this latest school governance and organizational reform is something to celebrate or watch with a wary eye.

2

Portfolio Management Models and the Political Economy of Contracting Regimes

Jeffrey R. Henig

There is nothing new under the sun but there are lots of old things we don't know.

—*Ambrose Bierce, U.S. author and satirist*, The Devil's Dictionary

Everything seems new and fresh in the eyes of a child. In this same sense, debates about education policy in the United States display an element of childish fascination. Policy entrepreneurs, foundations, and the media cycle through a succession of the latest and best new things, each greeted with wide-eyed enthusiasm.[1] Unencumbered by a historical track record, new reform ideas seem compelling and full of promise. When the neatness and coherence of idealized models hit the hard pavement of implementation, complexity ensues. But when each new idea is seen as *sui generis*, little learning accumulates. Naive hopes spawn disillusionment that, unmediated by any strong sense of history, sets the stage for the next new enthusiasm.

The portfolio management model (PMM) is currently gaining attention and momentum as a new approach for restructuring education delivery that advocates argue will expeditiously increase flexibility, competition, choice, efficiency, and student performance. Although the details vary from place to place, key features include shifting from a top-down, district-managed, and highly uniform educational delivery in favor of contract-like arrangements in which schools are granted increased budgetary and programmatic discretion in exchange for being held accountable for the outcomes they produce. Portfolio districts consist of a mix of types of schools, which may include schools managed by for-profit companies or nonprofit organizations, charter schools, or district schools that have been given special grants of autonomy.[2] As with a stock portfolio, managers (in principle) regularly intervene to weed out below-average performers and attract new providers that are expected to do a better job (see Bulkley, chapter 1, this volume; and Levin, chapter 8, this volume). In addition to leveraging a higher level of overall performance through a combination of competitive pressure and managerial oversight and intervention, proponents suggest that deliberate efforts to differentiate schools to appeal to particular types of families, so-called product differentiation, will better match services to children's individual learning needs.

It is too soon to tell whether PMM will deliver on these promises or prove to be just the latest in a series of school reform fads. But it is not too soon to raise the discussion to a more sophisticated level. One way to do so is to disentangle the actual mechanisms and underlying logic of the PMM from the language with which it is frequently described. For reasons I'll discuss, PMM is frequently presented as a variant of privatization, a strategy for shrinking the size and power of local public-sector bureaucracies by introducing the discipline of markets, competition, and choice. Rather than replacing local government with a family-based consumer market, however, PMM is better understood as a *contracting regime*.

Contracting regimes incorporate private providers and attempt to harness markets to public goals, but instead of bypassing government, they place government into the role of consumer supreme. The term *contracting regime* combines two distinct concepts, each of which brings to bear a substantial body of research and policy insights, and thereby offers us some opportunity to link the discussion to evidence gleaned from experience. Contracting arrangements have long been common in the provision of public services, wherein a unit of government essentially hires a private provider (or, in some instances, another unit of government) to offer a specified service to a specified population. Contracting out is similar in some ways to other so-called privatization or market-oriented reforms, but unlike the idealized market often conjured up in policy debates, the key consumers are not atomized students or their families but government entities, operating within legal, political, and institutional constraints.

Government entities differ from individualized consumers in a number of ways. Compared to individuals, for example, they are in a much stronger bargaining position: they have the resources to be more highly informed and the market power to extract concessions from providers that the average consumer cannot. Moreover, and more important, government preferences are not idiosyncratically held but are the outcome of complex political interactions involving voters, candidates, political parties, and interest groups competing, collaborating, and negotiating within an array of institutions intended to protect both democratic accountability and individual and civil rights. The concept of regimes emerged in the urban politics literature as a way to better understand how local political arrangements—not only the formal institutions and powers of government but the informal-yet-patterned interactions among government, business, unions, and the nonprofit sector—shape local policy priorities and the prospects for getting things accomplished.

Acknowledging the core differences between contracting and consumer markets means recognizing that much of the empirical and theoretical research that has emerged on the issues of school choice and privatization has only limited application for predicting the likely evolution and consequences of portfolio models and similar contracting regimes. In the remainder of this chapter, I provide some greater elaboration on contracting out and regimes as they have been applied to other areas of social policy and governance, draw implications about how PMM might evolve, and identify possible pitfalls and unintended consequences to bear in mind as policy makers at all levels of government, along with the citizens to whom they are responsible, consider whether and how to expand the approach.

The portfolio model is at high risk of being drawn into heated national policy debates ideologically framed around the claim and counterclaims that greater reliance on market dynamics is the best route forward for speedy and effective school reform. Rather than an all-purpose salve or universal threat, I suggest in this chapter that whether or not to contract out is often a pragmatic decision that should be made selectively and contingently, based on nature of the service, economic and social context, and the realities of governmental capacity.

Claims by some advocates to the contrary, adopting PMM will not take decisions about schools out of politics, but it is likely to shift them into a different set of political dynamics, reallocating access and influence among groups with competing views of what public education should entail. The outcomes of a more widespread adoption of the approach are not simply out there, waiting to be documented by research and evidence; instead, they will depend on decisions yet to make, lessons yet to learn, and battles yet to fight. This open-ended nature of the process makes it even more critical that public deliberation be both empirically grounded and framed sufficiently broadly so that important societal interests—interests that sometimes lack mobilized champions—do not get overlooked or obscured.

CONTRACTING ARRANGEMENTS VERSUS CONSUMER MARKETS

Market theories and reform ideas grounded in those theories have played prominent roles in education policy discourse over the past twenty-five years. Milton Friedman laid out the basic elements of the market perspective about fifty years ago.[3] They include the claims that: free interactions between suppliers and informed consumers are the most effective way to match services to desires; competition among providers produces efficiencies, innovations, and responsiveness; and government monopolies, because they can use taxing power to coerce payments even from dissatisfied customers, are even more insidious than private monopolies. Though frequently chattered about before then, these ideas did not really gain leverage in policy circles until the mid-1980s. The Reagan administration played a key role in this transition when, by linking market framing to magnet schools and other existing public school choice arrangements, it made the case that what previously had seemed abstract, academic, and risky not only was realistic but was already operating to good effect. If small doses of choice were associated with innovative programs, satisfied families, and integrated schools, it argued, imagine the benefits that might accrue if choice could be more fully unleashed as an antidote to the inertia and sameness associated with the bureaucracy and public monopoly typical of the standard school district.[4]

Part of the political appeal of the market model rests on the familiar metaphor of the consumer market in which firms compete for the patronage of informed shoppers. Even those whose eyes glazed over during classroom lectures about microeconomic theory grasp the basic logic of supply and demand. And the notion of parental choice has concrete and immediate attraction for families unhappy with their assigned neighborhood schools, whether they intellectually connect this with economic models or see it more simply and immediately as an attractive alternative to a manifestly undesirable situation.

This grassroots popular appeal of the market metaphor is conjoined with a different kind of appeal, one that matters more in elite politics than mass politics, more in national partisan debates than in localized tussles over school reform. At the national level, the metaphor of the consumer-driven market model integrates education policy ideas into the broader ideological battle pitting conservative proponents of privatization against liberal defenders of the idea of progressive government. Polarized politics at the national level makes this a high-stakes, winner-takes-all competition in which nuanced conceptions of mixed or "quasi" markets—in which governments create market arrangements and both compete and collaborate with private actors in an effort to harness the benefits of markets, while keeping government in the game to protect the public good—are regarded as watered-down compromises of purer and more principled conceptions, despite the fact that they are arguably the dominant expression of the contemporary state.[5]

Within this context, PMM has too readily and too closely been characterized as part of the market-based, consumer-driven, privatization movement. Like consumer markets, PMM emphasizes competition and choice as mechanisms for generating innovation, efficiency, adaptability, and quality outcomes. And the constellation of groups promoting PMM overlaps considerably with that behind vouchers, charter schools, and other reform notions more directly anchored in the ideas and images associated with consumer markets. But this alignment masks a central point: PMM puts government front and center—as the key contractor and arbiter—

and alters, rather than displaces, the role of politics in shaping the agenda and establishing priorities.

Table 2.1 highlights four important differences between consumer markets and the kinds of contracting arrangements that are at the core of the portfolio model. While the conventional market model envisions individuals (or families) as the critical decision makers, in contracting arrangements this role is played by government. It is government, not individual families, that decides whether or not to employ private organizations to manage schools or provide them with support services. For example, while family choice can play an important role in determining the viability of charter schools, in practice parents frequently stay loyal even to charter schools that are demonstrably bad; public-sector actions in selecting among charter applications, establishing and implementing oversight regimes, providing (or not providing) access by charters to public buildings or other forms of district-funded support, and closing or failing to renew charters can be much more decisive in determining their fate.[6] The role of choice is even less significant in district-managed schools, where parents' views may play a role in moderating central administrators' decisions about whether principals operating under empowerment or autonomy zone arrangements are meeting their contractual obligations, but in practice, the criteria applied in PMM districts weigh centrally designated criteria much more heavily.[7]

Microeconomic theory about consumer markets places individual preferences as the driving force dictating supplier behavior, but in contracting

TABLE 2.1   Consumer markets versus contracting regimes

	Market arrangements	Contracting arrangements
Key consumer	Individuals and families	Government agencies
Establishment of priorities	Family shopping for schools	Pluralistic politics
Primary indicator of dissatisfaction	Exit	Voice
Mechanism for improvement	Competition for customers	Government budgeting, oversight, regulation, and termination

arrangements, the priorities applied to assess performance emerge out of pluralistic politics, in which individuals' desires have impact only as mediated through the machinations of party and electoral politics, interest-group lobbying, judicial action, and other processes in which factors such as power, elite privilege, conventional wisdom, and precedent play direct and consequential roles.

In markets, it is the power to exit—for example, to move to another attendance zone, another school district, or a private or charter school—that is supposed to signal discontent and motivate providers to improve. Under contracting arrangements, collective expression of discontent—what Hirschman refers to as "voice"—plays a more central role.[8] Parent choice, a form of exit, can also play a role, but rather than operating directly on schools, it is filtered through the district's monitoring of enrollment patterns; requests to transfer become a signal of a problem and can both supplement and be supplemented by voice, a dynamic that Hirschman notes can be beneficial to both. Finally, the key mechanism for translating preferences and dissatisfaction into changes in product and performance varies between the two institutional arrangements. In conventional markets, competition and the desire to increase profits and market share act as the linkage between consumer desires and suppliers' adjustments of products and pricing. In contracting arrangements, government takes the priorities that emerge from pluralistic politics and converts them into policy changes—through its actions in raising revenue, devising budgets, setting and enforcing regulations, and its capacity to directly and authoritatively intervene by nurturing new providers and weeding out those who fail to perform.

Failing to appreciate the core differences between contracting and consumer markets leads to problematic inferences about the likely evolution and consequences of portfolio models and similar contracting regimes. School-choice researchers, for example, have focused tremendous attention on the question of whether parents measure up to the expectations of a healthy consumer market; do they act as informed and quality-conscious education shoppers whose expressed demands would drive providers in socially desirable directions?[9] As another example, charter school research has looked for differences between for-profit and nonprofit providers and between individual charters and those enmeshed in national networks.[10]

Findings from these kinds of studies are by no means irrelevant to the portfolio phenomenon, but they are misdirected in the sense that they leave the more critical issues in the shadows. The preferences and capacity of families *qua* consumers are less consequential if portfolio management systems take it on themselves to define and enforce performance. Differences in inclination or capacity between for-profit and nonprofits or between localized and national providers are less consequential if portfolio management systems define tasks, enforce contracts, and structure rewards and sanctions in ways that force participating organizations to conform.[11] What we need to know more about is the capacity that governments have or can develop and the ways in which that capacity—inevitably enmeshed as it is in political give-and-take—is likely to be steered.

CONTRACTING IN OTHER POLICY ARENAS

Government contracting with private providers is a widespread and growing phenomenon. Contracting with private providers is hardly new—Kettl suggests that governments "have always relied on private providers to provide key goods and services," but most observers suggest it is expanding.[12] Considering both the United States and other countries' experiences, O'Toole and Meier observe that "by most reasonable measures, this is the age of the contract." Not only do more governments contract, they observe, but "governments contract for more goods and services, and a larger portion of government benefits are allocated to contractual arrangements than ever before."[13]

Contracting out has been slower to infiltrate core aspects of public education than other services, whether because education has more of a public-goods component that policy makers fear will not be fully realized by competitive markets or because education decision making, in the United States, has been carried out in local, school-specific, and bureaucratic arenas where educators and teacher unions have been better able to protect their jobs. That does not mean that contracting has been absent. Ritter, Maranto, and Buck go so far as to suggest that "nearly all" public school districts rely on private contractors for some specific support functions like transportation, maintenance, food services, security, construction, payroll, legal services, and security.[14] Some districts have relied on contracting arrangements to handle more core educational functions, especially for students with special needs.

PMM, though, has been associated with a significant breakthrough of what had been the constraining barriers. Some districts are now turning to private providers to deliver services well beyond the standard peripheral service provision and services to niche groups of students.[15] Until recently, contracting in education was seen as a way for districts and schools to shed distractions and allow them to focus their attention on the things that really mattered: the provision of high-quality instruction to their more typical kinds of student.[16] Under PMM, nondistrict employees now are delivering core elements of teaching to substantial proportions of students. New Orleans is at an extreme here; the combination of Hurricane Katrina and the state's recovery policies left the traditional local district almost completely marginalized and completely opened the field for an array of new education providers (see Levin, et al., chapter 6, this volume).

Albeit less dramatically, a growing stream of other large districts is moving in the direction of having most students in charter or other privately operated schools and some would like to see that model extended to all students. In Washington, D.C., for example, more than a third of public school students are currently in charter schools, and Chancellor Michelle Rhee aspires to expand the district's contracting arrangement with private providers and support organization. Estimates are that about 30 percent of students in Milwaukee use publicly funded vouchers or other public school-choice options.[17] Even internally to the public system, some districts are adopting contract-like relationships, in which principals, and sometimes teachers, at so-called empowered schools may give up some job and assignment protections in return for greater authority conditioned on the school meeting specified performance goals.

Large-scale and sustained examples of contracting out core educational functions are still too rare or recent to provide a clear empirical record. Pioneer examples, like Baltimore's 1992–1997 management contract with Education Alternatives, Inc., or Pennsylvania's 2001 enlistment of Edison Schools to run almost all of the schools in the Chester-Upland district, were seen by some as disastrous, but the political battles that engulfed those efforts make it difficult to determine whether the failure should be read as indicating a flaw in the concept or the result of union resistance and sabotage.[18]

What then can we learn from the experiences of contracting in other are-nas that might inform our efforts to understand portfolio models and the ways they might develop over time? The first lesson is that *the nature of the service matters*. Contracting out is more likely, and more likely to have been found effective—especially in generating cost saving—in areas like trash collection, cleaning, and maintenance where the service can be easily speci-fied, where there are established measures of process and outcomes, where the causal relationship between service output and intended outcomes is direct and immediate.[19] Services that are labor intensive can be attractive candidates for contracting, presumably because lower salary scales in the private, less-unionized sectors offer greater potentials for lowering costs, but governments sometimes find it appealing to contract for services in which up-front capital costs are high or where technology frequently changes.[20]

Because private provision is more subject than public provision to inter-ruptions due to labor shortages or providers going out of business, services for which the tolerance for a discontinuity of delivery is low can be more risky for governments to contract out.[21] Finally, services differ in the ex-tent to which we care about process, as well as outcomes, and the extent to which doing the tasks well necessarily requires that providers exercise good judgment and have the discretion to adapt their behavior based on the vari-able characteristics of the situation and the context in which they operate.

Considerations such as these have led some to argue that contracting out is simply impractical for schooling, a service from which we expect many and elusive things. Americans want public schools to produce bet-ter workers, inculcate creativity and entrepreneurial spirit, build scien-tists, transmit culture and values, reinforce public health initiatives, and turn out informed and independent-minded citizens.[22] The system itself is famously "loosely coupled" making oversight problematic, especially at the classroom level.[23] And the ultimate test in evaluating schools is how students perform in various roles as adults, well after they have left the schooling scene. Further straining the portrayal of education as well suited for market transactions is that the direct and immediate clients are chil-dren, who are for the most part defenseless and uninformed about how to evaluate the quality of the services they receive. These various compli-cations make regulating process—punishment, prayer, gender and racial discrimination—more central and challenge the notion that contractors can be held responsible simply for the outcomes they produce.

Other social services have similar characteristics (e.g., they deal with young children or other clients, like prisoners, who are not able to exercise full exit or voice). Significantly, too, some changes in the national and state policy regimes may be working—self-consciously or not—to *remake* education into a service that more neatly fits within a contracting arrangement. State and federal efforts to increase accountability for educational outcomes have raised the prominence of reading and mathematics and increased the extent, precision, and consequences of measurements in those two areas. Although the elevation of standardized testing and the narrowing of curricular focus are controversial compared to ten years ago, there seems to be a broader consensus that proficiency in reading and math is a primary—or at least first-order—goal. And state and local officials have access to outcomes data that are unambiguously better than ever before. Nonetheless, we need to be wary of too facile an assumption that contracting out for schooling is a simple extension of a delivery model familiar in other service areas and likely to produce the same kinds of results.

A second lesson from the general literature on contracting out is that *claims of success are more often based on cost savings than on sophisticated measures of service quality or consideration of broader collective goods such as social cohesion and equity.* Focusing on cost savings may make sense for some housekeeping services like trash collection and road maintenance, where variation in quality is more constrained because bad service is more immediately apparent and standards and expectations do not vary substantially from place to place. Research focusing more on human services, such as hospitals and nursing homes, though, suggests, that for-profit providers are more likely than government or nonprofit providers to sacrifice quality for higher profits or lower costs.[24] Much more than most public services, schooling has been expected to play a role in promoting key societal outcomes, such as social cohesion, equity, and the inculcation of democratic values, but because it typically focuses on more mundane services that share more characteristics with private goods than public goods, the empirical literature on contracting out rarely takes these kinds of outcomes into consideration when making judgments about contracting success.[25]

Hodge, in one of the most extensive reviews, analyzed 268 studies that provided empirical data on the consequences of contracting out. Of the studies, most of which focused on the United States and most of which focused on the local level of government, about three-quarters zeroed in on economic outcomes, with the rest divided among those focused on social, political, democratic, or legal outcomes.[26] Such a focus on costs and individual outcomes may make sense in the broader contracting literature, precisely because those studies often focus on straightforward services where variation in quality is more easily perceived and the distribution of benefits and costs more readily discernable. The problem arises when indistinct claims of success are transported in a vague and facile manner into discussions of policies, like education, where quality and societal considerations are more critically in play.

A third general finding from the broader literature on contracting is that, even within specific types of services, the empirical record is mixed. This is a reflection of the fact that *both implementation and context matter.* Like most things, contracting out can be done poorly or done well. Hatry and Durman, for example, found that challenges on which some efforts foundered could be met and conquered by careful administration.[27] "To reap the benefits of competition," writes Van Slyke, in summarizing one strain of findings in the empirical literature, "government must be a smart buyer, a skillful purchasing agent, and a sophisticated inspector of the goods and services it purchases from the private sector."[28] One contextual factor that many analyses highlight is the number of providers able and willing to serve the area in question: when competition is low—because a jurisdiction is small, isolated, or unable to pay sufficiently high fees—contracting out may be impossible or may lock it into reliance on a single provider that can extract overly generous payments or disregard with impunity efforts to exercise effective regulatory oversight.[29]

Fiscal context can matter also. In general, governments seeking to cut costs in times of fiscal contraction have seen contracting out as especially attractive. Interestingly, though, analysis of historical trends suggests that reliance on privatization also has spiked at times of government expansions such as the New Deal and Great Society, and there is evidence that governments often turn to private providers when they are launching new areas of service provision where they lack a trained work force of their own and where they may prefer the provisional nature of contracting until it is clear that the new commitments will be institutionalized.[30] Political factors, including local political values and the presence and strength of public employee unions can also be critical (more on the political side of the equation later).[31]

The fourth lesson is that disappointing results, when they occur, can be *attributed to market failures or government failure or both.*[32] Proponents of an expanding welfare state frequently justify governmental provision by highlighting structural market failures, such as natural monopolies, inefficient handling of collective goods and spillover effects, and informational asymmetries that allow private actors to extract favorable terms or escape regulatory intervention. Proponents of privatization counter that government also exhibits structural failures (such as bureaucratic inefficiencies, self-interested public monopolies, and the intrusion of partisan politics). The empirical literature suggests that both kinds of failures are prevalent, and that, rather than being mutually exclusive, they often combine in ways that exacerbate one another and "may actually create 'hybrid' failures, thus creating entirely new pathologies for privatized arrangements."[33]

What remains contested is whether it makes sense to speak of market failures or governmental failures as inherently linked to particular services in ways that make either market or public provision the logical, objectively determined solution. The post-1980 resurgence of privatization as a countertrend to expanding government is in large measure attributable to the theoretical argument challenging the conventional notion that the potential vulnerability of a service to market failure is sufficient to justify governmental service delivery. Where market failures exist, Friedman, Savas, and others argued, government often can address them while leaving delivery to private organizations and private employees. If there is a public interest in ensuring equitable access to education, for example, government could offer vouchers that make the purchasing power of the poor greater; if there are legitimate public costs to racial or economic stratification, government could institute controlled-choice policies that ensure that school-level demographics do not deviate too much from those of the broader community.[34] Public responsibility, in other words, need not entail public delivery. By imagining that government would exercise this meta-responsibility well, however, critics charge that proponents of privatization implicitly rely on heroic assumptions about the capacity of the public sector to judiciously and effectively intervene and do so not only whenever required, but also only when required, to maximize the public good—an ironic assumption since the calls for privatization are so often linked to charges of governmental corruption and incompetence. Responding to democratic signals, respecting legal rights, and exercising stewardship in decisions where there may be uncertainty and ambiguity of values may be more difficult and costly if government gets out of the service delivery process and loses the ground-level information, the flexibility, and the public legitimacy to step in when private markets fail.[35]

The fifth and final lesson: contracting out—and privatization more generally—is *not unidirectional*; governments that engage in frequent contracting subsequently scale back that initiative and take on more of the direct delivery themselves. Hefetz and Warner offer one of the most focused empirical analyses of the dynamics of the contracting process.[36] They link local government responses to two surveys administered by the International City Managers Association (ICMA)—now International City/County Management Association—in 1992 and 1997. Respondents in 628 U.S. counties and cities answered, in both years, questions about whether they directly provided a list of more than sixty services (not including K–12 education) or whether they contracted for their provision to for-profit or non-profit firms. Most jurisdictions did not change their method of delivery for particular services over that five-year span: 44 percent of services were provided publicly ("stable public") and 27 percent privately ("stable private") in both years. However, there was considerable dynamism as well. In 18 percent of the cases, services were newly contracted out, and in 11 percent services that had previously been contracted out in 1992 were completely public by 1997 (what they label "contracting back-in").

The phenomenon of contracting back in is important, both as a possible indicator of conditions in which contracting may prove unsuccessful and as a challenge to those who see an air of inevitability around the shift away from government toward markets in a globalizing economy. Hefertz and Warner test a number of explanations for the variance in new contracting out versus contracting back in, finding, among other things, that governments are most likely to contract back in when they find it difficult to monitor providers, when more professional public managers concluded that monitoring was not working, and when in-house citizen complaint mechanisms revealed dissatisfaction.[37] Public managers, they conclude, make pragmatic decisions about whether and when to contract out or reverse the contracting process. The patterns are partly attributable to local specifics, but also point to a broader understanding of what contracting out entails. Public managers are not simply listening carefully to markets or applying a set of technical administrative criteria: they "do more than steer a market process; they balance technical and political concerns to secure public value."[38]

Taken together, these five lessons of contracting out show the limitations of evaluating PMMs exclusively on technical, managerial, or market criteria. Details of contracting arrangements, administrative infrastructure, and the interaction of supply and demand matter, but they are unlikely in themselves to determine either how portfolio models will evolve or whether they will succeed. Many of the critical levers and contextual factors lie within the realms of politics and governance.

PMMS AS CONTRACTING REGIMES

The evolution of PMM in large urban districts (see Part II in this volume) is often driven by pragmatic adjustment rather than abstract theories. When proponents discuss the approach with others, however, they tend to reach for more abstract rationales and theoretical grounding; "we made it up as we went along" apparently is not seen as a compelling narrative. When such rationales are presented, they most typically are constructed from theories and metaphors tied to economics and corporate management, and often draw strong support from the business community. As is the case with contracting out more generally, however, the changes associated with PMM are not merely technical decisions about modes of organizing and managing the delivery of a public service. Sometimes they are reflections of administrators' context-driven efforts to adapt original designs to concrete local circumstance.[39] They also have important political dimensions as reflections of existing power arrangements and as potential shapers of new power arrangements.

Attending seriously to the political dimensions of contracting can provide insights into two sets of issues raised, but not resolved, in the case chapters included in this volume. The first concerns the timing and pattern of emergence of portfolio management on the policy agenda: why is PMM emerging as a favored reform now and why has it taken root in the particular cities that have begun adopting it to date? The second relates to likely scenarios for the future. There are broad similarities in the language, rationales, and organizational structures associated with the portfolio approach in Chicago, New York, New Orleans, and Philadelphia—similarities that are owed at least in part to the role that foundations (see Reckhow, chapter 10, this volume) and educational entrepreneurs (see Burch, chapter 9, this volume) are playing in disseminating and promoting core ideas. Yet, the case studies also suggest, the way that portfolio models evolve on the ground can differ depending on the local political context and history; this is why seemingly successful models transplanted from one city to another often end up looking and behaving quite differently than anticipated. Consideration of the literature on contracting out in noneducation realms underscores the openness of questions about the future of PMM. Will the portfolio management approach continue to evolve and spread or will it spark the kinds of reassessments or countermobilizations that underlie the general phenomenon of contracting back in?

The concept of regimes emerged within the urban politics literature as a way to understand broad and relatively stable relationships between the public and private sectors. Regime theory starts with the recognition that the formal powers and resources of local government are insufficient for meeting ambitious goals. In order to satisfy campaign promises and their own commitments to making things better, local officials need to build informal alliances with nongovernmental interests that can bring additional resources to bear. This can be done on an ad hoc basis—for example, mounting a temporary collaboration to build a convention center or win a bid to host the Olympics—but establishing a broader and ongoing set of relationships can reduce transaction costs associated with building alliances from scratch. As key individuals and organizations become accustomed to working together, they establish channels of communication, reduce mutual suspicions of one another's motives, and accept short-term losses to the benefit of others in the rational expectation that others will reciprocate in battles down the road. These more stable relationships among public and private interests are what is meant by urban regimes. What earns individuals and interest groups entry into these regimes is partly their ability to help local officials get elected, but more centrally it is their ability to help them govern.

Urban regime theory initially developed as a way to understand the interplay of mayors and business around issues of urban economic development. Stone's seminal study of Atlanta, for example, helped explain the otherwise puzzling fact of the predominantly white downtown business community's continued political access and influence even when business interests may have been on the sidelines or backed a rival during the election of the city's early black mayors.[40]

More recently, the regime concept has been extended to explain the politics of coalition building for urban school reform.[41] Governance regimes for education policy can look different from those dealing with other issues in a city, especially when the formal institutions for making decisions about public schools are separate from those for general-purpose policy making, as is the case where school boards and superintendents operate largely autonomously from mayors, county executives, and city and county councils. Business continues to be an important component of school reform regimes, but its engagement can be episodic and it typically shares the stage—often as a junior partner—with teacher unions, parent and community organizations, and various nonprofit groups, including social service groups advocating for children and organizations representing racial and ethnic minorities.[42] These groups are part of the governance coalition because they care intensely about the issue but also because their cooperation (or opposition) can be critical in determining whether policies flourish or die on the vine. But some reformers—particularly those in the business sector and those operating at the state and national levels—have come to see these traditional, local education regimes as part of the problem instead of the cure. They argue that the balance of influence within these regimes is held by interests overly committed to the status quo, to looking at public school systems more as a source of jobs, political power, and neighborhood status than a vehicle for substantially raising academic achievement or closing achievement gaps.

Public employees typically are important parts of urban political regimes. This is partly due to their intense interest and the fact that their skills and cooperation can be critical determinants of an administration's success. It's partly due, as well, to the fact that public employee unions can muster disproportionate political weight by turning out members in elections, by endorsing and helping to fund candidates for public office, and by using their near-monopoly of information and expertise as a tool for gaining influence.[43] When local districts move toward a portfolio model and extended reliance on private providers and charter schools, the potential is high that they also will reconstruct their governance regimes. They might be forced to do so—because teacher unions will be unsupportive—or they may opt to do so, calculating that shifting their reliance onto a new set of actors may increase their flexibility, effectiveness, and power.

From this vantage point, the construction of contracting regimes in urban education both reflects and may help to support the emergence of a new kind of governance coalition. A governance regime built around contracting with a diverse set of providers has the potential to shift the balance of power and influence, less by directly confronting and defeating the organized interests central to the operation and maintenance of the traditional system than by inviting in new groups and thereby displacing the older ones from center to periphery.[44]

Table 2.2 illustrates this by contrasting a common version of the traditional school governance regime with an alternative alignment that might emerge in portfolio management cities. There are no ironclad rules for how governance coalitions are constituted, as local leaders have an element of discretion and use that strategically. While some may attempt to import models that they think have worked well in other places, they also respond to local political history, established channels of communication and trust, and the personalities and tactics of other actors with whom they are jousting for position and influence. The information in the table, accordingly, should be treated as suggestive of likely tendencies, rather than predictive in any detailed sense.

While the particular stakeholders likely to constitute the core of contracting regimes in particular cities will depend on local circumstance and the coalition-building strategies of local leaders, theories about coalition building in urban politics, combined with case studies of emerging PMM districts such as those in this volume, suggest some possible tendencies.

TABLE 2.2 Contracting versus traditional school governance regimes

	Traditional educational governance regimes	Contracting regimes
Core	• Teacher unions • Parent organizations • School boards • Superintendents and bureaucracy	• Superintendents • Mayors • National foundations • Service providers (for-profit and nonprofit; local and nonlocal) • Mobile business (financial, source of capital), investors • State and national advocates • More entrepreneurial elements of the private education industry (publishing, testing, professional development, management consultants, etc.)
Episodic and variable	• Mayors and councils • Youth advocates • Racial and ethnic advocacy organizations • Downtown business community (place-based source of resources and support) • Local foundations • Parents (as voters and supporters or opponents of local spending and taxation)	• School boards • Teachers unions • Parent organizations • Families as individual consumers • Nonparent citizens as voters (including advocates for lower taxes and spending)

Diminished Role for Traditional Core Participants

Teachers, parents, and school boards may continue to be important actors under contracting arrangements, but their access and influence are likely to be more attenuated. With system leaders able to turn to other groups for resources and support, parent and teacher organizations have to be more active and astute and more willing to join coalitions with others. With authority for many decisions dispersed to principals, charter boards, for-profit and nonprofit school managers, and private support organizations, teacher and parent organizations also lose the benefits of having a clear target and a single battlefield. Official parent-engagement policies in portfolio districts tend to encourage parents to focus their attention on their individual schools rather than engage in system-level activism. Because their ability to mobilize the necessary energy and leverage is finite, teacher and parent organizations in contracting regimes may find it harder to exercise a sustained voice; their influence may wax and wan with events largely out of their direct control.

Larger Roles for General-Purpose Governments and Multi-issue Organizations

The introduction of contracting regimes has tended to coincide with a shift of authority from elected school boards to general-purp
ose governance institutions such as mayors, city councils, governors, and state legislators. Chicago and New York City provide the preeminent examples of mayoral control and are among the United States' most aggressive pursuers of a portfolio management approach (see Gyurko and Henig, chapter 4, this volume; Menefee-Libey, chapter 3, this volume). In New Orleans (Levin et al., chapter 6, this volume) and Philadelphia (Bulkely et al., chapter 5, this volume), the propelling force for contracting arrangements and reliance on nontraditional providers came from the state, with governors and legislative leaders playing important entrepreneurial roles. The causal links behind this association are complicated and likely to run in both directions. For several reasons, districts in which general-purpose governments and officials play major roles may be more likely to apply the contracting model to schools. First, contracting out, as noted earlier, is a familiar and well-established policy tool in areas that municipal and state policy makers deal with all the time, such as urban service delivery, day care, transportation, and social services. Second, elected officials in general-purpose government can afford to be less wary about alienating teacher unions; although the unions are powerful in local and state general-purpose politics, candidates operating in those electoral arenas can find other bases for support from among a broad range of stakeholders, including many for whom schools may not be the highest priority. In general-purpose government institutions, both election to office and the capacity to get things accomplished require drawing support from a broad range of stakeholders, including many for whom schools may not be the highest priority. Third, elected officials in general-purpose institutions are

more likely to already be working closely with foundations, management consultants, financial institutions, and corporations that are proponents of privatization more broadly, whether out of a principled belief in its benefits or more direct and material incentives.

While mayoral and state control have facilitated the introduction of the PMM, moving in the direction of contracting and portfolio management might increase the momentum behind movements for stronger mayoral and state involvement both where they already exist and where it has not yet been instituted. Some supporters of mayoral control see it less as an end in itself than instrumentally—as a step that will make it easier for them to achieve specific reforms they favor, including charter schools and contracting. Reckhow documents the general phenomenon of foundation support for mayoral control and expands on this point in chapter 10 in this volume.[45] "Although most foundations do not publicly endorse a particular mode of governing school districts," she observes, the Broad Foundation's 2008 *Annual Report* says quite explicitly that, "We have found that the conditions to dramatically improve K–12 education are often ripe under mayoral or state control" (as cited in Reckhow, this volume).

Shifting Membership Within the Business Community

As noted earlier, the downtown office and commercial business community that Stone and others found to be critical in urban development regimes has been more peripheral and occasional in its involvement in school governance regimes. Contracting regimes are likely to draw business interests into a more central role, but the representation of the business community may shift. Urban regimes built around downtown development and urban growth tend to be centered on the manufacturing, retail, and commercial office sectors—groups that often are anchored in the local area and constrained in their ability to pick up and move in search of a more lucrative or business-friendly location.[46] In contrast, contracting regimes built around education are likely to be marked by greater involvement from the growing private education sector, including not only those groups that directly manage schools but also the wide array of businesses that sell products to support the education enterprise (publishers, professional training, testing services, etc.) and the broader financial community, which often serves as a source of investment capital and philanthropic support.[47] Groups like these tend to see contracting regimes as more hospitable markets than traditional systems that may provide services directly or use their public monopoly to support favored providers at the expense of new and more entrepreneurial firms.

Kelleher and Yackee provide some empirical support that contracting out opens a new pathway for organized interests, especially contracting firms, to lobby and influence public managers.[48] They look at the phenomenon at the state level and do not focus specifically on education or schools. A survey sent to all (1,175) state agency heads in 1998 and 2004 asked respondents to assess how influential certain categories of interest groups were in affecting overall budgets, budgets for specific programs, and major policy change. Agency heads were also asked how much time they spent interacting with interest groups. The analysis related an overall interest-group-influence dependent variable to state and agency characteristics including reported use of contracting out. In a multilevel analysis, controlling for other state and individual administrator variables, they found a modest but statistically significant relationship between the contracting scale and the overall influence of organized interests as perceived by state agency heads. Moreover, they found an interaction between contracting and time spent with organized interests, suggesting to them that contracting both increases the access of private organizations to public officials and that "more provocatively . . . government managers may—overtly or inadvertently—shift their management strategies, orientations, and decision making when government contractors are utilized."[49]

Larger Role for Nonlocal versus Local Actors

In general, school systems with heavy reliance on contracting might be less likely than traditional school systems to favor place-based actors for inclusion in their governance regimes. Traditional school governance systems were designed to reflect local values. This orientation toward localism was rooted in core American values, but also was hardwired into the institutions through which school boards are selected and school revenues derived.[50] In practice, this localism extended a favored place for individuals and groups with direct ties in and loyalties to the community. In extremis, this meant that superintendents tended to be hired from within;

jobs and other forms of patronage tended to be reserved for those with local political sponsors.

Contracting regimes create pressure to extend the geographic scope of efforts to solicit school founders, managers, teachers, and the providers of educational support services of various kinds. National organizations—such as the KIPP network of charter schools, Teach For America, The New Teachers Project, NewSchools Venture Fund, EdisonLearning, Inc., and national foundations like the Broad Foundation and the Bill & Melinda Gates Foundation—are not especially useful allies in the hurly-burly of local elections, but they can be critically important allies to mayors or school superintendents seeking to build governance regimes with the resources to get things done. One local newspaper, having examined Michelle Rhee's calendar as chancellor in Washington, D.C. (a district that has been moving in the direction of a PMM), characterized her as having become

> part of a vast network of education-oriented charities, think tanks, business interests, and "venture philanthropists." Her talks with and wooing of this educational-industrial complex have both enmeshed her in the for-profit and nonprofit sectors of her new city and have taken her across the country to speak to grad students, corporate functionaries, and masters of the universe.[51]

Among those with which she was reported to have had contact over the first seventeen months of her tenure were: the Gates Foundation (ten contacts), the Broad Foundation (eleven), Walton Family Foundation (four), NewSchools Venture Fund (eight), Venture Philanthropy Partners (nine), the Robertson Foundation (a major funder in New York City of both the Klein initiatives and New York charter schools (two), and New Leaders for New Schools (six). "I see fundraising as a big part of the job," Rhee told the paper. Fixing the system is her goal, she said, "and part of that certainly is trying to bring every resource you possibly can to bear."[52]

The kinds of resources that nonlocal allies provide to contracting regimes include direct financial support that is valuable beyond the dollar amount because it is more discretionary and less subject to veto efforts by unions and others with access to local elected officials (see Gyurko and Henig, chapter 4; Reckhow, chapter 10, this volume). Just as important, though, may be national networks for recruiting school leaders and accessing venture capital. Hill et al. emphasize that portfolio districts must aggressively intervene on the supply side, not only closing bad schools but continually attracting or creating new schools, new educational entrepreneurs, new teachers, and support services for testing and data management that are needed in order to institute an effective oversight and accountability capacity.[53] Alliances with national organizations can also add legitimacy to local education leaders, enhancing their ability to use the mantle of nationally recognized expertise to buttress their efforts and portray local opponents as parochial and out-of-date.

Incorporating nonlocal actors into an educational governance regime is a delicate and risky step, however. Localism is not dead, and political opponents can often mobilize resentment against outsiders and carpetbaggers who are "just in it for the money" and who "don't understand our community and our kids." One response is to openly extend an invitation to local organizations to compete for schools-related contracts; that has the twin advantages of reducing resistance and further extending potential supply. Yet, reflecting on the way this played out in Philadelphia, Gold et al. argue that the cost of gaining access to contracts may be a weakened ability of local organizations to aggressively exercise voice and influence within the governance regime: "[the] contracted group can easily be discouraged from criticizing the district."[54] To district leaders, muffling dissent might seem like an added bonus, but this may come at a societal cost if it prevents the airing of rival perspectives that would enrich democratic deliberation. "Furthermore," Gold et al. suggest, "by structuring relationships as district-to-partner or district-to-contractor, this process makes genuine collaboration and collective action more difficult."[55]

Larger Role for Citywide Organizations

The contracting regimes we see emerging under PMM aim to reallocate key decision-making responsibilities, simultaneously shifting some to the central office and others to the school level. Midlevel ranges of the education system bureaucracy are quite explicitly targeted for reduction in number and authority. Less openly discussed is the tension between the portfolio model and governance units and political organizations that represent geographic slices of the city larger than individual schools but smaller than the city as a whole. This includes formal structures like community advisory boards, wards, or community school districts such as those in New York City. It also can include other neighborhood and community-based associations that may lack a formal governance role but have well-established and loyal constituencies and serve as mobilizing platforms for projecting and protecting community voice.

Organizations that operate on these subcity geographic levels have their own perspectives on what constitutes good and bad policy. The most obvious flash points involve decisions about school closures, new schools, small schools, charter schools, and the deemphasis of community-based schools that serve a geographically defined area in favor of a differentiated array of schools that are open to students regardless of where they live. PMM proponents acknowledge that school closures and openings are controversial, but tend to dismiss resistance as knee-jerk, parochial, and self-interested turf battles that favor emotion over reason and threaten their efforts to do what is best for the city as a whole. Although New York City's history with community school districts is somewhat idiosyncratic, the self-conscious efforts by the Michael Bloomberg–Joel Klein administration to eliminate the community school districts (and, failing that, to shrink their authority), as discussed by Gyurko and Henig (chapter 4, this volume), likely reflects a common pressure in contracting regimes to frame problems and solutions in terms of functions instead of places.[56]

IMPLICATIONS FOR URBAN SCHOOL REFORM

This chapter has developed two broad themes. First, rather than a startlingly new and unique idea, the PMM being developed in some major urban school districts is broadly analogous to contracting arrangements that have long been common in other areas of state and urban policy. That they are not unprecedented does not mean that they are stale or unimportant; as noted, the education policy arena has been overly taken with the notion that new means better, and that has contributed to its tendency to waste energy spinning its own wheels.[57] What it does mean is that analysts and reformers seeking to understand or steer the phenomenon do not need to start from scratch. There are lessons from contracting arrangements elsewhere that can and should be brought to bear.

Second, understanding the emergence and future evolution of PMMs requires understanding how they are integrated with supporting networks of power and politics. This may seem ironic. Champions of the approach often portray it as a tool for taking political considerations out of the policy process. Like Cerberus, the three-headed creature who, in Greek mythology, patrolled the boundary between the Earth and the Underworld, the stern twins of competition and accountability are imagined able to sniff out and destroy influences based on partisanship, patronage, and political self-interest. Like any reform that proposes to change ways of doing business, alter decision-making criteria, and reallocate government priorities and actions, portfolio management threatens some political interests and holds out the promise of increased access and benefits to others. To imagine that politics would not play a role in determining the success and sustainability of that kind of reform seems either naive or disingenuous.

Let's be clear. Acknowledging the importance of politics need not mean cynically abandoning the ideal of aspiring to more informed and evidence-based reforms. It does not require abandoning the field to those with greater access and clout. From the standpoint of analysis and prediction, it means wrestling with the likelihood that idealized models will be pulled and tugged and reformulated as they are institutionalized, that the policy-in-practice that emerges will differ based on local context and local battles, and that the differences will *make* a difference the outcomes. From the standpoint of a reformer, acknowledging the importance of politics means recognizing not just the necessity but the appropriateness of using politics, because politics is not just about parochial interests blocking new ideas; it is also about animating new visions of the collective interest and mobilizing the support needed to propel and protect change in a pluralistic and largely democratic system.

It is too early to draw strong conclusions about the portfolio management model and its likely consequences. This chapter and the edited volume of which it is a part are intended to set the foundation for more research and more focused deliberation, not to rush to judgment about a phenomenon still in the formative stage.

PART II

Case Studies

3

—

Neoliberal School Reform in Chicago?

Renaissance 2010,
Portfolios of Schools, and
Diverse Providers

David Menefee-Libey

On June 24, 2004, Mayor Richard M. Daley and Superintendent Arne Duncan announced the launch of Renaissance 2010, a major new initiative they proclaimed as a way to replace or revitalize the worst-performing schools and turn around the Chicago Public Schools (CPS).[1] They argued that "Ren10," as it came to be called, would lead to the rebirth of the district through the creation of a hundred new schools by 2010, offering new choices and instructional programs to parents and children and sharpening the district's focus on schoolwide efforts as the principal means of educational improvement. The initiative drew heavily on recommendations from the Civic Committee of The Commercial Club of Chicago, which the previous summer had presented a stinging indictment of the district's performance in a report entitled *Left Behind*. That report showed that after eight years of mayoral control, poor children and children of color were still consigned to attend persistently underperforming schools in the most segregated neighborhoods of the city.[2] The committee recommended that the district stop wasting its time trying to improve such schools and instead close them and encourage the creation of new replacement schools modeled on the existing charter system. Daley and Duncan responded nearly a year later with Ren10.

This was not a revolutionary policy change drawn up from scratch, nor was it a thorough shift to a portfolio management approach for the district. The contemporary era of Chicago school reform had begun in 1988, and with strong support from foundations and elite advocacy groups, Ren10 adapted and redirected the existing school-level policies of CPS, including, principally:

- Test-based accountability begun by Superintendent Paul Vallas during the 1990s, which continued to evolve with changing curriculum standards, assessments, and proficiency requirements.

- Charter schools created under a 1996 state law, which was subsequently reinterpreted and amended to allow the creation of nearly eighty charter schools in the district.

- Contract schools first established in 2001 under an obscure provision of the 1995 state law granting mayoral control over the whole system.

- Human capital initiatives encouraged by Duncan to increase and improve the pool of principals and teachers capable of leading cohesive and high-quality schools.

Duncan pulled these policies together in Ren10 and worked to align the closing of underperforming schools with the creation of new schools to serve the predominantly low-income and minority students affected by the closings. Importantly, he also encouraged the differentiation of existing schools, using performance indicators to trigger intervention or autonomy from close district oversight.

Ren10 has proved to be a challenge both politically and as a policy initiative. Politically, it has confirmed the ongoing importance of the Civic Committee of The Commercial Club of Chicago and a broader network of business leaders in shaping CPS, solidified Mayor Daley's control over CPS, and drawn business and nonprofit leaders into collaboration with the district in unprecedented ways. This work drew national attention to a district, and its successful components helped propel Duncan into President Obama's cabinet as his Secretary of Education. On its headline educational reform proposal, the district has seen the creation of more than a hundred new schools. Several recent evaluations have found that Renaissance 2010 schools of various kinds have not substantially improved student outcomes in the aggregate, and there has been significant political resistance to school closings and the undercutting of the authority of the elected Local School Councils (LCSs) initiated by an earlier round of reform in the 1980s. This provoked speculation that Daley might be open to a change of direction after Duncan departed in early 2009. But there was enough good news in those evaluations to give Daley and his supporters reason to believe that the approach was working, and his new superintendent, Ron Huberman, signaled a consolidation of CPS management around differentiated interventions and autonomy.

Taken as a whole, Renaissance 2010 puts Chicago among the leaders in a new approach in school district reform described in this book: a blending of diverse public and private provision for students, and differentiation of entrepreneurial schools into a diverse portfolio to be managed by district leaders. In Chicago and elsewhere, this combination of strategies follows patterns of what is often called "the new governance" or a "neoliberal" policy approach common in businesses and governments across the developed world. Such policies often blend public and private provision, with public components increasingly staffed by conditional employees rather than career civil servants or union workers, subject to contractual accountability for outcomes, heavily focused on numerical data for bottom-line accountability, and subject to sharp fiscal management discipline from above.[3] To date, the leaders of Ren10 have embraced all of these components, but have only partially pursued other common neoliberal priorities such as transparency, public agreement on consistent indicators for evaluation, and "depoliticized" insulation from constituency-based politics.

In this chapter, I will first offer a brief introduction to the CPS and the three waves of reform that began in the late 1980s under Mayor Harold Washington. Next, I will describe Renaissance 2010 in more detail, exploring ways in which Duncan and other district leaders increasingly came to see the initiative as a portfolio approach to managing the district. I will then explore the political underpinnings of the reform and its grounding in a neoliberal approach to policy and public management.

WAVES OF SCHOOL REFORM: THE CHICAGO PUBLIC SCHOOLS

Chicago is perhaps the prime exemplar of the troubled big-city public school district in the United States. The district has been in a state of permanent crisis for decades: ordinary citizens and organized interests alike have come to believe that CPS does not perform at an acceptable level, and that the school system's leaders have proved incapable of reforming it from within.[4] In such a context, the school district has been continuously open to dramatically new ideas and major policy initiatives, especially from outsiders and entrepreneurial politicians. Since the 1980s, such initiatives have come to the district in waves, culminating in a third wave that includes Renaissance 2010.[5]

First, some background. CPS comprises the third largest school district in the United States, behind New York City and Los Angeles. During the 2009–2010 academic year, CPS had an operating budget of $5.33 billion and enrolled 417,855 students from preschool through high school.[6] Poor students and students of color are the large majorities. About 85 percent of children qualify for the federal Free and Reduced-Price Meals program. Just over 45 percent of students are African American, and 41 percent are Latino, while only 9 percent are white, 3.6 percent are identified as Asian/ Pacific Islander, and 0.2 percent are Native American. Though Latino enrollments are substantial, only 12.2 percent of students are identified as having Limited English Proficiency, a proportion far lower than many large urban districts in the United States.

The district had 43,731 full-time employees during the 2009–2010 academic year, including 23,110 teachers and 592 principals. The teachers are represented by the Chicago Teachers Union, affiliated with the American Federation of Teachers (AFT), and they work in the district's 675 schools, of which 482 are elementary schools covering kindergarten through eighth grade. The district has historically not had junior highs, intermediate, or middle schools, but it has 122 high schools covering ninth through twelfth grades. Five years into Renaissance 2010, the district includes a variety of other school forms, as indicated in table 3.1.

TABLE 3.1 Chicago Public Schools by type, 2009–2010

Elementary schools (K–8th grade)		High schools	
Total	524	**Total**	151
Traditional	395	General/technical	41
Magnet	36	Magnet	5
		Selective enrollment	8
Gifted centers	12	Achievement academy	8
Classical	4	Career academy	8
Small	4	Small	11
		Military academy	6
Special education	8	Special education	5
Charter	42	Charter	29
Contract	8	Contract	7
Middle	10	Alternative	8

Other "autonomous schools" designations	
Autonomous management performance schools (AMPS)	128
Innovation schools	22
Diverse provider network schools	11
Recognition schools	49

Sources: Chicago Public Schools, *Stats and Facts* (Chicago: Chicago Public Schools, 2009), http://www.cps.edu/About_CPS/At-a-glance/Pages/Stats_and_facts.aspx; Office of New Schools, "Charter and Contract High Schools Opened 1997–2009," *Chicago Public Schools*, December 22, 2009, http://www.ren2010.cps.k12.il.us/docs/Charter_and_Contract_High_School_Profiles_Public_Use_12_22_09.pdf; Autonomous Management and Performance Schools Office, *Autonomous Management and Performance Schools (AMPS)* (Chicago: Chicago Public Schools, 2009), http://www.cps.edu/About_CPS/Departments/Pages/AutonomousManagementandPerformanceSchools.aspx.

Note: Schools reported in "Other 'autonomous schools'" are also included in the elementary and high school counts above.

Wave One: the Chicago School Reform Act of 1988

The contemporary era of school reform in Chicago began with the Illinois state legislature's passage of the Chicago School Reform Act of 1988. The development of that law had been touched off by then-mayor Harold Washington, who convened a citywide summit in 1987 in response to public frustration with dismal school quality and persistent teacher strikes.[7] Even after Washington's death later that year, momentum continued, spurred on in part by U.S. Secretary of Education William Bennett, who called the district's schools "the worst in the nation."[8] The most powerful driver of reform after Washington's death, however, was a complex local coalition of neighborhood activists, nonprofit organizations, and business leaders, all of whom agreed that the time had come for major change.

Within months, they had successfully pressed the Illinois state legislature to enact the Chicago School Reform Act of 1988, which moved the district strongly toward a school-level approach to educational improvement. The law mandated the creation of elected LSCs, each of which was empowered to choose its school's principal and create a school improvement plan, then implement that plan in part through control over the school's share of state Title I money.[9] The sheer scale of innovation and grassroots mobilization was remarkable: hundreds of thousands of residents turned out in October 1989 to elect more than 5,400 LSC members to run the city's 550 schools.[10] This shift toward focusing on the school as the locus of reform was new to Chicago, but it was a hallmark of late-1980s and early-1990s reform in many U.S. cities: restructuring and decentralization of control over instruction to enable parents, teachers, and principals to develop an autonomous educational program best suited to the needs of local children.[11]

The legislation reached higher into CPS as well. Though the law continued the mayor's existing authority to appoint members of the school board, it mandated that he choose members from a slate nominated by the School Board Nominating Commission, which was in turn elected by LSC members.[12] The law also placed a cap on central office administrative expenses and required greater equity in the distribution of district funds among schools. It also required that the district develop systemwide goals for student achievement.[13] The CPS central office responded by developing an elaborate system of oversight for LSCs and schools but only very limited technical assistance, an approach that frequently drew objections from local parents and teachers.[14]

The 1988 law spurred other developments as well. It empowered a diverse array of nonprofit organizations to greater engagement in district developments—including Designs for Change, the Chicago Panel on Public School Policy and Finance, and Chicago United—and the local philanthropic community made substantial contributions to support the development of LSC capacity. The Community Renewal Society, a century-old church-based foundation in the city, founded *Catalyst: Chicago*, which evolved into an authoritative monthly news magazine and Web site focused entirely on CPS. Education policy researchers at the University of Chicago and other colleges and universities formed the Consortium on Chicago School Research (CCSR) in Hyde Park on the South Side.[15] CCSR quickly developed into a substantial policy development and evaluation organization, doing extensive research on the implementation and effects of the 1988 reforms and often collaborating with the district. Among other things, CCSR researchers found that the reform worked as intended at some schools, while others substantially failed to improve.[16] This drew disparate responses: some worked to improve LSCs and their capacities to improve schools, while others took it as evidence that such a bottom-up approach to reform could never work systemwide.

The LSC-based system was barely getting established when Daley won his first election as mayor in April 1989. Daley had expressed strong support for the reforms while running for mayor, and he gladly appointed an interim board to serve until the LSC elections could be held in October and an LSC-controlled School Board Nominating Commission could nominate longer-term members. Early in 1990, however, Daley began working to preempt the development of an LSC power base that might challenge his control over the district's headquarters and direction. The interim board appointed a new superintendent, Ted Kimbrough, in January, and in March, when the commission presented Daley with candidates to replace his appointees, he resisted.[17] Daley's relations with the LSCs and their supporters quickly soured, establishing a pattern that has continued to some degree ever since. Nevertheless, the five years of the first wave of Chicago school reform brought substantial school-focused innovation and development.[18]

Wave Two: Mayoral Control

The second wave of Chicago school reform began in 1995, spurred in part by the polarized partisan politics of the Bill Clinton–Newt Gingrich era. When Republicans swept to power in the 1994 midterm election, Illinois was the site of one of their greatest victories, as they won control of both chambers of the state legislature and every statewide office. In early 1995, Governor Jim Edgar and other Republican leaders negotiated with Daley on substantial changes to the Chicago School Reform Act, and the legislature enacted the result in May.

The core provision of the sweeping new law was mayoral control: it gave Daley the power to appoint the district's superintendent and a smaller school reform board to replace the existing Chicago school board.[19] But the law had several other major components. Some were targeted explicitly at the powerful Chicago Teachers Union and dramatically reduced its influence in the district. The law limited collective bargaining on many issues related to curriculum, assessment, and resource allocation within schools, and placed sharp restrictions on the union's right to strike.[20] It also freed CPS to contract out almost any kind of service, a provision that would become much more important later. Along with several fiscal provisions giving the district greater autonomy over its spending practices, the law also toughened state testing requirements and began to lay the groundwork for test-based accountability for students and schools.

Daley welcomed his new authority over the district and appointed his budget director, Paul Vallas, as the district's new chief executive officer and Gery Chico as reform board president in June. Vallas and Chico approached their work in the district's Pershing Road headquarters with zeal, initiating sweeping changes in several areas and bringing a bottom-line business orientation to the district's management.[21] They pressed for the contracting out of district services, initially for building maintenance and janitorial services, but ultimately for entire schools. They challenged the weakened teacher union by pressing for merit pay for teachers, and they challenged the lax educational culture of the district by requiring students to demonstrate academic proficiency before they were allowed promotion to the next grade.

With Daley's support, Vallas and Chico also worked to establish limits on LSC autonomy when a school's test scores and other measures fell below certain levels. The relationship between the LSCs and the central office deteriorated further when the reform board mandated CPS-approved training of all LSC members. In essence, Vallas worked to place boundaries on LSC autonomy to make it conditional on the performance of schools. This retained the school-focused logic of reform established in the first wave, but moved sharply away from the decentralization of control that had come with it. It was not an entirely punitive approach: with help from the Chicago Annenberg Challenge, the district sponsored support for the LSCs in developing plans for schoolwide improvement. But the bottom line was that Vallas wanted to differentiate schools by their performance and to conditionally grant autonomy or conduct aggressive interventions, depending on how they scored on performance indicators he was working to develop and control.

Such accountability was difficult in Illinois at the time. The state required that students take the Iowa Tests of Basic Skills (ITBS), a national norm-referenced test not closely aligned with state or district curriculum standards. Vallas worked with CCSR to develop alternative means of assessment, but until they were in place, any intervention focused on students or schools remained difficult. Nevertheless, high standards and accountability remained central to his vision for system improvement throughout his time as superintendent.[22]

A major part of Daley's and Vallas's vision of the district was the reinvention of schools themselves, and they were strongly influenced by views that large schools were an important problem. In an effort to create more human-scale and effective instruction, Vallas embraced the small-schools movement, which began in earnest in Chicago in the mid-1990s, partly through the district's collaboration with the Chicago Annenberg Challenge and other national reform projects, and partly through locally driven initiatives. Leadership for Quality Education (LQE), a nonprofit launched by the Civic Committee of The Commercial Club of Chicago, collaborated with Vallas on creating the program.[23] One major participant was the Small Schools Workshop led by Michael Klonsky and others, which worked with teachers and parents as well as principals.

Another major development during this second wave was charter school legislation enacted by the state legislature in 1996, which allowed for the creation of forty-five charter schools statewide, including fifteen in Chicago. State-level Republicans may have thought of charters as a partisan initiative, challenging what they saw as the Democratic party's attachment to conventional schools and school districts. But Daley saw charter schools as a tool for injecting innovation and improvement into the public school system and embraced them enthusiastically. After the passage of the law, Vallas and Chico arranged immediate contact with potential school providers and circulated a request for proposals. Thirty-eight potential charter providers submitted proposals, of which the district approved only ten in January 1997. During the following months, the providers and the district struggled and in many cases failed to find facilities to house the schools, and only six opened in September 1997. One quickly failed, but five more gained district approval and opened in the fall of 1998. It took four years for the district to reach its limit of fifteen, but the experiment was well under way.

The cap on charters had one odd side-effect. Daley and Vallas bristled at the limit because they thought charter schools were a promising means of bringing improvement. So they found two ways to increase the number beyond fifteen. First, Vallas began looking for ways to create something that might be as close to charters as possible without violating the cap. After consultation with the district's lawyers, he decided to draw on the provision of the 1995 reform law that allowed the district to contract out for services. If you can contract out for janitorial services, they reasoned, why not contract out for an entire school? Thus, a whole new category of schools was born in CPS: contract schools.

His first opportunity to put this idea into practice came through a collaboration with venture capitalist Martin "Mike" Koldyke, who "set out to create his own teacher training school for career-changers."[24] This led to the fall 2001 opening of the Chicago Academy, a hybrid organization in which a CPS school was staffed by teachers that included the trainers and trainees of a teacher academy. The principal of the school reported to the district, and its permanent teachers worked under a Chicago Teachers Union contract. The school's LSC lacked some of the authority of the standard council—the school was governed in part by a board of directors—and the school admitted students through a lottery rather than attendance boundaries. The arrangements were improvised and idiosyncratic, but the distinctive instructional approach and accountability system were perfectly consistent with a differentiated school-by-school approach to innovation and improvement, and did not conflict with Daley's and Vallas's desire for more charter schools.

Second, Vallas and his attorneys developed the notion that while the law might have limited the number of charters the district could allow, the law did not limit the number of schools each charter operator could run. There was nothing that said a charter could only operate on one school "campus." On the contrary, each charter should be allowed to "replicate" its model on multiple campuses. After months of discussion and negotiations, the first of these replication campuses opened in the fall of 2001, sponsored by the Chicago International Charter School (CICS) and the Lawndale Educational and Regional Network (LEARN).

Throughout this second wave of reforms, Vallas left no doubt about the political logic of his work. In a 1999 interview at the Manhattan Institute around the time Daley secured his third reelection, Vallas boasted of the district's improvement under his leadership, but insisted that:

> The credit for all this goes above all to Mayor Daley . . . In Chicago today, Mayor Daley is responsible for the schools—no debate. He appoints a five-person corporate board and a CEO. The CEO, with the consent of the board, appoints everybody else. We have a holy trinity—Daley, the board, and the management team I head. Before we go public with things, we always reach a consensus on what we want to do. We speak with one voice. So if the schools go bad, there's a political price to pay. The responsibility begins and ends with the mayor.[25]

This political logic presented an aggressive challenge to the conventional politics of public education, which was grounded in diffuse public support for the system and driven by interest-group politics dominated by teacher unions and grassroots community advocates. Daley built his successful mayoral campaigns with support from a long-established but significantly different political coalition, focused on the business community and the broader economic development of the city, and his business-oriented approach appealed to Vallas. The power of the business community in this Chicago school reform coalition is arguably more profound than in any of the cities highlighted in this book, and it has continued long after the departure of Vallas and Chico. By the time they resigned in early 2001, their performance had helped Daley take substantial control over the district and move it in entirely new directions.

Vallas's policy logic was equally aggressive, but less particular to Chicago. Like Daley, he rejected the worldview of the twentieth-century administrative progressives, who pushed school districts toward bureaucratic accountability built around a "logic of confidence" that good practice would bring about good results. Advocates of this view held that, as long as professional teachers and administrators in the system did their work well, one could have confidence that the system was performing as well as it could educationally, and expensive and data-intensive attention to outcomes was not worth the effort.[26] In contrast, Daley and Vallas sided with reformers who called on educators to move to a more business-oriented "logic of accountability." Advocates of this view held that the credentials and practices of professionals in the system were less important than the outcomes of schooling for students, and that reform and change should be accountable to those outcomes. Of course, detractors countered that this simply exchanged a logic of confidence in professional educators for a logic of confidence in managerial professionals, but in any case Daley and Vallas sided with the winners in this battle for control.[27]

Vallas continued to battle for nearly five years, but his patience (and support from Daley) gradually waned. Convinced that he had accomplished all he could as the district's CEO, Vallas announced his resignation in June 2001, and within a month he launched an unsuccessful campaign for the 2002 Democratic nomination in the Illinois governor's race. In July 2002, he was named CEO of the School District of Philadelphia.

Origins of Wave Three: Duncan and Differentiated Schools

After Vallas's departure from Chicago, Daley quickly replaced him with Arne Duncan, Vallas's thirty-six-year-old chief of staff. Duncan appointed former principal Barbara Eason-Watkins as his chief educational officer. Initially, it appeared that his major departure from Vallas's policies would be his insistence that the policies he inherited be supported by a broader approach to serving the district's children.[28] He proposed universal access to preschool and targeting wraparound services to the city's at-risk children.

Yet, while making some other changes—for example, ending school interventions because he said they didn't work—Duncan initially presented himself as carrying forward Vallas's reforms of the district or taking initiatives with approaches similar to Vallas's. Within his first year, Duncan and Eason-Watkins created eighteen Area Instructional Officers (AIOs) to assist in instructional improvements and help principals better manage their schools.[29] Duncan pushed the further development of assessment systems and data analysis, embracing the standards-based Prairie State Achievement Examination in 2002 and worked to develop more effective strategies for school improvement. His work was reinforced by the passage of the federal No Child Left Behind Act at the beginning of 2002.

Duncan also carried forward Vallas's commitment to charter and contract schools. Duncan viewed the creation of new schools—especially schools intended to serve low-income and minority students formerly enrolled in the closed schools—as the most powerful educational improvement tool available to the district. His view came partly from the performance of CPS initiatives under Vallas and partly from his own experience heading a private foundation, the Ariel Education Initiative, when it created the Ariel Community Academy as a magnet elementary school in 1996.[30] Duncan incorporated new school creation into his 2002 "Every Child, Every School: Education Plan for the Chicago Public Schools" after he became CEO.[31] And when the state legislature raised the cap on Chicago's charter schools to thirty in 2003, Duncan welcomed the change and encouraged new school providers to step forward.

But the publication of *Left Behind* by the Civic Committee of The Commercial Club of Chicago got Daley's attention in 2003, and he pressed Duncan for a more school-specific approach to reform that led to the launch of Ren10. One major catalyst was the *Left Behind* report's focus on huge swaths of the city's south and west sides, which were profoundly underserved educationally: there simply were no good schools for most students to attend. Duncan was already committed to starting new schools, but this catalyzed the mayor's attention and pushed this to the front of his schools' agenda. There were outside influences as well: Duncan had met with New York City Superintendent Joel Klein at a conference in Aspen, Colorado, and the two had discussed that city's reform initiatives. *Catalyst* picked up on Duncan's references to national school reform trends and reported that "[e]lements of the district's new schools plan are borrowed from similar efforts in Boston and New York."[32]

The ongoing role of philanthropy in school-based reform leading up to Renaissance 2010—and the establishment of new schools—is also substantial. During the 1990s, two major philanthropic initiatives helped lay the groundwork for Renaissance 2010. First, the Chicago Annenberg Challenge focused on schoolwide improvement in collaboration with the

LSCs. Next, with the assistance of the Bill & Melinda Gates Foundation, the district developed the Chicago High School Redesign Initiative (CHSRI). The conversion of three high schools—Bowen, South Shore, and Orr—began in the fall of 2002. This conversion strategy resulted in the creation of twelve small high schools. In 2003, the Gates Foundation awarded CHSRI an additional $7.6 million to support a "new school start" strategy. The strategy provided opportunities for small high schools to be created and housed in schools that were phasing out, vacant, or newly constructed facilities. Between 2003 and 2007, CHSRI supported the creation of twelve new starts.[33]

All told, foundations and philanthropists have contributed perhaps $200 million to school improvement in Chicago over the past two decades. This initially impressive sum pales when one considers that the district's annual budget has consistently exceeded $4 billion—the philanthropic contribution amounted to 0.25 percent of the roughly $80 billion spent by CPS between 1988 and 2008—but foundation grants did gain the attention of district leaders and shaped their initiatives, in part because the money was less encumbered by existing policy (see Reckhow, chapter 10).

By the spring of 2003, the components for building Renaissance 2010 were to some degree in place: a focus on schools as the locus of educational improvement, emerging systems for assessing and differentiating schools on the basis of student outcomes, several different ways of creating distinct schools, a variety of supportive services to help them improve, and a strong commitment of financial support from national and local philanthropies and local business leaders.

RENAISSANCE 2010

Newspaper headlines the day after the launch of Renaissance 2010 focused on new schools, but Ren10 is far more than that. At its core, it attempts to draw together school evaluation, school closings, and the creation of new schools in new and coordinated ways in order to spur continuous improvement in the district's educational outcomes for children. Though it took a few years for Duncan to develop such a cohesive explanation, ultimately Renaissance 2010 gradually converged into what we call a portfolio management approach to school reform and educational improvement.

A portfolio management district takes a strategic approach by focusing on the school—not the district, not the curriculum, not the classroom or the teacher—as the locus of educational improvement.[34] In theory, a portfolio management school district must do four things. First, it must evaluate schools by some agreed-on standards for attendance, curricular or school completion, testing, or anything else required by the district or state. Second, it must differentiate its handling of schools based on the evaluation outcomes, allowing satisfactory schools to go on doing what they are doing until the next round of evaluations, and intervening in underperforming schools. Third, a portfolio district must close schools that persistently fail to achieve required outcomes. And fourth, such a district must create or enable the creation of new schools. Following the logic of the theory, this approach leads to two simultaneous cycles: satisfactory schools engaging in continuous improvement, informed by regular performance assessments, and underperforming schools being replaced by new and more capable ones. A district may do any number of things to support these cycles, including, for example, curricular development, recruitment and training of principals and teachers, or the provision of wraparound social services. But all schools, according to this theory, develop to perform better on the required metrics and either gain autonomy or face intervention, depending on their performance.

Under Duncan and through Renaissance 2010, CPS pursued each of these four tasks and applied them to at least some of the schools in the district. None of these activities were new to CPS; all of the components had already been initiated before the launch in 2004. The important thing about Renaissance 2010 was the effort to pull them together into a cohesive strategy. Each of them proved to be technically difficult and politically contentious, and they continue to be so.

School Evaluation

As in many states and cities across the United States, student testing has evolved dramatically in Illinois and Chicago since the mid-1990s, when CPS embraced the ITBS as its principal instrument for evaluating students and schools. ITBS, a national norm-referenced test not closely aligned with state curriculum requirements, was supplemented at the high school level by the standards-based Tests of Achievement and Proficiency

(TAP). In 2002, Illinois and Chicago shifted to the standards-based Prairie State Achievement Examination.

Illinois has struggled with school evaluation for decades, lacking the uniform curriculum standards and sustained testing system necessary to enable performance assessments over time. CPS worked to establish its own standards and assessment systems, often in collaboration with CCSR, and in the past decade it has homed in on a more consistent set of measures for school performance.[35] The development of CCSR gave the district some autonomy from national and state debates over curriculum standards and assessments, enabling Duncan and CPS to integrate some CCSR analysis and ideas into its efforts to identify schools for intervention or increased autonomy under Renaissance 2010. The consortium also helped CPS identify essential supports of school improvement and helped develop tools to assess and document where performance was getting better and worse. According to interviews conducted for this study, CPS sought to create evaluation indicators robust enough to enable three very different purposes:

- Informed school improvement, which required data that could identify quality curriculum, effective instructors or instructional practice, or student performance, among others.

- District evaluation of schools to trigger appropriate grants of autonomy or interventions, up to and including school closings or revocation of a charter.

- Evaluation of schools and educational options by parents, students, and the broader public in order to inform attendance choice and public support for particular schools.

Thus, the district—often in collaboration with CCSR—worked to develop evaluation and performance data systems not just for districts bureaucrats and managers, but for broader audiences as well.

Both Vallas and Duncan had argued for a data system accessible to parents who wanted to know how their kids' school was performing, or wanted to be able to compare their school with others in the district. Research then and now suggested most parents knew little about school performance, so this was a major challenge.[36] Mayor Daley and the superintendents also pressed for school choice for students and parents, which they viewed as an essential element of school improvement and a potential political driver for continued reform. More broadly, they wanted the city's residents and voters to know how schools were performing as they made choices about where to live, whether to vote for the mayor in the next election, whether to support increased taxes for schools, or whether to support the people who worked for the district.

School Differentiation, Positive and Negative

Drawing on school-level aggregates of these assessments, the district worked to create tiers of autonomy and intervention for schools. Differentiation represented a fork in the road: schools performing to a satisfactory level would be treated differently from underperforming schools. Switching metaphors, Duncan and CPS worked to develop carrots as well as sticks.[37] The most visible carrot for satisfactory schools was freedom from central office interference. Duncan offered carrots through a new Autonomous Schools Office (ASO), which opened in 2006 to serve existing schools that performed well. The office's February 2009 brochure gave a sense of the scale and approach that had evolved by that time:

> There are 139 autonomous schools, classified into four categories based on how they came to be autonomous and their current relationship with the district (see p. 2). With an enrollment of just over 100,000 students, the autonomous schools serve one-quarter of all Chicago Public Schools (CPS) students; if they were a school district, they would be the 33rd largest district in the country. ASO runs on a lean budget of roughly $1.5 million, and more than 50 percent of that is distributed directly to schools, enabled by a tiny staff of four full-time employees. . . .
>
> Empowering schools works best when we collaborate with others also working to tackle tough issues. For that reason, ASO regularly convenes leaders from the Office of New Schools, the Office of School Turnaround, and various outside organizations to share what we learn and problem solve collaboratively on the difficult issues we all face. We are in the middle of a cultural shift: Schools are beginning to own their own successes and failures. Working together, we can make that possible.[38]

This positive component of school differentiation has been relatively noncontroversial.

School Interventions and Closings

In contrast, differential treatment of unsatisfactory schools proved difficult and controversial even before Renaissance 2010 got started. All aspects of policy presented challenges: how to identify unsatisfactory schools, how far to go with interventions while leaving the school intact, and how to handle school closings when a school seemed impossible to improve.

Like many other urban school districts, CPS had spent decades putting schools on watch lists and probation, sending in new principals or promoting school improvement plans. For example, the school board put 371 schools on an early warning list in 2001. With support from the Bill & Melinda Gates Foundation, in fall 2001 the district launched the CHSRI, which subdivided three high schools into clusters with specialized academies. Though the subsequent performance of the schools that replaced Bowen, Orr, and South Shore high schools was not encouraging, the district learned from the experience, and the Gates Foundation continued to fund more small high schools for several years before abandoning the project.[39]

Part of the problem with interventions was a lack of clarity in the theory of action. When the school was to be the focus of educational improvement, whom should be held accountable and how? A school was not a person you could offer incentives to, a person who could simply choose to act in a focused way to bring change for the better. On the contrary, schools often performed badly because their leadership and/or teachers were dysfunctional, unable or unwilling to recognize and solve problems regardless of outside interventions. Payne, in his research for CCSR, investigated schools targeted for intervention and concluded that many simply could not be "saved."[40]

For schools that did not respond to such interventions, a more aggressive approach was a turnaround through which the school remained available for currently enrolled students, but a new principal was installed and given the authority to replace any or all of the school's teachers and staff. Initially, Duncan intended to require a one-year delay between closure and reopening, with a closed school remaining fallow while the new principal identified new staff and developed a plan for improved performance. This proved extraordinarily difficult even when the district started with two or three turnarounds, however, because students from a closed school didn't necessarily have a better school to attend instead. Parents strongly resisted closures, arguing that school alternatives were too distant from children's homes or were unsafe because they required crossing gang turf lines. One of the few schools left fallow in 2002–2003, the Dodge School of Excellence on the west side, saw fewer than half of its former students return in the fall of 2003, and the district abandoned this approach.[41]

The district changed gears quickly and shifted to immediate turnaround and reopening, but substantial challenges remained. The turnaround approach proved to be deeply disruptive, creating difficult questions about what the district should do with tenured faculty displaced from a school, for example, and LCSs objected to their reduced authority over school operations. Approaches emerged, nevertheless. Many of the schools worked with a nonprofit organization called the Academy for Urban School Leadership (AUSL) in developing new plans for improvement. And the district consistently published requests for proposals from interested nonprofit organizations, in part because dozens of schools remained eligible for turnaround based on their test scores and other outcomes. To date, however, only AUSL has demonstrated the interest and capacity to respond. As a result, the district has used this intervention sparingly, applying it to only seven elementary schools and two high schools between 2006 and 2009.[42]

The most draconian response to poor school performance was closure. A school closing policy had been established before Ren10's launch, and Duncan made use of it almost immediately after taking office in 2001, carrying on where Vallas had left off. According to CPS policy at the time, a school could be closed entirely for two reasons: low enrollment or persistently low academic performance. Enrollment-driven closure could be triggered at the discretion of the board if a school fell below specific thresholds: less than 40 percent of capacity, or fewer than 250 students. The district applied the policy to several schools emptied out by the closure of public housing projects on the south and west sides, and the board's choices proved to be contentious: *Catalyst* reported that "over the past four years [2000–2004], CPS has closed about two dozen schools, including Terrell, Dodge and Williams elementaries; the latter two were reopened in 2003 as prototypes of Renaissance schools."[43] The closings led to lawsuits, demonstrations, and deep suspicion of the district in some quarters, but Duncan viewed it as essential to Ren10, a means for creating a fresh start.

School closings for academic reasons created even more controversy, but Duncan argued that such closings were just as essential. Like Vallas, he saw them as a top-down alternative to parental school choice. Advocates of bottom-up choice had long argued that giving children and parents a choice of which schools to attend would kill bad schools and encourage the creation of good ones: bad schools would lose enrollment and die, and good schools would gain enrollment and thrive. But Duncan recognized that there was little sign of this dynamic in Chicago, where students and families continued to select even incorrigible schools decade after decade.

Parents often made these choices despite the apparent presence of viable alternatives. Chicago had a vibrant system of Roman Catholic schools that drew more than a quarter of all enrollments throughout the twentieth century, and for more than twenty years before Ren10, the city had magnet schools that drew many of the best students away from conventional schools. Perhaps the Catholic and magnet school systems lacked the capacity to expand beyond a certain scale, so their competitive influence was limited. In any case, there was no evidence that the presence of Catholic or magnet schools gave any impetus for improvement in Chicago's conventional schools. So under both Vallas and Duncan, and then more cohesively under Renaissance 2010, the district began to exercise choice in ways that parents did not, could not, or would not. When Daley and Duncan announced the launch of Renaissance 2010, they promised to close up to sixty schools for underperformance.

Nevertheless, school closings for academic reasons were confounded from the start. One major problem was that the district's academic and enrollment justifications for closure were jumbled together. The day before Daley and Duncan launched Ren10, hundreds of angry parents and community advocates had descended on a school board meeting to demand that the board block the proposed closing of ten underenrolled and underperforming schools. Among the demonstrators' accusations: the district had manipulated enrollment and test score data to close schools in the neighborhoods of residents who didn't have the political clout to stop it.[44] The board voted to postpone most of the closures that year, and only a handful of schools have subsequently been closed for academic reasons.

By the time Duncan left office in early 2009, more specific rules were established and a more transparent, tiered approach to school closures was essentially in place: a final set of rules was published in December of that year.[45] But this did not quell the controversy. For the 2010–2011 school year, thirty-four high schools and forty-seven elementary schools are eligible for closure because their school performance data fall below district thresholds.[46] Yet there is little interest in closing many of these schools, in part because of a phenomenon documented by CCSR.[47] CCSR researchers found that students displaced from closed schools rarely have easy access to a school that would be much better. Most students from closed schools, in fact, end up in schools with very similar performance data.

New Schools

Despite the high-profile controversy, school closures were only one small part of the Renaissance 2010 strategy. Daley and Duncan instead wanted the public and the district to focus on renewal through the creation of a hundred new schools by 2010. The initial idea was that about one-third of those schools would be charter schools, and another one-third would be contract schools run by nonprofit organizations in collaboration with the district. They initially expected that the final third would be underperforming schools closed and reopened by the district as small, focused schools with distinctive academic programs, but they also embraced the creation of new, conventional schools of quality by the district.

Perhaps ironically, opening schools is the most familiar portfolio function of any school district. After all, districts have been creating schools for as long as there have been districts. Large urban districts like Chicago are quite experienced with creating differentiated schools, most significantly during the 1970s and 1980s, when they created magnet schools with specialized curricula and instructional approaches as means for luring students of color into predominantly white neighborhoods to comply with court desegregation mandates.[48] One could argue that CPS has an even longer experience with differentiation in its large comprehensive high schools. Like those common in school districts throughout most of the twentieth century, Chicago's comprehensive high schools were, after all, differentiated schools-within-schools, offering distinct tracks for college preparation, vocational training, and general education.

There were some school-creation continuities in Chicago during Renaissance 2010: CPS began expanding the number of district magnet schools in the late 1990s. But most new school openings of the past dozen years have broken the traditional mold and blended public and private provision.

Charter schools. Contrary to the initial plan, the most common path to new school creation under Renaissance 2010 turned out to be the establishment of charters. This was in part because state law and the city had already set up that model; as figure 3.1 shows, a substantial number of charters were in place well before the program was launched in the summer of 2004. Virtually all of these Chicago charters were homegrown. Though many of their leaders were well-connected with the national charter school movement, only one national charter organization—KIPP, or the Knowledge Is Power Program—currently runs a school in Chicago. The local scene seems not to be constrained by this lack of national players, as dozens of school providers have emerged.

FIGURE 3.1 Chicago charter school "campuses" opened, 1997–1998 through 2009–2010

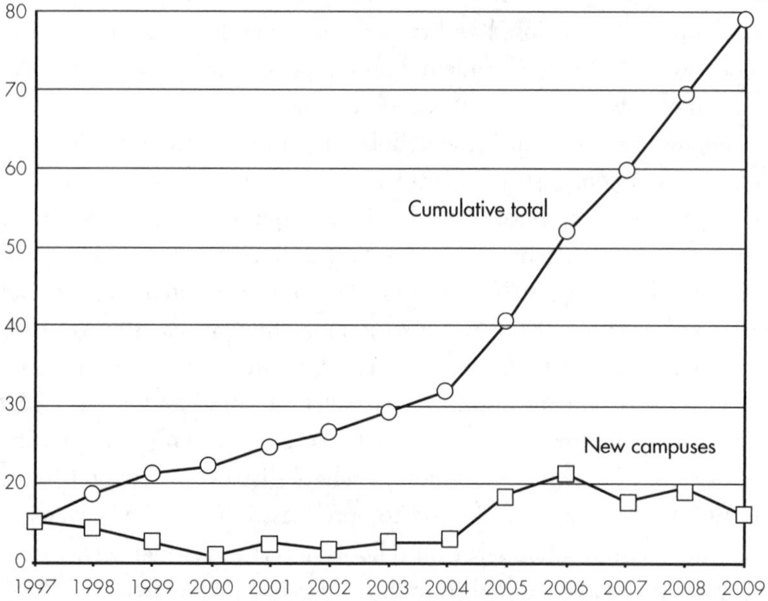

Sources: Office of New Schools, "Renaissance 2010 Schools Opened 2005–2009" (Chicago: Chicago Public Schools, 2009), http://www.ren10.cps.k12.il.us/Renaissance_2010_School_Profiles_Public_Use_12.22.09; Office of New Schools; "Charter and Contract Elementary Schools Opened 1997–2009," Chicago Public Schools, 2009, http://www.ren2010.cps.k12.il.us/docs/Charter_and_Contract_Elementary_School_Profiles_Public_Use_12_22_09.pdf.

As noted earlier, although the Illinois state legislature limited Chicago to fifteen charters in the 1996 law, Vallas interpreted the law as allowing a single charter holder to replicate and open multiple school campuses. Duncan and the district's Office of New Schools continued Vallas's replication practice, so that more than twenty charter schools were in operation in 2003 when the state legislature raised Chicago's charter cap to thirty. The new law, however, prohibited the fifteen future charter holders from operating more than one school. This left the fourteen pioneer charter holders in a uniquely powerful position, free (with CPS permission) to become something like small school districts operating many schools and open to enrolling a significant portion of the district's students. Chicago International Charter School (CICS) became the most prolific of the replicators, with fourteen campuses by the fall of 2009. The legislature further raised the cap to seventy in June 2009, but again it limited each new charter to a single campus.

One core problem for CPS in its relationship with charters proved vexing from the beginning and continued even after the launch of Ren10: ensuring that the new schools would serve the students who needed them most. This was first a location and facilities challenge, and second an enrollment challenge. The location and facilities challenge was stark in 1998, when some of the district's first charter schools could not open as planned for lack of facilities. The district was faced with terrible choices: leave dead-end schools open so that children in those neighborhoods had somewhere to go, or close those schools without being able to offer the children accessible alternatives. While private providers were under no obligation to create schools for anyone, CPS faced legal mandates (and, arguably, public obligations) to provide schooling for all children, especially the poor and minority children most likely to be served by a dead-end school. In collaboration with the nonprofit Illinois Facilities Fund, the CPS Office of New Schools director Greg Richmond developed a more systematic planning approach in 2003 and 2004, and the district worked to match school closings with school openings.[49]

The process of inviting and reviewing charter proposals, and the means of evaluating charter schools, has evolved substantially in Chicago. Interviews reveal that it was a somewhat informal process at first: the superintendent's office would reach out to community and nonprofit organizations it saw as capable of running schools, and encourage them to apply. The Renaissance Schools Fund, a private business-related philanthropy created to support Ren10, would often provide substantial seed money and technical assistance to organizations developing their applications. Other nonprofit organizations such as New Leaders for New Schools emerged to help prepare principals to run the proposed schools. Much of this process was not transparent to the public, and rumors and controversies abounded each year.

By the time Duncan left in 2009, the district had developed a far more standard (though not necessarily more transparent) approach to charters. It started with the publication of a request for proposals by the school board. Submitted proposals were then subjected to several reviews for their academic plans, business plans, enrollment areas, and facilities plans. The proposals were also subjected to public scrutiny, although the authority for final approval rested with the school board and superintendent.

Contract schools. As noted earlier, Vallas's and Duncan's desire to expand the number of charter schools beyond state-imposed caps led them to invent contract schools, an innovation unique to Chicago. The creation of these schools did not follow a single path, and they did not share a common description: some are full-service schools, while others are specialized academies.

Contract schools resemble charters in some ways. They are run by non-profit organizations with their own boards of directors and are exempt from some of the provisions of CPS collective bargaining agreements. The schools are not part of the CPS organizationally: their relationships with the district are mediated through a contract. As with charters, all of the organizations running contract schools are homegrown: no national charter operators have applied to run a school under this model.

Yet there are substantial differences. Charter schools are required by Illinois law to enroll all students who apply or, if more students apply than there are seats available, handle admissions through blind lotteries. In contrast, contract schools are allowed to have selective enrollment, which has enabled the creation of several magnetlike, specialized contract schools in the district. And unlike Chicago charters, contract schools continue to have LSCs, although LSC authority is limited. Under these hybrid governance arrangements, contract schools lack some of charter schools' autonomy from district policies.

Although Daley's and Duncan's initial description of Renaissance 2010 predicted that one-third of the district's one hundred new schools would be contract schools, in fact, only fifteen have been created in the district. All were created after Ren10 got under way, but it is not clear how many will continue as contract schools. When the Illinois legislature voted in June 2009 to allow the district an additional forty-five charters, a substantial number of existing contract schools signaled their intention to seek charters from the district, and several had won approval for that transition by the end of 2009. Though the district continues to open small numbers of contract schools, if charter caps continue to rise, the number of contract schools may continue to decline into a small remnant from a particular historical moment.

Performance schools. The final set of new schools created under Renaissance 2010 came to be called Performance Schools. The schools were expected to be similar to charters and contract schools in some ways, operating as small campuses with focused and innovative academic missions.[50] These similarities have in fact been retained: performance schools have been initiated and run by local leaders or groups chosen by the district to implement a particular vision for each school. Like magnets and some contract schools, some performance schools have been allowed to enroll students selectively by application, choosing those they have judged best qualified to take advantage of the school's specialized curriculum.

Performance schools have differed from charters and contract schools in important ways, however, by retaining many conventional links to the district. Instead of operating as independent organizations under contract with the district, performance schools are part of CPS, and all of their staff are CPS employees. Teachers work under the district's collective bargaining agreement with the Chicago Teachers Union. Performance schools also have distinctive LSC arrangements somewhat like contract schools, and the district rather than the LSC chooses the school principal.

When the first performance schools opened in 2005, several of them were carryovers from CHSRI, which the district ran in collaboration with the Gates Foundation. Four schools—the Infinity Math, Science and Technology High School; the Multicultural Arts High School; the School of Social Justice; and the World Language High School—opened on a new campus in Little Village after years of activism in that predominantly Latino neighborhood on the city's near-southwest side.[51] But most of the twelve performance schools that opened that year had been initiated by invitations from the district to current employees or local leaders who proposed to bring new curricula and approaches to specific campuses around the city. Interestingly, that first year saw the creation of the Rickover Naval Academy High School, the first of three military academy-style performance schools.

Thirty-one performance schools were launched between the start of Renaissance 2010 and the fall of 2009, and the district continues to circulate requests for proposals for more. The process of recruitment, development, and screening has become more routinized, but the distinctive characteristics of these small campuses remain. In contrast to contract schools, this component of the Ren10 program is likely to continue and grow.

Related Policies

The district was already substantially organized to enable Ren10's central office-guided focus on school-level improvement. Duncan had created a system of AIOs to serve the conventional schools of the district, and conventional schools governed by LSCs reported to them. Duncan also created the Office of New Schools in 2002 and the Office of School Turnaround in 2008. He added the Autonomous Schools Office described earlier to serve as a "substitute AIO" for higher-performing schools, to relieve them of some reporting requirements and give them more control over their professional development activities. The Office of New Schools also served as a communications link to the central office for private organizations running contract schools for the district.

Like other districts moving toward a portfolio approach, the leaders of CPS quickly found that the district lacked administrators and teachers with the necessary skills and attitudes to run differentiated schools of high quality for low-income students, students of color, and students with limited English proficiency.[52] The district has enabled substantial progress in the development of an administrator pool, most notably by supporting networks of communication and collaboration among people who lead or hope to lead improving schools in Chicago. The school district itself has done work like this on and off throughout its existence, and those efforts are now housed in the Office of Principal Preparation and Development. Similarly, there have been on-and-off efforts to assist LSCs since the passage of the Chicago School Reform Act of 1988, often with the assistance of the CCSR.

But there are even more substantial networks emerging outside the bounds of the CPS central office, often linked to the city's vibrant non-profit sector of churches, community organizations, foundations, and service groups. Some networks working on school improvement are mainly local, while others routinely communicate and collaborate with other organizations across the country, especially on issues relating to whole-school improvement or human capital. Local principal development and collaboration projects existed long before the creation of Renaissance 2010, and continue at the University of Illinois at Chicago's program on Urban Education Leadership, among other places. The passage of Illinois' 1996 charter school law led to similar work in the charter sector, for example, in New Leaders for New Schools. And the Academy for Urban School Leadership provides such a network as well for principals and teachers, spurred in part by CPS's school turnaround program.

A variety of groups have worked to expand the pool of high-quality teachers in the city. The district initially looked for nontraditional teachers, including new college graduates provided by Teach For America (TFA), others trained by organizations like The New Teachers Project, and middle-aged career changers willing to obtain alternative certification. But they also worked to resocialize incumbent educators. For example, the district contracted with a local organization called Strategic Learning Initiatives (SLI) to focus on instruction in struggling schools. SLI emerged during the first wave of Chicago school reform, and the components of its program draw on lessons learned since then: they focus on "shared leadership, targeted professional development, continuous improvement, and parent engagement."[53]

Such locally based collaboration and activism have long been a part of the Chicago scene, and Duncan worked to integrate it into Renaissance 2010. More broadly, this suggests that the shortage of human capital available to CPS in recent decades has been the school district's problem rather than the city's. Business, nonprofit, and neighborhood-based groups in

Chicago have long proved to have a deep capacity to generate people with the skills for creating and running effective organizations and schools. People from these various communities have always fought within and among themselves, so it has never been a simple task to draw on them to improve the city's schools. To some extent, Renaissance 2010 is the third wave of attempts to breach those boundaries, although in diverging ways.

RENAISSANCE 2010 AFTER DUNCAN, AFTER 2010

The election of President Obama in November 2008 and his naming of Duncan as his nominee for Secretary of Education one month later echoed throughout CPS. Like Vallas before him, Duncan had led the district in ways that reflected well on Daley, and Daley was reluctant to gamble on Duncan's successor. Even so, most observers were surprised when Daley named trusted ally and Chicago Transit Authority President Ron Huberman to lead the city's schools. Huberman, an immigrant from Israel and a former policeman, had served as Daley's chief of staff, but he had no experience as an educator. He became CEO of CPS in January 2009 and immediately set to work learning the system.

Huberman proved reluctant to speak publicly about his job at first and only began giving interviews in April 2009. When he did talk, he identified three central goals: improving safety in the face of a frightening number of murders of school-aged children in the neighborhoods around CPS schools, managing the district through the deep fiscal crisis brought on by the national recession, and carrying forward Renaissance 2010-style school improvements at a somewhat more cautious pace, with particular attention to its human capital initiatives.[54] He rarely mentioned Ren10 specifically, and he laid out a careful, managerial, and data-focused strategy when he spoke at the City Club of Chicago at the start of the 2009–2010 academic year.[55] Daley was less reticent, promising in early 2010 that the push to create new, high-quality schools would continue: "I hope there's a chapter two [of Renaissance 2010], a chapter three, a chapter four, five, six, seven, eight, nine, ten."[56]

Huberman faced challenges in carrying forward Renaissance 2010. A number of serious and substantial evaluations were published early in his term that found the deeply disruptive changes of Ren10's first five years had brought uneven results in the schooling provided to Chicago children. Most prominently, the research organization SRI had conducted a multiyear study of Renaissance 2010 in collaboration with CCSR, publishing its first report in April 2009 and multiple reports in August 2009.[57] Another major study on charter schools in Illinois and the United States, conducted by the Center for Research on Education Outcomes (CREDO) at Stanford University, came out in the summer of 2009.[58] RAND published a substantial research report on charter school performance in Chicago as well, finding uneven performance.[59] CCSR also published a major report in early 2009 on student transience, which differentiated schools are intended to reduce, finding little improvement.[60] Perhaps most stinging for Daley, his allies at the Civic Committee of The Commercial Club of Chicago released a June 2009 follow-up to their influential 2003 *Left Behind* report, calling it *Still Left Behind*.[61] Their research showed that even many new schools created under Renaissance 2010 continued to underserve poor and minority children in the city.

Practical Implementation Problems

Among other things, these reports revealed that huge technical implementation challenges remain for Renaissance 2010 and a portfolio approach to educational improvement in Chicago. Unsolved problems include sustaining and growing the pool of charter providers in the city, and creating the supports and transparency necessary for parental choice in the district.

Finding providers. As the district creates and encourages the creation of new schools, its leaders are explicitly seeking to find reliable and capable school providers inside and outside the district. Interviews suggest that they do not expect that school providers will grow to encompass the whole system. Skepticism runs deep in Chicago, and any theory that the district (or anyone) can or should "scale up" school improvement on its own carries little weight. School leaders and activists instead seem to embrace a more limited "diffusion of innovation" idea, that communication and collaboration among successful people inside and outside CPS will encourage the creation of new schools and better educational practices. But no one has claimed that anyone can command or even lead this diffusion. As the number of charter schools increases, it remains to be seen whether new school creators or leaders will be identified, recruited, or included in the networks of innovation and improvement. In particular, it remains to be seen whether the overall pool of Chicago charter providers—old and new—can survive without the heavy subsidies offered by the Renaissance Schools Fund and other private donors.

Reaching parents. Research also suggests persistent problems with choice and enrollment. Ren10 will have only limited impact if children do not attend the new schools, particularly if underserved children do not attend these schools. A March 2009 report by the Target Area Development Corporation suggests a deep disconnect between the substantial change described earlier and the children and families CPS serves.[62] There is strong distrust in many quarters about the district leadership's interest in poor children and particularly children of color, distrust easily visible in state legislation to limit school closings, or in public demonstrations about school safety during a year when dozens of CPS students have been murdered in the neighborhoods that surround the schools, or in protests over the potential gentrification of the Near South Side where ten years ago huge public housing projects once stood.

But this disconnect also tracks down to the level of individual students or families, most of whom have little information about the confusing array of school types: charters, contracts, turnaround schools, performance schools, magnet schools, neighborhood schools, and so on. It isn't clear how those families can be expected to exercise informed choices about the rapidly changing schools in their city.

THE POLITICS OF CHICAGO SCHOOL REFORM

A Politicized District in Permanent Crisis

Renaissance 2010 is not only an education policy initiative. It is also a core component of Daley's political program for the city; he says that he considers it one of the reasons he continues to seek and win reelection. The political situation in the district has been fraught for decades, but as of this writing, Daley is in clear control. Since his first election in 1989, Daley has developed a stable political coalition of white ethnic voters, downtown business interests, selected unions, and substantial segments of the Latino and some segments of the African American communities.[63] He has built this coalition carefully, adapting to the changing demographics of the city and its gradually deindustrializing economy, and he has worked to maintain that coalition's support for his efforts to reform the city's school system. Given the difficulty of improving a district in a state of permanent crisis, it is in some ways surprising that he has taken on the task in the absence of any catalytic event or outside pressure.[64]

Political opposition to Daley's control of the school system is weak at best. The once-strong Chicago Teachers Union is a shell of its former self.[65] State legislation in 1995 sharply limited union power in several ways. First, it limited collective bargaining on many issues related to curriculum, assessment, and resource allocation within schools. Second, it freed CPS to contract out services. The district first tested this authority in 1996 by contracting out some maintenance services. The district expanded this practice in 2001 to include contracting for the creation and management of entire schools. Union influence was limited further with the enactment of charter legislation in Illinois in 1997, which barred the CTU from bargaining collectively with any charter.

Community-based skepticism toward Daley's vision of the city's future remains substantial, despite his six consecutive elections as mayor. One persistent criticism is that Daley is too beholden to the city's business leadership, and that he is more interested in reassuring affluent and middle-class voters than in serving all his constituents. This view is shared by many who view the Chicago School Reform Act of 1988 as the foundation for effective, sustained, and inclusive educational improvement in the city.[66]

A more aggressive critique of Daley's leadership came to a head in his policies for low-income housing, particularly in the Chicago Housing Authority's management of public housing for the city's poorest residents.[67] Daley and the CHA launched a sweeping reform of public housing in 1999 that included the demolition of many of the city's notorious highrise projects. Despite repeated promises that the former residents of these projects would be provided "scatter site" housing in the city, large numbers of those residents ended up with nothing, and many had to find alternatives in low-income suburbs to the south of the city. This spurred suspicion that the mayor's housing reform program was in fact intended to drive low-income people from the city, and to create more attractive targets for real estate development for middle-class settlement and gentrification. In a city where race and poverty are closely tied, this critique has a sharp racial and ethnic component.[68]

Some critics view Renaissance 2010 in the same light, as less an education reform initiative than a power grab hostile to the interests of low-income people and communities of color. The group Parents United for Responsible Education (PURE) makes the argument most directly: "Renaissance 2010 is not an education plan, it's a business and real estate developer plan. This is Mayor Daley's plan to push poor African American and Latino residents out of the city . . . Students are being displaced and discarded."[69] PURE also argues that one of Daley's ultimate aims is to limit the authority of LSCs and thus limit the influence of local residents in the schools.

There is also substantial concern about violence around schools. More than thirty murders of CPS students were concentrated in low-income and minority neighborhoods during the 2008–2009 school year, which increased antagonism toward all the mayor's initiatives. The new superintendent, Huberman, a former police officer, has focused heavily on safety issues, but the violence continues. The beating death of student Derrion Albert on the street outside Christian Fenger Academy High School in September 2009, caught on video and posted on YouTube, drew particular attention. It provoked a reporter to ask now–Secretary of Education Arne Duncan whether students displaced from closed schools must move into schools where neighborhood and gang rivalries expose them to risk.[70] Such concerns have not derailed Renaissance 2010 or the cycle of school closings and openings, but they have fed a substantial opposition.

Portfolio Reform, Neoliberalism, and the "New Tools of Government"

The broader context. In the context of recent elementary and secondary education reform in the United States, Renaissance 2010 and portfolio reform can be seen as drawing on three of the four waves of reform that followed the famous *A Nation At Risk* report in 1983, the last three of which roughly parallel the waves of reform in Chicago.[71] Nationwide, first came the focus on states improving curricular standards and graduation requirements, which is presumed but not focused on by the portfolio approach. Next came "restructuring," which focused on the school as the locus of educational improvement and decentralized substantial authority over curriculum and instruction to principals, teachers, and parents, often encouraging the use of school improvement plans as blueprints.[72] Third came the move toward test-based accountability and school report cards, triggering state- or federally sponsored interventions to turn schools around, an approach most identify with the 2002 No Child Left Behind Act. At around the same time, states and districts pursued a fourth wave of reform by encouraging the creation of distinctive schools as charters or under other school-wide designs, giving students and families increased choice.

Portfolio reform in Chicago and elsewhere clearly draws on the last three of these, but synthesizes them in a new way that reflects broader trends in public policy both in the United States and in the developed world. Salomon calls this approach "the new governance," which draws on developments in business organizations since the 1970s, but whose public-sector version was initially identified in the United States with the "neoliberal" wing of the Democratic party.[73] The neoliberal origins of Renaissance 2010 contrast sharply with the worldview of the Administrative Progressives who most strongly shaped CPS and other big-city districts in the mid-twentieth century.[74] The Administrative Progressives had an equally managerial view of educational improvement, but they argued that the ideal district should be organized as a depoliticized public-sector bureaucracy, with a superintendent exercising top-down command and control over all functions within a standardized array of schools. The leaders of Renaissance 2010 have a no less managerial view: they certainly intend to manage the district toward educational improvement. But they see the previously conventional approach to district governance as not just technically impossible but also undesirable, particularly because they argue that district leaders lose their focus and a district underperforms educationally when they try to manage every aspect of schooling.

The neoliberal policy worldview of Chicago's major players. In our research on Chicago and other major U.S. school districts experimenting with variations on the portfolio approach, we identified a group led by Paul Hill that has found that these reforms are usually led by professionals from outside the conventional world of education policy, including lawyers, public managers, management consultants, venture capitalists, academics, and foundation leaders. These professionals are familiar with policy making that draws on data and incentives to optimize the performance of public- and private-sector organizations. By training and inclination, such professionals believe that strong incentives, transparency about performance, and freedom for school leaders to innovate are the keys to performance improvement. Hill has noted in an earlier analysis of urban school reform that there are major cultural gaps between such professionals and traditional educators, whose values and training emphasize the pursuit of multiple missions, interdisciplinary collaboration, mutual support, and moral commitment.[75]

This contrast in worldview is visible in something as simple as the word *portfolio,* which has distinct meanings. For new governance professionals, a portfolio belongs to the world of investors and venture capitalists, and has to do with maximizing returns by choosing good investments over bad. For most educators, in contrast, a portfolio is a compilation of one's own work as in creative writing or, more recently, a sampler of a student's work that enables more rigorous and thorough evaluation and grading. Thus, the phrase *portfolio district,* while evocative and meaningful for new governance professionals, might not even parse for traditional educators. To the contrary, it might lead educators to think of diverse and multidimensional approaches directly contrary to the standardized assessments and interventions of Renaissance 2010.

The Chicago case also demonstrates that such a focus on data-driven school improvement requires a narrowing of educational goals. Much of the public legitimacy of the education system since Horace Mann has rested on "strategic ambiguity," to borrow a phrase from policy scholar Deborah Stone.[76] Paradoxically, the strategic advocates for public schooling gained broad support in the nineteenth and twentieth centuries by encouraging different people to see schools as committed to disparate goals, and they avoided attempts to boil down the purposes of schooling unambiguously to any single formulation. Labaree suggests that this strategy worked: Americans do support public education even as they disagree about which of its goals is most important. He found that most Americans want some combination of collective economic productivity, collective civic capacity for self-government, and individual competitive opportunities.[77] Annual Gallup polls sponsored by Phi Delta Kappa have similar findings.[78] While agreeing to disagree, educators constructed a loosely coupled system in which local districts, schools, teachers, and even parents could simultaneously pursue disparate goals.[79]

This ambiguity was made easier by opacity: the absence of accepted assessment criteria, tests of system performance, and data systems to make the results of those tests widely known. In recent decades, with the rise of test-based accountability, however, the opacity is falling away. Policy makers have spent the years since *A Nation At Risk* getting more specific about the goals of education and the assessment of the system on its performance of those goals.

This is an essential part of Renaissance 2010. Its new governance or neoliberal approach to school reform requires detailed quantitative assessment that scores the performance of everyone and everything in the system, including children, teachers, schools, and school providers. At least some of the political conflict in Chicago and across the United States is over this effort to wring the ambiguity out of the system, and to name explicit standards and priorities, which requires defeating people and groups with alternative goals or priorities. The strategy carries political risks because it drives wedges into the pro-education coalition, but neoliberal reformers in Chicago seem willing to take that risk because the system faces a legitimacy crisis no matter what.

In sum, district leaders in Chicago bring together these two things: a new, simplified bottom line *and* a new governance approach to managing the district to maximize that bottom line. As one interview respondent told me, the indicators for school performance in Chicago are all established now, especially for the high schools. It's all about performance management now, to drive up those indicators.

This is essential as district leaders in Chicago seek to narrow their managerial focus and move to a contractual approach. Under Renaissance 2010, schools owned and run by CPS gain conditional autonomy based on performance (an extension of the School Improvement Plan approach of the 1990s), though it is performance on a set of indicators that may ignore the educational goals many parents or voters might view as essential, such as preparation for citizenship or well-paid work. But many Ren10 schools are not owned or run by CPS. These schools, owned and run by independent charter holders for a fixed period, keep their autonomy if they meet performance requirements on an even narrower set of indicators. The performance evaluation and the district's grant of a franchise to such a school are ideal mediators of this attenuated managerial relationship.

The political limits of neoliberalism. Political challenges remain as well. According to Hill et al., "A portfolio strategy transforms school districts in ways that upset established patterns, threaten many groups, create the need for kinds of expertise not traditionally used in public education, and render some forms of expertise obsolete."[80] School district leaders take substantial risks when they embrace a narrowed array of specific goals for schools and then gather detailed data on the performance of the district for those goals. They may lose the support of constituents who disagree with their educational goals at the same time they expose themselves to rigorous evaluation on the goals they have chosen.

It's important to note, however, that many Chicagoans remain mystified by the arcane details of the district's new management and welter of data. As Salomon has noted in his analysis of neoliberal policy making, once a public service is contracted out to private third parties, those contractors have a great deal of discretion over how they choose to do the public's business.[81] In actual practice, the resulting education system in Chicago may well be less accountable to the public and less transparent to children and parents seeking the best possible schools.

4

Strong Vision, Learning by Doing, or the Politics of Muddling Through?

New York City

Jonathan Gyurko and Jeffrey R. Henig

Michael Bloomberg took office as mayor of New York City in January 2002, having heavily emphasized school reform as a personal priority during a campaign in which education was a prominent issue.[1] New York City public schools have long been the object of politics and reform, with Tammany Hall's patronage-based control of schools for much of the 1800s and progressive reformers taking their turn well into the first decades of the twentieth century. In the early 1960s, the modern teacher union movement—denoted by collective bargaining—was launched from the city through a series of turbulent strikes. Later that decade, the state legislature divided the city into thirty-two separate community school districts after a failed experiment with community control degenerated into racially framed battles between parents and the teacher union.[2]

In the final four decades of the twentieth-century, high-profile turmoil, demographic change, and a perception of declining performance left much of the public teetering between fatalistic resignation to a continuing decline and readiness to accept strong measures that would previously have been infeasible politically. The system of thirty-two community school districts allowed some parts of the city to engage in innovative practices and maintain high-quality schools, but at the cost of corruption, patronage, and inattentiveness in other areas. By 1999, then-Mayor Rudolph Giuliani, aspiring to gain mayoral control of schools and reduce the system's bureaucracy, expressed a desire to "blow up" the board of education.[3]

Picking up where Giuliani left off, Bloomberg spent the first six months of his new administration fighting for formal control of the school system. Centralized mayoral control, he argued, was a prerequisite to breaking the patterns responsible for previous reform efforts that had been too weak, fragmented, or ephemeral to leave a lasting mark.

In June 2002, the state legislature gave Bloomberg the authority he sought: a mayoral control law empowered him to appoint the chancellor (i.e., superintendent) of the system; although the thirty-two community school districts remained, each district's board was eliminated and the chancellor would appoint each community superintendent.[4] The act sharply reduced the powers of citywide board of education—which Bloomberg renamed the Panel For Educational Policy—turning it into a mere advisory body with a majority of its members appointed by, and serving at the pleasure of, the mayor. Symbolically, Bloomberg equated the system to other mayoral agencies, referring to it as the "Department" of Education.

A month later, after a broad but tightly managed national search, Bloomberg announced the appointment of Joel I. Klein as chancellor. Klein, a lawyer, had almost no experience in the education sector; he was best known for leading the Justice Department's antitrust case against Microsoft. But in selecting Klein, the mayor made it clear that he saw the challenge as calling more for skill, tenacity, and a David versus Goliath attitude than for knowledge of curriculum and instruction. Klein quickly began to solicit advice from school reformers he admired in other cities, and he reached out to philanthropic foundations, the business community, and other local experts.[5]

With 1,200 schools, 80,000 teachers, 1.1 million students, and a wobbly history of overbureaucratization, overfragmentation, patronage politics, and stark inequities, New York City presented a formidable challenge. However, in Bloomberg, the city had a leader who had made school reform a top campaign priority; his election was interpreted as a democratic mandate to act boldly. The newly approved governance structure eliminated key points of friction that had stalled or moderated earlier reform efforts. Other building blocks of civic capacity were also in place: school reform was supported by influential foundations, such as the Carnegie Corporation of New York and Open Society Institute, as well as individual philanthropists, many with Wall Street fortunes, who supported market-based reforms.[6] Overall, the business community was inclined to support the new administration by dint of shared ideology and through personal connection to a mayor whom they considered to be one of them.

Despite this mandate and alignment of support, the new administration inherited preexisting collective bargaining agreements and would have to negotiate with the powerful United Federation of Teachers (UFT). This union still had substantial ability to block initiatives it opposed but also had a history of progressive pragmatism that distinguished it from the more knee-jerk adversarial stance characterizing its counterparts in some other U.S. cities.

Mobilizing these resources, the Bloomberg–Klein team launched a series of reforms that were grounded in management theories, articulated in corporate values and metaphors, informed by their interpretation of failures locally and in other cities, and planned by teams of external consultants. By 2008 and after two seemingly incongruous waves of reform, the result is squarely a form of the portfolio management model (PMM). Layers of school system bureaucracy separating the mayor and chancellor from city schools were eliminated. Autonomous schools and principals have greater control over their budgets and (to a lesser extent) staffing decisions, in return for more direct responsibility for performance.

In contrast to a more traditional command-control district structure, schools now self-affiliate into networks, buying administrative services from a district-designed marketplace of private and public school support organizations. A centralized information management system evaluates and compares student performance, assigns letter grades to schools, and has been used to justify controversial decisions on school closings. Alongside these reforms, a robust charter-school sector—operating as a separate portfolio of public schools—was encouraged aggressively by the administration, which pushed the state to raise the cap on the number of charters and provided charter schools with access to school buildings.

Many critics emerged to take issue with the process by which these reforms were hatched and carried through; they argued that student achievement outcomes were narrowly defined, substantively misleading, and artfully manipulated. What critics did not claim was that this was a do-nothing regime.[7] Bloomberg and Klein had delivered on the promises of being proactive and aggressive in establishing a new model for thinking about, delivering, and steering public education.

This chapter investigates the evolution of the city's current model of portfolio management. It is tempting to read New York as an exemplar of the rational-comprehensive model of decision making in action: of the benefits that can come when the best and the brightest, armed with theory, informed by scientific evidence, and protected from partisan distractions are given room to design and implement a newer and better way; in fact, this is precisely how the administration characterized the reform process.[8] Yet the current portfolio approach was by no means a foregone conclusion, particularly when compared to the city's first wave of centralizing policies. A more careful account shows a number of ways in which rational planning and imported models were frustrated by, layered onto, or accommodated to preexisting norms, institutions, and political processes.

We do not argue, here, whether New York City's version of portfolio management is or is not worthy of emulation. Rather, by analyzing the politics of Bloomberg's reforms, we argue that national, state, and local reformers put their efforts at risk if they adopt the naive lesson that reforming urban schools is simply a question of combining a clear plan, the right people, and steely resolve to see things through.

CENTRALIZATION IN THE HANDS OF THE BEST AND BRIGHTEST: THE FIRST WAVE OF REFORM, 2002–2004

Bloomberg had not yet provided a school reform road map when he named Klein chancellor in July 2002.[9] Unlike previous leaders who, in their first weeks on the job, grabbed headlines and courted allies by announcing dramatic changes, Klein conducted a four-month, top-to-bottom study of the school system. Entitled "Children First: A New Agenda for Public Education in New York City," this evaluation aimed to examine "every function of the school system," from teaching and learning to organizational structure and opportunities for community involvement.[10] For some, this methodical approach was itself validation of the apolitical promise of mayoral control. Kathryn Wylde, president of the New York City Partnership and Chamber of Commerce, commented that Klein, "[didn't] feel pressure from the mayor, the media, or other political forces to come out of the box with a strategy . . . it's very refreshing."[11]

Nor was this planning process like any other before it. Funded with $4 million in private philanthropy from The Broad Foundation and others,[12] Children First was led and staffed by a small army of private consultants and educators new to or from the periphery of the New York City school system. McKinsey & Company, the management consulting firm, provided analytical support. Leaders of school reform organizations, including New Visions for Public Schools, the Annenberg Institute for School Reform, and NewSchools Venture Fund, served on planning committees. Although some efforts were made to gain community input through meetings with parents and local groups, this appeared to be more pretense than engagement; there is little evidence that parents' views influenced the reforms.[13] By and large, the Children First working groups made decisions behind closed doors in a manner reminiscent of nineteenth century progressive reformers designing a system "for the people but not by the people."[14]

A Model for Centralization Takes Shape

On January 16, 2003, Bloomberg unveiled what would later be characterized as the first wave of his school reforms. At that time, there was little reason to believe that the city would eventually embrace a portfolio management approach. Instead, the reforms aimed to impose "rigorously centralized control" to "completely transform the structure and philosophy of a school system that long allowed localized decision-making about everything from budgets to textbook selection."[15] Highlights included replacement of the city's thirty-two and largely independent community school districts with ten regions controlling about a hundred schools each and led by a regional superintendent directly accountable to Klein. A new uniform curriculum in reading and math was implemented citywide to "ensure consistency for the many students and teachers who move around the system."[16]

NYC Leadership Academy, chaired by former General Electric CEO Jack Welch, was founded with private funding to train a new crop of entrepreneurial principals who would be "strong, effective, dynamic leaders."[17] In stark contrast to market-based reforms premised on differentiation and choice, or a portfolio model with schools granted autonomy in return for accountability, "coherence" and "alignment" were the guiding principles of the centralizing reforms.[18]

Winning Support

Although the administration characterized the reforms as apolitical solutions planned by the best and the brightest, the policy rollout was intentionally designed to garner public support. The mayor announced his plans in Harlem on the Martin Luther King Jr. holiday. Reforms were clothed in a civil rights garb; Bloomberg encouraged the city to "have the courage to stand up to the apologists, to the entrenched self-serving special interests, to the self-promoters and doubters and the apathetic."[19] In the process, this rhetoric served to undermine many practitioners across the system, painting them as impediments to black and Latino student achievement.

Despite the grand announcement, it did not take long for the political limits of the mayor's control of city schools to become apparent. Parent groups, backed by some state and local lawmakers, mobilized against the mayor's proposals; they argued that the ten-region "corporate model" was "ill-suited to a school system." The chairman of the state assembly's education committee criticized the mayor for acting with "absolute unilateral authority" and exceeding his statutory authority. The teacher and principals unions, originally supportive of the plan's emphasis on instruction, lashed out over their lack of input.[20] Even the chairperson of the city council's education committee, herself a strong supporter of mayoral control, commented on "a danger of a lockdown on information."[21] Throughout the fight, the administration staunchly defended its plan, arguing that the centralized regional structure "offers a far more manageable chain of command and clear accountability."[22] Klein acknowledged the need for parent involvement, but emphasized strategies to engage parents in the education of their *own* children rather than deliberating with them over policies. Klein placed parent coordinators in every school, who worked at the principals' direction, not as parent advocates. Although the mayoral control law established parent-elected advisory bodies in each of the community school districts, their legal authority was limited. The administration was clear that, once expressed, advice from these bodies need not be acted upon; Klein himself remarked that not every issue should "be put up for a plebiscite."[23]

By June 2003, a deal was brokered to end legal and political challenges to the reforms. In the settlement, the thirty-two community school districts would remain as geographic but not administrative or governing entities and with only nominal responsibilities. The resolution was a clear, if incomplete, political win for the administration.

Implementation of Children First

On the eve of the new school year, a "deep unease" pervaded the system as new programs were not fully developed, union relations were at a low, and there were high levels of parent confusion.[24] Against this backdrop, unanticipated consequences—hardly unavoidable in an undertaking this ambitious—took off some of the sheen of neutral expertise. These miscues provided fodder for critics and helped account for the administration's eventual decision to change course, shed much of its centralized structure, and adopt a portfolio management approach in which decentralization, empowerment, and accountability would be major themes.

For example, students' special education files and medical records were not delivered from the shuttered district offices to the schools for a number of months; referrals for disability evaluations went unprocessed. The principals' union president claimed that her members were "being micromanaged as never before" and had "little control over their school budgets."[25] The demands on teachers to implement new curricula in math and science across all grades were high. A breakdown in the school discipline process delayed the suspension of dangerous students. Paychecks and health benefits were delayed, and new school-support centers were slow to respond to administrative issues.[26] Despite these serious breakdowns, the administration was unwavering in its defense of the centralized structures and policies, minimizing the problems as "a few bumps."[27]

Assessments of the first full year of Children First reforms were less than glowing. The *New York Times* reported on the potentially "destabilizing" effect of turnover among Klein's senior staff, given the dismissal of many long-serving administrators and the loss of institutional memory.[28] Columnist Michael Winerip described it as a "lost year" for students with disabilities.[29] Randi Weingarten, president of the city's teacher union, blamed the reforms for creating "widespread mismanagement, overcrowding . . . [and] an inane micromanaging bureaucracy."[30] Education historian Diane Ravitch, at one time a champion of mayoral control, emerged as one of the most outspoken critics.[31] Even the business community, a heretofore reliable source of support for the businessman-turned-mayor, pulled back a bit. Kathryn Wylde of the New York City Partnership and Chamber of Commerce commented, "It's hard for the business community to be enthusiastic when the educational community appears to be spending more time fighting with each other than figuring out how to improve the schools and educate the kids."[32]

Dismantling the Old

There is little doubt that the first wave of Children First reforms brought sweeping change to the New York City school system. The thirty-two community school district boards and administrative offices, many of which had become symbolic bastions of political patronage and educational failure, were eliminated.[33] The system's senior administration was transformed into a young work force, loyal to the mayor and chancellor; many hailed from the private sector.

Under the mantra of coherence, centralizing structures and citywide policies promulgated a uniform curriculum, a "fair student funding" budgeting system, a centrally managed process for high school admissions, and top-down staffing mandates.[34] Breakdowns in implementation were characterized as minor hiccups, and the administration remained committed to its approach.

In retrospect, there is little to suggest that notions of portfolio management animated much, if any, of Bloomberg and Klein's earliest reforms. Arguably, the first phase of Children First was more about political accomplishments than educational ones. Although the legislature gave the mayor policy-making control over the schools, the breadth of that power had yet to be defined. By beating back political challenges to the replacement of community school districts with ten administrative regions, the mayor established a wide scope of administrative power. By replacing the existing management team with new appointments, the mayor secured the loyalty of his top bureaucrats.

It is likely that had the mayor not established this extensive authority to define and quickly implement school policy, New York City could not have eventually moved as swiftly as it did toward PMM. Moreover, reforms predating Bloomberg and Klein encouraged the city's ultimate shift away from a fully centralized system. The following section discusses these earlier reforms and their role in moving the city toward a portfolio approach.

MUDDLING TOWARD PMM

One need look no farther than the city's new Leadership Academy to find a paradox embedded in the first phase of Children First. Despite Klein's goal to prepare "strong, effective, dynamic leaders," the newly centralized systems of authority and decision making were at odds with the notion of empowered school leaders. This example suggests that the administration was grappling with more than just the challenges of implementation. What remained unresolved was how to best distribute authority and responsibility across a system as large as the city's to stimulate the radical improvements sought by the mayor and chancellor.

In the spring of 2004, Klein asked Eric Nadelstern, a thirty-year veteran of the system, to help answer the question by piloting a low-profile initiative called the Autonomy Zone. Within the Zone, about two dozen schools would gain autonomy from the recently created regional structure and gain more control over their school programs and budgets in return for heightened accountability for student performance.[35] Hardly a creation out of whole cloth, the Autonomy Zone emerged from or was inspired by several lines of local organizational practice, each with their own origins, champions, trajectory, and rationale. These separate streams were: (a) the New Century High Schools Initiative; (b) charter schools; (c) logistical and political accommodations made to institute the Children First uniform curriculum; and (d) the city's tradition of permitting niches for internal innovators to coexist with a system that more typically enforced bureaucratic uniformity.

New Century High Schools

The New Century High Schools Initiative involved replacing large, failing high schools with a campus of new small schools.[36] With support from the Bill & Melinda Gates Foundation, Open Society Institute, and Carnegie Corporation of New York, planning for the effort began under Chancellor Rudy Crew and was launched by Chancellor Harold O. Levy, Klein's two predecessors.[37] The third and key partner in the initiative was New Visions for Public Schools, an education nonprofit led by Robert Hughes, known for its work during the Annenberg Challenge of the 1990s for founding new, small schools.

The initiative combined a number of ideas that had been percolating during the city's and nation's experience with failed high school reforms. A key premise was that dysfunctional schools create dysfunctional cultures that are self-sustaining; accordingly, sometimes it is easier to start from scratch. But this was not just a plan to shutter schools in the hope that a thousand, better flowers would bloom in their place. Each new high school was to be designed around principles learned from the national literature on effective schools.[38]

After opening a series of small high schools in the Bronx, New Century expanded to Brooklyn, founding eighty-six schools in total. Encouraged by New Visions' success, the Gates Foundation funded other New York City organizations to also create new schools. These groups included the Asia Society, College Board, Replications Inc., Outward Bound, Urban Assembly, and Internationals Schools.

Although not formulated in the vernacular of portfolio management, New Century's strategy to replace large failing schools with a campus of small schools is a practice now identified with the portfolio approach. New Century also was a proving ground for a coterie of people who would contribute to the development of the city's emerging portfolio model. Michele Cahill went from being the Carnegie program officer responsible for New Century to one of Klein's top advisers. The small-schools offices developed by Hughes were prototypes of the school support organizations that would emerge in the second wave of Children First reforms.[39] Nadelstern headed the Bronx small-schools office, spending much of his time protecting the schools from the surrounding, albeit new and improved, bureaucracy.

Charter Schools

The slow and careful growth of charter schools in New York City was a second model informing the city's future portfolio arrangement. New York came late to the nation's charter school movement, passing its charter law nearly a decade after Minnesota adopted the first state charter statute. New York law allowed only a hundred charters to be granted statewide, earning it a "B" on the Center for Education Reform's ranking of charter law permissiveness.[40] An unsuccessful 2001 effort to convert five schools to charters run by Edison Schools, Inc., generated a hostile response from community organizations and the teacher union and further suppressed growth in city's charter sector.[41]

Yet in the years leading up to Bloomberg's administration, New York's charter school leaders raised the reputation of the state's charter movement by emphasizing the quality of school authorizing and accountability.[42] Detailed charter approval and renewal criteria were implemented, close fiscal oversight prevented the scandals that had emerged in other states, and a number of charters were closed on the basis of low academic achievement.[43] Charters were also a favored policy of the city's venture-capital-style philanthropies, such as the Robin Hood Foundation and the Robertson Foundation, whose support Bloomberg courted.

Despite the seeming inconsistency between chartering's radical form of school autonomy and the first wave of centralizing reforms, Klein and Bloomberg expressed early support for charters. In late 2003, the mayor and the chancellor announced a major initiative to open fifty new charter schools across the city. The effort gave charters additional funding for special education and school start-up, provided free-of-charge access to public buildings, and offered $250 million in capital funds.[44] A new charter school resource center, on whose board the chancellor would serve, was founded to drive the effort and was supported with over $40 million from local philanthropies. This push, along with financial and strategic support from groups like NewSchools Venture Fund, prompted new charter school creation, the replication of existing charters, and the emergence of charter management organizations (CMOs).[45]

At that time, the city's charter initiative (and new schools generally) was conceived as a way to solve the city's supply problem. The well-funded charter sector was stocked with entrepreneurs looking to take chartering "to scale" at the same time that Klein needed more good schools. The fact that charters would be sponsored by state authorities and therefore outside of chancellor's direct control was a secondary concern. Although the charter movement's raison d'être—autonomy for accountability—had not yet been fully considered as a governing principle for the entire system, the rapidly emerging charter sector provided Klein with a model of school-based empowerment.

Exemptions to Children First

A third stream offering policy and organizational precedents to the Autonomy Zone was Klein's exemption of two hundred schools from the new citywide curriculum.[46] This exemption was made despite the administration's overall emphasis on systemwide coherence and its defense of a uniform curriculum as a strategy to support students who move from school to school.[47] This decision was likely based on a combination of factors including a desire to not fix what was already working and to avoid opposition from parents in middle-class neighborhoods whose children attended functioning schools.

Intra-System Safe Havens

The final contributing stream was composed of a series of institutional niches for innovation that the system had spawned or tolerated over the previous three decades. These safe havens sheltered innovative, within-system efforts by individuals familiar with local history, institutions, and politics and who exemplified the spirit of entrepreneurialism that gets a lot of attention in today's school reform rhetoric.[48] Anthony Alvarado, Deborah Meier, and Seymour Fliegel's work in East Harlem in the late 1970s and early 1980s is a prominent example. Along with other educators, they founded about thirty small alternative schools that students attended by choice.[49] Many of the schools were protected in a special alternative-school district within the city, with later attempts to grant them further autonomy through an official "learning zone."[50]

The New Century High Schools Initiative, the city's charter school sector, the freedom granted to high-functioning schools, and institutional safe havens for within-system innovators all provided an organizational and theoretical counterpoint to the first wave of centralizing reforms. Across these four strands, the relative autonomy that educators earned and enjoyed was a *result* of successful practice and victories on legislative and bureaucratic battlefields. Their autonomy was conceptualized as a means to promote and protect good practices. Notably, as the mayor and chancellor drew on these four precedents to pilot the Autonomy Zone and to improve the first wave of Children First reforms, school autonomy and portfolio management was conceived and then institutionalized as a *means* and *source* of radical, nonincremental improvement.

REFORM'S SECOND WAVE:
PMM TAKES SHAPE, 2004–2007

In January 2006, Klein announced a second sweeping reorganization of the school system that he had established just two and a half years earlier. The proposal included $200 million in cuts to central and regional offices and increasing the Autonomy Zone to over three hundred schools. As with the original twenty-six schools in the Zone since September 2004, these additional schools would enjoy "wide freedom from oversight" in return for heightened accountability and a "ladder of consequences" ranging from the implementation of remediation plans, replacing principals, and closing schools.[51]

These structural changes, coupled with Klein's early emphasis on school leadership, sketched an emerging portfolio system premised on autonomous schools, empowered leaders, and more accountability.[52] The changes were also a response to breakdowns in implementation during the first wave of reforms, given that Zone schools were less dependent on regional offices and, in theory, more self-sufficient.

Although the Autonomy Zone was praised as "the one place" where teachers and principals felt respected, it remained an open debate whether greater autonomy—a central notion of PMM—would lead to improved student achievement.[53] By contrast, the *New York Times* ran an in-depth article on the work of Kathleen Cashin, one of Klein's ten regional superintendents with a track record of turning around low-performing schools. Part of Cashin's top-down approach (described as the "antithesis" of Klein's new reforms) provided principals with a "detailed [curricular] road map of what should be taught in every subject, in every grade." Although Klein was complimentary of Cashin's work, he suggested that it was still "incremental" and argued that by "devolving decision making and resources" to principals, larger gains would be possible.[54] From Klein's perspective, such empowerment was a "precondition of success."[55]

Regardless of the competing theories of change, a more pedestrian concern also played a role in the administration's shift from a centralized system to a decentralized portfolio management approach: private funds to key intermediary organizations like New Visions for Public Schools were drying up. Gates Foundation funding to nonprofits responsible for the launch and support of more than 180 new schools was scheduled to start phasing out in June 2007. These funds, totaling $100,000 per new school, were described as merely "catalytic."[56] As is common among education philanthropies, the Gates Foundation was not inclined to assume long-term responsibility for work that it considered a public expense.

Department officials considered the Gates Foundation intermediaries a "critical success factor."[57] Had these organizations been forced to retrench, the city would have had to deliver additional support services, a less than attractive option, given the mixed performance of the regional offices. Instead, the city contracted with a number of the groups to provide support services. The result resembled a marketplace of publicly financed school support organizations, originally created by the Gates Foundation and adopted by the city.

With these moves, the components of a PMM were taking shape. Nearly a quarter of the city's schools operated outside its regional governance structure. The nonprofit partner organizations offered a private alternative to the public bureaucracies that traditionally support schools. The final and necessary element was an accountability system to evaluate school performance, inform school practices, and guide decisions on school closings.

For this task, Klein hired James Liebman, a Columbia Law School professor, as chief accountability officer to develop "more sophisticated methods to measure individual school performance."[58] Over the course of the next few years, Liebman and his team instituted annual quality reviews modeled after the system of school inspections in the United Kingdom. They administered periodic, low-stakes standardized assessments to identify students' strengths and weaknesses. His office convened school-based inquiry teams to identify struggling students and develop data-driven interventions.[59] Liebman oversaw the development of the Achievement Reporting and Innovation System (ARIS), an $80 million system developed by IBM and Wireless Generation to collect, analyze, and compare student achievement data throughout the system. The city also began to assign letter grades—A through F—to schools, based on a combination of absolute student performance on standardized tests, progress measures, and the quality of the school environment.[60]

These building blocks allowed the city to announce, in January 2007, yet another comprehensive reorganization and a decisive adoption of PMM. The ten administrative regions and their school support offices—signature elements of the first-wave reforms—were scrapped. All of the city's twelve hundred schools and its additional three hundred new schools gained control over their budgets and hiring decisions. Moreover, the schools were no longer bound to geographic school districts or public service centers; instead they would purchase their support services from among public and private providers.[61] Choices included four city-run offices (consisting essentially of what had been the top-performing regional offices, including Cashin's); the Empowerment Zone (a renamed Autonomy Zone, still under Nadelstern's leadership); and six nonprofit "partner support organizations" under contract with the city. Table 4.1 provides a complete list of the eleven organizations.

Described by the *New York Times* as "a sort of inversion of the City school administration," the approach aimed to introduce market incentives to the provision of school support services and improve their quality. In a tacit acknowledgment of shortcomings in the original Children First reforms, Klein noted that "until now many educational decisions were made outside of the schools and classrooms"—a problem the new structure aimed to fix.[62] Yet this autonomy did not relinquish the mayor's ultimate authority over the schools, given that ARIS, the school progress reports, and other measures kept them squarely accountable to Klein and Bloomberg.[63]

TABLE 4.1 Organizations, focus, and number of schools served

Name	Type	Focus	Number of schools (2007–2008)	Number of schools (2009–2010)
Academy for Educational Development (AED)	Private, nonprofit	Youth development; middle schools	10	10
Center for Educational Innovation-Public Education Association (CEI-PEA)	Private, nonprofit	Customized support	52	77
New Visions for Public Schools, Inc.	Private, nonprofit	College prep; policy advocacy	62	76
Replications Inc.	Private, nonprofit	Strong, positive school culture	9	13
Community Learning Support Organization (CLSO)	Public, NYC DoE	Community engagement	163	156
Empowerment Support Organization (ESO)	Public, NYC DoE	Customized support; policy advocacy	477	526
Integrated Curriculum Instruction Learning Support Organization (ICI-LSO)	Public, NYC DoE	"New basics" model	364	354
Knowledge Network Learning Support Organization (KNLSO)	Public, NYC DoE	Content-rich curriculum (based on core knowledge)	96	93
Leadership Learning Support Organization (LLSO)	Public, NYC DoE	Leadership development	113	136
City University of New York (CUNY)	University	College prep; middle and high schools	13	18
Fordham University	University	Diagnostic model; early childhood	11	16

During the spring of 2007, the city, rather than individual schools, negotiated with the support organizations to determine the specific services each would provide and the fees each could charge to schools. A content analysis of each school support organization's advertised description of services indicates that all of the organizations provided a common set of basic services such as leadership and professional development, on-site coaching, and data analysis.[64] Organizations distinguished themselves through specialty services to support gifted and talented instruction, arts education, use of school technology, and parent and community engagement. Most services were programmatic; operational support for payroll, budgeting, accounting, and procurement was still provided by the city through new Integrated Service Centers. As presented in table 4.2, on average the most comprehensive set of programmatic services (thirteen out of seventeen functional areas) was offered by former regional offices.

Once each organization's suite of services was negotiated, all fifteen hundred public schools were required to purchase services from a provider, with fees ranging from $24,000 to nearly $63,000, depending on the size of the school and composition of supports. By and large, the public entities charged lower fees than the private organizations. Two years

TABLE 4.2 Summary by type of school support organization

	Private, nonprofit (4)	Public, NYC DoE (5)	University (2)
Number of schools (2007–2008)	133	1,213	24
Number of schools (2009–2010)	176	1,265	34
Average service areas offered (out of 17)	11	13	12
Average level principal satisfaction	93%	95%	93%
Fee (2009 pricing)	$35,717–55,746[a]	$29,943–47,350[b]	$37,574–40,617[a]

a. Pricing varies with school size.

b. Higher price includes additional services.

after this initial selection, schools were allowed to change providers, with about 126 schools (fewer than 10 percent) moving from one provider to another. (Providers added another hundred new schools to their networks between 2007 and 2009.)[65]

MANAGING THE PORTFOLIO, 2007–2010

The shift from a centrally run system to a portfolio of fifteen hundred autonomous schools, accountable to the chancellor and mayor through the city's data management systems and supported by public and private service providers competing for customers, is a major institutional change. But the point of the portfolio approach is not to *create* a portfolio structure, per se, but to *use* this governance arrangement to manage a system toward high achievement. At the time of this writing, New York City's experience with portfolio management is too premature for us to make any firm conclusions. But in three defining areas of this approach—school autonomy, the marketplace of support organizations, and school closings—political and practical realities are challenging the model.

School Autonomy

At times, Bloomberg and Klein have exercised their prerogative to set citywide policies, despite a stated commitment to school autonomy. In one high-profile instance in late 2006, the mayor made a sweeping ban on the use of cell phones by students in all public schools.[66] Parents protested and initiated a lawsuit against the policy, but the city held firm, going as far as conducting an unannounced sweep for phones at a Manhattan middle school in 2007 and winning the lawsuit in 2008.[67] More recently, the city strongly encouraged superintendents to hire Leadership Academy principals rather than other candidates.[68] Klein imposed a systemwide hiring freeze to force schools to hire from a pool of unassigned teachers, limiting principals' ability to recruit from the open market.[69] As these examples suggest, school autonomy within the city's portfolio model has its limits, particularly when it runs counter to the mayor's prerogative or when systemwide obligations and constraints need accommodation.

School Support Organizations

In an effort to eliminate the command-and-control structure and culture of the traditional school district bureaucracies, New York City's portfolio is buttressed by nearly a dozen school support organizations competing for school customers. Yet the creation of a providers market has not opened the system to a new set of actors and ideas. A closer look at the size, leadership, and satisfaction results of each school support network suggests the continuing relevance of practical know-how and insider expertise.

Former regional offices continued to support the lion's share of schools. In some instances, private providers negotiated limits to the size of their networks so as to not exceed their own organizational capacity. Such limits left schools with only a public-option; other providers' focus on middle and high school instruction left city elementary schools with fewer *real* choices of organizations from which to buy services. By the start of the 2009–2010 school year, over twelve hundred of the city's fourteen hundred public schools continued to receive support from a governmental subunit of the Department of Education.

School principals were surveyed three times from 2007 to 2008 on their level of satisfaction with their support organization.[70] The top-ranked organization was the Knowledge Network Learning Support Organization, a former regional office, with a near-perfect 99 percent of principals responding that they were "satisfied" or "very satisfied" with the overall quality of support. The high marks given to the public-sector providers suggest that insider knowledge and experience may be critical to high-quality services. Even the private, nonprofit organizations employ former city officials in key leadership positions. The department's former chief financial officer, corporation counsel, and other senior managers hold top positions at New Visions for Public Schools. The city's former executive director of financial operations leads the Center for Education Innovation–Public Education Association (CEI-PEA) school services alongside Seymour Fliegel, its president. An educator with decades of within-system experience runs Replications Inc.

This picture suggests that despite replacing regional offices with a new type of support organization, the city's original goal of a competitive school-service marketplace has yet to develop. Although it is too early to conclude that the capacity limits of a handful of private support organizations indicate a true market failure, there do not appear to be many other actors eager to bid on this work, engage schools as clients, and gain a share of the marketplace. For example, a number of the original Gates Foundation intermediaries chose *not* to become formal school-support organizations, in part because they viewed the funding as insufficient or the work did not align with their interests. Consequently, the traditional role of school district offices providing such services may be less a function of the logic of bureaucratic growth than it is the absence of others to accomplish work that is at times challenging and steeped in the arcana of curriculum, pedagogy, and local, state, and federal regulation.

Moreover, the next wave of structural reforms is already underway. Some school support organizations are looking to convert the district schools in their network into charter schools and themselves into charter management organizations. At the time of this writing, the city plans further changes to the school support model, as it creates new Children First Networks and plans to eliminate the Integrated Service Centers.[71]

School Closings

Few other attributes are as central to the portfolio approach as the opening and closing of schools. Just like an astute financial manager who sells off low-performing stocks, maintains an assortment of consistently strong performers, and adds new and promising prospects to the mix, superintendents working within a portfolio arrangement aim to do the same, albeit with schools.

Yet unlike a financial portfolio, where transactions can occur with relative ease, school closings are complicated. Closing decisions should be based on solid evidence, a rarity in the complex and contentious world of student achievement metrics. Even in the face of poor statistical performance, students, parents, and teachers are often loyal to their school and may protest the closing. Regulatory requirements for zoning and community hearings may further delay the process. Attractive alternatives need to be available to students. Moreover, despite the city's stated commitment to data-based decision making, critics charged the administration with targeting some schools for closure at least in part from an eagerness to generate space for favored charter operators.

Particular attention to the politics of school closings made for a relatively smooth process when the New Century High Schools Initiative replaced large high schools with a campus of new small ones. Community organizations were affiliated with each new school. Union officials were part of the planning process, and teachers retained placement rights within the system. A general consensus existed that the schools slated for closure either were beyond recovery or accommodations were made to preserve functioning programs within dysfunctional schools. Although the effort was not without its unintended consequences, including the overcrowding of existing high schools to accommodate a closing school's student exodus, New Century did not face the stiff opposition that has characterized more recent closings.[72]

For example, in 2009, the city planned to close three elementary schools on the basis of low achievement and replace them with charter schools. Parents rallied to keep the schools open, and the teacher union sued the city for violating state zoning regulations. Ultimately, the city withdrew its plans, and the lawsuit was dropped.[73] A year later, the three schools earned As on their city-generated report cards, up from Ds and an F the previous year, serving to undermine the city's data system and vindicate the schools' supporters.[74] In early 2010, a similar controversy exploded over the city's plans to close nineteen schools, including Columbus High School and Alfred E. Smith High School, despite the fact that some of the schools slated for closure received As and Bs on their city-generated report cards. Student, parent, community, and teacher union efforts to preserve the schools were all but ignored by the mayor's Panel For Educational Policy.[75] The city's plan to replace some of these schools with new charters raised further suspicions that the closures were driven by a political rather than educational agenda.

These three issues demonstrate the practical challenges of managing the portfolio approach and the limits of the portfolio metaphor. School autonomy is at times in conflict with systemwide obligations; private operators may not have the expertise or inclination to replace public bureaucracies; and the politics of school closings do not compare to the ease with which an investor can buy and sell shares.

More fundamentally, critics of these recent and controversial school closings have demanded to know what responsibility the chancellor bears, in a portfolio arrangement, for the success or failure of a school. Should the chancellor (or any superintendent working through a portfolio approach) actively work to support and improve schools? Or is the chancellor merely responsible, as chief portfolio manager, to open, monitor, and close failing schools, thereby leaving the work of instruction and improvement to principals, teachers, and other school-based staff? In New York City, where the mayor fought hard to win control of schools and takes credit for their successes, it seems inconsistent to assert that principals and teachers shoulder the blame when things go wrong.

PORTFOLIO MANAGEMENT AND THE POLITICS OF "APOLITICAL" REFORM

Like the traditional progressive reformers of the early twentieth century, both Bloomberg and Klein have been outspokenly disdainful of politics. The mayor frequently distinguishes his pragmatic and businesslike approach from the rigid, ideological, and self-interested behavior he associates with professional politicians. "[A]ny successful elected executive knows," he has said, "that real results are more important than partisan battles and that good ideas should take precedence over rigid adherence to any particular political ideology."[76] He went beyond rhetoric in pursuing this vision, for example, by investing millions of his own dollars in an unsuccessful effort to make the city's elections formally nonpartisan.

But unlike at least some of the traditional progressives, Bloomberg has not been naive enough to unilaterally disarm himself in the game of hardball politics. George Washington Plunkitt, the colorful Tammany Hall machine politician, once dismissed good government reformers as "morning glories" who "looked lovely in the mornin' and withered up in a short time, while the regular machines went on flourishin' forever, like fine old oaks."[77] As a case in point, in his first campaign, Bloomberg switched from being a registered Democrat to run for mayor as a Republican (in order to avoid a crowded primary field of candidates), and then ran for a second term as an Independent, backed by the power of his incumbency.

The Bloomberg–Klein team may have believed that rationally constructed plans based on good intentions and expertise would eventually win out, but they buttressed their plan with a distinctly political analysis of the obstacles they faced and devoted substantial resources to fighting political fire with fire of their own. The point, here, is not that they are hypocritical. Rather, would-be reformers studying lessons from New York City would be wise to learn from what Bloomberg and Klein *did* and not just what they *said*, lest reformers underestimate the obstacles to implementation and the range of tactics to employ or avoid.

In this concluding section, we distinguish among the politics of *adoption*, the politics of *implementation*, and the politics of *sustainability*. Bloomberg and Klein had the luxury to avoid many of the battles over policy adoption that often frustrate reformers. This allowed them to move initially to engage in the politics of implementation—trying to ensure that their initiatives were actually carried out—and the politics of sustainability, making sure that reforms would be sufficiently institutionalized and sustained after their terms of office come to an end.

The Unpolitics of Policy Adoption

Historically, political scientists have focused the bulk of their attention on the political conflicts and strategic maneuvering that determine which policies get debated and enacted. But the unusual combination of formal and informal power that characterized the Bloomberg–Klein regime eliminated or overwhelmed most of the common veto points, making the adoption of new policy less problematic than it had been historically in the city or than it is likely to be in most other places. As played out during the mayor's first two terms, the dynamics of policy adoption conforms to what has sometimes been referred to as *unpolitics*, a phenomenon in which power is asserted without having to be openly exercised and without substantial challenge.[78] Public deliberation, debate, and contestation were at a minimum, not because everyone was in consensus but because there was a powerful momentum and air of inevitability that made open challenge seem fruitless.

The formal structure of mayoral control was one important factor in eliminating points of friction in the policy-making process. Mayoral control had replaced the central school board with a thirteen-member Panel For Educational Policy (PEP), to which the mayor named eight, including the chancellor. Notions that the PEP would serve as an independent check on the mayor were disabused almost from the start. In July 2002, while introducing the first members, the mayor went on to say, "I do not expect to see their names—ever—in the press on the record or off the record. That's exactly what's wrong with the current system."[79] This was underscored some twenty months later when a few members of the PEP expressed doubts about approving the chancellor's plan to end social promotion for the city's third graders. As reported by the *New York Times*, the mayor simply "fired them, had three new members appointed and rammed his policy home—in one workday…"[80]

The administration's ability to plow through obstacles to initiating new policies did not depend on formal power alone. Even under mayoral control, for example, there were checkpoints that might have been activated if the mayor were perceived as politically weaker or his opponents more organized and unified. The city council still had the ability to challenge and constrain the mayor and chancellor via its formal control of the purse strings. In at least some other cities with mayoral control, city councils have stepped up to take on a more direct role in monitoring the education agency, airing critiques, and occasionally mounting direct challenges.[81] That this did not happen is partly attributable to the mayor's general popularity and partly to the factionalism and general weakness of the city council.[82]

Mayoral control of schools also confers an important set of informal powers. Unlike school superintendents or school boards, a mayor is in position to engage in cross-sector logrolling, using control of resources in other agencies to reward or punish local legislators. Council members and even locally elected state legislators depend on their access to a range of agencies in order to tender services to their districts and earn the loyalty of their constituents. That does not mean that none of them would challenge the mayor or his handpicked chancellor, but it certainly raised the anticipated costs of going that route.

Equally important may have been the ability of the administration to sidestep the approval, oversight, and regulatory mechanisms that come along with public funding. Ready access to substantial amounts of private funding made it easier for the administration to act quickly and flexibly. A primary vehicle was the Fund for Public Schools, a 501(c)(3) nonprofit that had existed since 1982 but which the mayor and Klein (who serves as its chairman) turned from a modest channel of support for individual schools and programs into a much larger engine for systemic change—going so far as to appoint Caroline Kennedy as the organization's chief fundraiser. As described on its Web site, the mayor and chancellor "established public-private partnerships as a critical lever for driving public education reform." The fund, by "raising more than $240 million for system-wide reforms and initiatives that support individual schools," took the lead.[83]

About $80 million of that amount went to support the NYC Leadership Academy, which the Bloomberg–Klein team marketed as a critical linchpin in the administration's plan to recruit and train a new cadre of principals focused on performance rather than compliance. Later as portfolio management took hold, Leadership Academy training was viewed as a way to prepare principals with the skills and values they would need to function in a decentralized portfolio environment where control over key resources was delegated to the school level.

The administration was able to use such private support as a form of venture capital, helping it to launch initiatives quickly without the normal political and bureaucratic checkpoints. Once established, marketed through extensive public relations as a success, the initiatives could be moved onto the public budget.[84] In June 2008, for example, the Leadership Academy was chosen—in what was described as a competitive multibidder procurement process—to become the Department of Education's primary provider of principal training, moving about $10 million per year (for five years) of its operating budget onto the public balance sheet and freeing the Fund for Public Schools to put its resources ($44 million was raised in 2008) to other uses. Hiring the nonprofit school support organizations as city vendors offers a similar case.

Bureaucracy Busting and Rewiring as Implementation Precursor

As Pressman and Wildavsky famously made clear, there are a Rube Goldberg-like series of trip wires and diverters between the announcement of formal policy and the changes that eventually take place at street level, where the intended features of government action eventually make or fail to make their mark.[85] Not all of Bloomberg's advantages in the policy adoption arena carried the same weight when it came to implementation, and moving from declared policy to implemented policy required greater attention. We suggest this was accomplished largely by delegitimizing or replacing individuals and institutions most likely to stall or redirect the administration's initiatives. But rather than sweeping clean and building anew (as one might expect from the continued evocation of the rational-comprehensive model of decision making), this stage involved considerable weaving and layering of new elements into institutions and actors that predated the administration.

In selecting Klein as his chancellor, Bloomberg opted for a paramount example of a nontraditional superintendent.[86] Over the past two decades, there has been growing openness to hiring superintendents whose records of leadership have been compiled in other arenas—business or the military, most notably. One rationale offered for doing so is that traditional superintendents, having been schooled in the conventional paradigms and having accumulated allies and interests through a career within the bureaucracy, are less willing and able to aggressively challenge the status quo and introduce innovative reforms.

Klein came to the job directly from Bertelsmann, Inc., where he had served for one and a half years as chairman and chief executive officer. Before that, he was assistant attorney general in charge of the Department of Justice's antitrust division during the Clinton administration, where he was most famous for leading landmark cases against Microsoft. "It's not an accident that the mayor selected the country's leading antitrust litigator and not a teacher to lead the DOE," one top department administrator noted. "What the mayor understood [is that] when you have a system with so much vested interest somehow you have to break through that."[87]

This antibureaucracy orientation was powerful in shaping the administration's restructuring, and serves as one of the core animating ideas behind both the first and second reform phases. Jack Welch, who helped launch the Leadership Academy, reportedly informed a team of district leaders that they should emulate GE's approach of "annihilating" bureaucracy. "We cultivate the hatred of bureaucracy in our company, and never for a moment hesitate to use that awful word 'hate.' Bureaucrats must be ridiculed and removed."[88]

A primary appeal of the first wave of centralizing reforms was that by structurally marginalizing institutional nodes at which the protectors of the status quo would be strong, they would make it possible to implement changes more quickly. In addition to attacking the bureaucracy and establishing new modes for recruiting and training a different kind of principal, the administration all but eliminated the thirty-two community school districts—another likely site for the mobilization of opposition.

From the standpoint of organizational theory, moving from thirty-two districts to ten regions could be seen as pretty incremental stuff. But the community school districts were political bodies with their own patrons and constituencies, capable of bucking the new reforms. By shifting to the new regions, these preexisting networks were disrupted; the new regional leadership was administrative in nature and unambiguously accountable to the chancellor. In addition, the regions were deliberate amalgams of the former districts, whose original boundaries were drawn up in the 1960s along racial, ethnic, and class groupings. Packaging different types of districts into each region created more internally heterogeneous units and facilitated a reallocation of resources and personnel to pursue greater equity.[89] In the process, administrative jurisdictions were unaligned from the communities and electoral boundaries that are traditional bases for political action.[90]

Marginalizing institutional obstacles makes the intentional derailment of implementation less likely. Bloomberg and Klein were still left with the challenge of creating an implementation framework and finding the people to make it work. The new cohort of Leadership Academy principals was a partial answer, but with roughly twelve hundred schools, this alone was unlikely to suffice. After six years, Academy alums constituted only about 13 percent of the city's principals and served less than one in ten of the city's students.[91] Consequently, the administration also needed to enlist individuals and groups with longer-standing roots in the system.

The rational-comprehensive approach is often tied to an economic perspective that emphasizes system design and incentive structures more than fuzzier concepts relating to organizational culture, local knowledge, and social capital. Get the rewards and sanctions properly aligned with the desired outcomes, the thinking goes, and the right kinds of behavior will result. By their statements and actions, it appears that Bloomberg and Klein had a somewhat more nuanced understanding of the role of culture, individuals, and relationships as mediators of organizational signals. As implementation continued, this led to a reduced reliance on outside experts and a greater cultivation of individuals and organizations that had retained an entrepreneurial orientation to successfully operate in niches under the previous, dysfunctional regime.

As characterized by Bloomberg and Klein, the animating forces for reform were the right people making the right judgments; the worst aspect of bureaucracy was its inculcation of a culture that systematically recruits and indoctrinates people who lack these qualities. The self-perpetuating culture of bureaucracy meant that changing incentives alone would not generate a behavioral response—or at least not as quickly as they wanted. Although their corporate backgrounds and suspicion of the educational bureaucracy encouraged them to reach out to corporate actors such as Jack Welch, consulting firms, and graduates of elite business and public policy schools, their approach also resonated among some key actors who were closer to the ground in New York City education.

Pre-Bloomberg, New York City was notable for its pervasive education bureaucracy. The former address of the central office, 110 Livingstone Street, was diagnosed by David Rogers as a "sick bureaucracy" and skewered by Bloomberg as the "Kremlin of the now-defunct Board of Education."[92] But within 110 Livingston were "guerillas in the bureaucracy," entrepreneurial leaders who had found niches within the organization where they could build and maintain innovative schools and programs; the central bureaucracy left them relatively undisturbed because either their work was sufficiently under the radar screen or they had influential political constituencies.[93]

This history gave Bloomberg and Klein like-minded allies within the system—individuals like Nadelstern and Carmen Farina;[94] Fliegel of CEI-PEA;[95] and Hughes of New Visions for Public Schools—who combined a belief that the existing system was incapable of reforming itself with the inside knowledge and credibility that the mayor and chancellor lacked. The Autonomy Zone, combined with the small-schools initiative and the intermediary groups operating there, provided a quick and ready holding area for some experienced school leaders who had long chafed under the old regime. Absent that safe haven, the centralizing aspects of the administration's first-wave reforms—precisely because they were pursued with more vigor and effectiveness—might have driven out these very individuals who were potentially the administration's best allies. Incorporating such individuals and groups did not just mean enrolling them in a mapped-out and fully developed scheme. These inside actors came into the process with their own understanding of reform, one more closely linked to research and practical knowledge accumulated within the education sector, and set an example of empowered leadership, drawing on their experience and insights to influence the city's evolving policies.

Looking Forward: The Politics of Sustaining Reform

The politics of sustaining the reform initiatives may have been low on Bloomberg and Klein's agenda in the first couple of years, but it became increasingly central and played a major role in shaping the PMM near the end of Bloomberg's second term. During the first two years of the administration, they focused on eliminating obstacles and putting new arrangements in place. But the electoral clock was ticking—by the time Klein came on board, worked through the Children First planning process, and resolved legal challenges to the reorganization plan, the mayor was already eighteen months into his first four-year term.

It is possible that some in the administration started off with the naive view—common among reformers—that once the up-front obstacles were surmounted and their people and policies in place, the benefits of reform would be so quick and clear as to create their own sustaining constituency. But events demonstrated soon enough that decisive action was insufficient to ensure sustainability. According to a *New York Times* poll taken just before Bloomberg's initial election, 73 percent of New Yorkers were dissatisfied with the quality of the city's schools (a figure roughly constant over the sporadic *Times* polls on this question since 1993). In April 2004, more than halfway through his first term and after many highly publicized reforms and challenges to the educational status quo, the number was virtually the same, 72 percent.[96] If the electorate was really going to reelect the mayor on the success or failure of school reform—which Bloomberg, in his first campaign, encouraged New Yorkers to do—there were good reasons to be concerned.

The predictable pressure to show results in time for the reelection bid was exacerbated by two factors relating to the city's governance structure at the time: term limits and a sunset provision on mayoral control of the schools. When Bloomberg took office, a city statute limited him and other locally elected officials to two successive terms, and the mayor himself was in favor of the limits, having said as late as mid-April 2008 that, "I'm looking forward to being mayor through midnight December 31, 2009 and then doing something else."[97] The state legislature had this in mind when it initially granted Bloomberg the power to run the city schools by including a June 2009 sunset provision. The stipulation, timed just as the city would be gearing up to elect Bloomberg's successor, would force a reconsideration of the governance model.

In no more than eight years, Bloomberg had to launch a radical restructuring, demonstrate real results, and justify mayoral control itself. Klein was particularly aware of the urgency, having followed and admired Alan Bersin's work as superintendent in San Diego, who was ousted by his school board before his initiatives could take root, but concluding that Bersin ultimately "got beat by the politics."[98] During the spring of 2008, rumors circulated that members of the mayor's staff were feeling out public and elite opinion about the possibility of Bloomberg pursuing a third term. By that October, the mayor announced that he had changed his mind, would seek a change in the term limits law, and run again. Bloomberg offered as his primary rationale for the reversal that he was uniquely qualified to lead the city during tough fiscal times due to the stock market collapse.[99] The mayor's supporters also pushed the message that the administration's schools agenda was not yet fully realized and vulnerable to backsliding. With private funding, they launched a major advertising campaign that linked claims of school improvement to the tag line, "Keep it Going."[100]

In late October 2008, the city council narrowly approved an extension to the term limits, making Bloomberg the presumptive front runner. To keep in place the school reforms he and Klein had implemented, Bloomberg also needed to negotiate successfully with the state legislature and renew mayoral control. Although almost no credible voices called for a complete return to the previous school board and community district structure, a combination of factors made the fight for extending mayoral control more difficult than many expected. Resentment lingered over the mayor's turnabout on term limits. A coalition of community-based organizations argued to keep but substantially reform mayoral control and emphasized the need for three kinds of changes.

First, the coalition members called for greater transparency on testing data, which they claimed the Department of Education was manipulating in order to inflate purported gains, and on budgetary data, to surface what they believed was a large and hidden reliance on costly contracts. The second push was for more checks and balances, particularly to make the Educational Priorities Panel sufficiently strong and independent so that it could serve as more than a rubber stamp for the chancellor's policies. And third, they wanted more parent participation, reflecting a broad sense of resentment in parts of the city over the Department of Education's perceived indifference to their concerns. Also complicating the extension of mayoral control was a series of chaotic shifts in majority control in Albany that left the legislature completely dysfunctional at precisely the time it was supposed to act on the issue.

Professions of antipathy to politics aside, the mayor and his team engaged in bare-knuckles politics to extend term limits and mayoral control of schools. The details are fascinating, but must be told separately.[101] For our purposes, it is only necessary to report that the administration and its allies mobilized their substantial resources to create a sense of urgency, sway public opinion, mobilize grassroots support, and consistently paint their critics as out of touch. With Bloomberg's subsequent reelection, the administration gained four more years to make permanent its reform agenda. By 2009, any presumption that rationally conceived policies and demonstrated outcomes would suffice to ensure continuation had long since dissolved. The portfolio management approach, in this context, needs to be understood as more than simply an alternative model of service delivery; it was also an important part of a political strategy for sustaining the administration's work.

PMMs as a Strategy for Policy Sustainability

PMMs of governance, as a particular form of contracting regimes, have the potential to alter the structure of urban school politics, both by shifting control of key decisions into new venues and by introducing new interest groups. The naive reformers that Plunkitt ridiculed for being "morning glories" counted on the power of the idea and the normative authority of "doing the right thing"' to carry the day. Whether by happenstance, opportunistic adjustment, or political design, the reform forces behind portfolio

management may be putting into place structures that buttress their perceived "right thing" with new arrangements of political power to maintain
momentum and defend their gains.

E. E. Schattschneider famously noted that "new policies create a new
politics."[102] Political scientists recently have been returning to this point to
emphasize the feedback loop by which policies change frames of reference,
interest group alignments, and decision-making venues that, in turn, may
subsequently determine whether those policies are amended, sustained, or
undone. Accordingly, as they "gauge how a new policy will affect social
problems," Soss and Schramm observe, "strategic politicians also consider
its potential to mobilize or mollify the opposition, create pressure for further action, appease or outrage the party faithful, redistribute political resources, change the terms of debate, and so on."[103]

One way that the establishment of a PMM may change the parameters
within which the politics of sustainability is played out is by *moving important resources and authority to more protected venues.* As one important
member of the Bloomberg–Klein team explained in an interview with the
authors, "Part of our job for the third and final term is to decentralize to
the point where the people who come after us cannot recentralize easily."
Asked how it is possible to embed the reforms so that a future mayor, chancellor, or more aggressive city council could not reverse them, he replied
that one way is to "position resources and authority outside the system. It
is not an accident that six of the eleven School Support Organizations are
not-for-profits and will continue to exist long after the chancellor and I and
the others we've worked with." He went on to indicate that the administration had already "repositioned" $400 million dollars that had been in the
regional and central offices. If a new administration tried to pull that back,
it would find it "harder to take money away from schools than to give it."[105]

In addition, the establishment of the portfolio framework appears to
have *created a new constituency* to protect the reforms. The district official quoted earlier went on to explain why it would be hard to reverse
the reforms: "The organizations represented by those partnership school
organizations—the organizations that partnered with us on 400 new
schools—have a lot of political influence in the city that would be hard to
ignore." Private providers including charter schools, school-support orga-

nizations, and other institutions that have been enlisted in district part-nership roles provide a readily mobilizable set of actors and resources and constitute a new base for political mobilization outside the normal chan-nels of the city's conventional party politics.

The actual mobilization of this new constituency was most readily ap-parent in the battle over the extension of mayoral control of the schools. Learn NY was the organization formed by allies of the mayor to give a grassroots face to the supporters of mayoral control. Its most prominent leader, Geoffrey Canada, is chief executive of the Harlem Children's Zone (HCZ), which runs two charter schools as well as network of health and social services. Various reports suggest that HCZ has received over $385 million in contracts from the city and Department of Education and at least a half-million in philanthropic support from the mayor himself.[105] One of Learn NY's co-leaders, Sister Paulette LoMonaco has been the ex-ecutive director of Good Shepherd Services for twenty-eight years. Good Shepherd was an early partner in the Gates Foundation small-schools ini-tiative, and one of Good Shepherd's leaders joined the Department of Education to work on alternative high schools.[106] In August 2009, it was revealed that Bill Gates and Eli Broad had quietly given millions of dollars to help launch and support Learn NY.[107]

Organizations that have benefited from Bloomberg's pro-charter poli-cies were also part of Learn NY's coalition. In addition to several relatively small operators of individual charter schools, coalition members include larger groups advocating for or supporting charter networks, including the New York City Charter School Center, the charter resource center on whose board the chancellor serves; Achievement First and Uncom-mon Schools, two charter management organizations with deep ties to the philanthropic community; Beginning with Children Foundation, another charter support organization operating two schools in Brooklyn; Civic Builders, a nonprofit developer of charter school facilities; and Ground-work, an East New York community-based organization whose founder also serves on the board of Achievement First charters.[108]

Noncharter school organizations in the Learn NY coalition include school partner and support organizations operating within the portfolio management system. Outward Bound and Urban Assembly were Gates

Foundation-funded developers of new small schools and continue to support networks of schools. Fordham University is listed as a coalitional supporter. Another SSO listed is Fliegel's Center for Education Innovation.

Still others are groups that rely heavily on Department of Education funding. Learning Leaders, whose mission is "to help New York City public school students succeed by training volunteers to provide individualized instructional support . . . and by equipping parents to foster their children's educational development," has received substantial philanthropic funding directly from the mayor in addition to public support.[109] The After-School Corporation (TASC) received millions in public dollars, including some via a no-bid contract awarded retroactively.[110] According to one online investigative blog associated with Columbia University's Graduate School of Journalism, "Nearly one third of the companies and nonprofits that are members of [Learn NY] . . . received no-bid contracts from the Department of Education since Mayor Bloomberg took control of New York City schools in 2002."[111]

CONCLUSION

Although celebrated as a rational, comprehensive approach that counts among its benefits a reduced role for political bargaining and compromise, our interpretation of the evidence suggests that the Bloomberg-Klein regime combined early twentieth century Progressive-style enlightenment, old-fashioned power politics, and pragmatic muddling. In addition, an intentional effort was made to structure a new set of politics in which contractual relationships, rather than formal political representation and direct bureaucratic authority, define interests and shape constituencies.

Political and economic advantages during the policy-formulation and adoption stage made it possible for the administration to push through a broad agenda of change with little resistance or negotiated compromises. Other districts seeking to emulate New York City's rapid launch need to be wary of the apolitical, rational-comprehensive framing; only a handful of administrations are likely to have the same luxurious circumstances.

The rational-comprehensive framing of the reforms can also mislead observers about the kinds of expertise required for implementation. Despite the "annihilate the bureaucracy" rhetoric associated with the first wave of reforms, implementation involved pragmatic steps that relied on educators and organizations that predated the Bloomberg–Klein regime. This brought to the table local knowledge, long-standing relationships, and different ideas about models for centralization and decentralization.

Some proponents of apolitical reform concede that power politics may be a necessary evil at the early stages, but hold to the expectation that it will become less prominent as entrenched elements of the old regime are marginalized in the face of improved outcomes. This would then allow further adjustments to be incremental, evidence-based, and delegated to those with the greatest technical expertise. But New York City's experience does not fit this pattern. As the Bloomberg–Klein team has shifted attention toward sustainability, the exercise of politics has become even more apparent. The battles over the requisite governance changes involved old-style power politics—attacking opponents, calling up favors, mobilizing allies, and heavy investment in public relations and political communications campaigns. The term limits and mayoral control extension battles may have been somewhat specific to the New York City case; alternately, the fact that key supporters of portfolio management are also pushing for mayoral control in other cities suggests that this linkage may occur elsewhere. Regardless, the stage of constituency building to sustain reforms is likely to be endemic.

We think the verdict is still out on the extent to which the portfolio management approach will result in the higher student outcomes. The contractual and political relationships central to the model are vulnerable to management lapses, undermined autonomy, and unreliable or discredited metrics. Scandals, such as rogue principals or support organizations misusing funds, cheating on tests, abusing employee rights, and disregarding dissatisfied parents, can plague—with disproportionate impact—the decentralization effort. As New York City's experience shows, these are not theoretical vulnerabilities; many of the lapses have occurred. These challenges do not necessarily discredit the portfolio model's core ideas of autonomy and empowerment, accountability, and private-sector activity. They do, in our view, suggest that districts contemplating this approach do so with open eyes and a realistic assessment of the obstacles to be confronted.

In New York City, the Bloomberg–Klein regime enjoyed formal and informal political power, philanthropic and civic support, a generally expanding financial base, and an education bureaucracy that, despite its reputation for rigidity, housed numerous individuals who retained an entrepreneurial orientation leavened by experience and know-how. Yet despite these unusual and largely unreplicable advantages, the need to build and maintain a supportive politics is ongoing, and scorch-the-earth strategies for clearing out potential obstacles risk driving away insiders who are needed to convert abstract ideas into working practice.

5

One Step Back, Two Steps Forward

The Making and Remaking of "Radical" Reform in Philadelphia

Katrina E. Bulkley, Jolley Bruce Christman,
and Eva Gold

The story of Philadelphia's portfolio model of school management is a remarkable one on at least three counts.[1] First and foremost, the model has evolved and expanded over four district administrations—a preacher, lawyer, and systemic reformer, David Hornbeck; two business-oriented CEOs, nationally prominent Paul Vallas, and interim CEO Tom Brady; and now a traditional education professional, Arlene Ackerman. Second, at one point in its history with portfolio management, Philadelphia represented the country's largest experiment in the private management of schools. Third, the concept of different kinds of schools and school management has taken root, even as district leaders have tightened the reins in many areas, most importantly, the managed instruction system (which includes a core curriculum and aligned assessments). These two seemingly contradictory reforms operating alongside one another led Boyd and colleagues to argue,

"The district has combined what Wong and Shen describe as the leading alternatives for reform strategies—market-based solutions along with a strong centralized authority model."[2] As this chapter will show, grappling with the paradoxes of these strategies is a central theme of the Philadelphia story.

Less remarkable is the fact that Philadelphia's particular version of a *portfolio management model in practice* diverges considerably from the *portfolio concept* that Hill, Pierce, and Guthrie originally put forward and Warren and Hernandez amplified.[3] Reform ideas often look quite different on the ground than on paper. Hill, Pierce, and Guthrie emphasized the importance of a strong supply of high-quality school options, choice for students and their families, and substantial school autonomy over personnel, budget, curriculum, and instruction. Their expectation was that choice and autonomy would spur innovation and differentiation based on demand. In their view, districts were responsible for accountability for school performance, including the willingness to close failing schools and replace them with a ready pool of alternatives. Warren and Hernandez argued that, in addition, districts must also manage the system of choice, periodically balancing the portfolio, to ensure that all students have quality choices that meet their needs and interests. In this chapter, we demonstrate just how Philadelphia's portfolio model in practice differs substantially from the portfolio model in theory. We also shed light on the many factors and their complex interactions that have influenced its ever-changing shape.

Currently, Philadelphia's portfolio of schools consists of:

- Regular district-managed schools that include both neighborhood and special admissions schools

- A group of low-performing schools slated for a complex, layered set of interventions that are designed, in some cases, by the district itself and, in others, by outside providers

- A growing number of alternative schools that serve students who have been removed from their schools for disciplinary infractions and over-age or undercredited students (alternative schools are managed by external providers from both the for-profit and nonprofit sectors).

- A thriving charter school sector that has grown exponentially and as of 2009–2010 included 67 schools serving nearly 37,000 students (18.5 percent of students in public schools in the city)

Despite this diversity of school types, Philadelphia's portfolio model has not yet made good on important promises of the original concept. It has not brought broad-based choice to students and families, except in the charter school sector. It has not introduced radical shifts in authority to schools or to the external providers that manage them, again, with the exception of the charter school sector. And, the district has not yet enacted a strong accountability framework for outside managers or for charter schools. Contract performance provisions for managers have been nebulous, and the district has, in numerous instances, chosen to continue with providers despite a lack of evidence that they are improving student achievement. And the district, which is the authorizer of charter schools in Pennsylvania, has until very recently, assumed a very light-handed approach to awarding and reauthorizing charters.

In the following sections, we tell the story of the portfolio model in Philadelphia, showing how multiple forces both within and outside the district interacted in ways that led to its current form. This evolution has been influenced at the local level by community protests, pressure from civic and political leaders, collective bargaining agreements, budget reductions, and CEOs who believe in the power of strong central mandates to improve school performance. While local pressures have been significant, the federal and state commitment to private engagement in public education and test-based accountability, fueled especially by the No Child Left Behind Act of 2001 (NCLB) and more recently by the Race to the Top competition, have played critical roles in shaping Philadelphia's reform.

Philadelphia's history with the portfolio management model (PMM) has included dramatic turning points and barely visible shifts. The model's evolution has been guided by moments of intention, but much has happened through serendipity. While there are currently indications that autonomy may figure somewhat more prominently in relationships between the district and successful schools and successful school managers, and that the district will use its authority to close failing charters and fire school managers who don't make the grade and take steps to engage local communities in the shaping of their schools, these developments are not a given.

All this said, the landscape of schools in Philadelphia is radically different than it was in 1997. Aspects of the district's role in improving schools have changed dramatically. An array of new players—for-profit companies, nonprofit reform support organizations, universities, and community-based organizations—is on the scene, attempting the hard work of making schools better at educating students.

This chapter is based on extensive research conducted by Research for Action (RFA), a Philadelphia-based research organization, over the last twenty years. Our sources include a substantial number of pieces (reports, journal articles, and book chapters) written by RFA staff and affiliated researchers, interviews and observations at the district level, and analysis of documents from the district, media, and elsewhere. RFA's data on the Vallas years are particularly rich and complete; due to the fact that the Ackerman era is still in the early stages, our data and analysis on this period are necessarily preliminary. We begin our story with two actions by the Commonwealth of Pennsylvania—charter school legislation in 1997 and state takeover of the School District of Philadelphia in 2001—that served as both catalysts and backdrop for all that followed.

CHARTER SCHOOL LEGISLATION AND STATE TAKEOVER: THE SEEDS OF PHILADELPHIA'S PORTFOLIO MODEL

We had a situation where more than 150 schools had over 50% of their students performing at below basic level on the PSSAs [the Pennsylvania state tests]. We believed that there was not the capacity on the ground to turn that situation around. We needed outside expertise . . . We believed that the private sector could do a better job.

—Secretary of Education Charles Zogby[4]

In 2001, the Commonwealth of Pennsylvania announced that it was taking over the School District of Philadelphia. At the time, Philadelphia was among the ten largest urban districts in the country, serving approximately 210,000 children in 237 district-managed schools and 40 charter schools and employing over 12,000 teachers. Low levels of student achievement and fiscal bankruptcy provided overt justification for the state's action. However, as Secretary Zogby's remarks suggest, other forces were also at play.

David Hornbeck, Philadelphia's superintendent from 1994 through 2000 and a staunch advocate of systemic reform, was in a contentious relationship with state leaders, most especially Republican Governor Tom Ridge. Hornbeck waged a loud and public battle with Ridge and legislators, insisting that the state, which had capped its education funding in 1993, was not adequately supporting Philadelphia's growing and increasingly impoverished student population. In 1998, Hornbeck announced he would not dismantle his reform efforts with further budget cuts. In response, a majority of state legislators, including both Republicans and Democrats, passed Act 46, authorizing state takeover of any district in financial and/or academic distress. And in May 2000, the legislature passed Act 16, the Education Empowerment Act, affecting Philadelphia and ten other school districts. Failure to produce turnaround results in three years would result in removal of local boards of education in these districts and state installation of new governance bodies.[5] Legislative changes in the school code sanctioned sweeping and unprecedented powers, including the right of the new governance structures to deny teachers the right to strike.[6]

In addition to their argument about fair funding, state leaders and Hornbeck were at odds over other big ideas circulating about how to reform schools and improve student achievement. Ridge believed in market-based solutions. He had tried to pass voucher legislation three times, but failed. However, in 1997, with strong bipartisan support, including Philadelphia's own Democratic and Republican legislative leaders, Ridge succeeded in passing charter school legislation. Although not a supporter of charter schools, Hornbeck did not exercise a rein on their growth during the remaining years of his tenure. He hoped that this hands-off approach would win him support in the state capitol for the fair-funding battle. It didn't.[7] Notably, close to forty charter schools were operating in Philadelphia at the time of Hornbeck's departure in 2000.

State leaders were not the only ones who doubted whether the education bureaucracies were capable of reforming themselves. The original support that Philadelphia's civic and business leaders had shown on Hornbeck's arrival had eroded as the funding battle turned nasty and Hornbeck did not win the labor concessions they believed necessary for meaningful change. They did not see the district as a viable change agent and offered no protest when Ridge turned to Edison Schools, Inc. to review district operations in preparation for a state takeover under Act 46.[8] Issued within six weeks at a cost of $2.7 million, Edison's report recommended replacing the existing elected school board with a five-member School Reform Commission (SRC), with four members appointed by the governor and the fifth appointed by the mayor. The report also proposed that significant district central-office functions and school management be turned over to an outside provider (the implication was that the outside provider would be Edison Schools, Inc.).

In October 2001, Ridge left Pennsylvania to become U.S. Secretary of Homeland Security, and lieutenant governor Mark Schweiker succeeded him. Schweiker moved forward with the recommendations in the Edison report, including plans for Edison itself to manage sixty low-performing Philadelphia public schools as well as to take over many central-office management functions. But a *Philadelphia Inquirer* article likened the expansive roles for Edison in both the central office and schools to the proverbial "fox in charge of a hen house." Student and community protests swelled over Edison's role, and the teacher union and other city unions and many from the education reform advocacy community joined them. Mayor John Street moved his office into district headquarters in a display of solidarity against the state and Edison. After negotiations, however, the state takeover was a "friendly" one, with the mayor gaining the right to appoint two members of the SRC instead of one, and both the city and state contributing new funding for the district. The diverse provider model, in which multiple outside providers (not just Edison) would manage district schools, was a compromise between the city and state and a response to the backlash against a more dramatic role for Edison.

PHILADEPHIA'S PORTFOLIO MODEL TAKES ROOT AND GROWS

Following the state takeover, the newly created SRC began work on multiple fronts. It set the diverse provider model in motion, issuing a request for proposals (RFP) to provider organizations to manage low-performing schools and it embarked on a national search for a new CEO to lead the district. James Nevels, chair of the newly created SRC and the only appointee at this point, saw the importance of finding a prominent, energetic reformer who would bring credibility to governance under state takeover and the SRC's radical privatization plan. The SRC settled on Paul Vallas, who had served as CEO of the Chicago Public Schools from 1995 to 2001; prior to his role in CPS, he was the budget director to Chicago Mayor Richard Daley and was known as a district turnaround specialist. In the summer of 2002, Vallas arrived in Philadelphia, demonstrating immediately that he was a master communicator and a strong-minded and tireless reformer. He quickly announced that Edison would not need to assume any responsibility for central office operations because that was his job.

The Diverse Provider Model Takes Shape

Finalizing district contracts with the providers was at the top of Vallas's to-do list. He wrote contracts with the for-profits and nonprofit educational management organizations (EMO), and memoranda of understanding with two universities. Provider responsibilities for the two universities were more limited in scope than the EMO contracts and the universities received less per-pupil funding. Allocations ranged from $450 per pupil (for the universities) to $881 (for Edison, Inc.). The district assigned the managers to low-performing elementary and middle schools, without any kind of consultation process with either school staff or parents and local community groups.

When the dust settled from the takeover and the RFP for outside providers, a total of eighty-six low-performing elementary, middle, and K–8 schools were targeted for interventions. All eighty-six schools received additional funding contributed from both state and city coffers. Ultimately, the state provided roughly $75 million in new funding to the district, and the city added $45 million, approving a substantial bond measure.[9]

The majority of the schools (forty-six) were assigned to outside providers selected through the RFP process: three for-profit companies (Edison Schools, Victory Schools, and Chancellor Beacon Academies), two community-based organizations (Foundations, Inc., and Universal Companies), and two universities (the University of Pennsylvania and Temple University).[10] Twenty-one schools were placed under the management of the newly created Office of Restructured Schools (ORS), a district-run alternative to the private managers that was designed to demonstrate the district's internal capacity. Of the remaining schools, sixteen received additional funding but no management changes and three were slated to move toward charter status.

This set of eighty-six schools, along with Philadelphia's existing charter school sector and a growing set of alternative schools, formed the foundation for a portfolio school model in the city as the district assumed explicit oversight of multiple models of public school management (EMO-managed, ORS-managed, university-managed, conversion charter, regular charter, etc.). Greater energy was placed on managing some of these models (especially those used in the diverse provider model (DPM) than others (including both charter and alternative schools).

Homogenizing Forces

Even as the School District of Philadelphia set the DPM in motion—a seemingly decentralizing reform that offered providers the opportunity to innovate and establish their own brand of school—district leaders and the provider organizations themselves took steps that ultimately diluted the differentiating effects of the DPM. First, in its contracts with the providers, the district limited their autonomy in important areas of operation, and soon Philadelphia's approach to outside management came to be known as "thin management." The district retained authority over and responsibility for facilities management, school safety, food services, the overall school calendar, and the code of conduct for teachers and students. Most important, teachers and principals in provider schools would remain employees of the district, contractual agreements with their bargaining units would be in effect, and hiring of new staff would go through the district's centralized system. A subsequent negotiation with the teacher union gave principals a little more autonomy over personnel by instituting a partial site-selection process.[11] The providers had complete authority over curriculum and instruction in their schools and professional development for staff.

Second, actions of the providers themselves minimized their potential differentiation. Most notably, with the exception of Edison, the providers elected to adopt, wholly or in large part, the district's managed instruction system (MIS), including its core curriculum and benchmark assessments (described later).[12] They took this unexpected step for a number of reasons. For one, the pressures of NCLB and test scores required curricula and assessments that were tightly linked with state standards, something many providers did not have, but the district's MIS offered. In addition, school-level actors pushed for integration with the district initiatives, in part because of doubts about the strength of the programs that providers were introducing, and in part because of their lack of confidence that the provider programs would remain in the schools. Ironically, while a lack of capacity within the district was an argument for introducing the DPM, the apparent lack of capacity of the providers led to greater reintegration with the district over time.

The adoption of the DPM, clearly a response to external pressures, greatly increased the number of new players in school management within the Philadelphia district. It also brought greater national attention to Philadelphia, where Vallas and Nevels had embraced NCLB and the pursuit of Adequate Yearly Progress (AYP) as an important, substantive goal for schools. The combination of the DPM and district attention to NCLB helped to bring Bush's first Secretary of Education, Rodney Paige, to a Philadelphia meeting on private engagement in education, where he strongly endorsed the city's efforts. Paige said, "This school district has embarked on one of the most aggressive implementations of NCLB . . . You have blurred the line between public and private. . . . Everyone in the nation should take notice of these partnerships. They are a new frontier in school reform."[13]

Philadelphia's Managed Instruction System

Vallas came to Philadelphia determined to put a districtwide curriculum in place. He had done so in his last two years in Chicago and believed that a core curriculum was central to improving instruction and raising student achievement. He found experienced and knowledgeable curriculum and instruction people in Philadelphia's central office who were ready to take the standards and curriculum frameworks developed under Hornbeck's administration to the next level. A district-wide teacher survey in 1998 had shown that a substantial majority of Philadelphia teachers wanted more curriculum guidance.[14] District leaders turned to a longtime partner, the Philadelphia Education Fund (PEF) for assistance in creating the K–8 core curriculum; Kaplan K12 Learning Serviceswas selected as the partner for the high school curricular work.[15]

The district piloted the core curriculum in the schools operated by the ORS in the first year of the DPM. In the second year, Vallas mandated its use across the district. The core curriculum became the centerpiece of what district leaders called an MIS. In addition to the core curriculum, the principal components of the MIS included a detailed instructional planning and scheduling guide, benchmark assessments aligned with the literacy and math curriculum and administered every six weeks in grades 3–8, and SchoolNet, a data management system that provided reports about student achievement and other student data to schools and families. These pieces were designed to bring coherence to the district's curriculum implementation and to align these efforts with the Pennsylvania System of School Assessment (PSSA) framework in order to help improve student test scores and the number of schools making AYP.

Expansion of the Charter Sector

As noted earlier, the charter sector continued to expand under state take-over. Furthermore, Vallas and the SRC discarded the hands-off attitude of Hornbeck and moved toward strategic collaborations with charter schools and operators they viewed as successful, inviting them to participate in an overall district strategy to create more options for students in all regions of the city. At the same time, they took some small steps toward stronger oversight of charters. This represented a second move toward greater intentionality in the district's management of a portfolio of schools, the first having been the establishment of the DPM. However, the word *portfolio* was still not in play.

Several factors contributed to the explosion of charter schools in Philadelphia. First, parents clearly wanted options for their neighborhood schools. Second, Hornbeck's laissez-faire policy toward the creation of charters eased the way for groups interested in opening them. And third, Foundations, Inc., a nonprofit organization based in Cherry Hill, N.J. (a suburb of Philadelphia) and staffed largely by retired district administrators, helped these groups to file their charter applications and negotiate the many regulations and day-to-day headaches of charter school start-ups. Like many other districts across the country, the vast majority of Philadelphia's charter schools were established and operated by local community organizations or groups of people who came together to create a charter school because they shared a common educational vision or wanted an alternative to their neighborhood school.

During Vallas's tenure, some Philadelphia charters began to distinguish themselves, even though the sector as a whole did not demonstrate stronger achievement gains than regular district schools.[16] (See section on the portfolio's track record for more detail.) Vallas did not hesitate to recognize those charters that he felt were good schools, and he invited Mastery Charter Schools, a charter management organization, to operate in a district-run school that was losing population. By 2007, at the district's invitation, Mastery had added two more district schools to its growing fleet.

Unlike the DPM, which was increasingly pulled into the centralizing forces of the district, the charter school sector remained distinct during this period. Charter schools exercised authority over staff, budgets, and curriculum. And some Philadelphia charter schools proved to be sites of innovation in personnel practices, allocation of resources, and to a lesser degree curriculum and instruction.[17] For example, ten charter schools received a federal grant to implement the Teacher Advancement Program (TAP), a comprehensive teacher appraisal system that connects appraisal to targeted professional development and introduces career lattices.

Addition and Removal of Schools in the Portfolio

While the School District of Philadelphia, like most other districts, has a long history of contracting with outside organizations for goods and services, Christman and her colleagues argue that the DPM served the district as a platform for launching many other partnerships with private-sector organizations that went deeper into the core of district operations.[18] Other forms of management or partnerships were used in additional district schools, particularly high schools, where Vallas was committed to providing more and better options for students. At the request of the district, two DPM managers, Foundations, Inc., and Victory Schools, assumed management of one district high school each.

Additionally, Vallas envisioned creating small high schools (defined in Philadelphia as those serving fewer than 700 students) as part of his high school reform plan. Between 2003 and 2007, twenty-five new small schools were created, including nineteen transitional small schools from previously existing schools and six brand-new schools. In contrast to other cities, such as New York and Chicago, small schools in Philadelphia were created without foundation support. "Small high schools" (fewer than seven hundred students) had existed before Vallas arrived in the form of six, small, special admissions schools; however, the new small schools expanded options for students well beyond those who met the criteria for the special admissions schools. This surge in small high schools meant that the district, in addition to having a sector of privately managed schools in its portfolio, also had a significant sector of small high schools. Both of these new sectors created different kinds of management and organizational demands on the district.[19] Some of the new small high schools were initially assigned a private-sector transition partner to assist them in adjusting to becoming small schools, but these were discontinued after a year because of budget constraints and, in some cases, dissatisfaction with their role. And some of the small schools were paired with cultural or advocacy organizations, while others were supported by youth organizing groups. For example, the National Constitution Center, The Franklin Institute, Public Citizens for Children and Youth (PCCY), and Youth United for Change (YUC) became significant and enduring partners in forming and sustaining some of the small high schools.

Vallas also increased the number of alternative schools that served students who had posed disciplinary problems in their home schools. Hornbeck had first contracted with a private, for-profit company to run a disciplinary school in response to pleas from the Philadelphia Federation of Teachers that such a move would improve school climate for teachers and students. As of 2005, all district disciplinary schools were under outside management by for-profit-companies (Community Education Partners [CEP], Camelot For Kids, and Cornell).[20] In addition, from 2004 to 2005, three accelerated schools—schools intended to meet the needs of overage, undercredited youngsters—were also opened under the management of outside providers. In sum, the period from 2003 to 2007 saw an unprecedented growth in private-sector expansion through contracting and partnership in Philadelphia. The overall waning of public outcry allowed the district to expand privatization with few political repercussions.

Finally, the ORS, which originally managed twenty-one of the original eighty-six low-performing schools, was disbanded in 2005, and the schools it had managed were mostly returned to regular district control.

This was a surprise move because the ORS model appeared to be successful. But, in fact, budget cuts had pushed Vallas into a corner. He could not terminate the contracts with EMOs because of their strong political support by state officials and some members of the SRC. Vallas explained his decision by saying that the district had, by this time, expanded the ORS model—meaning the MIS—to all schools and therefore the ORS model was no longer needed.

Struggling with the District Role in a Portfolio Model

The district struggled to figure out where the DPM and charter schools fit into its broader reform agenda and overall organizational structure. When the model was first launched in 2003, the providers were hired to manage schools, and all forty-six provider schools were under the jurisdiction of their geographic regions, just as they had been before being managed by providers. However, ambiguity about the role of the provider relative to the district arose in this first year—the mixed autonomy of thin management was at the core of these uncertainties. As reported by Bulkley and her colleagues, one of the most challenging aspects of the DPM for principals during this period was determining the roles and relationships among different actors in the system.[21] For example, despite being formally managed by an outside provider, relationships between principals and the central office remained highly important for school operations, and provider-linked schools were often affected by central district reforms. Since principals remained district employees, most looked to the district as the place in which they would move up the career ladder. One principal remarked, "There seems to be competition between the district and the EMO as to who is really in charge. There's a power struggle going on."[22] Principals' experiences showed that the DPM did not generally offer the clear division of responsibility, authority, and accountability that was originally envisioned by Hill, Warren, and their colleagues.[23] The assignment of providers to schools and the limited ability of providers to choose principals also meant there was no guarantee of alignment between school leadership and providers.

Recognizing the frustration and confusion at the school level, in 2003, Vallas designated the Office of Development to work with the providers to identify problems and smooth out relations within the bureaucracy. This newly created district unit, whose purpose included but was not limited to direct oversight of the DPM, was charged with developing and overseeing a variety of contracts between the district and outside organizations and encouraging those within and outside of the district to develop entrepreneurial relationships that would help forward the mission of the district.[24] The hope was that this primary point of contact within the district would lead to significant expansion of partnerships between the district and for-profit and nonprofit organizations.

Vallas considered "all [public] schools" (including charter schools) in the district to be district schools, regardless of management model, and supported the Office of Development taking an advocacy role within the central office on behalf of the providers in order to ensure that district obstacles would not prevent the success of the providers.[25] As the providers worked together as a group with the Office of Development, they began to identify collectively, talking about success at the level of the DPM, rather than at the level of the individual provider. However, it is less clear how successful the Office of Development was in terms of promoting a broader culture shift toward entrepreneurship and partnerships in the broader district.[26] From 2005 to 2008, after the providers were considered past the initial development phase, the district kept them together as a distinct set of schools, but removed them from the Office of Development and placed them in a separate EMO region intended to address their particular set of needs and challenges.

The Portfolio's Track Record Under Vallas

Beginning in 2007, discussion of the effectiveness of school models in the portfolio came to the forefront, following a series of reports analyzing student test-score data. Despite the continuing support of the district, and its attempts to buffer the providers within the context of the bureaucracy, several studies indicated that after five years, the provider schools, on average, were not performing any better or worse than district schools.[27] Overall, Philadelphia test scores improved following the takeover, with gains that were greater than elsewhere in the state from 2003 to 2005, but then fell into line with the state in 2006.

Three reports—one by RAND and Research for Action, one by the district itself, and one by the Accountability Review Council (which oversaw the state takeover)—found little evidence to suggest that students in schools managed by outside providers were performing better than their peers in other district schools (and found that, in some cases, they were performing worse), even when taking into account the fact that the provider-managed schools were serving students who were, on average, of lower socioeconomic status than in other district schools.[28] The study by Gill and his colleagues found that students in ORS schools performed slightly better in math than those in other district schools. Another study, by Peterson and Chingos, found that mathematics student test-score gains in schools managed by for-profit providers were higher than gains in schools managed by nonprofits.[29]

Christman and her colleagues examined the relationship between elements of the MIS and gains in student achievement.[30] Their analysis showed that extensive use of the core curriculum was related to gains in student achievement, providing evidence that at least one element of the district's MIS was having the positive impact that district leaders intended, a distinctly different finding than analyses of the effects of the DPM.

Based on the preponderance of reports finding few positive effects for the DPM, SRC member Sandra Dungee-Glenn proposed to continue only EMO–school partnerships that had been shown to be successful based on the district's report and the RAND–RFA report.[31] Some parent and community groups supported her proposal. Similarly, Vallas's proposed budget for fiscal year 2008 would have led to deep cuts in funding for providers. Nonetheless, political leaders at both the city and state levels continued to advocate for the providers and the providers received extensions for their services (with reduced funding) —albeit differentiated at the school level, depending on whether there was indication that the school was making progress in improving student achievement.[32] Nonetheless, by 2007, more than $107 million (roughly $22.7 million per year) had been poured into contracts with outside providers alongside the substantial funding diverted from district funding toward the creation and operation of charter schools.[33]

Like the evidence on the DPM in Philadelphia, research on charter performance has been mixed. While charter school advocates have pointed to charters' stronger track record in meeting their AYP targets, more rigorous examinations of performance have shown little difference between student achievement gains in charter schools and in regular district schools. In 2008, the RAND Corporation and Research for Action issued a report showing that students' average gains when attending charter schools were statistically indistinguishable from their gains when attending regular public schools.[34] Interestingly, the study also showed that charter schools were attracting students whose prior achievement levels (when they were in regular district schools) were slightly below the districtwide average, but higher than the average achievement levels of the traditional public schools they had left, demonstrating that charter schools were "creaming" higher performing students from on those schools.

A Research for Action study of small high schools that opened between 2003 and 2007 examined key student outcomes—student attendance, tardiness, suspensions, and algebra passage—among first-time ninth graders within each type of Philadelphia district-managed high school: the two variants of selective high schools, special admission and citywide admission, and the nonselective neighborhood high schools. Across all admission categories, the 2006–2007 data showed that small schools were beginning to make a difference for student engagement and achievement. The study also showed significant levels of parent and student interest in small high schools; many of the small schools received many more applications than they had slots, with acceptance rates as low as 15 percent. Nevertheless, these schools were enrolling students from across a range of achievement levels and special learning needs.[35]

Lack of Civic Engagement

Although the public initially pushed back against privatization, the establishment of the PMM took place with little public consultation. Decisions about the DPM were top-down and imposed on schools. Neither Vallas or other central office administrators nor the SRC consulted educators or parents from the schools' communities about their selection for inclusion in the DPM; these selections were based on test score data. Members of the SRC did attend evening meetings at the schools slated for takeover, where they often were greeted by crowds of wary, if not outright angry, parents and community members. Nonetheless, the process proceeded, and the district selected providers and matched them with schools.

In the planning phase, leaders at the state and local levels proposed the assignment of a community partner to each provider school. These groups, which were local organizations with close ties to the surrounding community, were to work with the provider to make sure it remained responsive to community concerns, thus ameliorating the lack of community input to the process. This idea quietly faded, however, due to budget realities and participation of these community groups not being a clear priority for the working of the model.[36]

Furthermore, there was virtually no public discussion of the contractual agreements and criteria for judging the providers' progress toward greater efficiency and efficacy. This lack of transparency—which denied the public the information it would need to make sound judgments about the efforts of the providers—greatly reduced the possibility for public accountability. Neither were there strong contractual ways for providers to seek parent feedback, although some providers did conduct parent satisfaction surveys. The feedback of parents became most relevant at the time of the five-year renewal of provider contracts. Some providers conducted their own parent feedback sessions, and the central office conducted parent focus groups in its research on the effectiveness of the providers.

Once schools were selected and providers assigned, the public fervor over contracting out school management died, only to flare up again at key junctures: for example, in early 2007, when a district budget deficit reappeared and parents challenged cutbacks at district-managed schools, rather than cutbacks to providers; and again later that year at the time of contract renewal, when parents and students, some district leaders, and some of the advocacy community challenged the efficacy of the providers. Several reasons might explain the general quieting of the public outcry. First, as alluded to earlier, SRC chair Nevels substantially reduced the role of Edison Schools, Inc., which was the primary target of the initial protests. This change in strategy distanced him from the state and helped to legitimate the initiative. Second, the providers were assigned to elementary, K–8, or middle schools. High school students had spearheaded the protests, and when the providers were not assigned to their schools, the students turned their attention to other battles. Third, over time, many of the education reform groups, longtime partners with the district, accepted contracts for services, which muted their voices as critics of the system.[37] Fourth, union objections to provider management dissipated. Resistance from principals and teachers was avoided when it was made clear that they would remain district employees, and collective bargaining agreements for salary and work rules would hold in provider schools. Finally, by summer 2002, when the DPM was being finalized, tensions between the city and state had subsided. The takeover had become a friendly one, with the city and state both working to increase funding to the city schools and operating as a team on the SRC.

The growth of charter schools did provide a number of parents, community groups, and civic and business leaders a new venue for engagement. Their involvement in charter schools, however, meant an almost exclusive focus at the individual school level, channeling involvement away from the welfare of the district as a whole.[38] The adoption of a policy to increase small high schools during the Vallas years, coupled with a generous capital plan, provided the high school student groups with a lever for engagement. Students from several Youth United for Change and Philadelphia Student Union chapters had already become convinced that breaking down their large, chronically underperforming neighborhood high schools into multiple small schools was a critical first step for school improvement. They began campaigns to bring small high schools to their underserved neighborhoods and to press the school district to support their efforts as part of the district's own small-schools initiative. In addition, they insisted the district accept a community planning process for the new small schools. Their progress was slow, but their community planning process won local support and helped to gain them legitimacy. In 2008–2009, ground was broken for a new small school in one community, and in another community, community members and the school were working together to develop small learning communities in preparation to moving into a new building.

The Vallas and Nevels years expanded the portfolio in meaningful ways, and the overall number of schools of different types increased during this period. Of particular importance was the introduction of the DPM, which has helped to create a much higher level of comfort with outside contracting for educational services than previously existed in the district. However, combining the DPM with the managed instruction system, both of which were (directly or indirectly) responses to the demands of No Child Left Behind, also set up one of the enduring tensions in the district—between a set of reforms designed to decentralize authority to schools and providers, and another set that focused a set of key decisions on curriculum, instruction, and assessment in the district central office. The district struggled with balancing these conflicting approaches to educational improvement, and those challenges have continued into the Ackerman era.

ARLENE ACKERMAN AND THE "SYSTEM OF GREAT SCHOOLS"

In the summer of 2007, Vallas left Philadelphia to become the superintendent of the Recovery School District in Louisiana. After five years as CEO, he left behind a district that had been changed in significant ways, most notably in terms of the DPM, the MIS, and a perception of progress fueled by rising test scores.[39] He also left a district that was continuing to experience large deficits. Now that the district had expended a $300 million bond created when Vallas first arrived, there was no easy source of revenue and there was no certain avenue for creating stable funding. Despite the fiscal crunch, the DPM continued, largely because the state legislature threatened to withhold the additional funding it was providing to the district as part of the state takeover unless the providers were sustained. Following his departure, Tom Brady, who had been hired to serve as chief operating officer, stepped into the role of interim CEO while the SRC searched for a replacement. Brady served as CEO until the selection of Arlene Ackerman in the spring of 2008.

Unlike Vallas and Brady, Ackerman's qualifications fit the more conventional education-oriented experience of most public school superintendents. She had been the superintendent in San Francisco and Washington, D.C., places where she earned the reputation of being a leader who focused on educational practice, but struggled with managing the challenging politics of leading in a big-city school district. Once hired, she established a transition committee that consisted of a number of major national figures in educational reform, but few members from Philadelphia. Ackerman's tenure has seen significant turnover in the SRC, including the departure of several critical members. In April 2009, Robert Archie, a local attorney and Philadelphia public school graduate, was appointed as the new chair of the SRC. He has taken a lower-profile role than did Nevels, and the role that he and the SRC are playing in shaping the district's direction is less clear than was Nevels'.

Remodeling the Portfolio of Schools

Ackerman's initiatives are embodied in her February 2009 strategic plan entitled "Imagine 2014"; the subtitle of the plan, "Building a System of Great Schools" (instead of a great school system), seems to reflect her openness to the ideas underlying a PMM.[40] Imagine 2014 incorporated plans to identify up to thirty-five low-performing Renaissance Schools for significant changes that might include conversion to charter status or outside management and a set of high-performing Vanguard Schools, which would be given added autonomy (see next section). It also called for the establishment of school report cards, continuation and refinement of the MIS and two new controversial instructional initiatives—corrective reading and corrective math—scripted remedial programs for students in the Empowerment Schools. Additionally, Imagine 2014 identified a number of initiatives designed to improve teacher quality and the ability of those at schools to select teachers (see discussion on the 2010 teacher contract in the next section on Renaissance and Vanguard Schools).

Within the context of Imagine 2014, in fall 2009, Ackerman charged the newly created Office of Charter, Partnership and New Schools with managing significant portions of the portfolio of schools, including charter schools and schools still managed by partners under the original DPM. She tapped Benjamin Rayer, a former leader at Mastery Charter Schools, to head that office as an associate superintendent. The release of Imagine 2014, the creation of this new office, and the hiring of a charter school leader to head it seemed to signal that Ackerman was embracing and planning to expand and more intentionally manage the portfolio of schools that had grown under Vallas.

Ackerman's philosophy toward reform in Philadelphia has been consistent with national changes promoted by U.S. Department of Education Secretary Arne Duncan. In fact, the connection is so strong that Duncan launched his "listening and learning tour," in which he visited districts throughout the country alongside the Rev. Al Sharpton and former

House Speaker Newt Gingrich, in Philadelphia. One knowledgeable observer commented that, "Ackerman likes whatever Arne Duncan likes."

Renaissance and Vanguard Schools

Soon after the SRC named her Philadelphia's new superintendent, Ackerman drew on her national, high-level transition committee to assist her in assessing the status of the district. In this section, we examine Ackerman's evaluation of how the external school managers had worked with the district and changes she made in the spring of 2010, in part based on the findings of the transition committee. First, she deemed that, going forward, providers needed to show a track record of success. Second, she re-thought the degree to which the providers had real autonomy in the management of their schools and to innovate. Third, she acknowledged the previous absence of community engagement in selecting schools and providers, matching them, and monitoring their efficacy. Fourth, she picked up on the notion of a district-managed alternative to private-sector management of low-performing schools (like the ORS during the DPM era) through the establishment of a model in which a set of schools falls under her purview. And fifth, she planned to impose stronger contracts and systems of accountability.

In Imagine 2014, Ackerman planned that the use of partners will also be central to a turnaround strategy for the very lowest-performing schools—called Renaissance Schools. Seeking to avert the community pushback that occurred around privatized school management early under state takeover, she and the SRC asked a Renaissance Schools Advisory Board to provide guidance on processes for Renaissance School selection, turnaround team recruitment, and community engagement and communications. To build legitimacy for their process and bring a wide circle of stakeholders under the tent, the district reached out to the mayor, a prestigious university, and a civic intermediary organization for leaders in the process. Lori Shorr, chief education officer in the Mayor's Office of Education; Patricia Coulter, president and CEO of the Urban League of Philadelphia, Inc.; and Robert Peterkin, director of the Urban Superintendents Program, Harvard University Graduate School of Education, cochaired the advisory board. The board was composed of approximately sixty members from area universities, civic and community groups, service agencies, reform support organizations, the district, the business sector, and charter schools. Notably absent were representatives from the educator unions. The student organizing groups that had mounted the original protest against privatization were not a part of the group either. In this case, however, they were already mounting an effort to challenge private-sector or charter management of low-performing schools, especially the high schools in which they are active, and believed it was important to maintain their independence in order to continue to effectively do so.

Based in part on the recommendations of the advisory board, district leaders announced in January 2010 that fourteen schools were eligible to become Renaissance Schools. There were four possible paths for the schools: conversion to charter status; management by outside organizations; district-management by a turnaround team that was, at least in part, selected by the community; or management by people selected by the superintendent or central office.[42] In the first two paths, the staff of the school would no longer be district employees. The final option, to be called Promise Academies, recognized district educators who had good ideas and had shown that they were capable of the steady work needed for school improvement. It harkened back to previous district efforts, including ORS, to create a stronger link between the central office and the district's lowest-performing schools.

Simultaneously, the district was negotiating a new contract with the Philadelphia Federation of Teachers (PFT). The contract was settled in January 2010, and its provisions allowed for the forced transfer of all teachers at Renaissance Schools. At district-run schools, teachers could reapply, but only half would actually be able to return. (Regardless of whether the teachers were rehired at the school, they would retain their seniority.) And teachers in these schools would work a longer school day and year, with additional pay. At schools that become charter or contract schools, teachers would not necessarily be union members.[43] These contract provisions reflected the tremendous pressures that the PFT and unions across the country were feeling as their districts applied for federal Race to the Top funding.

By spring 2010, the district had completed three major steps in its process for establishing Renaissance Schools. Teams led by the Boston-based SchoolWorks had completed school quality reviews assessing the strengths and weaknesses of the fourteen eligible Renaissance Schools. A district-appointed review committee had finished its examination of twenty-eight responses to a request for qualifications (RFQ) to external providers, and selected six as having enough of a track record to move forward to the request for proposal (RFP) stage. With the exception of the Diplomas Now model, all the others were charter school operators. According to comments by Rayer at a March 2010 meeting of the Accountability Review Council, these charter operators had a road map in place for setting up schools, while the other potential contractors explained that the time line was too short for them. (Rayer said that the time line in year two would be much longer, with the RFQ process starting in Spring 2010 and selection over the summer, which would allow for a full year of planning.)

The Renaissance Schools providers will all have greater autonomy than the DPM providers, primarily because of their charter school status. In addition, the Promise Academies will benefit from provisions in the new teachers' contract which extend the school day and school year. The district has also sought greater community engagement for Renaissance Schools, in large part through School Advisory Councils. The district provided one-day training at school sites for all those who expressed an interest in being on a council. The councils will be responsible for recommending a match between a provider and the school with one of the six providers. (The district-appointed review body decided all six providers that made the RFQ cut submitted strong enough proposals to run a Renaissance School.)

First, the district announced the five schools that will be Promise Academies and thus managed directly by the district. (Later, a sixth became a Promise Academy.) Then, the matching process proceeded with the remaining schools and was completed in early May 2010, with the exception of West Philadelphia High School, which was at first delayed, and then postponed a year as a result of a series of differences between the District and the School Advisory Council. In addition to this initial responsibility, School Advisory Councils (for both Promise Academies and Renaissance schools) will submit an annual school report, one tool the district will use to monitor the efficacy of the provider. Another tool will be reviews conducted by SchoolWorks every two years. The district is developing an index of accountability, with appropriate metrics and time frames, and according to Rayer, if schools do not reach targets, then the district will revoke the contract. This time, Rayer hopes, the contracts with providers will be as tight as possible, with the district responsible for regular monitoring and reporting. The District has named over a hundred community based organizations as qualified to be school support groups, and both Promise Academies and Renaissance Schools are supposed to work with at least one of them.

Ackerman's Vanguard Schools initiative addresses schools at the other end of the performance continuum. In January 2010, the district identified twenty-five schools to become Vanguard Schools; they have demonstrated either higher overall performance or substantial student growth in terms of test scores. According to Imagine 2014, these schools will have autonomy agreements with the district that combine additional flexibility from district requirements with expectations that the schools meet annual performance targets; thus, autonomy is a reward for success, rather than a prerequisite for improving quality.[44] Schools that have demonstrated the ability to perform well will be rewarded with increased autonomy.

In January 2010, teachers in Philadelphia ratified a new contract that has significant implications for Philadelphia public schools and particularly for the Renaissance Schools. Among its overall provisions, it provides the district the ability, beginning in 2010–2011, to grant bonuses to all teachers and other PFT members in schools with the best overall performance or high levels of student growth. The contract also provides for an overall expansion of site selection for teachers. In the more than ninety lower-performing schools in the district, the school year will be extended by a month (with extra pay for staff who work during this additional time), and all school vacancies will be filled through site selection. Additional provisions apply specifically to the Renaissance Schools, where "the entire staff can be forced to transfer out and only up to 50 percent rehired; others would have to take jobs in other schools. Teachers in Renaissance Schools also will have to work an hour more a day and possibly more days each year, but will earn additional money."[45]

This new contract, with provisions tied to some of the expectations set out in the Race to the Top competition, was called "groundbreaking" by Randi Weingarten, president of the American Federation of Teachers, in part because of the collaborative process used in its development.[46] Ackerman's openness to negotiating such a contract is consistent with her attention to new expectations coming from the U.S. Department of Education.

From Diverse Provider to "Partnership" Schools

While Ackerman's focus has been on the new initiatives proposed under Imagine 2014, she decided to alter but not eliminate the original partnerships between outside providers and the remaining schools in the DPM. In the fall of 2008, under Ackerman, the district central office returned the schools managed under the DPM to their original geographical regions. District central office staff explained this shift as a move to clarify authority within the district, but it also removed some administrative costs in a time of fiscal challenge. This administrative shift accompanied a slow attrition of schools from the DPM that had begun under Vallas. By May 2009, twenty-eight of the original forty-six schools remained in the hands of the providers, and annual additional spending on the DPM schools under Ackerman dropped from roughly $22.7 million per year to less than $6.5 million per year.[47]

At that time, Rayer, who had oversight of schools managed by providers, spoke at an SRC meeting about the DPM. He provided student achievement data that once again suggested a "mixed bag" at best for provider-managed K–8 schools, with many doing worse than comparable schools in the district.[48] Despite these results, he, like others before him, recommended that the SRC approve additional one-year provider contracts for the schools that did not already have contracts past June 2009. Rayer also proposed altering the district–provider relationship so that the providers—now called "partners"—would offer discrete services to schools based on their strengths, rather than overall management. In exchange, they would be paid $500 per pupil, consistent with spending in the 2008–2009 school year. At the following SRC meeting, Rayer argued that the original DPM (which he called the EMO model) had been poorly implemented and supported. He suggested that it needed to be transformed, rather than disbanded, as one SRC member had suggested.

As of December 2009, the district's plan was to have the Office of Charter, Partnership and New Schools work closely with the regional superintendents on what were now called the Partnership Schools. Based on lessons learned, the district intended that the 2009–2010 school year be one in which the district and partners focused on alignment of efforts, roles, and responsibilities. One significant policy change required outside partners to use the district's core curriculum and benchmark assessments, and the regional superintendents would have rating authority for principals, with partners providing input into the evaluation process. These changes further decreased the autonomy seen by the DPM schools under Vallas and shifted the schools away even more from the high levels of autonomy that Hill and his colleagues envisioned. They also appeared to contradict Rayer's own assessment that the providers under Vallas had not had sufficient autonomy to innovate.

Rayer explained that he saw his mandate as a transition of the EMO model to something new and better, thus contributing to the institutionalization of charter and private sector engagement: "Hopefully getting to a place where we set things forward and then other people taking the ownership to continuously improve it. Nothing works right the first time. And the EMO model is a classic case of that. What makes things right is fixing them over time."[49]

The district will extend the partnership concept to other district schools as well, especially with schools slated to pilot weighted student funding, which will grant them greater discretionary funds to spend. Clearly, Rayer believes that that a commitment to revising and refining the district's approach to privatization will ensure that it will last.

Charter Schools

With regard to charter schools, Ackerman pursued Vallas's lead, choosing stronger oversight and strategic collaborations. She asked charter operators to consider district needs as they decided where to locate the schools. She also invited successful charter managers to join district turnaround efforts by assuming responsibility for Renaissance Schools. By appointing a former charter school leader, Rayer, to a top post in her administration, Ackerman signaled openness to charters and private providers to powerful charter school advocates in the state legislature, city council, and community organizations. She also established a task force that consisted almost totally of charter school advocates to examine the relationship between the district and the charter school community. Their recommendations included streamlining operating agreements, providing charter schools with timely feedback on late filing of reports and audits, and conducting mini-reviews halfway through the five-year period before a charter came up for renewal. However, in August 2009, the SRC stalled, taking the recommendations under advisement.

The district then asked the SRC to approve a policy that would allow charters to expand their enrollments or change their grade configuration only at the time of charter renewal and that would require a demonstration of adequacy to accompany such requests.[50] Here, Ackerman acted consistently with district administrators who viewed these requests for stronger district oversight as reasonable, given recent discoveries of abuses by some charter schools. Beginning under Vallas, accountability issues had become increasingly important in the charter school sector, as the district more rigorously implemented the existing review process, seeking to ensure that all required documentation was in place, financial arrangements were transparent, and academic quality met minimum standards. As a result, two charter schools were not renewed due to the poor academic performance of their students. Soon after, the *Philadelphia Inquirer* ran a series of investigative articles about the Philadelphia Academy Charter School; this investigation was triggered by parent allegations of financial irregularities and nepotism.[51] As a result of a federal investigation, the board was reconstituted, one school leader was sentenced to two and a half years in prison, and another committed suicide before trial. By early 2009, there were five charter schools under federal investigation for financial irregularities and by spring 2010, the number had increased to 18. In response to these allegations, state legislators proposed new charter legislation that would put in place a state-level office with the authority to investigate complaints that charter schools were not meeting state laws or the terms of their charters. The legislation also offered incentives to accompany the increased oversight, including the proposal that universities and colleges could issue charters and that renewal periods be lengthened to as many as ten years.

A few charter operators also demonstrated enthusiasm for expanding to other neighborhoods and an appetite for working with the district to introduce charters where the district wanted them. In a 2009 *Philadelphia Inquirer* article, Mastery Charter School's CEO Scott Gordon explained the CMO's mission in Philadelphia: "We'd like to take on the most difficult schools. We'd like to have both elementary and high schools, and we'd like to take on the most difficult areas of the city."[52] Likewise, KIPP, a national charter management organization, has been responsive to district requests to create more charters.

Other Forms of School Management

Disciplinary schools managed by outside providers have existed in Philadelphia since before Vallas. However, there has been growth both in these schools and in accelerated alternative high schools that serve overage, undercredit students. These accelerated schools were begun in 2004 and have been developed in collaboration with the Philadelphia Youth Network, a local intermediary organization. Like the disciplinary schools, they are provider managed. Sixteen such schools now operate, serving nearly four thousand students.[53] The partner-providers have considerable autonomy in these schools in the areas of personnel and curriculum. These schools fit into the district structure differently than do the other district-managed schools that partner with external providers, in that their district directors report to the chief operating officer. They are not included in the work of the district's newly established Office of Charters, Partnerships and New Schools, discussed earlier. Their connection with the overall portfolio of schools, and the extent to which they are managed as part of the "system of great schools" that Ackerman envisions, is limited and still evolving.

Despite the specifics offered in Imagine 2014, it is still too early in Ackerman's tenure to clearly see her vision for the district overall. Her commitment to the idea of a portfolio model, in particular, is uncertain. Consistent with research on contracting out more broadly, Ackerman's focus with the Renaissance Schools (including her openness to outside providers), as well as other changes in school management, appears to be based more on the pragmatic needs of individual schools than on a broad ideological belief in outside contracting (see Henig, chapter 2, this volume). Some of what she has done (i.e., hiring Rayer and proposing the use of outside providers and charter status for Renaissance Schools) moves in direction of a portfolio model with distinct and autonomous schools, but she appears less interested in offering greater autonomy to the remaining DPM schools or to other schools in the district, except in the case of the Vanguard schools. A shift toward small schools, especially small high schools, began under Vallas. However, Ackerman has not shown the same enthusiasm for such an approach, and has largely turned the district away from these efforts

A COMPLEX AMALGAMATION

Over the past eight years, the School District of Philadelphia has changed from a conventional system of district-run schools (with a thriving charter sector that operated almost completely separately from the district) to a complex amalgamation of delivery models. As table 5.1 shows, the overall number of public schools in Philadelphia has grown from 281 to roughly 355 schools in less than a decade. One consequence of this shift is that many Philadelphia schools now operate well below capacity. (For example, Philadelphia's large, comprehensive high schools now serve less than half the student population they once did.)

Pragmatic responses to federal mandates, the need for additional state funding, and local context rather than ideology have played the starring roles in the evolution of the portfolio model in Philadelphia. Additionally, numerous tensions have marked the model's evolution from the beginning. First is the continuing tension between centralization and decentralization, as district leaders and institutional arrangements (particularly

TABLE 5.1 Delivery models for public schools in Philadelphia

School delivery model	2001	Estimate 2010–2011
District-only management without additional autonomy or oversight	237	204
Charter	40	67
Partnership Schools	0	28
Outside-managed accelerated/ disciplinary schools	4	17
Renaissance Schools (including Promise Academies)	0	14
Vanguard Schools	0	25
Total public schools	281	355

Source: District sources.

district–union bargaining agreements) have considerably narrowed the autonomy for schools and the groups that manage schools. A second tension relates to accountability and the difficulty of closing schools or firing outside management organizations when they fail to perform as a consequence of the mandate for performance accountability, given the highly institutionalized nature of public schooling. A third tension is between vesting strong decision-making authority in a small set of powerful actors and broadening the governing coalition in ways that enhance civic capacity and enable a meaningful role for the public. Finally, a fourth tension involves responding to national (and especially federal) expectations about the shape of school reform as opposed to those expectations that arise more locally.

Promoting Reform from the Bottom Up or the Top Down?

Throughout the period discussed, district leaders have championed two seemingly contradictory efforts—promoting reform through outside providers and enhanced autonomy, consistent with a portfolio model, and seeking educational improvement through the increasingly centralized managed instruction system. While Vallas gave some attention to the idea of autonomy for schools, he was less comfortable providing it in practice. And early indications of Ackerman's preferences suggest that she is willing to offer autonomy, but only as a reward for success rather than a condition of it.

While charter schools have retained roughly comparable levels of autonomy from the district throughout the development of a portfolio model in Philadelphia, district leaders have struggled with how much autonomy to provide schools in other delivery models (including the DPM). Throughout this period, the practices of the providers have increasingly aligned with the broader district reforms. With the exception of Edison Schools, Inc., the providers adopted many aspects of the district's managed instruction system, including its core curriculum and benchmark assessments. In addition, providers increasingly adhered to other central office mandates, deferring to district staff in areas such as compliance with special education and English language learner state mandates, food, facilities, and transportation services. Despite the diversity of organizations that served as providers, they were less distinguishable from each other and from district schools than was anticipated by advocates.[54] In many ways, providers became part of the "fabric of the system, voluntarily relying on the district for many functions and programming."[55]

While contracting became part of the fabric of the district, the district also continued and, we argue, expanded its own guidance and authority role with vendors, creating greater mandatory centralization. For the DPM, thin management became even thinner. Going forward under Ackerman's administration, partners will choose the schools with which they want to work and the services that they will provide to those schools. However, they will also be required to use the core curriculum and, while they will participate in the evaluation of principals, they will not have rating authority. The recently ratified teachers' contract opens up new possibilities for autonomy, but it remains to be seen how this will translate to school and provider autonomy. A question that remains open is, what exactly are the partners in charge of?

As for the district, it had its own set of implementation issues to resolve as it struggled with what it meant to have schools that were operated by the district, but distinct in important ways from conventional district-operated schools. District leaders responded to this dilemma by alternating between placing these schools into a conventional organizational structure and putting them into separate places on the organizational chart. At times, the DPM schools (commonly referred to as EMO schools, despite the fact that universities and community-based organizations were among the providers) were placed in separate parts of the district organizational structure with the hope of building different kinds of relationships and supports between district and schools, while at other times they were placed in regions alongside district schools. In the latter case, they fell into the traditional lines of district authority, with regional superintendents having the authority to rate principals.

One of the arguments for shifting school management to outside providers was that the School District of Philadelphia (in particular, the central and regional offices) did not have the capacity to turn around persistently low-performing schools. By this argument, outside providers would bring new expertise and capacity that would enhance the schools and bolster achievement. In practice, this has so far not proved to be the case. Outside providers, at least in the DPM, brought expertise in specific areas but not the comprehensive expertise necessary for school turnaround. Hence, the turn to the district's managed instruction system, developed by district staff in conjunction with more conventional outside organizations.

As Sclar and others have argued, contracting with outside organizations in a manner that can lead to positive outcomes requires significant, and significantly different, forms of expertise in the government sector.[56] At a time when district staff has been cut significantly, it is not clear that the district central office has the capacity necessary to serve this new and distinct role. A number of questions remain about the district central office's role in the evolving portfolio: How will it evaluate the management of the new partners, given that each partner is pursuing its own set of improvement activities? Will it be able to establish a rigorous process for writing and reviewing contracts to hold partners accountable for their efforts? Will it be able to figure out how to be helpful to a range of partners, each with its own strategies and activities for school improvement? Perhaps most importantly, will the district be able to continue to build its legitimacy and credibility as an institution able to effect positive changes in classroom instruction, school leadership, district management, and student achievement?

Assessing Effectiveness: Issues of Accountability

Hill and his colleagues stress the importance of districts' roles in ensuring accountability within PMMs: districts must be willing to shut down failing schools and must be able to generate sufficient high quality options to replace those that they close. Such systems are ideally dynamic and change in response to both market demands (as expressed through school choice) and the ability of schools to meet district performance standards. Other theoreticians of privatization have warned that marketization can compromise the important role of the public in holding democratic institutions accountable for the public good.[57] Our own work as well as that of others shows that this occurs as market forces narrow accountability to the contract between the vendor and the district, leaving little room for public engagement. Public accountability is further weakened when there are restricted opportunities for public participation in decision making and as many community-based groups became service contractors to the district; they are therefore constrained in their ability to challenge the district.[58]

As power became concentrated at the CEO–SRC level, several studies by Research for Action[59] suggested that the top-down decision-making structure instituted by Nevels and Vallas, in combination with increased contracting, may actually have stifled civic engagement and diminished the possibility for public accountability.[60] Many of these contracts were written behind closed doors, and district contracting with grassroots and community groups to provide services made it difficult for these groups "to perform their traditional role as activists and critics, even while it offers employment to depressed communities and resources to financially strapped organizations."[61] In addition, the increases in student choice in the district that have emerged, largely through the growth of charter schools, also resulted in parental input being channeled away from concern with broad-based district issues and toward a focus on individual schools.[62]

Evidence was ample that mechanisms for accountability within Philadelphia's portfolio model were weak. In the case of the DPM, the result was that the model survived and was increasingly accepted as "the way we do things around here," regardless of the evidence that these schools were not outperforming district schools and that public accountability had been compromised.[63] For charter schools, the district moved towards creating some accountability where little had previously existed, but still did not have in place the kinds of rigorous performance-based accountability charter advocates envisioned.[64] In both of these cases, the providers themselves have become sufficiently part of the standards operation of the system of schools and have garnered strong allies, to the extent that closing them or ending contracts will take far more political effort than a simple decision based on performance.

Building a Narrow or Broad-Based Governing Regime?

Stone and his colleagues, among others, have suggested that sustained educational change requires effective governance that is supported by a strong and broad governing regime and considerable civic capacity.[65] Bulkley argues that Philadelphia under Vallas shifted toward a "contracting regime," in which public and private relationships are central to district functioning and the primary decision makers are those with the formal authority to form relationships through contracting.[66] The core of the contracting regime in Philadelphia was largely limited to the CEO and the members of the SRC.[67] Other actors, including the mayor and governor, who appoint SRC leaders, as well as union leaders and state legislators, also play important roles but are not in the core of decision makers. While Stone and his colleagues place considerable emphasis on the business community as a partner in a strong regime, such involvement has not been substantial in Philadelphia. The dominance by district actors has been aided by what Cucchiara and her colleagues describe as the "development of new mechanisms that channel participation and information along narrow, district-directed lines."[68]

The corporate management style of the SRC led its members to make decisions behind closed doors because, as one SRC member explained, engaging the public "is messier . . . outside our control."[69] This decision-making process, in combination with procedures for contracting out schools that provided for only minimal transparency, left the public in the dark, deprived of the information it needed to engage productively with the district. Thus, as scholars of privatization have warned, the quest for speed and efficiency in reform meant that the public could no longer play its crucial role as a check to ensure that contractual relationships were meeting social purposes, such as effectiveness and equity. As Minow warned, there was a clear danger that "public control and review . . . diminish as previously public activities fall under private management and control" in an environment averse to public participation.[70]

Ackerman has sought to address some of the concerns about the narrowness of the governing regime. The city has taken a more activist stance, and the superintendent is working closely with the mayor's chief education officer. Together, the district, city, and private sector have established working groups to shape reform approaches. The superintendent has met with parents periodically throughout the city to hear their concerns. And the 2010 contract with the teachers showed a higher level of collaboration than the city has witnessed in the past. Yet, the devil is in the details, and whether this collaboration with the union can be sustained through implementation is an open question. Many organized advocacy, youth, civic, and community groups still feel as though they are on the sidelines and their value is being questioned, as Ackerman works to establish her own support base directly with parents, rather than through organizations that represent them. A remaining open question is whether the initial efforts to engage a broader constituency—city, district, school communities, and the private sector—in reviewing plans for reform and in selecting providers and matching schools with them will translate into a public that can provide robust supports for reform efforts *and* has the information it needs and accessible venues for holding the district accountable for equity and the quality of the district's schools.

Privatization had initially been met by fervent protest, and the DPM had been implemented without much consultation with schools or communities. The lack of public consultation—and ultimately public accountability—was a widespread complaint about round one of the portfolio model. As a result, the Renaissance advisory board recommended mechanisms for much greater consultation at the school community level. School Advisory Councils are being formed as a result. Yet, the devil is in the details, and whether the district effectively mounts the kind of extensive and authentic civic engagement that is needed to ensure the demand for strong schools and the resources to support them is still to be known.

National Influences on Local Change

Both core reform ideas at work in Philadelphia during this period—the shift toward a portfolio model with outside providers and increased autonomy and accountability, and the implementation of an MIS for use in many of the district's schools—have strong connections with both specific federal policies (especially NCLB; see Burch, chapter 9, this volume) and with the general directions advocated across both the Bush and Obama administrations. This is unsurprising, considering that Vallas and Ackerman have both paid considerable attention to the national context for reform. For example, Vallas and Nevels embraced NCLB and the idea of AYP, using them as motivators for creating district change. The DPM under Vallas was also consistent with ideas of contracting out for school management for persistently low-performing schools, one of the options for restructuring offered (but seldom used) under NCLB; a visit by then-Secretary of Education Paige demonstrated national recognition of this particular effort. Ackerman's actions have also been consistent with the expressed desires of the Obama administration, with a strong focus on school turnarounds that involve outside providers and charter schools, as reflected in Imagine 2014, and the new teachers' contract that is being hailed as a national model. However, this attention to national directions has sometimes led to local tensions, especially when community groups have been wary of the engagement of providers that are not locally-based.

CONCLUSION

By April 2010, it was clear that, despite some tweaking along the way, many of the central ideas of a PMM had become institutionalized in Philadelphia. There was broad acceptance that a variety of delivery models for schooling should be provided within the district, and that outside providers—whether from the for-profit or nonprofit sector—should continue to add value to the school district by taking responsibility for core service functions to schools. However, the Philadelphia version of the portfolio model is coupled with some strong centralizing reforms that mute the autonomy of schools that remain under the direct control of the district. For PMM advocates like Hill, such muted autonomy (along with the minimal role for school choice, which Hill and his colleagues argued was a key accountability mechanism) significantly compromises the fidelity of the Philadelphia reform to an ideal model of a PMM. However, to those on the ground in Philadelphia, the shifts toward a PMM have had significant impact.

The pieces of the model came together not as a result of a grand plan driven by ideology (although certain aspects of the reform, especially the creation and continuation of the DPM, are tied to advocates acting on ideological grounds), but as a series of policy changes and political adaptations that resulted in a district that functionally had multiple delivery models and has now decided to move toward weaving them together into a system. The active participation of the office of the mayor and key Philadelphia education intermediaries in shaping the next iteration of the PMM provided evidence that ownership of privatization had indeed expanded. Ackerman's strategic plan, Imagine 2014, confirmed the continuation of private management of district schools and demonstrated that contracting out school management had a life beyond Nevels and Vallas.

While district leaders had removed some of the original schools from outside provider management due to poor performance, they had also announced that outside partners would play a key role in reviving a handful of the district's lowest-performing schools, Renaissance Schools. They were in conversations with successful charter operators to scale up their efforts both inside and outside district governance. District leaders asserted that they well knew the failings of the diverse provider model, individual providers, and the district itself in its contracting and oversight role. They intended to correct the situation by capitalizing on partner assets rather than asking them to do everything, improving district oversight and partner accountability, smoothing implementation, and erasing ambiguity about roles and responsibilities.

This chapter describes how the portfolio of schools model in Philadelphia is not static and, as it is currently enacted, does not conform to the ideological viewpoint of either marketplace advocates or advocates of democratic participation of school-level practitioners and parents/community members in the governance of their schools. The portfolio continues to evolve, with actors inside and outside the district playing important roles in the deals that are cut and the organizational arrangements that are made to sustain the central idea of Philadelphia's portfolio model. New players in the public, for-profit, and nonprofit sectors are increasingly viewed as having a legitimate, albeit sometimes limited, role in reforming the city's public schools.

This chapter also describes how, in the early stages, community groups (unless under contract to the district) and school-level practitioners have not been seen as critical to shaping remedies for Philadelphia's failing schools. Hints at shifts toward a broader community role are visible in Ackerman's decisions in early 2010, but where those shifts will lead is still uncertain. Some questions remain: In what ways will the Partnership, Renaissance, and other district schools gain autonomy in the next iteration of the portfolio model? Will this happen incrementally through negotiation and compromise across stakeholders or dramatically through the fiat of state legislation and the court consent decree? Will accountability for performance and issues of underenrollment lead to school closures (a critical piece of the PMM idea, but one as yet little utilized in Philadelphia)? Will choice for families and parents become a more substantial piece for reform in the city? Will district leaders continue to support and broaden the portfolio, or will they pull back schools that are granted additional autonomy as they have with the partnership schools? Despite the uncertainties about the shape and breadth of Philadelphia's portfolio of schools, the continuing existence of a portfolio—largely established under the guidance of Nevels and Vallas—with new kinds of schools, management, and governance is not in question.

6

A Diverse Education Provider

New Orleans

Henry M. Levin, Joseph Daschbach,
and Andre Perry

In August 2005, Hurricane Katrina descended on New Orleans and the Gulf Coast, resulting in one of the largest natural disasters ever to hit the U.S. mainland.[1] The devastation wrought by the levee breaks in New Orleans was catastrophic. More than half the population suffered serious housing damage, and many others left because of the public dangers and loss of services.[2] Of the estimated 485,000 persons living in New Orleans before Katrina struck, only about 91,000 were living there four months after Katrina. Five years later, the effort to rebuild the City of New Orleans is still underway.

A major component in the rebirth of New Orleans has been the rebuilding of its public education system. Local and state education authorities have adopted a multiphase facilities plan to renovate and rebuild the school system that will cost nearly $2 billion.[3] But school facilities were not the only aspect of the system that was in need of repair. Public schools in New Orleans had been considered deeply troubled, even before Katrina.

In 2005, over half of all New Orleans students taking Louisiana's high-stakes Louisiana Educational Assessment Program (LEAP) and graduation exit examination (GEE) tests scored below the basic level in English, mathematics, science, and social studies.[4] According to 2005 state education accountability standards, 68 of New Orleans' 120 public schools had been labeled as "academically unacceptable," and over 100 were ranked below the state average. In July 2005, just before Katrina, the Louisiana Department of Education (LDE) brought in financial consulting firm Alvarez & Marsal to help turn around the Orleans Parish School Board's (OPSB) dismal financial management, which included mismanagement of Title I funds and projected deficits of nearly $30 million.[5]

Against that backdrop, the Louisiana legislature passed Act 35 in November 2005, which enabled the state to take over more than a hundred low-performing schools and place them into the state-run Recovery School District (RSD).[6] The legislature granted the RSD the decision-making authority on land, buildings, facilities, and the management of the schools. The decision to transfer those schools was consistent with the state's treatment of what it considered a failing school. The consequent state takeover of the majority of the district's schools led to the unpredictable growth of a highly decentralized system. New Orleans now comprises a combination of centrally managed schools and privately managed charter schools, all subject to market decentralization through parent choice. Governance of schools is also mixed, with both state and local agencies providing direct school oversight and monitoring of charter schools. This assortment of providers establishes New Orleans as perhaps the most complex system of management and variety of schools in the United States.

The purpose of this chapter is to document the emergence and development of that complex approach. In the context of this volume, the public education system in New Orleans appears to be teetering between a managed portfolio of educational providers and an unmanaged diverse provider system in which market decentralization and choice rule the day.

BACKGROUND

Katrina made landfall in August 2005 with 145-mile-per-hour winds accompanied by prodigious rainfall and storm surge. The flooding damage to New Orleans from the levee breaks was immense. One-third of the schools were destroyed, and the vast majority of the other school buildings sustained serious damage that would require considerable repair and reconstruction. The lack of students and usable buildings and the issue of public safety in the weeks following the storm led to the closure of all public schools and, later, the layoff of almost all New Orleans Public School employees.

The strategy for resurrecting the school system was to permit a combination of authorities to reopen and operate schools with the intention of accommodating the unpredictable flow of returning students from Baton Rouge, Houston, and other destinations of refuge from Katrina. The New Orleans Public Schools (NOPS), the central district governed by the Orleans Parish School Board (OPSB), reopened four schools, all as selective-admission magnet schools, as well as several charter schools. The state's RSD filled the remaining gap with both directly operated and chartered schools. The RSD, governed by the Board of Elementary and Secondary Education (BESE) and created prior to Katrina, is a state-run entity originally formed as a remedy for improving schools that were considered "academically unacceptable" for four or more years under the state accountability system.[7] Such schools were considered "failing schools" and were eligible for placement in the RSD.

No one could predict the rate of returning New Orleans families, nor could anyone forecast the resources needed to open a new district. The RSD had been constructed in 2003 as part of state takeover legislation, which encouraged chartering as an intervention. The University of New Orleans became the first organization to take over a failing school under that legislation by assuming control of Pierre A. Capdau Middle School. Members of the state BESE saw chartering as a convenient way to give access to providers with capacity to open up schools as families and students returned. This also opened a window of opportunity for a range of nonprofit and for-profit providers to fill market needs.

This highly decentralized strategy served three goals: repairing and opening up schools quickly in order to accommodate the flow of families returning to New Orleans; maximizing families' school choice by increasing the diversity in educational offerings; and making a concerted attempt to raise overall educational quality of schools and student performance.

By 2009–2010, public school enrollments had risen to 38,000, from about 26,000 in 2006, and a bit more than half of what they had been prior to Katrina.[8] Of the eighty-eight schools, fifty-one were charter schools serving about 61 percent of the school population. In addition, there were several alternative schools and magnet schools with another thirty-one schools still run directly by the RSD, but subject to choice. Only four schools were operated directly by the OPSB.[9]

Looking forward, both the superintendent of the Recovery School District, Paul Vallas, and the state superintendent, Paul Pastorek, have referred frequently to converting most of the remaining noncharter schools to charter school status through the RSD takeover process. They have also suggested minimizing the size of the central authority of the district, a perspective supported by other groups contemplating the future of New Orleans schools.[10] Their comments suggest that New Orleans will continue to rely on a variety of educational providers for both direct operation of schools and for educational support services previously provided by a central district office.

Emergence of a Diverse Management Approach

Reliance on charter schools as alternative service providers began in New Orleans long before Hurricane Katrina. In 1995, the Louisiana legislature passed the "Charter School Demonstration Programs Law," a pilot program to allow up to eight school districts to voluntarily participate in the creation of charter schools. Under the law, local school districts in the program either could grant charters to eligible groups or could apply directly to the BESE to operate a charter school themselves. The law was revised in 1997 to allow all school districts in the state to participate, but the total number of charter schools allowed was capped at forty-two. The 1997 amendment also allowed for the creation of four types of charter schools:

- Type 1 charters are new schools operated under a charter between the nonprofit created to operate the school and the local school board.

- Type 2 charters are new or preexisting public schools that are converted and operated under a charter between the nonprofit created to operate the school and BESE. Type 2 charters are "appeal-type" schools and must first attempt a charter agreement with a local school board.

- Type 3 charters are preexisting public schools converted and operated under a charter between a nonprofit corporation and the local school board. Type 3 charters require the approval of the existing faculty and staff and of the parents of existing students.

- Type 4 charters are new or preexisting public schools that are converted and operated under a charter directly between a local school board and BESE. If the school is a conversion from a preexisting school, the charter must be approved by the faculty and staff and by the parents of existing students [Louisiana R.S. 17:3973.2(b)].

Legislative acts passed in 1999 and 2001 made additional changes to Louisiana's charter school law, mostly through clarifying existing ambiguities in areas such as funding and facilities. In 2003, charter law was amended to create a fifth category of charter schools. Type 5 charters are preexisting public schools that have been transferred to the RSD and are operated under a charter between a nonprofit corporation and BESE.

Prior to the 2005 school year, only a few charter schools existed in New Orleans: two Type 2 charter schools authorized directly by BESE; two Type 3 charter schools authorized by OPSB; and four Type 5 charter schools in the RSD. Few public options existed beyond the schools that OPSB operated. The system of public schools that emerged after Katrina looks dramatically different. The prototypical, centralized, local school district has been replaced by a system of schools that includes both local and state-authorized charter schools as well as schools under the centralized management of the RSD. However, there is no a clear picture of the future configuration of New Orleans schools because market drivers mitigate school officials' efforts to manage the district as a portfolio management model (PMM). With multiple authorizers and the lack of a central authority, the development has been more happenstance than guided by a plan.

Post-Katrina Expansion

The dramatic expansion of the RSD was primarily due to the passage of Act 35 in November 2005 (see the appendix). Under Act 35, the legislature expanded its previous definition of a "failed school." According to the new definition, any school operated by a local school district in "academic crisis" was eligible for takeover if its school performance score (SPS) was below the state average (as opposed to below 60). A local school district was considered in academic crisis if it operated more than thirty academically unacceptable schools or had more than 50 percent of its students in academically unacceptable schools. At the time of Act 35's passage, NOPS was the only school district in the state identified as a district in crisis. As a result, the majority of NOPS schools came under the jurisdiction of the RSD. Of the sixteen schools remaining under NOPS control, four were reopened as district-operated schools. The remaining twelve schools were granted Type 3 or Type 4 charters by OPSB. The passage of Act 35 sent a strong message that the legislature did not have faith in OPSB's ability to successfully manage schools.

Two characteristics now distinguish schools in New Orleans: the level of government in charge of the schools and the organizational structure for managing the schools. Figure 6.1 shows a matrix of the public schools in New Orleans along governmental and organizational lines. Table 6.1 compares the dramatic change in the distribution of school sponsorship from the period just before Katrina (2004–2005) to the present (2009–2010).

FIGURE 6.1 Public school governance in New Orleans

		Organizational structure	
		Centralized	Decentralized
Political control	Local	OPSB operated by New Orleans Public Schools (4 schools)	OPSB charter schools (12 schools)
	State	Recovery School District (RSD) (33 schools)	BESE (Type 2 and Type 5) charter schools (39 schools)

TABLE 6.1 Distribution of school sponsorship before Katrina and in 2009-2010

Public schools in New Orleans pre- and post-Katrina

School year	OPSB-operated	OPSB charter	BESE charter	BESE RSD charter	RSD-operated
2004–2005	112	2	2	4	0
2009–2010	4	12	2	37	33

Source: numbers from *Parents' Guide.*

Designing the System

In early 2006, at least two organizations endorsed the adoption of a market-oriented approach under a complex governing structure to rebuild public schools in New Orleans. Mayor Ray Nagin's Bring New Orleans Back Commission (BNOB) established an education committee of local, state, and national experts. This committee supported the creation of an "education network model," under which "various entities can operate schools and the central office plays a strategic role—delegating much authority to the schools but retaining system wide consistency in key areas."[11] Details on how systemwide consistency was to be established were not forthcoming.

Similarly, the Recovery School District Advisory Committee (RSDAC) endorsed the creation of a "charter school network," consisting of several networks of schools run by charter school management organizations or CMOs. Both BNOB and RSDAC pointed to the diverse provider model as responsible for successful reforms in urban school systems like Philadelphia, Oakland, and New York City. They also highlighted the need to allow external providers to compete with central offices for the provision of shared services such as food service, transportation, and professional development.

Figure 6.2 shows the organizational chart of the RSDAC's proposed charter school network.

Under the network model, the RSD superintendent would supervise a number of small networks, including one run directly by the RSD. Separate managers would run each of the other networks. The proposal identified three networks by name.[12] The University of New Orleans and Middle

FIGURE 6.2 Proposed charter school network's organizational chart

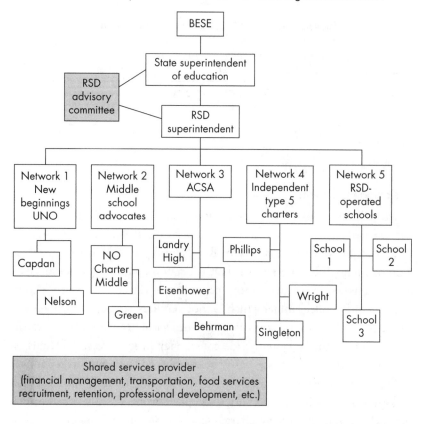

Source: Recovery School District Advisory Committee (RSDAC), Louisiana Department of Education, Committee presentation: Transfer of schools, 2006, http://www.louisianaschools.net/lde/uploads/8632.ppt

School Advocates[13] had both been operating charter schools in New Orleans before Hurricane Katrina, and continue to do so in the current system of schools. The Algiers Charter Schools Association (ACSA), formed in the immediate aftermath of Katrina, was chartered to provide schools under two different governing structures, Type 4 schools with OPSB and Type 5 schools with the RSD. The independent Type 5 network in the model represents stand-alone charter school operators that, along with the RSD network, would independently operate any remaining schools.

A shared-services provider to accompany the model was proposed, but never adopted. It was supposed to support the individual networks and the RSD in obtaining high-quality services and the benefits of economy of scale. This support was intended to include nonacademic services such as management support, transportation, and food, as well as academic supports such as teacher recruiting, professional development, and leadership training.[14] Although the shared-services operation was never implemented, these early advisory groups recognized that individual schools could not provide all the services needed without assistance from a broader institutional base. To some degree, schools have reached out for the provision of such assistance, as evidenced by many schools' reliance on a nonprofit independent source to evaluate the needs of students referred for special educational services, Serving the Unique Needs of Students (SUNS).

Educational Vouchers

The State of Louisiana provided the final component of this complex portfolio model—educational vouchers for students in New Orleans.[15] Even prior to his election in 2007, Governor Bobby Jindal had expressed his support for educational vouchers. In June 2008, he was successful in getting the legislature to approve a voucher bill with a state appropriation of $10 million that would provide fifteen hundred publicly funded educational vouchers New Orleans students in grades K–3 could use to attend private schools. Vouchers were restricted to families with incomes no higher than 250 percent of the poverty line (about $53,000 for a family of four). The relatively late date of the legislation in 2008 meant that only about 650 students found voucher places in private schools for 2008–2009, mostly in Catholic schools. That number was expected to double for the 2009–2010 academic year. It is unclear whether the state will expand educational vouchers from the relatively nominal number currently awarded to more in the future.

CONTROL OF SCHOOL POLICY

Unlike New York, Chicago, and other cities, the mayor of New Orleans has not been granted powers to run the schools. Nagin's name rarely even entered in conversations about the present and the future of the schools.

Nagin might have had a bully pulpit if he had been a stronger force in the reconstruction of New Orleans, but his approval ratings, already below 50 percent in 2006, had dropped to 31 percent in 2008.[16] Mitch Landrieu, elected to replace Nagin in May 2010, may change the mayor's role in school reform, but that is not clear at this point. The OPSB, the locally elected board in charge of NOPS, is also a very weak player, with direct operation of four schools and responsibility as an authorizer for a minority of the city's charter schools.

Clearly, most of the present and future decision-making power and organization of the schools is vested in the BESE, located in Baton Rouge. Superintendent Pastorek is a prominent New Orleans lawyer who previously chaired the RSDAC, an unpaid position. He devoted almost two decades of work to education as a school volunteer, headed a nonprofit group that supported school improvement, and served as a member of the BESE. In March 2007, he was appointed state superintendent and reappointed in January 2008. Although situated in Baton Rouge and accountable to the state of Louisiana, he is regarded as being highly committed to New Orleans and its schools.

In 2007, Pastorek hired Vallas, then-CEO of the Philadelphia schools, to become superintendent of the RSD. As head of the RSD, which is headquartered in New Orleans, Vallas is directly responsible for the operation of thirty-three public schools.[17] This gives the RSD considerable power in setting overall educational policy in New Orleans, and Vallas reports directly to Pastorek and to BESE, which ultimately has authority over most of the other schools.[18] Vallas is a former businessman and is best known for his role as CEO of the Chicago Public Schools where he guided the Chicago reforms, including the establishment of community schools and charter schools. He was then appointed CEO of the School District of Philadelphia where he helped implement a diverse provider model. Under the School Reform Commission jointly appointed by the governor of Pennsylvania and the mayor of Philadelphia to take over the financially bankrupt Philadelphia schools, he faced formidable challenges, both fiscally and educationally. Among his many actions, he helped to establish contracts with for-profit and nonprofit organizations to operate a large number of Philadelphia schools.

Finance and Performance

The RSD is spending significantly more in operating costs than the pre-Katrina New Orleans Public Schools did.[19] However, what must be understood is that financial comparisons become difficult because funding comes from many sources, including hurricane recovery funds from the U.S. government. Moreover, there are start-up costs for opening schools that will not be needed once schools are established and continuing operation.

Compounding the present situation are the uncertain magnitudes of returning students and locations of returning families with school-age children. The RSD must maintain a reserve capacity to accommodate new enrollees that arrive during the school year. This means not only retaining an excess physical capacity for new students, such that some schools will be substantially underenrolled and unable to operate with economies of scale, but also requiring employment of additional contracted teachers who must be hired at the beginning of the year to be assigned to specific school placements during the year as families enroll their returning children.

Estimates of per-pupil expenditure for 2008–2009 vary from about $13,000 per student to as high as $20,000.[20] When reconstruction costs are included, the estimate is closer to $32,000 per student. Precisely how these costs are estimated is not clear, so they should not be compared directly with pre-Katrina expenditures or those of other school districts that did not experience the natural disaster. A recent analysis by the Cowen Institute for Public Education Initiatives at Tulane University estimated that the New Orleans schools were spending about $15,500 per student on operating costs in 2007–2008, more than 50 percent higher than the average for the state of Louisiana.[21] In contrast, before Katrina, the New Orleans schools spent about the state average. Charter Schools in New Orleans had operating costs of about $10,000 per student.[22]

Louisiana summarizes school performance by combining results of a number of different tests, attendance, dropout data, and graduation rates in a single index, the SPS. In 2007–2008, the performance of all New Orleans schools on this index was 66.4, well below the state average of 86.3, but above the performance of 56.9 in 2004–2005 (pre-Katrina). It should be noted that the performance rose in the pre-Katrina period of 2002–2005 by about 10 points. In 2009, 41 percent of the schools were academically unacceptable, with a score below 60 relative to 64 percent of schools with that designation in 2005 prior to Katrina.[23] Comparing the relative change in the post-Katrina period with the pre-Katrina period is not a straightforward exercise because the population is changing and not comparable with the earlier time period. Details on demographic change among students since Katrina are not precise enough to venture a guess on the relative school-preparedness of enrollments. But one thing appears constant; overall, New Orleans still lags the state of Louisiana substantially in its most recent performance data as the state SPS continues to rise over time.[24]

VIEWS OF LOCAL CONSTITUENCIES

The chaotic development of the New Orleans rebuilding effort occurred without the usual stakeholders and consumers who participated in the previous system. As schools were being repaired and reopened, new charter schools also came online, and the RSD grew in staff, leadership, and stature. Community participation in this evolving entity was limited. Not all former residents could return, and the typical structures of traditional, consolidated school board meetings were defunct or powerless. The rapid decentralization of schools and emergence of new charter schools limited the access of organized groups of parents, community groups, the teacher union, and other stakeholders. At present, no single governing body exists to respond to public concerns about the school system. Instead, the system of schools comprises a number of stand-alone entities with no collective responsibility to deal with the public apart from their own constituents.

We conducted a pilot study in the summer of 2009 to capture the communities' perceptions and expectations of the new charter district as well as their experiences within it. The pilot study examined the overall effectiveness of the new school configuration and RSD stewardship, by administering an open-ended, interview protocol for focus groups. We recruited nonprofit groups that provide educational services to schools to participate via letter, e-mail, and phone, yielding eleven participants from various nonprofit organizations. Seven parents were recruited among school leaders from RSD and OPSB charters as well as RSD schools. Six parent liaisons from various school types also participated, along with academic officers from charter management organizations (CMOs). A union representative, three principals, and a city councillor also participated in the interviews. In all, thirty-two people, representing multiple organizations, took part. We developed much of the following section from this pilot study, which is not meant to represent the overall constituencies from which participants were drawn.

Community groups and other stakeholders reacted differently to the school reforms. In particular, parents, teachers, politicians, the local teacher union, and various advocacy groups displayed different attitudes toward the reforms, based on their pre-Katrina roles. However, many new organizations have been established to address the post-Katrina phenomena, and they compose a growing and more unified voice across the educational landscape. As a teacher who arrived in 2008 stated, "There are thousands of 'newbies' across the city just like me . . . We don't get caught up in the battles. We just teach kids."

Teachers and other former employees of NOPS, including custodial and cafeteria workers, bus drivers, and support staff, received only a single paycheck at the onset of the academic year in September 1, 2005. After the levee failures caused by Katrina, most NOPS employees were terminated, and hundreds of workers did not receive official notification of the district's decision to cancel employment and pay. The pay cancellations and lack of communication added insult to injury to an already displaced group of working- and middle-class employees. The teachers who did return and who later attended open meetings of the NOPS board directed their anger toward the board. The firing of a largely black teacher base, one of the major sources of black professional and middle-class employment in New Orleans, and the absence of a requirement for schools to hire the laid-off employees of the former system enmeshed the reforms in complex currents of racial politics and cleavages between carpetbaggers and true residents. It created an entrenched and dedicated opposition among a well-networked set of local actors with long traditions of political involvement and influence.

The United Teachers of New Orleans (UTNO), the local teacher union, fought vigorously against the reforms that led to the termination of teachers. UTNO started a statewide campaign titled, "Refuse to Lose." On June 30, 2006, the UTNO contract with NOPS expired, and the NOPS board did not vote to renew the contract, in a city with extensive union membership. With a significant reduction in membership due to the transfer of schools to the RSD and no collective bargaining agreement, the union saw its influence evaporate.[25]

Although former teachers projected their anger toward NOPS, local board members were not responsible for the state governance changes, and they vocally opposed Act 35 and the consequent service-delivery changes that the state legislation and the RSD created. School Board President Torin Sanders and Superintendent Ora Watson were on the losing side of a four-to-two vote to create a charter network in Algiers, a neighborhood that was only minimally affected by Katrina. The board president and superintendent sought to retain four of the thirteen schools in Algiers that would eventually fall under the auspices of the RSD. Sensing a loss of local control, a group of mostly black business leaders, activists, and religious leaders successfully filed an injunction to stop a plan to transfer control of the schools to the charter managing organization. The injunction eventually expired. The group staged opposition to the decentralized model with charter networks as a fight for local control. The charter network was ultimately established as the ACSA.

The transition to a choice-based, diverse provider arrangement created early resistance from parents, who saw the system of schools as fragmented and poorly prepared for serving the needs of students. For example, in January 2007, BESE and the RSD placed over three hundred children on waiting lists, as the state-run schools rushed to open additional facilities and find more teachers. There was no systemwide policy to ensure seats, particularly among charters, for increased enrollment. On the one hand, charter schools were permitted to set their enrollment intakes at the time of annual registration—in the spring prior to the next school year— with closed registration when those limits were reached. On the other hand, the RSD was required to accept students no matter when they enrolled and regardless of how much excess capacity was available in RSD classrooms. As a result, the RSD did not have the enrollment capacity to accommodate the large and often unpredictable number of students seeking to enter schools when they returned to the city during the school year, even though the RSD's responsibility.

The dearth of certified teachers and quality staff also contributed to the lack of capacity to serve students. Scarce human resources in the two years following Katrina clearly limited the RSD's ability to enroll the returning students efficiently and in timely fashion. The waiting lists exposed holes in the early hybrid model of relatively autonomous charter schools and traditional schools of the RSD, where many of the charters maintained selective admissions and low student-–teacher ratios. As a result, returning parents and parent groups voiced opposition toward a decentralized system as they saw their children falling through the cracks or being placed in schools of last resort, those left with enrollment openings.

In addition, the speed of the transition away from centralized control confused parents and families seeking to enroll their children in schools. Many parents did not know where to voice questions, as the traditional forum of the OPSB board meeting was unavailable. The terms "charter," "RSD," and "ACSD" confused parents as to where and how they should send their children to school. It was not until 2007 that New Schools for New Orleans, a nonprofit group, produced the *New Orleans Parents' Guide to Public Schools*, barely in time for the 2007–2008 school year.[26] While many parents saw hope in the reform efforts, a lack of clear information and the problems surrounding enrollment created persistent criticism of the new system. Increased choices did not necessarily improve access if the new options were distant. Parents who could not choose a school were more likely to express these concerns.

The lack of clear information about the new system of schools also gave rise to organizations like Save Our Schools New Orleans Louisiana (SOSNOLA), which emerged with the explicit aim of giving information and access to parents in the public school system. The organization offers workshops and meetings to support "a community of informed parents, residents and partner organizations to leverage their collective knowledge and influence toward ensuring equitable, excellent public schools for every child in New Orleans."[27] Similar organizations arose, like the Center for Action Research on New Orleans School Reforms and the New Orleans Parent Organizing Network, to seek greater parent participation on charter school boards, financial transparency, and equity between school types, as well as consistent discipline policy and overall instructional improvement and appropriate placements for special needs populations.

Other groups representing parents also voiced opposition or skepticism and concerns about the direction of this highly decentralized model.

For instance, after BESE and RSD released information regarding waiting lists of approximately three hundred students for admission to RSD-operated schools, the NAACP Legal Defense and Educational Fund, Inc., filed a lawsuit against the RSD, OPSB, and state education officials. The lawsuit aimed to ensure that students would not be denied access to public schools in the future.

Negative attitudes were also directed at the elected officials who shepherded legislative components of New Orleans education reforms. Karen Carter (now Karen Carter Peterson) and Ann Duplessis, who sponsored the original State House and Senate legislation that created the RSD, were attacked by political opponents who took aim at their support for decentralization, particularly Duplessis' support for Act 35. During their respective elections, their political rivals attempted to mobilize teachers who had lost jobs after the takeover. Carter-Peterson competed for incumbent William Jefferson's seat in the 2nd congressional district. Incumbent State Senator Ann Duplessis fought challenger Jon Johnson, who was endorsed by United Teachers of New Orleans. Carter Peterson lost her prospective bid, and Duplessis retained her seat in a runoff. The results from the races suggest that a voting, black middle-class base opposed key supporters of the reforms.

One New Orleans–elected member of the BESE also voiced opposition to the rise in charter schools post-Katrina. Board member Louella Givens spoke at a two-day summit entitled, "New Orleans Education Summit: Equity, Access and Community Participation," and was quoted in the *Times Picayune*: "I have voted against every charter, against anything that took away the right of the citizens of this parish to decide."[28] She was also quoted in the same article: "I don't want to experiment with children. We've been stigmatized in the Legislature as being thieves, as not caring about our children."

Despite the early negative reactions to decentralization, general public opinion may be turning. Parental backing for the charter schools seems to be growing as local leaders like Doris Hicks of the Dr. Martin Luther King Jr. Charter School for Science and Technology in the Lower Ninth Ward and Sharon Clark of the Sophie B. Wright Charter School garner parent voices to place political pressure on BESE members and other elected officials to support charter schools. In addition, with evidence of charter school performance outpacing RSD scores, parental satisfaction in charters is gaining momentum, although it should be noted that charters may attract more selective enrollments than students assigned to RSD-operated schools.[29]

Other community organizations are also supporting reform efforts. The Business Council of New Orleans, Baptist Community Ministries, and the League of Women Voters have financially and politically supported charter schools and general reform. In a 2009 public opinion poll conducted by the Cowen Institute for Public Education Initiatives, "66 percent of registered voters agreed with the state's decision to take over the majority of New Orleans public schools . . . However, 57 percent of African American voters agreed . . . compared to 80 percent of all other voters."[30] Support could be due as much to opposition to the NOPS board and structure as to support for charters and decentralization, but these organizations' support for reforms lends credibility to decentralized governance and the high prevalence of school choice in New Orleans. With the obvious exception of those who lost influence, power, and employment as a result of reform, many in the larger community, and particularly families who send their children to charter, private, and parochial schools, generally support the changes in public schools.

CURRENT CHALLENGES AND DILEMMAS

The new regime of schools in New Orleans faces at least three challenges. The first is restoring the connection between local communities and their public schools—a connection that some see as undermined by the transformation from schools that NOPS operated to those that the relatively autonomous charter schools and the RSD operate. The second is that decentralization has shifted school employment and operations from the local population to outside groups of organizations and consultants. This not only has placed the schools in the hands of outsiders, but also reduced significantly the educational employment of the more established New Orleans population. The third is that there is not yet a plan to provide a cohesive and efficient governance structure to coordinate the system of schools in terms of its finance and operations.

Loss of Political Links to Local Community

Although we might view schools as largely independent of other entities in the community, they are not. Schools are dependent on the overall support and connections that they have with various community institutions and constituencies. They depend on local taxpayers for financial support. They draw on assistance from community volunteers and community institutions such as churches, youth organizations, and other government agencies like those committed to health, social welfare, and housing. To a large degree, the portfolio approach to schools has hampered the traditional relationship between the schools and local community structures and organizations. Since the schools are largely independent of each other, many overall relationships between NOPS and the network of supportive organizations must now be established on a school-by-school basis. This requires a special effort and shifts the focus from overall support for the New Orleans schools to selective support for individual schools. It raises the question of how to address equity among schools in both inputs and results when large differences emerge, particularly substantial differences in philanthropic support. Individual school support was always an option in the past, but there was also symbolic and concrete support for New Orleans school children more generally and the schools that they attended. That relationship has become far more abstract.

Perhaps even more controversial than the seeming disorganization of the decentralization itself is the loss of employment for longtime New Orleans residents. Traditionally, the bulk of teachers and school personnel in New Orleans was drawn from the local population. After Katrina, the lack of suitable school buildings and the dramatic loss of enrollments led to massive layoffs by the NOPS. With the rebuilding of the school system primarily into a loose portfolio of charter schools and RSD schools, the new schools are able to choose their own personnel and seek teachers and administrators nationwide rather than recruiting in New Orleans.

One might argue that expanding the pool of human capital for teachers and leaders has had a positive impact on schools, and that it was a calculated step toward improving school performance. The local teacher union and the established teaching force were stigmatized by previous school failures throughout the pre-Katrina public school system. Thus, it has become common for schools to spread the recruitment net by vigorously seeking national and regional prospects rather than recruiting locally. Teach For America and New Leaders for New Schools have energetically recruited teachers and school leaders nationally to serve the emerging school expansion in the city. Whatever the justification, the changes have resulted in a serious erosion of one of the most important, traditional, and stable sources of employment for educated New Orleans residents (and especially the black middle class). The changes have also provided an image of carpetbaggers and opportunists, who will not make long-term commitments to New Orleans, taking over local schools. Most important, these changes do not seem to reflect a strategy of building long-term employment for native residents through training, promoting, sustaining, and upgrading a local corps of professional educators and appear to undermine the building of local capacity.

Building Local Capacity

Five years after the tragedy of Katrina, the recovery of New Orleans is still a part of the national awareness. Large amounts of government and philanthropic funds have been committed to the overall resuscitation of the economy, institutions, and infrastructure of the city. New institutions have been implanted in New Orleans to assist with recovery. All these efforts have certainly contributed to a more substantial rebound than would have happened in their absence. However, there is also a cost to this phenomenon if such endeavors are temporary and displace the local institutions and potential actors that are needed to build a more permanent capacity.

The efforts made to rebuild the educational system of New Orleans have responded to the emergency, and they have been well meaning and sincere. Both the federal government and the state government in Baton Rouge have been attentive to the need to rebuild and reestablish schools in New Orleans and have made considerable investments in doing so. Many nongovernmental organizations have arisen or expanded to meet the educational crisis. And philanthropists from far away have provided massive contributions to buttress the support provided by these organizations.

However, the inescapable consequence of all this external support is the loss of local influence; the expertise and capacity of the schools heavily depend on outsiders and potentially nonpermanent personnel. In particular, the national organizations of Teach For America (TFA), The New Teachers Project, and New Leaders for New Schools and their New Orleans branches and the offshoots of the national CMOs such as KIPP represent the main forces for recruitment, selection, and training of teachers and principals. All are dedicated to good schools, good teaching, and good leadership, commodities that were considered by many to be in short supply in the pre-Katrina period. All seek national recruits for the New Orleans schools and new sources of talent.

But there is concern that the tenure of these personnel will be short-lived, as new staff, after gaining their first experiences, will leave for other destinations after a few years. While the records of New Leaders for New Schools and The New Teachers Project are too brief to provide a pattern of longevity of placements, TFA has a much longer record in cities such as Houston. Two studies of TFA in Houston found that the tenure of its teachers was very short. Depending on the school, between 50 percent and 90 percent of TFA teachers had left after only the second year of teaching, and between 72 percent and 100 percent had left after the third year.[31] A different study of TFA in that city found similar results.[32] There is a serious challenge to build a permanent and stable educational capacity with commitment to New Orleans students, institutions, and culture, given this turnover, despite the very good intentions of TFA and the young professionals who are inspired by it to teach in New Orleans.

The same is true with regard to the external nature of governance and funding of the New Orleans schools. Only four schools are under the direct authority of the locally elected OPSB, although this entity serves as authorizer for an additional twelve charter schools. The remaining schools are under the authority of the BESE in Baton Rouge, operating as charter schools or as schools directly managed by the RSD. Local boards of directors do govern the charter schools, but the state develops the policies that govern those boards. Vallas, who arrived in New Orleans as a turnaround specialist and who has hinted that he has his eye on elective office or other positions in the long run (most likely in his home state of Illinois), directs the RSD schools.[33] And, Vallas is answerable to the BESE in Baton Rouge, not a local governance body.

Further, as one might expect, the public funding for rebuilding and operating the schools is mainly derived from the federal and state governments, and much of this financial flow is not permanent because it is based on the emergency response of both levels of government. Philanthropic funding also comes from afar and is based on the funding programs and philosophies of the foundations. In December 2007, the Broad Foundation of Los Angeles, Doris-Donald Fisher Fund of San Francisco, and the Bill & Melinda Gates Foundation of Seattle gave $17.5 million to New Schools for New Orleans, New Leaders for New Schools, and Teach For America to continue and expand their roles in New Orleans. The Walton Family Foundation has also provided large flows of support for charter schools and the RSD.

While all this funding from external sources is welcomed, it is accompanied by two cautions. First, foundations have an external influence on operations and policy by providing funding only for the programs and approaches that they support, distorting decision making in the direction of available funding. Second, because foundations' priorities shift, they are not likely to maintain similar levels of investment over the long run. As well meaning as the intentions of these foundations and paradoxical as it may seem, their efforts may actually delay the building of long-term, effective capacity at the local level to staff and operate the schools in a more stable environment. Again, strong market forces and concurrent political winds limit the efficacy of long-range planning.

One major challenge, then, is to begin to build long-term capacity, attracting educational talent that will stay in New Orleans. A second is the coordination between local and state authorities to build operations that are more focused on overall decision making in New Orleans and links to its institutions. Perhaps these will happen over time, but the instruments of transition do not yet seem to be in place.

Cohesive System of Governance

The advantages of a portfolio district premised on student choice are many. Schools can specialize in filling the educational needs of particular types of students and interests. Competition among schools for students may improve productivity.[34] And, if a school is not appropriate for a particular student, that student need not be held "captive" because the family can move her to a preferred school. Teachers also have the benefits of a teacher market in which they can stay in the district, but seek out the best positions in terms of salary, benefits, and teaching conditions. Thus, in theory, the system can provide the incentives for good teaching performance and discourage poor performance in a competitive labor market.

However, to benefit from such possibilities, semiautonomous schools must operate within an overall system of governance in which there are clear rules and procedures that make funding and operations efficient and equitable. In much of the rhetoric surrounding portfolio or choice districts, this concern has been forgotten. Act 35 has a provision for returning RSD schools to the "local system." For schools taken over by the RSD in 2005, consideration would begin in 2010. However, Superintendent Pastorek has indicated that such a transfer of authority from the state may be postponed for several years.[35] The need for a more cohesive system of governance of the New Orleans schools, with greater local control, is a pressing one.

When each school is given maximum autonomy, the differences that arise can have the opposite consequences for the system as those that were intended. How can students switch schools if curriculum and school practices vary so immensely from one school to another that there is little or no possibility of transition between schools? How can schools compete for teachers who must relinquish valued accumulation of pension and other benefits when switching to a school with different arrangements? Good choices require good information. How will the overall system collect accurate information on school options and disseminate it to students, parents, and teachers? Access to choice requires transportation. But, school vehicles crisscrossing the entire city are redundant, environmentally damaging, and costly, leaving fewer resources to be spent on instruction. Dependence on private transportation as an alternative also has challenges, favoring the more affluent and increasing problems of safety, traffic congestion, and parental costs. Students with special needs may require resources that are unavailable in small schools, and they are not accommodated in schools that may lack capacity or interest in serving them. How will provisions be made so that they are accommodated in the overall system?

These questions weigh heavily on how the overall system will perform. Lack of access to transportation and useful information will reduce educational equity. Extreme uniqueness of school curriculum and instructional approaches and lack of portability in teacher benefits will reduce the putative gains of competition for students and staff. At the present time, there is only piecemeal attention to these concerns at an official level. (See Levin, chapter 8 in this volume, for the economic considerations in designing a central governance unit.) In some cases, nongovernmental agencies have taken responsibility, resulting in, for example, the *New Orleans Parents' Guide to Public Schools* produced by the New Orleans Parent Organizing Network.[36] The Cowen Institute for Public Education Initiatives has accepted responsibility for developing data analysis of system functioning. But both of these organizations depend on philanthropic funding and unofficial or advisory authority, neither of which can be counted on in the long run. For this reason, the establishment of an overall system of governance of the New Orleans schools, quite unlike the traditional institution of the schools and school board of the past, is necessary. There has been little evidence of response to this long-term need.

OVERCOMING THE CHALLENGES

The evolving arrangement of schools and the uncertainty of central governance makes it difficult to place New Orleans in the category of a portfolio management model with other cities. New Orleans has a unique history and rationale for having moved in this direction. The decentralized system in New Orleans was an emergency response to disaster rather than a carefully planned and executed managerial change. But, the district or system is far from finished. Only its magnitude and form have come into being. There most likely will be considerable trial and error before it reaches long-term stability. The true test will come when existing and future crises in other domains (e.g., the national economy, global warming, persistent warfare, natural disasters, terrorism) have drawn attention away from the 2005 disaster, as funding and sympathy are undermined by competing challenges. At that point, it is hoped that New Orleans will have grown sufficient local capacity to meet the needs of its students and to obtain the exemplary educational results that it seeks.

Chapter 6 Appendix

Louisiana Act 35, Effective November 30, 2005

§10.7. School and district accountability; schools in districts in academic crisis; transfer to Recovery School District

A.(1) Each elementary or secondary school that participates in a Spring cycle of student testing and has a baseline school performance score below the state average and each alternative school, established pursuant to R.S. 17:100.5, that provides educational services to students a majority of whose test scores are reported back to such an elementary or secondary school under a uniform statewide program of school accountability established pursuant to rules adopted under authority of law by the State Board of Elementary and Secondary Education, referred to in this Section as "the state board", that is a school in or granted a charter by a city, parish, or other local public school system that has been declared to be academically in crisis pursuant to R.S. 17:10.6, and that has at least one school eligible to transfer to the Recovery School District pursuant to R.S. 17:10.5, shall be designated a failing school and shall be transferred to the jurisdiction of the Recovery School District established in R.S. 17:1990. The Recovery School District, referred to in this Section as "the recovery district", shall provide all educational services required of any city, parish, or other local public school system in order to meet the educational needs of all students residing in the jurisdiction of the transferring local school system who were attending a transferred school or who would have been eligible to attend such transferred school because of the residential location of the student or as the result of any other option or program available to the student.

(2) On and after November 15, 2009, no additional schools shall be transferred to the jurisdiction of the recovery district pursuant to this Section.

B.(1) Any school transferred to the recovery district pursuant to this Section shall be reorganized as necessary and operated by the recovery district, pursuant to its authority, in whatever manner is determined by the administering agency of the recovery district to be most likely to improve the academic performance of each student in the school.

(2)(a)(i) The recovery district, as directed by its administering agency, shall manage the schools so transferred in a fashion that provides the best educational opportunity to all students who attended or were eligible to attend such schools without regard to the attendance zones related to such schools prior to the transfer. The authority provided in this Paragraph includes the authority to determine and act on which schools should be operated, which schools should be closed, which schools should be relocated or rebuilt, and what range of grades should be operated in each school.

(ii) However, the recovery district shall provide for and ensure that schools of appropriate grade that have open enrollment policies are operating and available for the enrollment of students in reasonable proximity to the neighborhoods where concentrations of students reside. The recovery district shall use the best information available to make the determinations of the location of such neighborhoods. The requirements of this Item shall be reflected in all planning, presenting, reviewing, and approving required by Subparagraph (b) of this Paragraph.

(b)(i) Within six months after the transfer of a school to the recovery district pursuant to this Section, the recovery district shall develop and present to the state board, for its approval, a plan for the operation of all schools transferred. The plan shall be annually updated and reviewed by the state board.

(ii) The plan required in this Subparagraph shall address each of the following:

(aa) The educational needs of all students.

(bb) The number and location of schools to be operated to provide appropriate educational services to all students. This plan element shall include provision for changes in the student population being served.

(cc) A method for maintaining clear communication among interested parties, including the recovery district, the Louisiana Recovery Authority, the chief executive officer of the governing authority of the relevant municipality or parish, the parents and guardians of children for whom the recovery district is required to provide educational services, and the city, parish, or other local public school board from which schools were transferred.

(iii) The requirements of this Subparagraph shall not preclude the operation of a limited number of schools prior to completion and approval of the required plan provided that such schools are operated in direct response to the present needs of students and provided that the operation of such schools is approved by the state board after a review by the board of the data presented by the recovery district supporting the operation of the schools and review and consideration by the board of the efforts made by the recovery district to seek and consider input from the community and its leaders and the input gained from those efforts.

(3) The recovery district shall make an annual report to the House and Senate committees on education concerning the status, management, and operation of any school transferred to the recovery district pursuant to the provisions of this Section.

C.(1) The recovery district shall retain jurisdiction over any school transferred to it for a period of not less than five school years not including the school year in which the transfer occurred if the transfer occurred during a school year. At the end of the initial transfer period, the school may be returned to the system from which it was transferred unless the school is continued in the recovery district in accordance with the provisions of Paragraph (3) of this Subsection.

(2)(a) No later than nine months prior to the expiration of the initial or subsequent transfer period, the recovery district shall make a report to the state board.

(b) The report shall include at a minimum each of the following elements:

(i) The status of each school transferred, the nature of its faculty and administration, the demographics and size of its student body, its organizational and management structure, whether there has been improvement in student academic performance and, if so, how much and, if not, why not.

(ii) A recommendation as to whether the school should be:

(aa) Continued in the recovery district pursuant to its reported operational status.

(bb) Continued in the recovery district with a change in its operational status and the nature of the recommended change.

(cc) Closed and the reasons therefor.

(dd) Returned to the administration and management of the transferring system with proposed stipulations and conditions for the return.

(3) No later than six months prior to the expiration of the initial or subsequent transfer period, the state board shall take action on the recommendations of the recovery district. Additionally, no later than six months prior to the expiration of the initial or subsequent transfer period, the state board shall conduct a public hearing within the jurisdiction of the city, parish, or other local public school board from which the school was transferred relative to whether the school should be continued in the recovery district or returned to the system. The state board by a majority vote of its membership may continue any school in the recovery district for additional periods of five years.

D. At the time of the transfer of a school to the recovery district, the parent or guardian with responsibility for decisions regarding the education of any student attending a transferred school or any student who would be assigned to attend a transferred school shall be able to continue to have their child enrolled in and attend a school under the jurisdiction of the recovery district or may exercise an option, if one is made available by the city, parish, or other local public school board from which the school is being transferred to have the child enroll in or attend another school operated by the school board.

Acts 2005, 1st Ex. Sess., No. 35, §1, eff. Nov. 30, 2005; Acts 2008, No. 737, §1, eff. July 6, 2008.

PART III

Crosscutting Issues

7

Where's the Management in Portfolio Management?

Conceptualizing the Role of Urban School District Central Offices in Implementation

Meredith I. Honig and Michael DeArmond

Portfolio management reforms aim to strengthen urban schools district-wide in part by fundamentally changing how school district central offices participate in school improvement. For the better part of the twentieth century, for example, urban school district central offices have treated schools as relatively permanent investments, primarily maintaining and otherwise working with the schools they had and not opening and closing schools to help leverage school improvement. Portfolio management reforms by contrast call on school district central offices to oversee and support a dynamic system of schools—helping schools build their capacity for improvement, closing those that underperform, and opening new ones in their place. School improvement approaches for decades have involved the participation of external support providers in reform processes but mainly in marginal ways; under portfolio management reforms, school district central offices are to proactively encourage outside organizations not only to provide support for schools, but also to operate entire schools and networks of schools.

Educational research suggests the potential of these reforms mainly by negative example—instances in which school districts' central offices have not operated in the ways portfolio management reforms demand. Such results have been so common that some reformers have begun to question whether or not district central offices *should* play central roles in educational improvement efforts and to suggest that educational systems might better realize the goals of portfolio management reforms by intentionally limiting central office participation.

This chapter starts from a fundamentally different assumption, motivated in part by the designs of many portfolio management initiatives: namely, educational systems that are serious about taking a portfolio management approach must engage their central offices in their ongoing implementation. After all, research and experience have shown that school improvement under various reform banners typically does not penetrate more than a subset of district schools absent support from school district central offices for broader implementation.[1] The promotion of differentiated schools through other policy mechanisms has depended substantially on staff throughout central offices changing various central office policies and practices to enable schools to deviate from standard operating procedures.[2] Such policies and practices are nearly impossible to predict a priori and typically involve the launching of schools by local leaders and central office administrators mining schools' experience to identify policy and practice changes that might enable implementation.[3] Many portfolio management reform designs seem to reflect these important roles for central offices and call on them to engage in particular activities as part of implementation, as described later.

Ultimately, time will tell whether or not district central offices are up to the demands of portfolio management reforms. In the meantime, given past experience, reformers, researchers, and others might do well to clarify what more specifically portfolio management reforms demand of central offices and what it might look like if central offices were taking on those demands. This chapter addresses these issues central to the implementation of portfolio management reforms. We examine: What specific demands do portfolio management reforms place on school district central offices? What do central offices in urban school districts do when they do participate in implementation in the ways the reform designs intend? What conditions help or hinder them in the process? What are the implications for education policy and practice?

Given the limited research base on the implementation of portfolio management initiatives, we addressed these questions using research on the design of these initiatives, as elaborated in the case chapters, and research on the participation of school district central offices in other reform strategies with similar design features as those of portfolio management reforms.

Our review of research on the design of portfolio management initiatives suggests that portfolio management places three key demands on district central offices: first, these initiatives ask central offices to engage in capacity-building partnerships with groups inside and outside of the district focused on improving performance and expanding high-quality schooling options; second, they ask central offices to use evidence of school performance to support improvement efforts and to hold schools accountable for performance; and third, they ask central offices to manage the strategic closure of schools with chronic performance problems. Our review of the broader literature on district central offices suggests that meeting these three demands will likely require substantial changes. In particular, we argue that meeting these demands will require central offices in many urban school districts to fundamentally change their day-to-day work practices, especially the ways in which they interact with schools and outside organizations. Given the deep and broad scope of these changes, portfolio management reforms are likely to struggle with implementation if central offices relegate responsibility for these initiatives to a single office or set of staff and do not create formal and informal systems throughout the central office to support implementation. We describe these changes and derive selected implications for the research and practice of portfolio management reforms.

DEMANDS ON SCHOOL DISTRICT CENTRAL OFFICES AND EXPERIENCE TO DATE

As the other chapters in this volume suggest, the designs of portfolio management reforms vary across the country and call for numerous changes at the school level. However, the early initiatives place three common demands on school district central offices to support implementation. Unless central offices meet these demands—either with their own staff or through strategic partnerships with outside organizations—portfolio management reforms are unlikely to be fully implemented, let alone successful in meeting school improvement goals.

For one, these initiatives call on school district central offices to cultivate relationships with schools and outside groups to support the creation of high-quality and differentiated schools districtwide. Unlike some school-choice initiatives of previous decades (e.g., charter schools and vouchers), portfolio management initiatives do not rely solely or even mainly on the market or student/family demand to drive change. Instead, these initiatives seem to proceed from the assumption that school district central offices have key leadership roles to play in strategically shaping school supply—in helping schools and outside school providers build their capacity for designing and implementing high-quality school options in their districts. We call these relationships "performance partnerships" to emphasize their focus on central offices working to support schools and outside agencies in building their capacity for producing demonstrable improvements in school performance rather than, for example, traditional top-down regulatory relationships that emphasize unilateral monitoring of procedural compliance.

For instance, the Chicago Public Schools (CPS) New Schools Office identifies as one of its main goals the creation and support of

> quality schools through a comprehensive approach that recruits high-quality school operators, evaluates school proposals through a rigorous request for proposals (RFP), supports approved schools through planning, incubation, school opening, and school operation, and ensures accountability through regular monitoring of multiple measures of success.[4]

In the School District of Philadelphia, the district's Imagine 2014 strategic plan calls on the central office to "train, provide resources, and support the district's highest performing schools to operate more autonomously from the District and/or to replicate their work as successful school choice models."[5] In New Orleans, early proposals for the post-Katrina recovery also describe a model in which the "various entities can operate schools and the central office plays a strategic role—delegating much authority to schools but retaining system wide consistency in key areas." (See Levin, chapter 8, this volume.)

Two, central offices must develop, or already have in place, accountability systems to support the new performance management system. Such accountability systems would produce timely data relevant to gauging student learning in a system with approaches to teaching and learning at least somewhat differentiated across schools. For example, in the New York City Department of Education, the Office of Accountability has launched a major initiative to develop and oversee the implementation of four different accountability tools designed to assess school performance and inform support and accountability decisions: progress reports, which assign letter grades to schools based mainly on student test gains; quality reviews, which use on-the-ground observations to produce qualitative assessments of individual school strengths and weaknesses; periodic assessments in math and reading, which aim to inform instruction without formal penalties for poor performance; and the Achievement Reporting and Innovation System (ARIS), which provides various customized reports on student performance trends over time. In addition, under its Children First Intensive program, senior achievement and technology integration facilitators from the department's Office of Accountability work with external support organizations to provide professional development to schools on how to use these accountability tools to shape improvement efforts.[6]

Third, the designs of portfolio management initiatives assume that central offices will actually close schools that do not meet their performance targets. For example, the original design of CPS's Renaissance 2010 initiative explicitly, at least initially, called for the closure of low-performing schools. (See Menefee-Libey, chapter 3, this volume.) Similarly, written descriptions of the School District of Philadelphia's Imagine 2014 plan describe "a system of schools in which great schools are rewarded and replicated and failing schools are closed or transformed."[7] Philadelphia's initiative calls on the district to "renew or cancel agreements [e.g., earned-autonomy agreements] or contracts [for charters and contractors] with schools based on performance data. Internal and external turnaround partners must meet District targets annually for three consecutive years to ensure a second contract."[8] Descriptions of consequences for low-performing New York City Public

Schools similarly specify that "over time, school organizations receiving an overall grade of F are likely to be closed."[9]

What does research teach about the experience of central offices in meeting such demands? The emerging literature on portfolio management reforms mainly consists of descriptive case studies, such as those in this volume, and some extended analyses, both focused on the design of such initiatives and some information about early implementation dynamics. These pieces tend to identify key formal structures within school district central offices and formal agreements with outside groups as essential to central offices implementing portfolio management reforms.[10] For example, Hill and his colleagues suggest that central offices create new units to manage relationships with schools and outside organizations involved with their portfolios, revise employment contracts for teachers, create innovative school facilities agreements (for example, leasing commercial space to house schools), and invest in longitudinal data systems that can measure school and student performance gains. The case studies in this volume describe districts that have put in place many of these ideas. As Bulkley, Christman, and Gold (chapter 5 in this volume) describe, Philadelphia has recently created an Office of Charter, Partnership and New Schools to expand and support school-choice options in the district. In CPS, the New Schools Office plays a similar role.[11] In the New York City Department of Education, the chancellor created an Office of Portfolio Planning to assess the need for new schools in various communities, to work with potential school providers to develop new school plans, and to oversee the district's new school proposal process.

The case study accounts also show that districts are making significant investments in information technology to help generate and manage student performance data. For instance, Bulkley, Christman, and Gold (chapter 5 in this volume) describe how Philadelphia invested in the SchoolNet information system to manage student performance data, making it accessible not only to educators but also to families in the system. More recently, School-Net has also become a repository for resources on instruction and curriculum. Other examples include New York City's ARIS system and Chicago's recent initiatives to ensure the integrity of its various data systems.[12]

To enhance capacity for new schools and better enable school closures, some of the case districts are beginning to revise the formal policies and procedures governing human resources to enable teachers to flow into and out of schools based on local needs, including the need to close certain buildings, rather than seniority preference and job guarantees. For instance, in 2005, New York City Public Schools renegotiated its teachers' contract to: (1) allow schools to hire teachers regardless of seniority; (2) end the "bumping" process in which a more senior teacher could unilaterally claim a more junior teacher's position; and (3) require "excessed" teachers (those who lost their positions for a variety of reasons, including enrollment declines or school closures) to apply for vacancies instead of being assigned to them.[13] New York is also aggressively using alternative certification programs such as Teach For America and its own Teaching Fellows program to bring new types of teachers into the system.[14] Through such changes, the school district central office aims to facilitate the relatively flexible hiring and firing and strategic deployment of teachers that portfolio management systems seem to demand.

The development of these formal structures—new offices, technologies, and policies—makes sense as key supports for the implementation of portfolio management systems. After all, portfolio management places demands on central offices that their formal infrastructures were not necessarily set up to handle. For instance, educational research across disciplines has long recounted how inefficient technologies and standard operating procedures within the human resource units of central offices, buttressed by teacher union contracts, can lead to long delays in hiring and firing teachers and otherwise hamper dynamic school openings and closures.[15] District data systems notoriously fail to produce timely relevant student performance data of the kind that portfolio reforms call for.[16] Accordingly, many central offices interested in pursuing these reforms likely must make substantial investments in developing new data systems that can capture various levels of student, teacher, and school performance to help target supports and consequences at different levels.

At the same time, broader research on central office participation in ambitious change strategies suggests that while changes to these and other formal office structures are important, they alone are insufficient for enabling implementation. As Spillane and Honig have shown over a series of studies and policy cases, whether or not school district central offices participate productively in the implementation of education improvement efforts depends substantially on what organizational sociologists call the *informal* structures within organizations like central offices—how central office administrators understand their work and policy demands, what they do day-to-day, and how they relate to schools.[17] These informal central office structures include, for example, how people within central office interact with and actually use the new offices and units, technologies, standard-operating procedures, and other new formal structures in ways that may be more or less consistent with policy goals. The importance of informal structures to implementation raises questions for portfolio management districts not simply about whether they have created central office subunits focused on implementation, but about what people within those offices actually do in practice to seed and support the creation of new, high-quality, and differentiated schools. Analyses of portfolio management reforms thus far have shed little light on these human dimensions of central office participation in implementation. Accordingly, we focus the rest of the chapter on the human dimension of reform in the central office.

INFORMAL CENTRAL OFFICE STRUCTURES TO SUPPORT IMPLEMENTATION OF PORTFOLIO MANAGEMENT

To illuminate these human dimensions of central office participation in implementation of portfolio management and the importance of developing an empirical base on these dimensions, we reviewed literature on school district central offices that addresses what central office administrators do when they participate in reforms with demands at least partially similar to those of portfolio management reforms. More specifically, we asked: What does research teach about what central office administrators do day-to-day when they relate to schools and external organizations, use evidence to support school accountability, and productively close schools, all in ways consistent with portfolio management reforms? What conditions help or hinder them in engaging in such activities? We focused our review on a small but growing subset of empirical research on school district central offices that specifically reveals individual central office administrators' work practices and activities, as opposed to, for example, formal central office structures or broad overall district policy decisions.

In the sections that follow, we argue that when central office administrators engage in the demands associated with portfolio management, they participate in specific types of ongoing activities aimed at shaping the flow and substance of information and relationships between the central office and groups inside and outside the district. The administrators' productive participation in these activities seems to hinge on the availability of new formal structures and also on other kinds of social and institutional supports for their engagement in new, nontraditional roles and routines.

New Performance Partnerships with Schools

The research on school districts is replete with instances of central offices engaged in top-down regulatory relationships with schools, even under reforms that are ostensibly based on empowering schools.[18] However, a handful of studies reveal what central office administrators do when they engage in supportive, capacity-building partnerships with schools similar to the performance partnerships encouraged in the designs of portfolio management reforms.[19] These studies are beginning to show that such relationships depend not only on the creation of a new unit within the central office but on how specific, dedicated administrators work between the central office and schools to facilitate new roles and relationships between the two that support implementation. These individuals are sometimes called "boundary spanners" or "boundary crossers."[20]

Honig identified specific activities involved when central office administrators work as boundary spanners to help schools build their capacity for designing and implementing their own approaches to teaching and learning improvement, including designing new, small, autonomous schools.[21] First, boundary spanners enable implementation of such reforms when they bridge or link their central office and schools together in particular ways. Boundary spanners do this by engaging with other central office administrators to examine information from school sites to help spark and guide the development of policies and practices supportive of school designs and implementation. Such bridging work involves both searching for information about school goals and experiences and also translating that information for the central office to help inform district policies and practices.[22]

Bridging activities seem particularly important in the context of port-folio management, where a system of diverse, high-quality schools may conflict with current policies and practices and require central office administrators to facilitate myriad policy and practices to support the design and implementation of new, diverse schools. This finding also reinforces that productive development of policies and practices to support diverse, high-quality schools may involve some a priori policy and practice development. However, particularly given the diverse range of schools that districts intend to include in their portfolio, central office administrators will be unable to predict in advance the various policy and practice changes that those schools might need to grow and thrive.[23] In such complex environments, central office administrators must continuously learn about what is and is not working at particular schools and use that knowledge from experience to inform central office supports.[24]

Second, Honig found that boundary spanners' bridging activities help enable implementation when they help build central office administrators' knowledge and relationships with participating schools that promise to facilitate the future development of policies and practices supportive of implementation.[25] After all, the authority and resources necessary to implement a reform as complex as portfolio management rest not with one or two central office units, but instead, the necessary authority and resources are spread among various administrators throughout a central office. Engagement of these additional administrators in developing policies and practices supportive of implementation may hinge substantially on the extent to which they understand what portfolio management reforms demand and the implications for their own units. Such engagement may also depend on the extent to which these other administrators have relationships with individual schools and the boundary-spanning administrators that facilitate the trust often necessary to prompt coordinated action throughout complex organizations.

Third, boundary spanners' bridging activities may also enable implementation when the spanners communicate central office requirements to participating schools.[26] Such activities may be particularly essential in the case of portfolio management initiatives that aim in part to open up opportunities to design and run schools for people and organizations without traditional school system experience. As Honig found in the context of new autonomous schools initiatives, the principals of some of these new nontraditional schools may not yet have essential knowledge of federal, state, and district policies fundamental to appropriate uses of public funds, even in a context that aims to prompt innovation. Boundary spanners may serve as main conduits of such information.

Boundary spanners also enable implementation by buffering or strategically limiting contact between central offices and participating schools. Buffering activities include working in coaching assistance relationships with schools to help build their capacity for high performance and thereby avoid central office intervention. Such activities also involve essentially vouching or covering for schools when they deviate from standard operation procedures or dip in their performance but otherwise seem to be on a trajectory toward improvement. In these ways, boundary spanners help create a space for schools, free of some outside interference, to enable implementation and, in some cases, innovation.[27] Such activities, too, seem particularly relevant to portfolio management reforms. As noted earlier, designs of these reforms seem to reflect the recognition that if central offices expect such reforms to help generate high-quality school options, central office administrators may need to engage with participating schools in hands-on assistance relationships to help build their capacity for results. Likewise, especially early in implementation when central office (as well as federal and state) policies and practices may not yet fully support the portfolio management schools, boundary spanners may enable implementation by standing between participating schools and such outside influences and helping schools pursue promising strategies not necessarily authorized (but also not explicitly prohibited) by such policies and practices.

These boundary-spanning activities are both helped and hindered by various resources and conditions, including the formal organizational structures of school district central offices.[28] For example, central offices tend to hire boundary spanners into new positions and subunits such as those formed to implement the portfolio management reforms. They also tend to hire into those positions and subunits people with little or nontraditional experience in education. Early in his tenure, New York City Chancellor Joel Klein, for example, replaced some of the school system's key management corps with people who had legal and financial backgrounds rather than experience in schools. More generally, Hill and colleagues note the presence and prevalence of "MBAs, public policy experts, or educators with unconventional backgrounds, for example Teacher for America (TFA) alumni" in portfolio district leadership teams.[30]

By hiring noneducators and nontraditional educators, central office leaders hope to aid implementation by entrusting it mainly to new central office staff who are likely not to be hampered by old, long-standing central office routines that threaten to impede implementation. On the hierarchical margins of the central office, boundary spanners may find freedom for taking risks in their own work essential to enabling implementation. On the flip side, these strategies may also hamper boundary spanners' participation in implementation. For example, their status as new nontraditional employees in hierarchically marginal positions means they do not necessarily have the positional power to effect some of the changes throughout the central office necessary for implementation and they may lack knowledge of long-standing policies and practices essential for changing them. As new employees in hierarchically marginal positions, they may lack the relationships and networks throughout the central office necessary for effective policy changes supportive of implementation.[31]

Honig's studies suggest by negative example that boundary spanners might manage this paradox productively and otherwise support implementation if, among other things, they had available to them new models of central office practice consistent with reform demands. She also argues that relying mainly on boundary spanners to spearhead implementation of reforms that require involvement of all central office units is fundamentally limited; their work would be significantly aided by additional intensive efforts on the part of superintendents and other central office leaders to engage the whole office in reforming their work practices and relationships with schools in support of implementation.[32]

New Performance Partnerships with External Organizations

What does research on school district central offices suggest administrators do when they forge relationships with outside organizations that seem associated with positive school outcomes—or at least with creating conditions theoretically conducive to such outcomes? To address this question, we turned to research on reforms that, like portfolio management, demand that central offices engage in performance partnerships with various kinds of external organizations. This research includes studies that address school district central office engagement with charter schools and private school management organizations as well as nonprofit school reform support providers.

Overall, we find that when central offices engage with such organizations, especially organizations that take on key roles and responsibilities within the district system to support school improvement, central office administrators do not simply write contracts and monitor compliance. Rather, they participate in ongoing negotiations with members of the external organizations about the terms and focus of the relationships, even once formal contracts are in place. The contracts involved in educational improvement initiatives such as portfolio management are likely to be "incomplete contracts," in part given the difficulty and the impracticality of crafting a contract that details all the activities of the contractor. Studies of contracting in social services more generally highlight that such open-ended contracts are unavoidable when dealing with complex services with multidimensional outcomes.[33] Such contracts are a far cry from the arm's-length product-exchange relationships implied by some market-based contracting models.[34] Accordingly, central office administrators in partnership with members of external organizations likely must continually assess the terms of the partnership and how to grow and change their relationships as implementation advances and conditions change.

Research on school district central offices provides some illustrations of these dynamic human dimensions in how central offices engage in relationships with outside organizations that seem to help them realize their school improvement goals. Supovitz, for example, described an ongoing and evolving partnership between Duval County Public Schools (DCPS) and the National Center on Education and the Economy (NCEE).[35] He showed how, over the course of four years, central office staff first moved away from purchasing instructional materials from NCEE and attempted to develop those materials in-house but then over time reverted to purchasing the materials from NCEE, though reserving the right to customize those materials at their discretion. Supovitz underscored the continuing and complex nature of these relationships when he observed that "when the thing that is outsourced is a service . . . then the outsourcer [in this case, the district central office] needs to remain intimately involved because of the on-going nature of the transaction and the need for [it to be] . . . integrated with other resources."[36]

Similarly, central office administrators in Oakland Unified School District in California and a long-standing school reform support provider in Oakland (the Bay Area Coalition for Equitable Schools, or BayCES), established an initial memorandum of understanding between themselves and Oakland Community Organizations that specified distinct roles and responsibilities for each party in the implementation of new, small, autonomous schools.[37] Over time, the relationships were far more dynamic than that. For instance, early in implementation when the central office had little internal capacity for such activities, BayCES designed and ran an incubator for new schools to help school design teams develop new, small, autonomous school designs. As central office staff developed the capacity to run the incubator, they became the primary people running it, and BayCES turned its attention to other areas of implementation. Honig and Ikemoto call such work on the part of external organizations "adaptive assistance," to capture its dynamic nature.[38]

Various conditions mediate the extent to which central offices and external organizations engage in such dynamic partnerships. For instance, in an effort to keep their relationships dynamic, central office administrators and members of outside organizations sometimes do not specify goals, roles, or responsibilities in a contract, and the absence of such starting or temporary agreements can frustrate the relationship.[39] As Bulkley, Christman, and Gold (see chapter 5 in this volume) and others note, in the early years of Philadelphia's portfolio management initiative, the central office and external partners did not have a clear agreement about their roles and responsibilities.[40] In part as a result, the various parties sometimes fell into outright conflicts over the terms of their relationship, particularly over the resources the central office was supposed to provide the diverse provider schools. Similarly, Rhim revealed how the state-appointed Board of Control in charge of restructuring Chester Upland School District in Pennsylvania set the stage for conflict when it decided to preserve that district's central office, even as it hired Edison Schools to take over most central office functions.[41] The central office and Edison continually clashed over issues such as who had access to particular forms of technology like the district's Internet services and who controlled decisions about the hiring and firing of school personnel.

Partnerships can also be frustrated if central office administrators fall back on long-standing institutional patterns, such as command-and-control relationships with schools and outside groups, which run counter to portfolio management reform demands. The administrators participating in portfolio management reforms may be particularly susceptible to such conservative tendencies. As research on decision making outside education has long shown, when organizational actors face new, nontraditional demands coupled with high stakes for failure and limited or ambiguous feedback on their performance, they tend to pursue activities they believe they can carry out easily and well and that follow patterns of familiar practice, even if those activities do not promise to help them realize their new goals.[42] Honig found similar patterns among new central office administrators, even those with nontraditional backgrounds in new positions and units.[43] Though not directly supported empirically, the availability of role models and ongoing supports for alternative forms of central office administration may enable implementation.

Accountability Systems to Support Improved School Performance

As noted earlier, building the kinds of accountability systems that performance management reforms call for likely requires substantial investments in computer hardware and software and instruments for collecting school performance data. Beyond these formal structures, research on districts, like broad research on decision making in bureaucratic organizations, also emphasizes that the power of such systems for actually informing school improvement hinges substantially on how people interact with them, including how people use evidence from these systems to ground their actual decisions. This research suggests that such evidence-use processes involve the ongoing search for various forms of evidence and central office administrators' efforts to grapple with whether and how to incorporate that evidence into their decision making.

When central office administrators engage in evidence-based decision making, they intentionally or sometimes unintentionally search for information to ground their decisions. In the context of portfolio management reforms, the administrators might search for information about how well schools are performing against objective performance measures. They might also gather evidence about school goals and strategies and what actually happens day-to-day in individual schools to help them understand why schools may be performing at certain levels and what kinds of supports might help them improve their performance. Recent studies of central offices suggest that the lessons central office administrators learn from their experience working with schools provide essential evidence for grounding administrators' efforts to improve the supports they provide to schools.[44]

As Honig and Coburn describe in a comprehensive research review, central office administrators routinely rely on "working knowledge," the knowledge teachers and other practitioners gather routinely as part of doing their work, to help them fill the sometimes substantial gaps in the information available through formal data systems.[45] Such knowledge includes information on individual students' strengths and weaknesses not captured by standardized tests as well as their prior knowledge of school conditions that might be helping or hindering student progress.[46] The importance of such evidence from experience or working knowledge to central office decisions suggests that emphases in some policy texts on building better student data systems address only part of the challenge central office administrators face when trying to use evidence to make decisions in portfolio management contexts.

Evidence use also involves central office administrators intentionally incorporating evidence into central office policies and practices.[47] Processes of social sense making are especially important to incorporation. That is, when administrators encounter information, its meaning is rarely self-evident, especially in complex social policy arenas such as education where school performance has multiple, complex root causes and influences. In such contexts, administrators and other decision makers must render information meaningful by grappling often with others about how to interpret particular pieces of information. For example, Coburn, Toure, and Yamashita revealed how district central office administrators all agreed that a particular school had low math scores, but they understood the same scores as stemming from different conditions and suggesting different remedies.[48] Drawing on decades of research on social cognition, Spillane and colleagues have shown how such dynamics are not fundamentally problematic but rather the unavoidable result of human cognitive processes that involve decision makers filtering new knowledge in terms of their prior knowledge and understandings.[49] The work contexts and professional norms of different administrators also shape their interpretations.[50]

This line of research on incorporation processes reveals that leaders and others enable evidence use when they create opportunities for central office administrators to come together with their colleagues and others to make sense of various forms of evidence.[51] For example, Spillane and Thompson revealed, by negative example, that absent such opportunities for social sense making, administrators and other decision makers are particularly likely to fall back on their own individual frames and interpret new information as confirming their existing practices and worldviews.[52] This suggests that portfolio management reforms need to address the time and other resources central office administrators likely will need to work ably with various forms of evidence in a portfolio management system.

Central Offices and the Strategic Closing of Schools

Compared to research on capacity-building partnerships and evidence use, research on central office administrators and school closure is relatively limited. Researchers have examined how school closures, including those imposed through reconstitution, affect community members, school personnel, and students.[53] However, central offices tend to appear in the background of these studies, if they appear at all. Despite these limitations, this literature does reveal that school-closure decisions tend to be politically and emotionally charged events that create particular challenges for central office administrators. Given the centrality of closures to portfolio management reforms, these challenges may be relevant to central office administrators implementing those reforms.

When schools close, teachers and administrators lose jobs and students experience disrupted routines. Researchers have argued that these consequences constitute costs that give the affected groups strong incentives to protest the closure process. These protests may become especially charged when closure decisions involve an overlay of racial politics. As an example of the latter, Menefee-Libey describes how some community groups in Chicago saw the closure of some schools under Renaissance 2010 "as less an education reform initiative than a power grab hostile to the interests of low-income people and communities of color." (See Menefee-Libey, chapter 3, this volume.) For example, one advocacy group in Chicago, Parents United for Responsible Education (PURE), characterized CPS's school closures under Renaissance 2010 as "part of Mayor Daley's war on Chicago's low-income families."[54] During protests over closings at the Chicago Board of Education, community activists accused board members of educational treason for supporting school closure and of "messing with the stability in the community."[55] Levin, Daschbach, and Perry's (see chapter 6, this volume) account of New Orleans shows that closures can threaten "stability in the community," in part by threatening employment opportunities; when school closures and reform threaten the jobs of local teachers and school personnel, they argue, the stakes—and the potential for conflict—become even more intense. These conflicts arise even in places where coalitions may form to support the closure of low-performing schools.[56]

These findings suggest that school closures under portfolio management reforms may demand that central office administrators launch significant efforts to address and otherwise manage such tensions so they do not derail the reform and, where possible, so that they marshal support for the reform. Along these lines, New York State revised New York City's mayoral control legislation to require local hearings in communities before closing a school or making other structural changes (e.g., co-locating schools or moving sites).[57] In response, the district has designated central office administrators to oversee public hearings on each school identified for closure. During these hearings, the administrators explain the district's rationale for closing particular schools and provide opportunities for community members and others to respond. Still, these hearings are hardly peaceful events.[58] For example, according to an account of one hearing, when a central office administrator tried to speak, "boos cascaded across the auditorium."[59] "Closing a school," says Klein, "is worse than a root canal. You're disrupting people's lives."[60]

Given these challenges, central office administrators might decide to avoid the school closures that are part of the theory of action of portfolio management reforms. As the chapter on Chicago elaborates, Renaissance 2010 as originally designed called for school closures, but recently has shifted its emphasis from school closures to turning around schools, an approach in which students are allowed to remain in the same building and school staff are replaced.[61] Experience shows that school closures have been relatively rare in school districts and the charter school sector.[62]

Assuming that school closures should be a part of portfolio management reforms, how might central office administrators productively manage the conflicts and tensions that seem part and parcel of such efforts? Research on how central office administrators manage such political dynamics is limited. However, a small handful of studies, coupled with emerging policy analyses, suggest that such management is a profoundly human and social process calling for administrators to continuously forge coalitions, partnerships, and other relationships with various community members. For example, Malen revealed how the passage of a reconstitution policy in a Maryland school district hinged substantially on the superintendent and others striking various agreements and deals to bring different stakeholders on board with the initiative.[63] However, in part because the superintendent did not do similar legwork during implementation, unproductive conflict arose between the central office and various school and community groups in ways that stalled and ultimately squelched implementation.

Similarly, Kowal and Hassel argue that central office administrators can minimize community opposition to closures if they actively involve community members as advisers or collaborators in the process, either in the development of closure criteria or in closure decisions themselves (other researchers warn of the perils of community involvement in closures).[64] As part of recent school closure processes, some school districts have assigned school district central office staff to facilitate community engagements about school performance data to educate community and school members on low-school performance in their neighborhood and to seek their input on responses. When state law requires that schools be closed, central office administrators in some of those districts have strategically positioned themselves between the community and the state, working to help engage community members in the closure, providing opportunities for members to process the loss and participate in the development of next steps for improving educational opportunities for young people in their neighborhoods.

Such activities seem to reinforce the importance of administrators playing boundary-spanning roles as part of the closure process. For instance,

Kowol and Hassel argue that district central offices can minimize the conflict surrounding school closures by communicating clearly with school communities about the closure process, the rationale for particular cases of closure, and the plans for moving forward (e.g., how the district will transfer student records, help place students in new schools, and—if needed—liquidate the school's assets).[65] This recommendation echoes the importance of some of the bridging activities noted earlier, in which administrators communicate and sometimes translate complex information about closure decisions to the public.

Although there is little evidence about how district leaders might support the effective participation of the central office in school closures, some of the same supports mentioned earlier seem applicable. The central office administrators in the specialized boundary-spanning roles in implementation might be particularly well suited to managing the political conflicts noted earlier. Given the high profile of school closures, however, superintendents and other executive central office leaders can support those staff by participating centrally in the closure process and ensuring that all central office staff are on the same page and delivering the same message about which schools will close and why. When superintendents publicly override school closure decisions announced by other central office staff, they risk undermining the credibility of those staff and fueling tensions between them and the community members and school leaders they aim to support.[66]

SUMMARY AND IMPLICATIONS

In this chapter, we started with the assumption that central offices have vital roles to play in the implementation of portfolio management systems. In virtually all districts, only the public system has the authority to open and close public schools in the ways that the portfolio management reforms demand. Furthermore, the kinds of intensive, ongoing policy development in support of school implementation assumed under portfolio management require substantial involvement by central office administrators, who must work those changes through the systems in which participating schools operate. However, meeting these demands poses significant challenges for school district central offices. Administrators may address those demands in part by developing particular formal structures such as new units to manage the portfolio. However, informal structures within central offices—that is, how people within the central office go about their work—are arguably more consequential to implementation. For example, specialized units within central offices may or may not enable implementation, depending on what staff of those units actually do day-to-day and how they relate to schools and external organizations. In our discussion earlier, we have elaborated some basic work practices that seem consistent with demands of portfolio management.

This analysis has several implications for the practice and research of portfolio management. First, the work practices we begin to elaborate may provide a useful guide for practitioners interested in implementing portfolio management reforms. These work practices suggest, for example, that staff of dedicated portfolio management offices might think of themselves as boundary spanners working between the central office and schools and external organizations to improve the flow of information among those organizations and otherwise to help build all participants' capacity for seeding and supporting high-performing schools. Those boundary spanners or perhaps other central office administrators should anticipate significant conflict around school closures and develop processes appropriate to their communities for mediating those conflicts in productive ways.

But boundary spanners cannot go it alone. Their work is fundamentally contingent on the engagement of other central office administrators in other central office units that interface with schools. Other administrators in units related to finances, human resources, and facilities, for example, oversee resources and have authority to change policies that may help or hinder the implementation of individual schools in a portfolio. Their participation in implementation becomes especially important if those schools are realizing the promise of portfolio management reform designs and taking innovative (or at least nontraditional or uncommon approaches) to school improvement that do not fit neatly into existing central office resource-allocation or policy patterns. The second implication for practitioners then is that central offices may not participate productively in implementation if they relegate implementation just to a dedicated unit or if they treat portfolio management as a discrete program, rather than as a more fundamental cross-cutting approach to rethinking how schooling happens in whole district systems.

215

For researchers, our review suggests the importance of extending the descriptions provided in the current wave of portfolio management case studies to include more detailed analysis of implementation dynamics, particularly within central offices. Such research demands looking in depth at the day-to-day work of central office administrators in portfolio management districts as they support, assess, and hold schools accountable. Potentially productive questions to anchor that research include: In those settings, which central office administrators actually participate in implementation? What work practices do those people engage in? With what results? Do those work practices seem to help enable implementation, or are there ways they frustrate implementation? In sum, as these fundamental questions suggest, the main implication of this chapter for both research and practice is that both arenas need to pay more careful attention to the participation of school district central offices in portfolio management as fundamental to supporting and understanding how that reform unfolds.

8

—

A Framework for
Designing Governance in Choice
and Portfolio Districts

Three Economic Criteria

Henry M. Levin

Traditionally, school districts developed enrollment policies for their schools by setting attendance boundaries for most students according to their neighborhoods of residence. Some larger school districts provided a few schools that focused on specialized subjects such as the sciences, performing arts, or academic giftedness, allowing students to compete for places. And students with moderate or severe disabilities were typically assigned to schools with at least some specialized capacities to address their needs. In the latter part of the twentieth century, some urban school districts established choice options among a limited number of magnet schools across diverse neighborhoods, mainly to reduce the racial concentration associated with student segregation in neighborhood schools.

Starting in the 1990s, the United States witnessed a major shift from school assignment by attendance area to an increase in school choice based on parents' selection of schools for their children from a portfolio of different types of schools. Such schools, though supported by public funds, included not only schools operated directly by the school district but also private, nonprofit, or for-profit entities through district contracts or charter schools. Charter schools refer to schools operated independently of the local school district under state laws that waive most state and local regulations in exchange for a commitment to meet certain standards of service and performance.

In contrast with traditional assignment to neighborhood schools, district models based predominantly on choice make it possible for families to choose among district schools located in different neighborhoods, charter schools, and schools established by contracts between school districts and private providers. Presumably, the overall quality of education is improved through a closer matching of parental and student talents, interests, and learning styles and the schools of choice. And, competition for students among the different schools is expected to create incentives leading to higher school effectiveness and performance than with a district monopoly over educational provision.

More recently, there has been discussion of districts establishing all schools as based on parental choice. A particular approach to a choice district is the portfolio management model. This model combines choice at the level of students and families with the district intentionally managing the supply of available schools. School districts now considered to have adopted portfolio approaches include New York, Philadelphia, Chicago, Los Angeles, Washington D.C., New Orleans, and Hawaii, the only state that also functions as a school district. Currently, school districts that have employed the portfolio model still administer most of their own schools even if they promote choice among them, and there also exists a range of other publicly funded alternatives such as charter schools.

An important distinction between choice districts and portfolio districts involves the role of the market versus that of the central office. Full-choice approaches embrace consumer demand as expressed through the market to play the dominant role in determining which schools and types of schools to open or close. In portfolio districts, the central office actively manages the portfolio, both closing schools (operated by either the district or a private provider) that do not meet district expectations for performance and opening new schools or contracting with other organizations to open new schools. Thus, for portfolio districts, choice by families and students plays a less central role in ensuring the quality of schools available in the district, and government officials must have the capacity and will to make informed decisions guided by a set of criteria that is aligned with the collective well-being of the jurisdiction and open to public scrutiny and debate.

School districts that have employed the portfolio model, still administer most of their own schools even if they promote choice among them, and there also exists a range of other publicly funded alternatives such as charter schools. But, more recently, there has been discussion of establishing full systems of school choice, so-called choice districts in which all schools would operate independently from the traditional governance of the district. Of course, this raises the question of what role the school district might play in this form of organization. Hill, Pierce, and Guthrie have suggested that the district's role would be primarily to solicit, select, and establish contracts with providers and evaluate the subsequent performance of the schools for prospective contract renewal or replacement.[1] But, there has also been discussion of charter school districts, ones that would be comprised completely of charter schools. Presumably, the district administration would be responsible for converting its existing schools to charter schools as well as encouraging the establishment of new charter schools following state procedures for doing this. Once having done this, the charter schools would operate under the authority of the chartering school agency, usually an office of the state government.

The largest U.S. school district that has undertaken the path to become a choice district, after first having established itself as a portfolio district, is New Orleans, pressed by a calamitous natural disaster.[2] The devastation wrought by Hurricane Katrina in August 2005 led most of its residents to flee the city. More than half of the population suffered serious housing damage, and many others left because of the loss of services and of public dangers.[3] Prior to Katrina, New Orleans had 128 public schools serving 65,000 students in a school district that had been losing enrollment while experiencing high educational failure and substantial corruption.[4] The Louisiana Department of Education viewed a majority of schools as academically unacceptable, and failures on the high school exit exams were more than 90 percent in both reading and mathematics, with high dropout rates as well. Katrina spared only 16 schools, the rest sustained serious damage, and one-third were left unusable. The exodus of students along with the general population led to the closure of most schools and the layoff of almost all New Orleans Public School employees.

The strategy for resurrecting the school system was to permit a combination of authorities to operate the schools, with the New Orleans Public Schools maintaining five magnet schools and the state's Recovery School District (RSD) operating many schools directly. In addition, three different authorities—the New Orleans Public Schools, the RSD, and the state's charter school agency—have authorized a large number of charter schools, comprising more than half of all New Orleans schools.[5] This highly decentralized strategy had three goals: repairing and opening schools and enrollment places to keep pace with the largely unpredictable flow of families returning to New Orleans; flexibility in order to be accessible to family location decisions and provide educational offerings to meet student needs; and an attempt to raise overall educational quality of schools and student performance. Much of the strategy was based on providing some competition among schools for students through choice.

By 2009–2010, enrollments had risen to thirty-eight thousand, a bit more than half of what they had been prior to Katrina. Of the eighty-eight schools, fifty-one are charter schools serving 61 percent of the population. In addition, there are several alternative schools and magnet schools, with another thirty-one schools still run directly by the RSD, but subject to choice. An overwhelming portion of the students are minority and are eligible for the Free and Reduced-Price Meals program, an indicator of poverty. Although no official plan is evident for complete conversion to a choice district, both the CEO of the RSD, Paul Vallas, and the state superintendent, Paul Pastorek, have referred frequently to converting most of the existing schools to charter schools, a perspective supported by other groups contemplating the future of New Orleans schools.

The New Orleans case brings into high relief both the need for and the puzzling absence of serious efforts to envision the governance challenges presented to districts that sharply increase their reliance on consumer demand and actively managed supply. Despite the radical changes already in place, current leaders' indications of an intention to move further, and the fact that the current governance arrangements are ad hoc and considered to be transitional toward resumption of some kind of more locally centered home rule, there have been few attempts to explicitly plan for what overall governance of such a district would entail. Part of the explanation for the lacuna probably is specific to New Orleans, where sensitive issues of race and class make school governance a hot potato that few political actors are eager to grab. Another, more general explanation is that discussions of choice districts often have relied on simplistic notions about self-governing markets in which less government is always preferable to more.

What kind of governance authority would be needed, and what would its roles be? The purpose of this chapter is to begin to address the need for an overall governance framework by drawing on some broad purposes of education, roles that are designed to satisfy their purposes, and the assignment of specific dimensions of educational operations to individual schools, the marketplace, and a more central authority.[6] I will draw guidelines from the economic concepts of economies of scale, externalities, and transaction costs and argue that all three of these principles must be considered to create an efficient quasi-market or choice system for education.

PURPOSES OF EDUCATION

Before addressing the ramifications of a dramatically different approach to organizing education and school operation, one must ask a larger question: to what end? Education is a productive activity that draws on resources such as personnel, facilities, equipment, materials, and intellectual property that have other uses in society.

Clearly, it is assumed that educational activity yields benefits that are expected to exceed the value of these resources, and changes in the organization of education are undertaken to enhance the putative benefits of the educational system. In reorganizing education, we wish to take account of how the changes can maximize the value of these benefits, relative to any additional costs.

Perhaps the key feature for addressing the benefits of education and schooling is that they encompass both private and public dimensions. Private benefits include those that are conferred on and limited to the individuals being educated and their families. Families usually favor specific approaches to the rearing of their offspring, and they prefer schools that promote similar perspectives in the schooling process. Students who receive more and better schooling benefit from greater understanding of themselves and their society and are able to convert their skills into private gains of higher income, better occupations, favorable personal contacts, enhanced health, and greater political efficacy.[7] These benefits can be substantial for both educated individuals and their families.

But, mass education is also the major mechanism for mounting a society that is educated to understand, accept, and function within a universally accepted set of institutional premises. A smoothly functioning society means that all or most of its members accept a shared understanding of the values and premises that underlie the legal, political, social, and economic foundations that constitute the society. Much of the educational process is premised on creating a common experience for all of the young that enables them to understand these institutions and prepare them for effective participation. This goal is the rationale for the repeatedly heard aim of "education for democracy."[8] In short, a major function of the system of schooling is to reproduce the most basic functions and institutions of society from generation to generation through the common socialization of the young.

In addition, schools are charged in democratic societies with being the major social intervention for giving all of the young a fair chance of obtaining life's rewards or equality of opportunity. This mission entails adoption of various approaches to creating equity in the allocation of resources and educational outcomes to compensate for initial differences among children in family resources at birth and in early childhood.[9]

Much of the tension over the organization of schools and the purposes of schooling can be understood by realizing that individual educational goals and aspirations of students and their families may be in conflict with societal goals of equity and the integration of all of the young into societies' most fundamental institutions. For the individual and the family, the solution is for schools to provide a diversity of educational choices, encouraging schools to match as closely as possible their private aspirations and capabilities. For society, the solution is to provide a common educational experience that will introduce all of the young to the fundamental institutions that comprise society with the capacity for full participation in those institutions.[10]

We can see these tensions more clearly if we evaluate the functions of schools according to four commonly asserted criteria: (1) freedom to choose; (2) productive efficiency; (3) equity; and (4) social cohesion. We can use these criteria to see how well any particular system of education performs.

1. *Freedom to choose.* This criterion places a heavy emphasis on the private benefits of education and the liberty to ensure that families choose schools that are consistent with their child-rearing practices. Just as families wish to set the type of conditions that will influence their children's growth and development overall, they wish to choose schools that reinforce their values and goals. Purely market-based choice systems elevate this value above all others, but pragmatic and democratically responsive choice systems and those incorporating active management of supply treat freedom of choice as an important consideration that is at times in tension with other equally important values.

2. *Productive efficiency.* This criterion refers to obtaining maximum educational results for any given resource constraint placed on the schools. With a provision of similar resources, some forms of school organization are viewed as being more productive than others. Advocates of choice believe that competition among schools will increase productive efficiency relative to the central administration of all schools by matching students to schools more effectively. In contrast, proponents of portfolio management approaches believe that unconstrained competition can be destabilizing, that consumer exit is an unreliable instrument for ensuring educational quality, and that nurturing the conditions for productive efficiency can require direct intervention.[11]

3. *Equity.* This criterion refers to the quest for fairness in access to educational opportunities, resources, and outcomes by gender, social class, race, language origins, disability, and geographical location of students. Education is one of the key attributes of a person or group that can be used to more nearly equalize opportunities of individuals or groups born with unequal advantages. Here, the definition becomes important because many advocates of choice, such as Milton Friedman, have argued that choice itself provides equity in the sense that the same options are theoretically available to all.[12] This interpretation is challenged

by those who argue that families with greater resources, knowledge, access to information, and experience with consumer choice are best situated to take advantage of a choice solution and obtain the most favorable options.[13] That is, choice may tilt the playing field in favor of more advantaged families and outcomes, perhaps even more than the current system based on neighborhood of residence.[14] Portfolio management may dedicate deliberate efforts to recruit schooling providers that are able and willing to locate and have success in communities and for niche populations that market forces leave inadequately served.

4. *Social cohesion.* This criterion refers to the provision of a common educational experience that will orient all students to grow to adulthood as full participants in the cultural, social, political, and economic institutions of our society. In turn, this goal is usually interpreted as requiring common elements of schooling with regard to curriculum content, embedded values, goals, language, and political socialization. Choice advocates argue that social cohesion requires only minimal curriculum requirements in terms of exposure to subjects.[15] Others such as Barber, Dewey, Goodlad, and Gutmann assert that social cohesion and democracy require a much fuller common process and deeper content than a listing of general curriculum requirements.[16]

Instruments of Design

To a large degree, it is possible to design forms of school organization and responsibility that balance the choices of families' with the goals of a publicly accountable school system. This can be carried out by employing the three instruments of policy design: finance, regulation, and support services.

Finance. The level and distribution of financial support can make a large difference in both public and private benefits. The higher the level of finance—whether for existing public schools, charter schools, or vouchers—the larger the variety of educational choices that can be offered to families. With greater financial provisions, suppliers will offer a richer range of alternatives. This is true for both public and private choice where additional resources permit suppliers to offer a higher quality and greater range of educational strategies for both communities and individual children. This is also true for the education of students with special needs, where additional funding increases both the choices for those families as well as the likelihood of increased equity.[17]

The presence and form of financial incentives to improve education can affect the productive efficiency of schools. It is possible to provide financial incentives to schools that demonstrate success in given educational domains.[18] Equity can also be affected by finance. For example, whether philanthropists assist in financial support of schools and whether parents are permitted to pay for additional services will affect equity to the degree that these options will depend on family income and philanthropic relationships. Children in poorer households are unlikely to be able to benefit as much from schools requiring parent contributions as are students from wealthier families, resulting in stratification of schools by family income. Of course, if philanthropic funding or public funds were used educationally to compensate for lack of family resources of low-income families, they could be used to improve equity.

Regulation. Regulation largely ensures the provision of public benefits. States commonly create requirements for curriculum, testing, personnel qualifications, and student admission that will ensure equity and social cohesion. Although different regulations may be attached to private schools, voucher schools, and charter schools than to public schools, all types are regulated to some degree by the states.

Not all regulations have implications for public benefits, so there is no reason to believe that the present mix of state laws and local regulations is optimal for that purpose or even fully appropriate. Many regulations were established at the behest of specific constituencies, such as educational professionals and providers, or specific populations with the political power to lobby for advantages for their members. These may even have negative consequences for both private and public benefits of education. Nonetheless, specific types of regulation can be forged for designing the level of and balance among public and private benefits.

Curriculum and testing requirements may be introduced in behest of establishing public accountability for resource use and efficiency, greater equity among students, and social cohesion in terms of exposing all students to at least some elements of a common educational experience. Friedman suggests that a minimal required curriculum content is necessary to ensure the acceptance of a set of common values for democracy to function.[19] Such curriculum and instructional requirements also are designed to assure that children with disabilities receive an appropriate education, a concern for equity.

Support services. Support services refer particularly to those that enhance effective decisions in choosing schools. In particular, choice does not work well unless there is a wide range of options and choosers are informed about differences among them. In most cases, this suggests a system of transportation to provide student access to a reasonable range of schools as well as a system for providing accurate and useful information on alternatives. Such support services contribute not only to better school choice, but also to productive efficiency in promoting competition. Moreover, they support equity because especially the poor, minorities, and less educated lack access to transportation and have the least knowledge of differences among schooling alternatives.[20] Support services in portfolio districts can also include more conventional district support such as technical assistance and teaching resources to raise quality in schools that are deficient.

Some portfolio management systems bring to the fore a different kind of support services, in which schools rather than students become the key target. The system in New York City is an example of a portfolio model that shifts control over many budget elements to school-level decision makers, requiring them to purchase support services (e.g., professional development, teacher recruitment, targeted instruction for special populations) from public and private providers. Here, as with other policy instruments, experience suggests that the landscape of service providers must be cultivated, weeded, and pruned periodically. The purpose of this activity is to ensure that important decisions about whether and how to maintain a public-support option, ensuring balance between local and nonlocal providers, and assuring that schools have the information and capacity they need to make their choices well.

Trade-offs and Preferences

There are many ways that the policy tools of finance, regulation, and support services can be used to address the four criteria outlined. Some detailed examples are found in the application of this framework to the design of educational vouchers.[21] In theory, it is possible to design approaches to school choice that provide an appropriate balance among the various public and private benefits. However, there can be tensions and even contradictions between fulfilling some types of benefits and fulfilling others. This means that intrinsically there may be trade-offs in choosing among benefits and their specifics. Some goals cannot be fully attained without sacrificing others.

For example, freedom of choice could be expanded by allowing families to add their own financial resources to whatever the government provides and allowing schools to make supplementary charges, as Friedman suggests for his voucher plan.[22] Such a plan would certainly increase the range of choices for many families, but not for poorer ones. Moreover, it would likely lead to greater income stratification and segregation in schools than the current residentially based system. This would mean that the advantage in increasing private benefits through greater choice would be offset by greater inequality and stratification of students among schools, undermining public concerns of equity and social cohesion.

Or consider a plan to increase social cohesion by requiring a common curriculum, teacher credentialing standards, testing, and admissions that limit racial and social class segregation through the use of a lottery to choose among applicants. Such a plan will tend to make schools more uniform in their offerings and instructional approaches, thus raising social cohesion and equity, but it will reduce freedom of choice as all schools are beset with greater uniformity and may lead some private providers to refrain from entering the local market if their established practices and "brand" might be compromised. Likewise, trade-offs will be necessary for enacting a plan to increase equity by increasing funding and support services such as transportation and information services for students from low-income and minority families and those with special needs. The impact of these provisions might raise equity and increase freedom of choice through greater accessibility and the addition of an intensive information system with interactive Web site, print, radio, television, and counseling personnel that would benefit, especially, the most disadvantaged families. But the very high costs of transportation and information would reduce productive efficiency of overall resources by leaving a smaller share of the educational budget for instruction.[23]

There is no optimal system that provides maximal results among all outcome criteria. Ultimately, the selection of design features and their consequences must depend on specific preferences and values as transmitted through democratic institutions, a reality that is presently reflected in the differences in educational provisions that exist among the states and local educational entities. As school choice and portfolio management expand, it is necessary to consider the consequences for both private and public benefits and how these can be balanced. And it is important to remember that there are many major and subtle features of finance, regulation, and support services that can be enlisted to achieve this balance.

ROLES AND RESPONSIBILITIES

Obtaining balance between a system predicated on freedom of choice for both families and schools and a system that meets the goals of productive efficiency, equity, and social cohesion is a formidable challenge. Unlike laissez-faire choice systems, a key premise of portfolio management is that society cannot depend on unregulated markets to settle on the best balance. In the following, accordingly, I will assume that it is necessary to have a central governing unit (CGU) that will ensure that this balance is met and that roles are assigned to both individual schools and the CGU, and perhaps intermediate service units, to ensure that the challenge is met. In this section, I will introduce many of these roles and set out criteria that might be used for allocating them to the two principal levels. The term *CGU* is used here to be clear that central governance need not be relegated to an existing or traditional school board, but whatever arrangement is established by the responsible authorities at the state and local levels.

Roles

Among the roles needed in providing education in a choice system are the following:

- Choice rules and procedures
- Curriculum and instruction of schools
- Funding and financial accounting

- Provision of information
- Student accounting
- Personnel requirements, screening, selection, and portability of benefits
- Adjudication of disputes
- Transportation
- Admissions decisions
- Purchasing
- Accountability for educational outcomes
- Treatment of special populations (ELL, special education, gifted and talented)
- Technical assistance

All of these capacities must be established for any choice district, such as one based strictly on the emergence of charter schools. But, when the choice system is based on portfolio management of offerings, there are other roles to consider. These focus on the deliberate attempt to balance available offerings in terms of location and availability as well as to assess performance and gauge fulfillment of public-goods dimensions of education. In a portfolio-managed district, it is necessary to actively contract with school suppliers for the range and quality of school services and to evaluate their performance as well as to calibrate the mix of schools and to have the capacity to minimize disruption if contracted or charter schools depart suddenly.

- Establishing and monitoring performance contracts for school management
- Actively managing supply
- Retaining core public-sector capacity to ensure continuity

Even a cursory review of this list suggests some roles that must be satisfied within schools and some that require the CGU to establish greater uniformity of system operation and a level and effective playing field. Further, there needs to be coordination and collaboration between the two levels. Clearly, a portfolio-managed district will require far more centralization in meeting its obligation than one based exclusively on charter schools. This does not mean that there are only two levels. Some of the best solutions might be to let the market or intermediate institutions or cooperative arrangements address these roles and responsibilities, but even these would have to be monitored because of public funding and the public interest in outcomes.

Before addressing the issues of responsibilities, it is important to set criteria for considering which of these entities should undertake these roles and responsibilities. Three organizational concepts, widely used in economics, are helpful for establishing operational guidelines: (1) economies of scale, (2) transaction costs, and (3) externalities.

Economies of scale. The economies of scale of an activity refer to the magnitude of production of a particular product or service that is compatible with the lowest average cost per unit of production. All productive activities are characterized by a fixed cost, which is the minimum resource required to sponsor the activity. That is, these resources must be in place before any productive activity can take place. But, in addition to fixed costs, additional resources are needed to accommodate an expansion in output. These are known as variable costs, which increase with the scale of output. In general, the fixed costs for a given production unit do not change for any specific range of production, meaning that the average fixed cost per unit of output falls as fixed costs are divided by more and more units of output. But, variable costs associated with each successive unit of output may be constant or rising. Average fixed costs per unit of output and average variable costs per unit of output comprise the average total cost per unit of output.

In general, the average cost per unit of output follows a standard pattern or U-shaped curve in which average costs fall as more and more units are produced and average fixed costs per unit fall. As output expands, the variable cost per unit (the cost of the next unit or marginal cost) rises. This rise in the average variable cost is due to many factors and ultimately offsets the falling average fixed cost as productive output rises. At some point, when combined, the two types of costs reach a minimum average cost per unit of output and then start to rise as the increasing average variable costs outweigh any decline in average fixed costs. This level of output is associated with the lowest average cost per unit of output and is considered the level at which one benefits from economies of scale. Beyond this level of output, diseconomies of scale set in, and average costs per unit of output rise. Thus, one wishes to take account of the level of activity that is at or close to the level where economies of scale are maximized. Although this is usually viewed as a unique output level—the lowest point on the U-shaped average cost curve—it is better thought of as an approximate range at which lower costs prevail.

Economies of scale characterize many productive activities. Special education provides a good example. Let us say that all individual schools are expected to provide special education services for any student who requires them. What if the parents of a student with a severe disability choose a particular school, and the student is enrolled, but no other students with similar disabilities enroll. The minimum provision for this kind of disability is a separate classroom with appropriate learning materials and equipment and a trained teacher. These are fixed costs that would be divided by the one student to get an average cost per student for this program. Assume that these fixed costs are about $100,000 a year for up to six students and only an additional $4,000 a year for materials for each student beyond the first one—so-called variable costs. Then the total cost per enrollee of one student with that disability at that school is $104,000 a year, rising to a total of $124,000 for six enrollees. The average cost per student in this program shows strong economies of scale, falling from $100,000 for the first one to about $20,000 when six are enrolled, the limit that can be managed by a single teacher.

This would mean that to operate such a program at the lowest cost per pupil (quality held constant) would require six students. And, there are many different severe disabilities (as well as moderate and minimum impairments) that are addressed among specific special education students, each requiring a program that benefits from economies of scale up to some maximum enrollment. Clearly, schools with modest overall enrollments would be unable to sponsor programs for every disability at the level that would benefit from economies of scale, so decisions need to be made about the special education roles and responsibilities for individual schools. This is further complicated by the issue of externalities, the benefits of such students receiving some or all of their education in environments with nondisabled students as required by law (Public Law 94-142), rather than being segregated in schools only with other special education students. In a choice environment, virtually no school is likely to have the optimal enrollment numbers for each disability where program economies of scale will be realized. In fact, for prospective students with severe disabilities or even moderate ones, a school may view the optimal enrollment as zero. Unless mandated to serve such high-cost students, potential new school providers might define their missions to shift that responsibility to others by refusing to accept students with that disability. If they are required to take any student within their enrollment capacities, they may discourage families from enrolling such students by suggesting "better" schools for that type of disability. Sharply graduated payments to schools to cover educational costs of appropriate programs for students with special needs might overcome some school-based selection biases, but if the underlying economies of scale are unfavorable, this will come at the cost of inefficiency at the system level.

Transaction costs. A second economic concept that underlies the appropriate establishment of roles and responsibilities is that of transaction costs. Although we may think that the cost of any transaction is just the price on an invoice, there are many other costs. Transaction costs for a good or service include a range of necessary efforts for establishing a complex purchase or contracting arrangement. First, there must be a specification of the good or service to be purchased as well as a search for providers and an evaluation of the qualities and costs and dependability of different sources. Such efforts entail the expenditure of time and effort to gather and assess information. Further, negotiations with potential providers may be required to get the best combination of price and quality. Finally, the transaction may require monitoring and enforcement to ensure that the services and goods meet specifications and the imposition of sanctions if they do not. All of these are considered to be transaction costs, and they explain, in part, why purchasers often stay with traditional suppliers that seem to charge somewhat higher prices, but have been shown to be reliable, and avoid the additional costs of search, negotiation, monitoring, and sanctions in the quest for a new supplier.[25]

Consider transaction costs from the perspective of parents searching for a school for their child. Good decisions are informed decisions, and the more alternatives that are available, the more information the parents need. One possibility is for the CGU or a contracted designee to gather a comprehensive set of general descriptions for all available schools that will be useful to parents in selecting, at least, initial prospects. The CGU could provide such information in printed materials and electronically on the Internet with the assistance of information counsellors, if needed. Even then, parents may need to fine-tune their knowledge by visiting schools to translate the information into its likely impact on student experience and learning or to seek additional information. In the absence of a more centralized approach to disseminating comparative information, each parent would have to carry out these tasks separately, imposing high total costs on the population.

The main transaction costs derived from the resources devoted to centrally gathering and compiling the information include the participating schools' efforts to provide the standardized data, editing and preparing the data in a usable and comparative format, and disseminating the information, as well as parents' time to evaluate the choices and, possibly, to contact schools for more information and to visit individual schools. There are many transaction costs involved in this CGU endeavor, but far more if left to parents to gather the data on each school individually, in the absence of CGU intervention. Consider how parents' efforts and time would multiply and how schools might be inconvenienced by a multiplication of individual requests for information, even if each had its own Web site or brochure. For example, if some schools lacked readily available data on dimensions of interest to some parents, it is likely that those parents would make additional demands on school personnel. And, such a system might be inefficient from a competitive perspective because the limited resources of parents would constrain them to consider fewer schools than if the CGU provided a wide array of information on all available schools.

In both cases, there are transaction costs, but it is likely that a well-designed, centralized, system providing comparable information among schools and with a sound dissemination system would reduce the need for parents' special efforts and schools' responses to impart commonly sought dimensions of schools. Centralizing the data system under the CGU as well as reporting the procedures for choosing a school would reduce or avoid many parental transaction costs that a system of individual parental initiative imposes. In a portfolio-managed system, the CGU's monitoring of schools and reporting of comparative measures of performance would also serve to reduce the costs of parents' individual search efforts.

Externalities. Externalities refer to the impacts of decisions made by and in behalf of individual entities, for example, a consumer or a firm, that may affect others who are not involved in that decision.[26] Externalities can confer benefits or costs on others. If a decision has a positive impact on others, it is viewed as an external benefit; if a decision has a negative impact, it has an external cost. Consider a neighbor who carefully maintains his home and property, with a magnificent garden and manicured lawn. Such a neighborhood presence will confer external benefits on surrounding homes, not only aesthetically, but also on the values of adjacent properties. Contrast this situation with the presence of a neighbor whose unpainted house is badly maintained, with trash in the yard and weeds replacing the lawn. In this case, there will be negative externalities or costs conferred on the neighbors in terms of their property values and vistas.

The justification for public funding of education is that it confers external benefits to society beyond those received by the individuals receiving the education. Friedman acknowledges this impact as a "neighborhood" effect that justifies public funding.

> A stable and democratic society is impossible without widespread acceptance of some common set of values and without a minimum degree of knowledge and literacy on the part of most citizens. Education contributes to both. In consequence, the gain from the education of a child accrues not only to the child or his parents but to other members of the society; the education of my child contributes to other people's welfare by promoting a stable and democratic society.[27]

Clearly, Friedman is referring to the criterion of social cohesion as the major justification for which he argued that government should fund basic education, although he also refers to concerns for equity in other passages.[28] A productive society that functions effectively requires a universal understanding and acceptance of a common set of values and knowledge that allows participation in the universal institutions that bind a society together, such as language; social, economic, and political institutions; and culture. These dispositions and knowledge are largely acquired through a common exposure to an education that integrates the young into these institutions so that they can function effectively as individuals and in concert with others. The universality of these experiences produces an external benefit by which a society is molded to function effectively in sustaining its basic social, cultural, economic, and political institutions, a benefit to society that goes beyond the sums of the individual benefits of education. Even a person who has not participated in the educational system receives the benefits of a better functioning society.

In addition to these direct and purposive external benefits of education, there are other external benefits that seem to arise indirectly from education. One of these is the impact that education has on the economic productivity of a society, even beyond the sum of the increased productive capacities of the individuals who receive the education.[29] Educated societies have greater economic productivity and other societal gains, even after taking account of the measurable economic benefits reaped individually.[30] More educated societies are healthier, reducing the demand for resources devoted to health as well as the transmission of disease among members, and they have higher levels of economic growth.[31] They also appear to have lower levels of corruption.[32]

Responsibilities

The central task of organizing a choice or portfolio district is that of specifying and reviewing carefully the operational roles and responsibilities that must be discharged to address the four criteria and satisfy the three policy-design dimensions of finance, regulation, and support services. Since the states are constitutionally responsible for the schools, it should be expected that many of the policy design decisions will be made at the state level. That is, the state normally determines how schools and much of the support-service requirements are financed and regulated. Even so, some of the financial support for schools is derived from the local level, usually from property taxes, and the local level can set its own additional regulations and support services such as information, transportation, and technical assistance for schools.

It is important to emphasize the lack of precedent for designing a local system based completely on choice and schools that are quasi-independent, although portfolio school districts can base some of their operations on the traditional distribution of responsibilities between schools and the central office. But, there is no precedent in the United States where a school district or state has provided funding but relinquished most educational decision making to individual schools. Chile has a voucher plan in which all schools, including municipal and for-profit ones, have great autonomy within a regulated market.[33] Holland sponsors a complete system of choice among public and nonprofit schools. Both have extensive regulations including curriculum and mandatory national testing. In the case of the Netherlands, there is also regulation of admissions, class size, and personnel qualifications. That is, although choice is integral to the Dutch system, bureaucratic regulation of schools exceeds that in the United States on such central matters as curriculum and personnel.[34]

In what follows, I will consider the specific functions of a system of school choice to consider which levels should take responsibility for the function. The illustrative nature of this exercise should be emphasized. Depending on the history, context, state educational regulations, and specific goals of the choice system, the roles and responsibilities may differ. In each of the following cases, I will suggest how the principles can be applied to particular functions regarding roles, governance, and decision making for "choice districts." However, the examples are meant to be guiding and instructive rather than specific for all situations.

Choice rules and procedures. These dimensions represent the overall framework of rules and regulations that choice schools must operate within. They establish the rules of the game and the scope within which individual schools must operate to participate. For example, they include the broad regulatory criteria regarding admissions policy, accountability, required components of the educational program, scheduling, testing, personnel qualifications, and other boundaries on school operations. Typically, these will set out criteria such as the minimum hours and days that the school must be in session or the minimum qualifications for personnel or the minimum curriculum or testing requirements. These responsibilities must be charged to the CGU, whether that is a local or state entity. In addition, the rules of the game must be set at this level with respect to the establishment and operations of schools and the rules of competition for students. Economies of scale, reducing transaction costs, and capturing externalities are justifications for placing these responsibilities with the CGU rather than at decentralized levels.

Curriculum and instruction of schools. At the heart of the educational enterprise is curriculum and instruction. The roles and responsibilities for this function are multilevel. The CGU must require a common experience for all students for at least part of the learning experience in order to meet the external requirements of education for contributing to democracy and social cohesion. Beyond that, there must be some commonality in curriculum offerings so that students can shift from one school to another if the school that they are attending is inappropriate. If each school creates an educational structure that is completely independent of that of other schools, it will inhibit the dynamics of competition and limit student choice by imposing serious transaction costs on switching. Thus, some commonality in curriculum and instruction is required for both democratic participation and competition among schools.

Beyond these broad goals of curriculum and instruction, individual schools can set their own unique approaches with specializations in particular subjects, explorations through field studies and research, or highly structured approaches to traditional subjects. Further, they can implement all curriculum and instruction themselves or contract with others such as private firms or community-based organizations for portions of educational activities. Some of their responsibilities can be shared with other organizations that have advantages in instructional specialization and scale economies rather than requiring individual schools to produce all instructional services themselves. In summary, the CGU, individual schools, and intermediate-level organizations need to undertake appropriate roles within the different components of curriculum and instruction to satisfy goals of choice, efficiency, and democracy. Balancing these may be made even more challenging when private providers claim proprietary rights over elements of their curriculum, setting limits on the degree of overlap possible and introducing both legal and training obstacles when teachers move across providers and build on previous experiences.

Funding and financial accounting. Funding of schools is largely a CGU activity if the resources are derived from public sources such as state and local taxes. Clearly, the authority to take up such tax collection for schooling purposes is empowered by state constitutions and state laws, and it is based on generating external benefits of education as well as on taking advantage of economies of scale and reducing the transaction costs of revenue collections. But, to the degree that schools are also permitted to obtain philanthropic and private funding, that responsibility will fall heavily on individual schools or intermediate organizations, although the CGU can also solicit philanthropic funds to be shared among all schools.

As public entities, the schools must be publicly accountable for their financial status. Every state has rules with respect to allowable classes of disbursements and the various protections that are required for public funds. Clearly, this responsibility must be charged to the CGU, using a uniform set of accounting procedures and rules as well as a system that makes it easy to comport with the financial requirements. Individual schools can pay expenses directly or authorize payments that will be disbursed by the CGU and duly approved and recorded. This system will capitalize on economies of scale and reduction of duplication of activities embodying transaction costs. Even philanthropic funds that are received by a public entity need to be accounted for in this manner, although the rules for spending may be more liberal.

Provision of information. Good educational decisions by parents and schools are necessarily informed decisions. As discussed earlier, both economies of scale in providing information and minimization of transaction costs support the development of a centralized provision of information. This overall information system can be supplemented by parent and school efforts, including collaboration among networks of parents with specific interests or schools that share common goals or sponsorship. The CGU or its designates, such as contractors collecting and disseminating information that will become available in usable form to all parties, should undertake the development of an information system that provides details on school characteristics and performance. Where principals are empowered to choose among service providers or support organizations, they, too, need high-quality information on providers and cannot depend alone on that offered by vendors. Usable information may also require the establishment of a user-friendly system of dissemination through provision of easily understood materials, abundant use of the popular media, and information counsellors to assist comprehension, especially for those audiences who do not have English proficiency. In fact, in areas with large concentrations of immigrants, an effort should be made to provide information in the key languages of those populations.

Student accounting. Both schools and the CGU need a record of school placements of students and their progress. For the CGU, all students subject to the compulsory attendance law must be in a recognized school. For schools, it is necessary to have background details on students, including their past educational records and details on their participation and accomplishments. Under both choice districts and portfolio districts, enrollment counts for more than one time period may be necessary to ensure that schools receive the per-pupil funds to which they are entitled and that the system recaptures funds if enrollments decrease. This suggests that both the CGU and individual schools share those parts of the student database that record student registration and progress. This may also be required for accountability, since the CGU will be responsible for the overall performance of the district's schools in terms of student placements and performance and such outcomes as graduation rates. Schools will also expect to share information from the CGU on students' past educational participation and performance in order to accommodate their needs.

Thus, student accountability will be a collaborative responsibility where the schools and CGU will share the information pertinent to their functions, but maintain confidentiality where such information is pertinent only to their own operation. By sharing the necessary information, transaction costs for acquiring data and constructing student records can be reduced, and economies of scale can be utilized for the overall maintenance of student records, but the financial incentive for schools to exaggerate enrollments means that the CGU will need to make arrangements for oversight and investigation.

Personnel requirements, screening, selection, and portability of benefits. Another area of collaborative endeavor is that of recruitment, screening, selection of personnel, and portability of benefits. Schools will choose their own teachers on the basis of the unique needs of the school and the fit of prospective teachers to those needs. In choice and portfolio systems, there are compelling arguments, and sometimes legal requirements, for locating these responsibilities at the level of the school or network provider. But, economies of scale and reductions of transaction costs also argue for a CGU role in widely recruiting a talented pool of teacher prospects and initial screening for eligibility. The CGU will also be responsible for setting or monitoring personnel requirements in terms of qualifications of candidates and verification, as well as criminal checks and other requirements such as those relating to nondiscrimination. Candidates who meet these criteria will be available as a pool for schools to interview, and schools will choose their staffs. Individual schools or networks can also seek their own candidates and refer them to the CGU for screening eligibility. One strategy would be to band with similar types of schools to form a network for seeking teachers. Even this would reduce transaction costs and take advantage of scale relative to each school recruiting alone.

In order to enhance competition among schools for teachers, it is important to consider establishing a system of portable benefits. Although each school or provider network might set its own pay and benefits package, some or all of the benefits should be portable so that a teacher can access accumulated benefits if he or she moves to another school. For example, vested pension benefits should be available if a teacher decides to take a teaching position elsewhere or if a school closes. This ability to make a transition will increase competition in the teacher labor market and make employment in that market more attractive by increasing alternatives if a particular placement does not work out. However, it will also require the CGU to establish a benefits framework—particularly provisions for pension—that can be adopted for all schools. Of course, participation in a state employees' pension system or a 401(k) could be used to address this end.

Adjudication of disputes. Just as students now switch schools because of disappointing educational results, safety reasons, or residential shifts, there will be cases when parents wish to switch schools under a district choice plan. Yet, the transfer from one school to another during the school year may entail conflict. This is particularly so if the school must commit resources for the entire year for each student, but receives reimbursement only once or twice during the year. After the reimbursement period, schools may be unwilling to transfer a portion of those funds back to a family to follow a student to another school. In this case, a dispute will arise, and the CGU must adjudicate it to make legitimate transfers from one school to another possible. One option is that the CGU retain a small amount of the overall school funding for such a purpose, so that the initial school can retain the funds that will cover its fixed costs, even when it loses a few pupils. The role of the CGU is based on economies of scale for this function and reducing the transaction costs of both schools and parents at adjudication. The need to anticipate legal costs associated with disputes will likely be greater in portfolio districts, where for-profit providers and charters and nonprofits linked within networks may have substantial legal resources to bring to bear. The CGU will also have to be prepared to judge parental challenges that schools have breached the overall rules, such as that required of student selection by lottery if applications exceed enrollment capacity.

Transportation. A major contributor to freedom of choice is access to transportation. If provision of transportation is minimal, an equity problem arises because only those with sufficient resources can seek multiple schooling options. At the same time, restriction of access also undermines productive efficiency by reducing competition among schools. But, transportation is very costly, particularly if each school is required to provide it to students from anywhere in a large school district. It is important to note that transportation costs are likely to rise considerably in a choice district because of more students being transported, the need for longer and irregular routes, and many small vehicles, each with a driver, replacing fewer, but larger school buses now used on regular routes. Further, the fact that routes may change continually as student and school patterns shift is also a source of uncertainty and higher costs.[35]

A compelling case for the CGU to provide transportation in conjunction with schools' needs is premised on all three economic guidelines as well as a typical feature of the market for transportation supply. Because of the high fixed costs of establishing a transportation network, there are economies of scale that extend considerably beyond individual schools and even small networks of schools. Transaction costs are also reduced by a CGU endeavor, because individual schools need not devote resources to searching for, negotiating contracting with, and monitoring transportation providers. And, external benefits are achieved by reducing overlapping transportation routes, resulting in less congestion, pollution, and needless waste of public resources. Avoiding congestion and pollution are particularly significant when one considers the intensive time period in which school buses operate—the commuter rush hours. Further, the high fixed costs to establish a company for school transportation have led to markets that are dominated by just a few firms with great market power over individual schools, but much less in relation to a larger bargaining unit, the CGU, that has the threat of setting up its own transport service.

There are at least two other reasons that the CGU can provide lower transportation costs and shorter travel times, leaving more educational resources that can be utilized for instruction. The first is that a CGU can divide the territory into geographically competitive sectors where there are adequate numbers of schools to establish meaningful competition, but not so much territory to be covered by transportation that time requirements for student commutes and costs are overwhelming. For example, the CGU could divide a city like New Orleans into three sectors, still providing thirty schools per sector for choice. Alternatively, a CGU could establish a hub-and-spoke system where students are first brought to a limited number of hubs and then distributed by dedicated routes directly to their schools. The CGU can implement this completely, or the schools can carry out transportation from the hubs to particular schools. In either arrangement, there would be great savings of money and student travel time as well as conferral of external benefits to the public.

Admissions decisions. Virtually all choice systems in the United States have restrictions on the degree to which individual schools can choose from among their applicants. The purpose of these restrictions is to give all families a fair chance of getting into their school of choice as well as to restrict schools from stratifying populations by race, ability, or social class. The main approach is to require that schools that have more applicants than places admit students by lottery. Clearly, it is important that an independent authority implement and monitor this policy because of the temptation for schools to deliberately select their students along race, class, and ability dimensions and because a fair lottery is associated with an independent agent. The CGU can contract with an independent entity to monitor applications, lotteries, and school rosters. The centralization of the lottery will reduce transaction costs of individual schools as well as provide economies of scale in procedures and implementation relative to each school undertaking this task (and provide an external benefit of fairness to the overall system).

Purchasing. Schools should have the options to purchase goods and services directly in the marketplace, in cooperatives, or by establishing consortia among schools to gain market power. In special cases, the CGU may be able to provide certain goods and services directly. Individual schools purchasing supplies or services from a market where there are few sellers will face less competitive prices than if intermediate units or (in a few cases) the CGU bargains in their behalf. Transaction costs may also be reduced through this arrangement. But, most importantly, the purchasing decision from alternative suppliers, including the CGU, should be completely discretionary on the part of the schools.

The only mandatory involvement of the CGU is in its financial accountability function, where it needs to monitor and review school purchasing decisions for unusual transactions. Many charter schools in the United States pay management fees to groups to operate their schools for very high fees. In some cases, these are special arrangements, not subject to market competition, in which family or close associates of the charter boards or staff are involved. The CGU should monitor these irregularities whenever it appears that transactions appear to be unusually costly or not directly related to school purposes.

Accountability for educational outcomes. To the degree that a choice district is viewed as an overall school system, or to the degree that portfolio schools receive rewards or sanctions based on performance contracting, the CGU must take responsibility for measuring and reporting educational results, a requirement also based on economies of scale. There are at least two parts to this role. The first is that of measuring results, which means all important categories of educational outcomes required by the state and public policy constituencies and families. This accountability information not only must serve the requirements mandated by higher levels of government, but also must contribute to the information system that parents and students use to assess educational performance in their choice of schools. If important outcomes are left unmeasured, schools will have an incentive to reallocate efforts in order to maximize the results that matter more to the visible bottom line.

The CGU must also assure the authenticity of the data by establishing consistent procedures for measurement, collection, and reporting of data and certify that assessment procedures are legitimate. It should establish a common process for measuring achievement and other performance criteria, for example, by establishing testing procedures and monitoring that assure common conditions in testing students from different schools. Unfortunately, the incentives for individual schools may not induce them to always meet the strict requirements by which tests are administered.

Treatment of special populations. There is a dilemma in requiring schools to accept all applicants or to abide by lotteries to determine admissions if there is an excess of applicants. Schools may not have the specific capabilities required to serve student populations with moderate to severe disabilities. In order to serve such populations, they would have to invest a substantial amount in personnel and, in some cases, facilities and equipment. To justify this investment, they need to have adequate numbers of students with similar disabilities. This economies-of-scale situation, which I discussed earlier, also has deep implications for equity. The rare incidences of a wide variety of such disabilities being present in adequate numbers in a typical student population mean that most schools will not have the economies of scale to accommodate every request for special education. Almost all of the schools that arise under charter legislation are small schools that can accommodate students with minimal disabilities, but not moderate and severe disabilities. To a lesser degree, the same challenge may occur for students who are English-language learners, and gifted and talented students, but most schools can find ways to accommodate these students.

In these cases, a choice district has to determine how to address the education of special needs populations. If such children are turned down by many individual schools for lack of capacity, it is clear that they become the responsibility of the CGU. The CGU must either arrange for specific schools to specialize in and address the needs of students with particular classes of disabilities or establish special schools to accommodate them. The placement of students in schools exclusively devoted to their disabilities would violate the requirements of Public Law 94-142. That law requires that such students be given an appropriate education in the least restrictive environment, a mandate for including such students in regular classrooms and among conventional school populations whenever possible.[36]

Portfolio districts sometimes also face questions relating to populations defined by their past behavior, for example, students who have had trouble with the law. Philadelphia, for example, contracts with private firms to run its special disciplinary schools. These do not raise the same legal issues as do schools that would concentrate students with disabilities recognized under federal laws, but they introduce their own set of complications, relating to social goals of rehabilitation, neighborhood anxieties about safety, and the limited ability of those students and their families to exercise either exit or voice in the same degree available to other families. Whatever the solution, in all of these kinds of cases, the CGU will have to decide how to handle this type of dilemma.

Technical assistance. Individual schools may need different types of technical assistance in the areas of financing and managing a school, personnel, curriculum, instruction, teacher evaluation, test preparation, and others. Portfolio districts may provide these services to reduce inequalities in initial school functioning or shift responsibility to schools for purchasing technical services previously offered by the central office, which can exacerbate the consequences of cross-school inequalities. Schools can rely on private consultants or firms in the marketplace or form their own collaboratives, with primary reliance on these intermediate organizations. However, to the degree that the CGU sets out a common set of experiences for social cohesion and democracy, it may also be important for the CGU to provide materials and training or to work with local colleges and universities to provide both pre-service and in-service professional development. This is a discretionary category that may or may not be needed, but will be particularly salient with large turnover in teaching forces among schools and can benefit from economies of scale at the CGU level. The portfolio districts discussed in this volume provide considerable technical assistance to all types of schools. Nurturing local institutions as sources of expertise may be especially important to districts concerned about disruptions that might lead outside vendors to shift to other markets. As I discuss later, concerns of this type may also lead a CGU to consider the need to retain its own pool of expertise.

Added Responsibilities of Portfolio Districts

In contrast to a choice district—comprised completely of charter schools—a portfolio district must undertake three other responsibilities in its key role to sustain and manage educational choice. It must have the ability to design and oversee performance contracts for contracted schools and plan and manage supply through the creation of new schools and the closure of low-performing schools. Finally, it must retain capacity to undertake core instructional services if providers experience chaotic operations or serious lapses in performance.

Performance contracting for school management. Contracting out to private providers is nothing new for local governments. For many decades, municipal governments have contracted for such services as vehicle maintenance, streetlight repair, parking enforcement, refuse collection, legal services, and data management. Nor is it new to many school districts, which frequently have contracted for services like school maintenance, facilities repair and refurbishment, construction, cafeteria management, and school bus transportation. The move toward portfolio management, though, is notable for both the quantitative and qualitative shifts entailed. Especially important is the movement toward contracting for core instructional components rather than more peripheral support services.

Van Slyke, in reviewing the general empirical literature on privatization, highlights a common finding: "To reap the benefits of competition, government must be a smart buyer, a skillful purchasing agent, and a sophisticated inspector of the goods and services it purchases from the private sector."[37] Applied to portfolio systems, this lesson is a reminder that designing, overseeing, and enforcing contracts, including terminating contracts with failing providers and closing or radically reconstituting underperforming schools, likely calls for technical expertise, administrative capacity, and political will. These requirements may differ in kind and degree from those typically available in traditional districts and from those demanded in more market-based choice systems in which supply-and-demand interactions between families and individual schools are presumed to be the driving force of adaptation and change. The qualitative shift toward contracting for services more directly related to core instruction makes the need for special skills and capacities even more critical. Evaluating performance is more complex because of the presence of many potentially competing goals, the overriding importance of long-term consequences, and the complexity of judging what constitutes "good teaching" based on observation and measurement. These features add considerable transaction costs to contracting of education relative to public services with straightforward outcomes.

Active management of supply. The management of school supply refers to the development and balancing of the school portfolio among district-managed schools, magnet schools, contracted schools, charter schools, and other alternatives. Each type of school entails different district capacities for establishing a school, monitoring or managing it, and assessing performance. Districts need to recruit educational entrepreneurs to initiate new schools and transform existing ones and to assist providers with start-up capital and facilities or other assistance. These roles require resources that go beyond those normally found in conventional and static school districts that lack these dimensions and dynamics.

Experience with charter schools, for example, has made it clear that authorities cannot simply wait until a school withers and dies based on the exit of dissatisfied parents. Even when the schools in question are deeply dysfunctional, charter authorizers have discovered that many parents remain loyal and angrily oppose attempts to intervene. Evidence suggests, moreover, that turning around failing schools is much more complicated than commonly thought or than starting good new schools from scratch. For example, as part of Chicago's portfolio management strategy demonstrated, the simple announcement of an impending closure had negative consequences for learning, with dislocated students typically ending up at schools that were little or no better than the ones closed down.[38]

Retention of core public-sector capacity. Intellectually honest proponents of market arrangements concede that the competitive dynamics that they count on to generate innovation and efficiencies can also be disruptive and destructive, particularly in the short run. A supermarket closes down in an inner-city neighborhood, for example: eventually this may open up an opportunity for a locally rooted entrepreneur, but in the interim, families have to absorb substantial costs of inconvenience and higher prices. Public entities, however, are expected to maintain services and even step in to smooth out market-generated disruptions. Portfolio systems could suffer sharp disruptions, for example, if providers decide that it is no longer profitable to manage schools or shift their attention to other cities or regions or if private donors who have helped underwrite the costs of starting new small and charter schools shift their philanthropic strategies. They could suffer a possibly more gradual interruption in capacity if central office personnel with the knowledge and expertise to effectively bargain with and oversee private providers are lured away to work for those providers, leaving the public authority at a relative disadvantage, or if changing fiscal conditions lead state or local legislators to cut funding needed to maintain CGU databases or enforcement teams.

The threat of disruptions in service—combined with the legal, moral, and political pressure to ensure continued provision of education services—may mean that CGUs will have to maintain a certain degree of slack resources and capacity: keeping on their payroll school leaders and teachers who can step in to take over a school, for example, where a private provider suddenly opts out of the business (or is revealed to be engaging in improper conduct). To maintain such capacity may raise costs by requiring the district to invest in extra personnel and to maintain salaries and benefits adequate to keep such talent in competition with independent, portfolio school employers.

USE OF THIS FRAMEWORK

The purpose of this chapter is to demonstrate the need for designing a governance framework for choice or portfolio school districts. "Pure" choice districts comprise only quasi-autonomous charter schools authorized by the state to compete for students in a market environment. Such schools would be subject to the overall rules and regulations under state law, but would not be managed directly by the school district. In contrast, a portfolio district undertakes the design and management of a mixture or combination of different types of schools run by different operators, according to its perceptions of families' and students' needs and desires. Some schools are operated directly by the district. Others are given considerable autonomy as district magnet schools or are established by independent contract with outside educational providers; some are charter schools. What both types have in common is that whether moving toward universal choice such as occurred in New Orleans or establishing portfolio districts as in Chicago, New York, Philadelphia, and Los Angeles, there is little evidence of systematic and comprehensive planning of the needed changes in governance. Instead, it appears that trial-and-error adjustments are made idiosyncratically, rather than with systematic consideration of how to construct an efficient, effective, and equitable system. I have argued that by the use of specific criteria such as freedom of choice, productive efficiency, equity, and social cohesion, it is possible to set guidelines for the desirable function of a choice system. These can be combined with principles of economies of scale, transaction costs, and externalities to design finance, regulations, and support services and relegate functions to particular organizational levels of choice districts generally and portfolio districts specifically. The details presented here on roles and responsibilities and their disposition should not be viewed as complete, nor should the illustrative applications be considered concrete recommendations. Rather, I have designed the chapter to illuminate the issues surrounding the governance of such districts. The specific steps that are appropriate in any context need to be addressed by a properly constituted governance body. I hope that this framework demonstrates how goals and economic criteria can be used to draft the design of an overall governing and organizational system.

In a recent interim summary of portfolio school districts, Hill and his colleagues warn of problems in sustaining portfolio school districts:

> There are ways to design local governance so that it sustains rather than destroys a portfolio system. But these require careful design, including explicit limitations on board powers. Today it is not clear whether any locality is working toward a permanent governance system that could maintain a system of highly autonomous schools held accountable only for performance.[39]

I hope that the discussion in this chapter serves as a potential road map for action.

9

Convergence or Collision

Portfolio Districts, Education Markets, and Federal Education Policy

Patricia Burch

Dramatic changes are underway in the governance of K–12 public education.[1] We are nearing the end of a quarter-century of increasing federal and state policy directed at improving local instruction. On the one hand, the federal government has become increasingly engaged in education at the state and local levels and directive in so doing. The No Child Left Behind Act (the 2001 reauthorization of the 1965 Elementary and Secondary Education Act) tied federal funding for economically disadvantaged communities to test-score performance and introduced progressive consequences for schools, districts, and states found to be out of compliance with the law's directives for student academic performance. The American Recovery and Reinvestment Act (ARRA), passed into law in February 2009 under the Obama administration, provides stabilization funds to local education agencies (LEAs) through a targeted education and finance program.[2] With the encouragement of Secretary of Education Arne Duncan, the National Governors Association and the Council of Chief State

School Officers have drafted national content standards to guide instruction across the fifty states—an initiative that some have viewed as a step toward a national curriculum and national tests.[3]

Standing partially in tension with this centralization (or more centralized authority at the federal level), private engagement in the governance and administration of public education is expanding and evolving. Schools, districts, and states always have bought goods and services (food services, maintenance, texts, equipment, tests, curriculum, professional development) from private providers. The main difference in this area has been the extension of these activities to the practice of core instruction.[4] School districts and individual charter schools are contracting with private firms for in-school and after-school remedial instruction. They are contracting with private firms to design and operate the systems by which teachers administer periodic assessments in their classrooms—systems used by administrators to monitor teacher performance and redesign systemwide objectives. They also are contracting with private firms to design and manage virtual learning spaces, where students attend public school via an Internet connection. They are contracting with firms to hire teachers and manage in-school programs to help high school students progress toward graduation.[5] Firms are contracting with districts to operate schools perceived as alternatives to traditional district public schools, including charter schools, turnaround schools, empowerment zone schools, and hybrid schools.

The term *privatization* has many meanings both within education and outside education.[6] The aspect of privatization that I emphasize is one that in other work I have termed the *new educational privatization*. Under the new educational privatization, government is directly involved in creating new markets for school improvement and managing the flow of public funds to private contractors to support these markets. The contractor may be a for-profit or nonprofit organization, or some hybrid of the two, such as a private for-profit firm that has as part of its portfolio a nonprofit entity. As I describe in more detail later, federal policy simultaneously encourages and restricts the new privatization—proclaiming the virtues of a free marketplace, while mandating contracting arrangements that make government, rather than the parent, the primary consumer within these markets.[7]

The landscape of market-oriented and quasi-market-oriented education reform is changing, and the origins of those changes are complex, involving both local and national policies and actions of governmental and nongovernmental entities. This chapter considers federal education policy, in particular the No Child Left Behind Act (NCLB) of 2001, as a prelude to and influence on the phenomenon of portfolio districts described in other chapters in this book as unfolding in Chicago, New York, Philadelphia, and New Orleans. I identify pathways of influence of current federal policy on local efforts and discuss several implications for the portfolio management model (PMM).

FRAMING IDEAS

The relationship between federal policy and local policy and action has long concerned implementation researchers.[8] Research on the impact of federal policy on local action concurs that policy is transformed as it works its way down the system—from the federal level to the classroom level.[9]

The implementation-as-negotiation model of studying policy has strengths. However, it has neglected an important middle layer or ground of education public policy. This is the space where government and nongovernment organizations interact in school improvement. Institutional theorists refer to the landscape in which different organizational players interact as the organizational field.[10] As a sector in society, the organizational field includes suppliers, consumers, and regulators that interact in the work of education. Exchanges or interactions within organizational fields are understood as contributing to institution building—at times introducing change and at other times, reinforcing existing routines.[11]

While there are many players in any organizational field, the actions of the government are endowed with an assumed legitimacy. Consequently, if and when governments take action within organizational fields, their actions carry much weight. Whether or not government policies are fully implemented, they can help set standards for future practice and contribute to institution building.

In my view, the concept of the organizational field as developed by institutional theorists can help education researchers better understand a persistently neglected dimension of education reform—the ways in which the private sector and government interact in the work of school improvement. I use the concept of the organizational field to frame my level of analysis of portfolio districts. I attend to both the lateral and vertical organizational interdependencies and interactions that are central to what is happening at the national level and in cities such as Chicago, New York, Philadelphia, and New Orleans. This means I look at not only what districts or the federal policy makers are doing to stimulate markets, but also how private firms are responding to incentives. Clearly, we are in an era where one institutional form or logic of schooling—the market metaphor—is becoming more dominant.[12] And, as I argue later, NCLB exemplifies the legitimizing of that form by federal policy. However, both governmental and nongovernmental organizations shape and reshape the market metaphor as they design public policy and as they implement policies originating at higher levels—blunting or sharpening these policies for their own purposes.

It is in such a broader organizational and regulatory context—the institutional context—that we must situate the PMM and other market-oriented reforms, both in education and in other institutional sectors that parallel it.

PMMS AND THE EXPANDING FEDERAL ROLE IN LOCAL INSTRUCTION

Federal public policy toward the contracting of local instructional services is changing. The larger context for these changes is an expanding federal role in matters of local instruction. The founders of the education system in the United States left public education to the states. However, for several decades, the federal government has acted via spending conditions and new policies to influence what happens within classrooms. This movement built steam after the publication of *A Nation At Risk* and subsequent state activity to increase high school graduation rates and implement high-stakes exit exams. In the 1990s, with the passage of Goals 2000 and the Improving America's Schools Act (IASA), federal and state policy pressed for new systems of student accountability and the development of state-level standards.

NCLB extends federal and state involvement in local matters of instruction. As McDonnell has argued, rather than a first foray into an interventionist federal role, NCLB represents the extension of a decades-long trend.[13]

> Although NCLB has expanded federal regulation, this newest version of ESEA represents an evolution of the federal role rather than a radical redefinition. This evolution has changed the ways that at-risk students are targeted and served, and it has moved the federal role closer to the instructional core of schools and classrooms.[14]

This influence is exerted in part through increased conditions on the spending of funds used as inducements for broad categories of activity. In the very early stages of ESEA, funding conditions were tied to categorical funding. However, relatively few spending conditions linked to the regular education program were appended. Under the Bush and Clinton administrations, Title I goals were tied to state education goals via requirements that states receiving Title I funds create a single statewide system for measuring student performance (federal funds that state and local governments receive based on a designated funding formula). These spending conditions enabled the federal government to influence activities at lower governmental levels, while remaining a relatively junior funding source (7 percent to 10 percent) in overall education spending.

The passage of reforms such as IASA and Goals 2000 represented a defining moment in the history of education contracting in districts. On the one hand, under these policies, states were expected to establish challenging content and performance standards, implement assessments that measured student performance against standards, and hold schools and school systems accountable for the achievement of all students. NCLB pushed forward with an agenda of performance-based outcomes with greater confidence, given federal mandates requiring annual testing of children in grades three through eight, including children in non-Title I schools and two populations previously excluded from testing—special education students and English language learners (ELLs).

In this regard, NCLB intensified the centralizing logic of school reform and expanding federal and state roles. However, simultaneously, and much less visibly, NCLB greatly increased the role of market-based reforms in ways that are not easily visible to the public and thus not subject to much political debate or opposition.[15]

CREATING NEW MARKETS WITHIN THE SCHOOL IMPROVEMENT INDUSTRY

Before NCLB, much policy talk was organized around the question of whether we *ought* to increase private engagement in the design and delivery of educational services. A decade later, conversation has shifted to *how* districts should organize and coordinate the engagement of private firms in the operation and management of pubic schools.

Many of the issues discussed in the city case study chapters (in this volume), such as the opening of charter schools, the contracting of district functions, or the closing of failing schools, historically have been politically controversial ideas. While public school choice might be increasingly and widely supported, the other reforms introduced—the idea that some schools should be freed from government regulations, that these schools can be focused on the needs of individual students rather than the wider community—have been hotly debated and resisted. While contracting with private providers certainly does not go as far as vouchers, it does fall generally into the category of using public funds to pay for private interests (in this case, to maximize revenues of private firms for services not proved to be superior to those of public provision).

It is as yet unclear whether the portfolio district will prove a reform alternative that garners widespread political support and presses for greater system change or one that is fiercely resisted and becomes a passing fad. However, it is significant that some of those doing the practical work of portfolio districts (and perhaps some of those who support these developments from outside districts) view the policies of school closure, district contracting, and charter school management as established, acceptable strategies for improving educational and social outcomes for the poor. In the current climate, the introduction of these reforms might require some accommodations on the part of policy elites, but they are perceived as politically feasible. They are not pilot projects, but have been incorporated into the toolkit of districtwide strategies for instructional reform.

For example, in New York, Mayor Michael Bloomberg and Chancellor Joel Klein are described as muscling forward a model of reform; as Gyurko and Henig state in chapter 4 of this volume, "grounded in management theories articulated in corporate values and metaphors." These reforms included downsizing the central office, recentralizing community schools, and relying on the private sector to fund activities typically paid for with government dollars. In Chicago, under Renaissance 2010, Duncan extended a test-based accountability system and introduced a model whereby schools designated as underperforming would be replaced with schools operated by outside providers.

In contrast to earlier forms of contracting, like the Edison experiment in Philadelphia, these reforms were introduced and implemented with rapid speed. NCLB helped established a different moral or political climate for local contracting reforms. Controversial reform ideas, such as charter schools, the contracting out of core education services to private firms, and policies of school closure do not simply descend on education. In every phase, they require political and institutional work.

THE ROLE OF FEDERAL POLICY IN CREATING NEW MARKETS

NCLB helped accomplish this political–institutional work for local reformers in two primary ways. First, NCLB created new markets for the school improvement industry. Educational privatization has a long history in the United States. In the past decade, much public and academic attention has been focused on educational management organizations or EMOs. These firms typically assume full responsibility for all aspects of school operations including administration, teacher training, and noninstructional functions such as building maintenance, food service, or clerical support. However, with the passage of NCLB, the current chapter of education contracting is being written by firms of a different kind, which have received less attention from the press but cannot be ignored. These are specialty service providers. Similar to other forms of district contracting, involving contract schools, districts in principle maintain control of funds by putting out bids, writing contracts, and overseeing payment to vendors. Some firms specialize in a particular niche of specialty or wraparound services such as virtual schooling (K12) and learning software (Blackboard). Increasingly, as I argue next, firms in the K–12 education marketplace also are operating across multiple segments of the market and selling an array of products (à la carte) within one school district and/or across multiple school districts.

Until the mid-1990s, district contracts with specialty service providers represented a small slice of the privatized sector in education and involved things like food service, transportation, and driver education. However, since 2003, specialty service providers have become vital players in the K–12 education market. By some reports, school and local governments now spend approximately $48 billion per year to purchase food and products from the private sector.[16] While food service, transportation service, specialized instruction, and standardized tests account for a large part of that figure, in the past decade, other sales linked to high-stakes accountability reforms have become fast-growing segments of the for-profit K–12 industry. While districts historically have contracted with vendors to develop and administer standardized tests and to check the validity of test items, in recent years, the market for test development and preparation has exploded.[17] Key suppliers within this segment include test content and exam providers, standards-alignment providers, and suppliers of interim assessment technology. In 2006, the top vendors in the testing industry reported annual sales in the range of $200 to $900 million.

Specialty services now include after-school tutoring, school improvement and management services, charter schools, alternative education and special education services, professional development for teachers and administrators, and educational content providers. Some firms in the industry are well-established players such as textbook publishers and test publishers. This includes firms such as Houghton Mifflin, established in 1832; Kaplan, established in 1938; and Princeton Review, established in 1981. However, also represented are many new companies that were established since 1990 and even since 2002. This includes firms such as Educate! (2003), K12 (1999), Blackboard (1997), and Connections Academy (2001). New privatization firms also represent a range of industries including home entertainment, Internet services, and leisure products.

Thus, the K–12 education market, which Wall Street analysts termed sluggish a decade ago, is exploding through a rapid influx of capital investments and public policy revenue. Specialty service providers establish a somewhat different contractual relationship with the district than do EMOS. They may sell particular functions separately that are rolled together in a conventional school management model. Alternately, they may provide wraparound services (e.g., data analysis and management services, professional development, teacher recruitment, and after-school tutoring) that are supplemental to total school management contracts. Thus, as the concept of the portfolio district takes root in a variety of forms throughout big-city school systems in North America, the private-sector industry of school improvement is being transformed from an industry formerly clustered around two extremes—noninstructional functions such as food services and transportation and contracts for whole school management—into a more diversified industry attracting new kinds of organizations and, selling new kinds of products and services, supported in part by demands created through federal policy. The firms operating in this industry are selling to both individual schools (e.g., charter schools) and large, urban school districts (including those profiled in this volume). These firms include contracts for both whole-school management and wraparound services.

These organizations draw on districts, state, and federal funds to support their operations. In 2008, the Education Industry Association stated

> Education is rapidly becoming a $1 trillion industry, representing 10% of America's GNP and second in size only to the health care industry. Federal and State expenditures on education exceed $750 billion. Education companies, with over $80 billion in annual revenues, already constitute a large sector in the education arena. The education industry plays an increasingly important role in supporting public education by meeting the demand for products and services that both complement and supplement basic education services.[18]

As you look across the activities of these firms, the trend suggests that firms are increasingly selling across different segments of the market, as opposed to concentrating on one segment. Thus, rather than primarily selling textbooks, a firm will also sell online curriculum as well as stand-alone assessment, management consulting, professional development, and after-school tutoring. Examples of firms already selling across different segments of the market include Princeton Review, which sells tests, curriculum, application software, and school management, and Educate!, which sells after-school tutoring, teacher recruitment, and NCLB services for nonpublic schools

The trend toward specialty service providers in districts' contracting models is discernible in the case studies, although to different degrees and assuming different forms. Reformers in New York City have assumed a high-profile approach to working with specialty service providers. From the start, the New York reform, Children First, has been staffed and organized by private consultants and firms that originate from outside of the New York City school system and its infrastructure. The district hired McKinsey & Company, the management consulting firm, to assist in the design of Children First, in addition to enlisting large nonprofit organizations such as the College Board to create new small schools. The changes introduced to district management included the firing of staff with traditional oversight of government-contracted services—including transportation and food services—signaling the administration's eagerness to shift responsibilities for specific district functions (rather than whole-school management) to the private sector. The city also adopted contracting procedures that further reduced the transparency of the contracting process, for example, a no-bids contracting format. These changes reflected the behind-the-scenes approach of firms established or restructuring in the post-NCLB era.

The trajectory of Philadelphia's reforms represents a distinct shift from the EMO model (whereby the district contracted with one firm, Edison Schools) to manage and operate most of its contract schools to more of a specialty service provider approach. Under Superintendent Arlene Ackerman's plan, rather than contracting out for all services, the district contracts out for discrete services identified as "adding value" to the district. (See Bulkley et al., chapter 5, this volume.) In New Orleans, the movement toward contracting out of school services emerged from disaster—Hurricane Katrina. New schools managed by external authorities opened under five different authorities with a voucher program. In Chicago, the trend toward specialty service providers appears less pronounced. Renaissance 2010 has been built, in large part, around the concept of closing failing schools and opening new schools, either as charter schools or other kinds of schools that have more autonomy. Districts may create schools themselves or turn to outside providers. Thus, in Chicago, the trend of whole-school management remains very pronounced. However, this may be changing, particularly as firms such as K12 and Princeton Review become more aggressive in selling to urban school districts via contracts for remedial math, hybrid schools (online credit-recovery programs), and summer and after-school tutoring.

Thus, the context for the PMM is one in which the business model in K–12 education services is being transformed.[19] Firms that once specialized in whole-school management are turning to less visible, lower profile strategies where they contract with multiple districts for multiple specific functions in each. However, some are indirectly maintaining their strategies for comprehensive school management. In some instances, the firms have given subsidiaries a variety of independent names.[21] Consequently, the public, or even district personnel, cannot easily see that a single for-profit firm is providing a large array of often interlocking, educational services to a district.[20] Alternatively, instead of specializing in school management, firms offer a variety of services in other areas, such as summer and after-school programs and tutoring support. These services are called wraparounds by some testing companies and are a major source of income and rationale for getting the testing contracts from states and districts. They automatically promote the other products and services to prepare teachers and students for the tests.

The public cannot easily see that a single for-profit firm is providing a large array of educationally central services to a district. Thus, while a district may establish various contracts with seemingly different businesses and running for different terms, they could all be subsidiaries of a single company.

Consider this example. As noted, in the 1990s, Edison was a leading firm in the business of contract school management. It was a high-profile firm, but then suffered financial losses and became privately held. In 2003, the firm announced a new business strategy aimed at expanding its customer base while keeping a much lower profile. In a Form 10-K filed in 2003, Edison stated,

> We have historically focused on the direct management of public schools in the United States. Although we expect that school management will continue to be a major contributor of future business growth, we have developed strengths and capabilities through running schools that we believe can help students in other ways. We have begun to offer a variety of services in other areas such as summer and after-school programs and tutoring support.[22]

The firm sells these different products under various brand names. The Newton Learning division provides school districts with extended learning programs, including summer school, after-school, and supplemental education services. The Tungsten Learning division provides school districts with consulting services, test preparation services, and assessments. Edison's original business—the full-service management of schools—has been reorganized under a new division, which the firm calls its "district partnership division."

In its statements to shareholders, Edison specifically describes its growth strategy as "behind the scenes":

> This business line [Tungsten Learning] developed over the past year, is built on the intellectual property developed in our directly managed schools. We are now offering these resources to entire school districts on a consultative, *behind-the-scenes* [italics mine] basis. The initial product offering is built around our Benchmark Assessment System that provides teachers and administrators real-time data on students' learning progress against year-end standards, thereby providing a powerful tool to help teachers adjust their teaching strategies to accelerate student achievement. Our service includes professional development and achievement support.[23]

The firm describes a business model in which it takes services formerly sold under its school management model and sells them to districts à la carte on a behind-the-scenes basis.

Edison is not the only company taking this approach. It also is a strategy being employed to varying degrees by Plato Learning, Educate!, Princeton Review, Kaplan, and Pearson Education, among other firms. As in the case of Edison, they are selling the products under different brand names, but the products interlock in the sense that they are all tied to high-stakes accountability mandates. Second, while sold under different subdivisions, the services are all part of the same company. They are driven by the same corporate management structure. While the revenue from various products and services flow to the same parent company, the full reach of that company is not immediately apparent to the public. As a testing executive explained, "Each of the products are sold under different brand-names, but they are all part of a bigger business strategy that is engineered at high levels of our organization."[24] Another executive described how his company used contracts for after-school tutoring (and NCLB mandates) to make inroads into districts that it might otherwise not have a reason for approaching, stating,

> We approach the district we have been working with in one area, and say listen, "We are already working in your buildings; we already are working with your educationally disadvantaged students, let's think about how we can approach these problems collaboratively and this is what we are selling." So our contract with the district in one area becomes the direct outgrowth of a sale in another. It gives us a reason to go back to them.[25]

From a business standpoint, this is a very smart strategy. When a firm sells a school district an assessment, it also gains entrée to selling the district a curriculum linked to those assessments. When a firm sells a school district after-school programming that is supposed to prepare students for doing better on tests, it gains entrée to selling the district classroom assessments to measure progress toward the tests. And as in the example just offered, when a firm such as Edison sells assessments, it already is planning for the next contract with the district. In this regard, the firm may call the strategy "behind the scenes," but the ultimate goal is the same: to become a major supplier of education services to a district.

There is more. The products sold under different brand names interlock and are designed in ways that will encourage consumers to purchase more than one product. For example, Renaissance Place is a Web-based tool that is aimed at enabling districts to centralize curriculum and assessment information in a single database. The Web-based platform is designed to incorporate other Renaissance products, such as Standards Master, Accelerated Reader, and Accelerated Math. As another example, K12 sells technology-based services to virtual charter schools that work best when used in conjunction with K12's other products such as its online student enrollment and assessment system.

The examples provided highlight the tension between the realities of purchasing interdependent products (product A requires product B to work properly) with a more idealized market vision that assumes that purchasers have the option to purchase "unbundled" services from different providers if and when they find it advantageous to do so. The idealized market assumes that districts can contract with one firm for school management services, from a company like Edison. It assumes that they can then turn around and purchase online content from K12 and contract with Princeton Review for after-school tutoring or credit-recovery programs. In practice, all but the largest urban districts are confronting a situation where they are under pressure to purchase more from one vendor.

In sum, mirroring broader patterns in the education marketplace, there is a broad tendency of some of the early entrants to the PMM to move away from direct school management to selling distinct services to districts. One reason for this is that these activities are *less* politically visible and strategies for holding specialty service firms accountable for outcomes are in the embryonic stage.

These developments have several implications for portfolio districts. One implication is that the logic of portfolio management includes the notion that nonperforming contractors are eliminated. However, if these contractors are also selling the district a range of interlaced and integrated services—professional development, and so on—the spillover cost of terminating a school management contract might be greater. In other words, districts may find that they lack the flexibility to pick and choose which services work and may get maneuvered into package deals—either formally or because of feasibility and pressure.

Alternatively, proponents of the portfolio district may see increased activity within the private-sector school improvement industry as a very supportive development. Where there is competition and increased supply, as the theory goes, there also should be organizational churn and innovation. From this perspective, the rise of specialty service providers simultaneously creates a challenge and a solution: competition from private providers puts more pressure on the district to improve, but at the same time it enriches the pull of human and intellectual capital on which the district can draw in doing so.

Apart from simply increasing the supply of firms, the rise of specialty service providers may contribute greater political support for officials who have promoted a portfolio district as well as greater political pressure for changes in policies that expand even further the incentive to rely on private providers to meet public goals. The more that firms differentiate, and the more that firms proliferate, the more likely that there will be increased pressure on districts to secede full responsibility for the management and operations of schools to private-sector firms. In the same sense that text-book publishers became a powerful lobbying force in state curriculum debates, specialty service providers are likely to emphasize district rede-sign via contracting as a prominent educational strategy. Indeed, since the enactment of NCLB, the interest groups typically representing the school improvement industry (such as the Education Industry Associa-tion) have reorganized to better position themselves to encourage mem-bership among smaller specialty service providers, and thus to increase both their influence to coordinate activities within the private sector and their power vis-à-vis every level of government. However, it may also be the case that differentiation and specialization among private firms would require a greater role for the district. The more specialty service providers proliferate, the more they could create a cacophony of directions that will again require significant and far-reaching public management.

OVERLAY WITH CIVIL RIGHTS LANGUAGE

NCLB not only introduced and supported a new array of market practices that make contractors an integral part of the new patterns it requires. Its proponents also found numerous strategies to legitimize these new prac-tices by linking them with the quest to improve civil rights and improve poor and minority children's access to quality education. Many NCLB proponents strategically invoked the language of civil rights and the col-lective goals of education in advancing support for their reforms. When critics of NCLB's testing mandates voiced concern about the law's im-pact on poor and minority students, then-Secretary of Education Rod-ney Paige and others countered with arguments about the "soft bigotry of low expectations." They described the goals of the legislation in terms that linked the goals of market-oriented reforms to the ethical commitment of the federal government to protect the poor and underserved populations. They positioned the conventional district as presenting an obstacle to this stewardship. Thus, in defending policies of parent choice in Title I, former president George W. Bush stated,

> And when we find a child that needs extra help, there's money to do so. And
> there are options for parents . . . A parent can enroll their child in a free

intensive tutoring program. If your child is not up to grade-level, there is extra help for each family to do so . . . You would be amazed at the number of districts that don't take advantage of the money. Oh, they'll figure out ways to spend it, don't get me wrong. But the money is aimed at having an individual succeed and it's the cumulative effect of bringing these students to grade level to say we are all more competitive for the future.[26]

The law and its rhetoric helped link the idea of the private-sector engagement in the governance of public education to a collective and very public set of goals, including increased access to quality education for the poor, parent empowerment, and a more informed citizenry. As I have argued elsewhere, firms contracting with districts under NCLB also have explicitly leveraged the civil rights language of ESEA to maximize their revenues and to build confidence and legitimacy for their selling strategies.[27] For example, in statements filed with the U.S. Securities and Exchange Commission, K12, the virtual school provider, states,

> We were founded in 2000 to utilize the advances in technology to provide children with a high quality public education regardless of their geographic location or socio-economic background . . . These concerns were reflected in the passage of the No Child Left Behind Act in 2001 which implemented new standards and accountability requirements for K–12 public education.[28]

These statements and others like them offer telling illustrations of how NCLB has helped proponents of increased contracting in public education to make their agenda more politically acceptable. Through NCLB and through the efforts of private firms, the idea of contracting out core district functions *at scale* becomes a possibility. Further, the intended output of district contracting at scale is conceived as much more than a *local* efficiency question. It is framed as a cost-efficient way to increase the quality, access, and participation in public schooling for the very poor nationwide and to increase the nation's *global* competitiveness.[29]

What I am suggesting is that part of the reason that district portfolio advocates in Chicago, New York, and Philadelphia could push forward with otherwise controversial reforms is that they were in good company in terms of federal policy. Even though federal policy tends to be diluted as it works its way down the system, and even though federal policy counts for only a small percentage of districts' operating budgets, as a strategy of government, it endows otherwise controversial ideas in education policy with a form of legitimacy. In 2004, the public policy community still lacked any definitive evidence about the value of charter schools or contract schools as strategies for improving schools for the poor. However, then-Superintendent Duncan could proceed with Renaissance 2010, Mayor Bloomberg and Chancellor Klein could move forward with a large contract with McKinsey, and Superintendent Ackerman could push forward with the next stage of the portfolio model, in part because the federal government was acting as though the question of whether to move forward with market-oriented reforms was a moot point. Furthermore, the very fact that NCLB shoehorned the idea of district contracting into Title I of ESEA, a well-established reform designed to benefit the poor, into the broader goal of helping the United States compete in a globalized economy elevated the idea of contracting to the status of a national equity-oriented reform, as opposed to a local management decision of whether to make or buy.

PRIVATIZATION POLICY UNDER THE OBAMA ADMINISTRATION

The use of spending conditions in federal policy to encourage states and local districts to use market or quasi-market strategies are part of a school improvement agenda that continues under the Obama administration (with some important variations, as I note later in the chapter). Signed into law by President Obama in February 2009, the education component of ARRA includes the following: approximately $48 billion in state stabilization funds to address the immediate budget shortfalls and reductions in elementary, secondary, and higher education; $10 billion in additional funds for Title I grants to local education agencies; $3 billion for Title I school improvement grants; $12 billion for Individuals with Disabilities Education Act (IDEA) programs; $5 billion nationally in incentives grants to be distributed competitively to states that pursue standards-based reforms—higher standards, quality assessments, data systems, and teacher-quality initiatives.[30]

The U.S. Department of Education outlined four general principles in the use of ARRA funds. Funds must be (a) used quickly; (b) used to improve student achievement; (c) ensure reporting, transparency, and accountability; and (d) used as one-time funds, in other words to supplement rather than supplant existing district and state commitments. In these ways, ARRA can be described as maintaining the accountability markets that NCLB generates and stimulated by NCLB. The education component of ARRA (and policy makers' discussion of the rationale and goals of ARRA) includes frequent reference to the importance of data and maintaining the demands on districts for the reporting of data. Again, schools and districts have always bought tests and data services from outside contractors. The impact of federal policy (both NCLB and ARRA grants) is that it mandates increasing focus on data as a central lever for school improvement and, through the rules and language of the law, connects these activities to the central work of teaching and learning—the core work of instruction.

Further, beginning with NCLB and continuing with ARRA, federal policy paves the way for the expansion of contracting for school services, in particular, charter schools. Both President Obama and Secretary Duncan have long been vocal supporters of charter schools and have pushed legislation to increase both direct and indirect federal support for charter schools. Specifically, the incentive grants prioritize funding for states that have supportive charter school laws; guidance on the use of state stabilization funds requires that states take the necessary measures to ensure that charter schools (in particular, newly opening charter schools and charter schools with a record of achievement) receive funds. Further, the state stabilization funds include provisions aimed at maintaining the current contracting provisions of NCLB. Specifically, local education agencies are required to apply for waivers in order to use additional Title I funds on services other than supplemental educational services.

To summarize, beginning in the 1990s, one impact of a stronger federal role in education policy has been to increase the legitimacy of private-sector reforms via the overlay of civil rights language on market and quasi-market school improvement initiatives. Federal policy has exercised its influence via mandates that increase the demand for services for which schools and districts long have contracted, such as test administration, curriculum development, and data analysis and reporting. It also has exercised this influence via mandates and spending conditions that involve new markets and extend the trend from more traditional services of private providers into core instructional services of the school, such as mandated after-school tutoring for Title I students and school management.

COMPLICATIONS AND CONTRADICTIONS

As noted earlier, portfolio districts and recent trends in federal education policy are part of a larger movement that calls for more involvement of private firms in providing goods and services that cut close to the instructional core. I believe that it is important to view portfolio districts in the context of broader privatizing schemes as a step to better understanding the strengths and limitations of the basic logic that underlies different kinds of market and quasi-market approaches to school reform. A second important task is to analyze and compare the underlying assumptions—goals, rationalizing theories, implementation structures—that fall under the umbrella of market-oriented and quasi-market-oriented education reforms. As discussed next, there are both important similarities and differences.

Managerialism

NCLB expands and legitimates the role of the middle manager in school improvement. The law creates an incentive structure that involves nearly every level of government—state employees, district employees, and school employees. The responsibilities of middle managers across these levels are tied tightly to test-score performance. Government middle managers now have much of their work defined by test scores. There are rules about what percentage of students must take the tests (95 percent) if districts and states are to avoid sanctions. There are rules about when data must be reported, how they must be reported, how they must be analyzed, and the comparison groups included in the analysis.

NCLB ties the role of government employees more tightly to data by narrowing existing procedures. The law's redefinition of technical assistance illustrates this strategy. For much of ESEA's history, state education agencies have been required to provide technical assistance linked to districts and schools. NCLB defines technical assistance in very precise terms tightly linked to the law's accountability mandates. In the language of the law,

Technical assistance shall include assistance in the analyzing of data from the assessments required under 111b3. It also must include technical assistance to select methods of instruction based on scientifically based research and that have proven effective in addressing specific instructional issues that caused the school to be identified for improvement.[31]

Undoubtedly, program managers under ESEA always have been responsible for reporting and monitoring compliance. Under NCLB, the perceived necessity of this work is heightened. Not only are managers responsible for monitoring compliance; they are responsible for monitoring school performance (outputs) that is tied to the NCLB broader incentive structure. Further, rather than granting managers more autonomy in how they support the work of local sites, NCLB attempts more tightly to prescribe the activities of school, state, and district managers. One effect of this orientation is a flood of rules and regulations that can dislocate public administrators from their immediate political and social environment. Regardless of where they are located, state and district managers are expected to play the same roles; the idea is that they should all begin to look the same way and concentrate on the same kinds of work. A second consequence of the NCLB approach is that it more tightly constrains the work of public officials and therefore their flexibility to deal with and manage the private sector.

The emphasis on managerial incentives evident in NCLB also is a central component of portfolio districts. Portfolio districts, like NCLB, employ theories of strong management in the context of a reform design emphasizing the goal of parent choice. However, in contrast to the 2001 variants of NCLB, the designers of portfolio districts also take the approach that the existing district regime cannot be relied on to make these changes. As part of the reforms in each city, existing district staff have been fired or reassigned. Take, for example, the ways in which New York City officials treated the role of district managers in their reforms. The middle layers of central office bureaucracy were implicated as part of the problem and viewed as contributing to an unresponsive undifferentiated system. Bloomberg and Klein fired or reassigned many central office managers and instituted reforms that would diminish their influence.

The dislocation of *public* middle management is further reflected in the events that unfolded in Chicago before and after Renaissance 2010. In the first wave of reform, the central office was downsized and some of its authority transferred to the school level through the establishment of local school councils. As part of Renaissance 2010, Duncan pressed to establish schools that were run and operated by private providers, not district management. The district established an office of autonomous schools serving one-quarter of all Chicago Public School students. Policy statements by staff in the Autonomous Schools Office (ASO) put it this way, "ASO runs on a lean budget of roughly $1.5 million and more than 50% of that is directly distributed to schools, established by a tiny staff of four full time employees." (See Menefee-Libey, chapter 3, this volume.)

In New Orleans, at the time of writing, both the superintendent of the Recovery School District, Paul Vallas, and the State Superintendent of Education, Paul Pastorek, called for minimizing the size of the central authority of the district as part of a broader plan to convert noncharter schools to charter schools. This emphasis on local authority in PMM stands in stark contrast to NCLB and to lesser extent, ARRA. NCLB includes strong incentives for district managers to manage the flow of test-score data, and they are directly accountable for student and school performance on tests. However, particularly in comparison to earlier iterations of ESEA, NCLB favors the role of the state education agencies (SEAs) in the design and administration of school improvement initiatives.

Parent Choice

Although with important differences in degree and emphasis, both NCLB and portfolio districts pair the idea of parent choice (and differentiation in school type) with centralizing reforms that expand the role and influence of managers in school reform activities.[32] For example, as described in an earlier section, under NCLB, parent choice is introduced as a critical element in the dynamics of school and provider churn; it is viewed as essential to creating a competitive environment and improved outcomes. Parents of students in underperforming schools are given the choice of transferring their child to another school and, in the third year, given the option to choose an after-school provider for their child with funds paid by the district. NCLB creates other rights for parents in access to and usage of data. Under NCLB, parents have notice rights to their child's test score data, data on school performance, and the qualifications of their child's teacher.

Early variants of PMM espouse charter schools. However, their vision does not appear to align well with that of a true market believer who thinks that it would be great if families choose to exit the public school system and that exit from a school is a sufficient indicator of the need for a school closure. Like advocates of the PMM idea, Duncan and Obama, in celebrating charter schools, appear to be thinking more about a Harlem Children's Zone–style version of parent choice (choosing charters *that are linked* to the neighborhood) rather than a model that totally unlinks school from community (for example, as evidenced in Obama and Duncan's proposals for "promise neighborhoods"). Further, at the time of writing, the proposed Title I reauthorization significantly downplayed the parent option, in failing schools, to move to another school.

What does it mean when quasi-market education reforms pair the goals of parent choice with strategies of stronger managerial incentives, including incentives to contract with private firms to manage schools? What room does this arrangement (emphasis on managerialism paired with parent choice) leave for the policy influence of parents and communities as collective groups (e.g., low-income parents)? In sorting through these questions, it may be helpful to make a distinction between favoring public school choice as a sorting mechanism and escape valve (as reflected in the original version of NCLB) and favoring public school choice as a quasi-market mechanism (albeit imperfect) for generating better schools. In principle, the PMM's twist on public school choice is to lean heavier on the idea of school choice as generating a more diverse supply of schools than as an escape valve *from* public schools (à la NCLB and its choice provisions). However, if PMM reforms evolve further toward the ideas of the new managerialism and educational choice as enabling exit from public schools, portfolio districts may blend into the slow steady march in U.S. K–12 education toward neoliberal market education reforms.

Laissez-Faire Regulation

One argument for a strong managerial role in reforms employing parent choice and contracting is that some kind of systemic oversight by districts is needed to mitigate the profit-maximizing behavior of firms hired to provide school or supplemental services. Another argument is that in a reform where both government and private firms are central actors in the design and administration of services, government is more likely to protect or respond to the demands of organized industry and big business than individual parents.

The prevailing view of private-sector accountability under NCLB is that accountability is something that is done to the public sector. The private sector is buffered or bracketed from regulations. As I argued in *Hidden Markets*, the law privileges the rights of private firms and underwrites risks for firms in several different aspects of the law.[33]

Mandates for after-school tutoring under NCLB provide a good example of this orientation. Under the supplemental educational service (SES) provisions, schools that do not make test-score targets for three years or more must make after-school tutoring available to students in the school, paid for by the district.[34] Under certain conditions, the district may provide services. However, districts that do not make test-score targets for three years or more are prohibited from providing these services themselves, although they still must pay for them. There are no parallel accountability standards for the outcomes of private-sector tutoring; overburdened state bureaucracies are simply given vague directions to approve their inclusion in a statewide list each year.

NCLB also signals through its regulations that the access of private firms to public funds deserves governmental protection. First, as part of its responsibilities under the law, the SEA is required to provide annual information to vendors about contracting possibilities. In other words, the responsibility of the SEA as defined by law is to make sure that potential vendors are aware of the policies that could provide them participation in public practice and accompanying revenues. LEAS also are required to notify parents of eligible children about the availability of services provided by private contractors.

The law is very specific on this point. States must make this information available to vendors on an annual basis. The importance of making sure the private sector has the information that it needs is not a footnote in the policy; it is identified as one of the state's major responsibilities. Further, the law requires that districts that have schools with choice and SESs must ensure that all eligible students participate in the program. Second, under the regulations, if the district has demonstrated that there is demand for these services and does not meet demand (students are not enrolled; the money set aside for SES is unspent), then the district is considered out of compliance and can face sanctions.

Thus, NCLB represents a clear attempt to protect the rights of these firms, even if it comes at the expense of local needs and concerns. Specifically, states are strongly encouraged to set ranges rather than absolute values on pricing so that providers' service-delivery options will be as broad as possible. In response to comments, final regulations attempt to make more explicit the responsibility of SEAs and LEAs to ensure that ELL students and students with disabilities receive appropriate educational services. However, the nonregulatory guidance of NCLB takes pains to exempt private providers from the civil rights responsibilities required of *government* SES providers. The guidance states that SES providers are in principle not required to follow civil rights statutes because these statutes only apply to direct recipients of federal funds.

Experimentation with the portfolio district model in cities such as Chicago, New York, Philadelphia, and New Orleans generates a similar accountability problem: how to ensure that public money used in contracting is spent on public purposes. However, the case studies in this volume suggest that reformers in these cities are approaching the problem in a slightly different way than the designers of NCLB. That is, in contrast to NCLB, in the local experimentation described in the case studies, private firms are expected to display *some* accountability for performance-based outcomes. For example, Renaissance 2010 faced a problem when charter schools failed to open in the very communities in which children had few options in terms of neighborhood schools.

The private providers were under no legal obligation to serve the students. However, rather than ignoring the problem, the district responded. In partnership with the Illinois Facilities Fund, the Chicago Public Schools put together a response aimed at preempting problems in the future. The goal was to make sure that where schools closed, there would be new schools opening. In the most recent phase of Renaissance 2010, Superintendent Ron Huberman publicly announced that he is as willing to close charter schools as he is public schools. (See Menefee-Libey, chapter 3, this volume.)

Philadelphia assumed a somewhat different approach, but as with Chicago and New York, appears to be at least weighing different solutions to the problem. In Philadelphia, the role of the district, while challenged, was not displaced. As described by Bulkley et al. (chapter 5, this volume), to a greater extent than in the other cities, the providers offering instructional services became part of the fabric of the school system and therefore subject to the same performance standards. When evidence emerged that students in schools managed by providers were not performing better than peers in other schools, the proposal was made to eliminate contracts for providers not making progress. In the face of political opposition, the School Reform Commission backed away from this original proposal and voted to maintain all contracts, regardless of performance. Under the new Ackerman administration, more evidence was released that suggested mixed effects at best for provider-managed K–8 schools, requiring a response from the district. The new administration made incremental steps toward deciding what to do with the providers that were not performing. These steps included work to clarify the nature of the provider–school contract and limiting contracts to those areas in which providers added value. Provider performance was assessed on the basis of providers' contribution to school achievement, in particular the school in which they are working.

CONCLUSION

The landscape of educational privatization is expanding and changing. Portfolio districts are part of this trend. In this chapter, I have argued that as opposed to being a completely new institutional form, portfolio districts are part of a broader movement in the use and perceived legitimacy of market and quasi-market strategies in K–12 education. Portfolio districts have overlapping features with NCLB. They pair the goal of expanded parent choice with an emphasis on heightened managerialism. As in the case of NCLB, the new managers responsible for improving schools include individuals representing both the public and private sectors. In addition to these similarities, portfolio districts exhibit some important differences with the NCLB approach, most particularly in their stance toward state education agencies and willingness to hold providers accountable and theory of action of parent choice (as one strategy to encourage school differentiation, as opposed to the invisible hand approach to improving public schools).

Based on the perspective that portfolio districts and federal education policy share both convergent and divergent elements, I argue that policies that further legitimate or expand aspects of the new privatization agenda at one level affect the trajectories of market-oriented reform agendas originating at other levels. Both NCLB and portfolio districts are examples of market-oriented reforms that involve private enterprise *and* government entities in the design and administration of schools and supplemental services. As suggested by the case of NCLB and the districts profiled in this book, this category of quasi-market reforms presents both advantages and limitations. One advantage may be the ability of government to use its authority to establish new markets and in this way help stimulate the kinds of schools and array of services from which parents can choose. A critical issue to address is the role of public policy in enhancing the system's responsiveness to individual and/or collective parent interests and mitigating the overriding influence of big business.

LOOKING AHEAD

For various reasons, at both the national and local levels, the mantle of education reform is currently being worn by individuals who see existing local government (particularly elected boards and teacher unions) as part of the problem rather than part of the solution. Under former president George W. Bush, and for conservatives generally, the favored alternative was markets—with a heavy emphasis on the for-profit side (and theoretical models or metaphors based on consumer markets). President Obama and Secretary Duncan share much of the reticence about the old local regimes, but seem to be searching for a response that recognizes the limitations of laissez-faire and EMOs and that elevates nonprofits and charter management organizations. Against this backdrop, the PMM emerges as a seemingly good fit for the current direction of federal policy. It may share some principles with the NCLB privatization regime but also soundly rejects the idea of the invisible hand. What remains as yet unclear is whether and how the federal–local linkage via the PMM will surmount the problems historically associated with efforts to keep local reforms *local* and steer them away from the constrictions and standardized clamps of federal policy.

10

—

Disseminating and Legitimating a New Approach

The Role of Foundations

Sarah Reckhow

The tenth annual NewSchools Venture Fund (NSVF) summit in May 2009 epitomized the emergence of nontraditional private actors in public education reform. Close to five hundred participants attended the meeting, including foundation program officers, charter management organization leaders, nonprofit organization leaders, and heads of urban school districts. The rising prominence of NSVF was clearly on display when Secretary of Education Arne Duncan announced via videoconference to the summit that the chief operating officer of NSVF, Joanne Weiss, would oversee the Department of Education's multibillion-dollar Race to the Top program. Duncan explained that his choice represented a strategy to bring new, nontraditional actors into the bureaucracy: "Recruiting successful professionals from the entrepreneurial community is one way we will change the culture and our way of doing business at the Department of Education."[1] The summit showcased other members of this "entrepreneurial community" with several awards: Jon Schnur, cofounder and CEO of New Leaders for New

Schools was named a "Change Agent of the Year"; KIPP DC was recognized as the "Entrepreneurial Organization of the Year"; Don Feinstein, director of the Academy for Urban School Leadership was named "Entrepreneur of the Year"; and Don Shalvey, cofounder and CEO of Aspire Public Schools received an "Entrepreneurial Career Achievement Award."[2]

These organizations and individuals are part of what is sometimes referred to as the diverse provider movement in public education; some operate charter schools and others provide services, such as human capital development, curriculum, and school turnaround strategies, within urban districts. So-called diverse providers are private entities—nonprofit or for-profit—that offer some component of public education, usually under a contracting or charter arrangement with a public agency.[3] (See Bulkley, chapter 1, this volume.) Although diverse providers work in public school systems and often receive public funds, many diverse providers depend on private sources of funding for start-up costs and to supplement public funding. Each of the NSVF award recipients—along with many others represented at the May event—has received substantial funding from major national foundations. Furthermore, NSVF receives millions of dollars from major foundations to support its own "venture philanthropy" investments. Through the concerted efforts of funders, such as the Bill & Melinda Gates Foundation and the Broad Foundation, diverse providers are part of an emerging organizational field in education reform involving "self-referencing, mutually dependent organizations."[4]

This chapter empirically assesses foundation grant making to show how major foundations have helped to develop and legitimize the field of diverse provider organizations. I show how major foundations have shaped the diverse provider field in three key ways.

First, foundations aim their grant making for diverse providers toward a select group of urban school districts with specific political characteristics. Typically, these are districts where mayoral or state control of the public schools has replaced or diminished the power of elected schools boards. In these districts, as a result, the expanding use of diverse provider organizations is shielded from the kinds of interest group pressures and political entanglements that can effectively veto systemic reforms under more typical governance arrangements.

Second, foundations target grants toward specific types of organizations within these districts. The distribution of grants within districts is increasingly focused on diverse providers and other nonprofit organizations, rather than funding the public school district directly.

Third, foundations have promoted the legitimacy of the diverse provider model by converging on similar grant-making strategies and promoting relationships among grantees. The presence of private actors—both nonprofit and for-profit—in urban education is not a new phenomenon. Nonprofits were the main recipients on the Annenberg Challenge grants for urban education reform in the early 1990s. The growing field of diverse providers includes nonprofits, such as Success for All and KIPP charter schools, as well as for-profits, such as EdisonLearning and Kaplan. The market for school-improvement services that many of these organizations provide has expanded substantially "from virtually nothing as recently as 1995 to $1.5 billion in 2002."[5] Nonetheless, there is enduring political opposition to private actors delivering public education services, particularly from unions. As foundations have committed more grant dollars to enlarging this field of organizations, they are also working to strengthen ties among diverse providers and promote a shared national agenda.

In taking on the particular mission of seeding greater diversity of providers into the education landscape, however, foundations face some special challenges. As DiMaggio and Powell explain, maturation and legitimization of organizational fields tend to promote homogeneity, seemingly a paradoxical result in an effort built around the concept of diversification. In this instance, foundations want to promote diversity *within local districts*, while legitimating private providers on the national front.[6] Seeding diversity within traditional public school districts means confronting resistance by local actors who may have stakes in protecting the status quo. Building support for reliance on private provision nationally requires just the kinds of quality control and standardization *across localities* that DiMaggio and Powell describe. Large foundations often act as "institutional entrepreneurs" or "field builders," by awarding grants to certain types of organizations, establishing common standards, and facilitating interaction among those organizations.[7] Thus, foundations are able to guide the field-building process. Selective grant making designates certain organizations as legitimate members of the field, and building relationships among these organizations creates a shared sense of mission and identity.

DATA AND METHODS

I assembled the data on funding for diverse provider organizations in different school districts by examining the grants major foundations reported on their tax returns. I collected the data from the 2000 and 2005 Form 990-PFs filed by the fifteen foundations that gave the most money for K–12 education.[8] I used lists compiled by the Foundation Center to identify the fifteen largest donors in both years; those donors are listed in this chapter's appendix.[9] On the Form 990-PF, foundations report every grant they disbursed during the fiscal year. For each grant that directly funded K–12 education, training and support for K–12 personnel, K–12 policy advocacy or research, or supplementary education services for K–12 students, I recorded the amount of each grant, the recipient, the recipient's location (when available), and the purpose of the grant (when available). For cases when the recipient's location and/or the grant purpose were not included on the tax form, I conducted a Google search to identify the grantee and obtain information about the grantee's location and purpose.[10] For 2005, the dataset includes nearly sixteen hundred grants totaling over $660 million. For 2000, the dataset includes over twelve hundred grants totaling over $380 million. I coded each grant recipient into one of forty-six categories; the categories are based on the grantee's function or role; some examples include: public school, school district, publicity/media, local nonprofit organization, civic education, arts education, and legal advocacy. In order to determine the total grant dollars devoted to grantees in a given school district, I isolated all the grants in categories that were geographically constrained at the school-district level. I also searched in all of the other grant categories for grants that mentioned a specific school district in the description of their purpose. I grouped all of these grants based on the locations of the grantees, then totaled the grants for each school district.

To assess the development of an organizational field, I applied social network analysis, using UCINET software Version 6.216.[11] The network data were drawn from the data on major foundation grants. I identified all of the organizations that received grants from more than one major foundation. Among these organizations, I developed affiliation networks to plot relationships between organizations that received grants from two or more of the same major foundations. Thus, if organizations shared at least two major funders, I proposed that these organizations share some characteristics that are attractive to a certain set of field-building foundations. Within the networks, I highlighted the organizations that acted as diverse providers in urban school districts. The networks demonstrate the development of the diverse provider organizational field from 2000 to 2005. For 2005, I also collected data on foundation representation on the boards of major foundation grantees. To identify these ties, I conducted searches online for the board members of each grantee in the network.

Also, I conducted interviews with several foundation program officers and foundation grantees in 2008 and 2009, and I read the annual reports of several major foundations. Drawing on the interview material, I show how each set of actors is working to shape this new organizational field and responding to new pressures as the field develops.

DISSEMINATING: THE SPREAD OF FUNDING FOR DIVERSE PROVIDERS

Major foundations are disseminating diverse provider organizations in two key ways. First, they are targeting more dollars at fewer districts that share specific political characteristics. This selectivity builds up more resources for diverse providers in certain locations. Second, major foundations have shifted more funding toward nonprofits and charter schools, rather than the public school districts. This suggests that they are focusing more on building the capacity of the diverse provider types of organizations, rather than the capacity of districts to manage these organizations.

Between 2000 and 2005, the top fifteen education foundations increased the amount of dollars they allocated but directed that funding to a smaller number of districts. In 2000, grantees in forty-seven of the one hundred largest school districts received some philanthropic support from the top fifteen K–12 grant makers. By 2005, grantees in only thirty-four of the one hundred largest districts received funding. Although the total grants allocated by the fifteen largest donors grew by nearly $300 million from 2000 to 2005, these grants were less widely distributed among the one hundred largest districts in 2005. Thus, the level of support for grantees in certain districts increased substantially from 2000 to 2005. Figure 10.1 shows the top twenty districts based on grant dollars per student in 2000, along with the grants per student that grantees in each district received in 2005. Seattle's dramatic shift from top recipient in 2000 to much fewer grant dollars per pupil in 2005 reflects the Seattle-based Gates Foundation's growing national ambitions.[12] Overall, the distribution of grant funds in 2005 varies more widely than it did in 2000. Some districts, such as Cleveland, Detroit, Miami-Dade, and Tucson lost most of their major foundation grants from 2000 to 2005. Meanwhile, other districts, such as Oakland, Boston, New York City, and Atlanta, doubled or tripled their per-pupil grant levels from 2000 to 2005.

FIGURE 10.1 Foundation grant dollars per pupil, 2000 and 2005

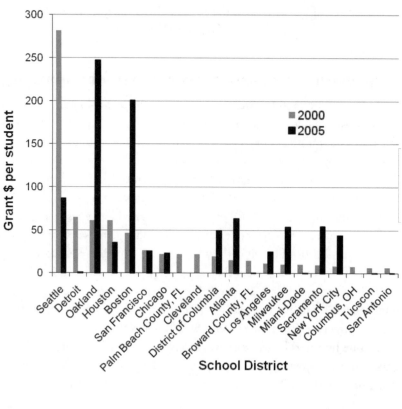

In some places, such as New York City, the increase in grant dollars parallels an increase in the number of diverse providers receiving funds. In 2000, one major nonprofit organization—New Visions for Public Schools—received major foundation grant funds, along with a handful of independent charters that received small start-up grants. By 2005, several nonprofits received grants of over $1 million to support the formation of new, small, public schools in New York City, including New Visions for Public Schools, Urban Assembly, Replications Inc., Institute for Student Achievement, and Outward Bound. New Visions for Public Schools has opened eighty-six New Century High Schools.[13] The Urban Assembly manages twenty small high schools and junior high schools, five of which are also New Century High Schools.[14] Replications Inc. and the Institute for Student Achievement each support more than twenty small high schools and junior high schools in New York, and Outward Bound operates nine schools.[15] Similarly, in Los Angeles, the increase in foundation dollars parallels an increase in grants to several new diverse providers, particularly charter management organizations.

The grant-making strategy looks quite different in Oakland and Boston, which were the top two recipients of grants per student in 2005. In these two districts, most foundation funds in 2005 were targeted at one or two major nonprofit organizations that provide services to the district: in Oakland, Bay Area Coalition for Equitable Schools; in Boston, Jobs for the Future and the Boston Plan for Excellence in the Public Schools. It is likely that local conditions are an important factor in shaping these two strategies. New York and Los Angeles are the two largest public school districts; they are more likely to have both the capacity and the demand to support a wider array of diverse providers. Boston and Oakland are much smaller districts, with student enrollment around fifty thousand; the "diversity" component of the diverse provider model may be less feasible under these circumstances.

Why do some districts get substantially more major foundation grants than other districts? Figure 10.2 displays total funding from the fifteen largest K–12 grant makers to districts where diverse provider organization types—nonprofits, charter schools, and charter management organizations—received more than $1 million in 2005. The graph also highlights

FIGURE 10.2 Total foundation grant dollars from 15 largest K–12 grant makers to districts and diverse providers, 2005

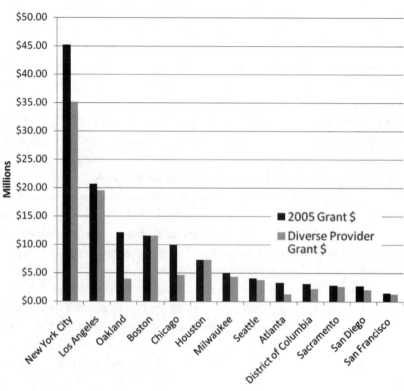

the amount of funding in each district that supported only diverse providers alongside total grant funding to the district. In most of these districts, funding for diverse provider types of organizations composes the majority or even the total amount of grants in the school district. Many of the districts that receive substantial support for diverse providers are districts with mayoral or state control. In 2005, New York City, Oakland, Boston, and Chicago all had full mayoral or state control; Washington, D.C., had partial mayoral control. In New York City, Boston, and Chicago, funding for diverse providers composed nearly 50 percent or more of all major foundation grants for K–12 education. In a multivariate model predicting major foundation grant dollars per student in 2005 to the one hundred largest school districts, mayoral or state control of a district is a strong predictor of per-pupil foundation funding.[16]

Although most foundations do not publicly endorse a particular mode of governing school districts, the Broad Foundation's 2008 *Annual Report* is quite explicit on this matter:

> Our work in this handful of cities—including Chicago, New York City and Oakland, Calif.—has deepened over time as we watched their progress. These cities have a common distinction: the school systems in New York City and Chicago are under the control of the mayor, and the school system in Oakland was placed under state control after facing bankruptcy. We have found that the conditions to dramatically improve K–12 education are often ripe under mayoral or state control.[17]

The Broad Foundations' 2009–2010 *Annual Report* reiterated and elaborated on the foundation's preference for mayoral or state control:

> But observing the frequent political turnover on school boards (and often the resulting shakeup in a school district's leadership or reform agenda) and the lack of focus on student achievement led us to conclude that a more successful governance structure than the country's 14,000 school boards was mayoral, gubernatorial or state control. So our work evolved into supporting mayors and governors in cities and states like New York, Boston, Washington, D.C., Chicago and New Orleans, where their education reform efforts are supported politically in a more sustainable way.[18]

These comments from the Broad Foundation reports and my interviews with program officers point to two seemingly contradictory factors that make districts with mayoral or state control seem ripe for grant makers—change and continuity. First, in districts where foundations hope to catalyze dramatic reform, the disruption provided by a change in governance offers an opportunity to shape new policies and introduce new actors into district-level decision making. According to Michele Cahill, vice president for national programs and program director of urban education at the Carnegie Corporation of New York, the reorganization of New York City's school district governance in 2002 enabled a major mayoral-led reform that was a break with the status quo.[19] Yet foundations also prefer mayoral or state control because they view the leadership in these districts as more stable and centralized than districts with elected boards. According to Constancia Warren, the former senior program officer and director of urban high school initiatives at Carnegie Corporation, foundations assess the strength and sustainability of leadership capacity at the district level: "Does [the district] have the underlying professional and political capacity to implement the change the foundation is supporting—or any kind of meaningful reform?" In particular, Warren added, foundations may avoid sites that are "fragmented and disorganized."[20] In other words, foundation leaders are interested in continuity and avoiding districts with "frequent political turnover." Yet changing a district to mayoral or state control does not always go hand in hand with leadership continuity. During five years of state control in Oakland, the district had three different state administrators. Nonetheless, a few prominent examples of mayoral control in cities with well-known multiterm mayors (Daley in Chicago, Menino in Boston, and Bloomberg in New York) may have advanced the notion that school governance change can foster leadership continuity.

Major foundations are not only increasingly selective when targeting grants at districts, but are also giving less funding directly to school districts and more funding to nonprofits. The amount of grant dollars for traditional public schools (via school districts, state education departments, and their respective foundations) was nearly 40 percent of major foundation grant dollars in 2000, but it was less than a quarter of grant dollars in 2005. Meanwhile, funding for charter schools, charter management organizations, nonprofit public school developers (such as New Visions for Public Schools), and venture capital for education nonprofit start-ups (primarily through NSVF) has increased substantially from 2000 to 2005. For example, the share of major foundation funding for charter schools and charter management organizations nearly tripled from 2000 to 2005.

Foundation leaders prefer to fund nonprofits because they think the relative impact of grant making outside the district will be greater. According to Janice Petrovich, who served as the Ford Foundation's director of education, sexuality, and religion until April 2008, "Most foundations are not providing direct support to the school system. They are supporting organizations outside the school system that have an impact inside the school system."[21] Petrovich explained that large urban districts, such as New York

City, have very large budgets, "so giving money to a school system is a drop in the bucket." She added that the strength of outside organizations is their innovative capacity. Another reason foundations favor investing in outside organizations is frustration with the slow pace of change in traditional school districts, particularly districts governed by elected school boards. The Los Angeles-based Broad Foundation has rarely donated to the Los Angeles Unified School District, but Broad has invested more than $50 million in charter schools in Los Angeles. According to an article in the *Los Angeles Times* about a recent announcement of a new Broad charter school grant: "Broad's gift to [the] Alliance [for College-Ready Public Schools] is the latest indication that he views the work of charters, and not the efforts of Mayor Antonio Villaraigosa or the district's Board of Education, as the best chance to reform the nation's second-largest school system. 'Certainly the brightest hope for students in Los Angeles are high-performing charter school organizations,' Broad said in prepared remarks."[22]

The focus on funding nonprofits rather than making direct grants to school districts suggests that major foundations are more focused on building capacity in the diverse provider field, rather than building the capacity of districts. Furthermore, as Petrovich explains, major foundations may be wary that their money will have less impact in a large and complex public bureaucracy. Nonetheless, a handful of major foundation grants in 2005 were directly targeted at building the capacity of districts to coordinate with diverse providers or to support the development of portfolios of schools managed by the district. Two examples are grants in 2005 to schools districts in Oakland and Milwaukee. A $4.7 million grant from the Gates Foundation to Oakland Unified School District was intended to "launch a model urban school district comprising of a lean central office, a school support services organization, and networks of increasingly high achieving and equitable schools."[23] The grant to Milwaukee Public Schools, also from the Gates Foundation, was slated to "expand and support Milwaukee's portfolio of high school options by converting comprehensive high schools into small learning communities."[24] Thus, a limited share of major foundation grant making has focused on school district capacity in relation to diverse providers.

Among three of the school districts highlighted in this volume—New York City, Chicago, and New Orleans—there are several examples of foundation support for diverse providers. In New York City, most of the diverse providers that received major foundation grants are organizations that open and operate new, small high schools in the district. In Chicago, foundation funding has also supported the creation of new schools operated by diverse providers, including both charter schools and contract schools that are managed by nonprofits. Foundation funding for these efforts has been channeled through the Chicago Community Foundation, which comanaged the Chicago High School Redesign Initiative along with Chicago Public Schools. In 2005, the Gates Foundation provided more than $2.5 million for this initiative. Although Philadelphia has opened up many schools to management by diverse providers, these organizations have received relatively few major foundation grants compared to New York City and Chicago. This is somewhat surprising, because Philadelphia's schools are under state control; major foundations have shown a preference for state control in other contexts, such as Oakland and New Orleans. One explanation for this discrepancy is that Philadelphia has contracted with several for-profit diverse providers, but foundations typically fund nonprofits due to restrictions on the types of grants that qualify for tax-exempt status.[25]

The 2005 foundation grant data do not capture the large increase in major foundation grants for diverse providers in New Orleans after Hurricane Katrina. Since the disaster, major foundations have poured millions of dollars into New Orleans to support the formation of new schools and the recruitment and training of new teachers and principals. Based on data available from the Foundation Center, both the Gates Foundation and the Broad Foundation have supported diverse providers in New Orleans. For example, in 2007, the Gates Foundation gave $5.4 million for a nonprofit, New Schools for New Orleans, to incubate new public schools and charter schools. In 2006, the Gates Foundation gave $2 million to New Leaders for New Schools to support recruitment and training of new principals in New Orleans. The Broad Foundation gave $750,000 in 2007 to support the expansion of Teach For America in New Orleans. Thus, foundations have recently granted substantial support for a number of diverse providers in New Orleans.

Foundations have provided very high levels of funding for diverse providers in a handful of districts, particularly those with mayoral or state control. Yet the involvement of foundations in supporting diverse provider organizations goes beyond the choice to fund certain organizations and not others. Increasingly, major foundations are seeking nonprofits with the capacity to rapidly expand services and meet specific goals. Furthermore, foundations are converging on a common set of grant-making strategies that form the backbone of a new network of diverse provider organizations.

LEGITIMATING: BUILDING A FIELD OF DIVERSE PROVIDERS

Foundations have been funding nonprofit organizations that work with school districts for many years. In the 1990s, the Annenberg Challenge grants were mostly distributed to nonprofits in large urban school districts. The $500 million Annenberg Challenge supported public–private partnerships between school districts and collaborating nonprofit intermediaries. According to Cervone, the Annenberg Challenge sought to avoid moving a large share of dollars "through existing bureaucratic channels," although public school districts were the primary target of the reform efforts.[26] Yet the Annenberg Challenge did not develop strong mechanisms to link these organizations or promote common standards and practices across the sites. As Cervone explains, the Annenberg Challenge allowed each site to "rely on local invention and design . . . which inherently pushed against the values of consistency and coherence."[27] The track record of major foundation involvement in urban education reform has often been assessed as inconsistent and fleeting:

> At best, [foundation] investment has yielded the rare and too often temporary "islands of excellence"—schools with a brief, shining moment of exemplary practice and performance that usually revert to the norm. Little in the way of improvement seems to stick. Today, there is little dispute among leaders in the field of school reform that the social return on philanthropic investment has been grossly inadequate.[28]

Since the Annenberg Challenge, the landscape of major education philanthropies has shifted, and the Gates Foundation is currently the dominant grant maker in the field. In 2000, Gates distributed about $74 million in K–12 education grants; by 2005, the foundation's tax return shows $280 million in K–12 grants, topping the second largest grant maker in

2005 (the Walton Family Foundation) by more than $200 million. New philanthropies, such as the Gates Foundation, Broad Foundation, and Walton Foundation, have also started to frame their grant making in a new way—as venture philanthropy. According to Scott:

> Like venture capitalists, venture philanthropies expect aggressive returns on their investments. They measure such returns not necessarily by profit generated but by growth in student achievement, expansion of particular educational sectors, such as educational [management organizations] or charter schools, and the growth of constituencies who will place political support on public officials to support particular educational reforms.[29]

Or as Dan Katzir, managing director of the Broad Foundation stated at a Democrats for Education Reform event in March 2009: "[Eli Broad was] particularly interested in venture philanthropy: funding or creating out-of-the-box solutions to chronic problems, and then measuring the student 'return on investment.'"[30] Of course, using the language of "investments" and "returns" does not directly translate to changed practice, and the Broad Foundation did not suddenly become the Goldman Sachs of philanthropy. The Broad Foundation *Annual Report* for 2009–2010 makes many claims about successful investments in education reform, but these are mostly presented in the typical anecdotal fashion of glossy foundation reports. Although the report speaks frequently about "investments" and the foundation's "theory of action," the report lacks a hard-nosed calculation of "return on investment" that Katzir describes. This does not mean that the rise of "venture philanthropy" as a common framework among foundations is unimportant. Rather, the fact that multiple foundations, such as Gates, Broad, and Walton, claim to share a common grant-making strategy points to an important new convergence in education philanthropy. Furthermore, the emphasis on grants as "investments" puts new pressures on grantees to demonstrate some type of measurable returns. Through shared grant-making strategies, foundations are building a field around a core set of nonprofits and promoting the legitimacy of these organizations.

Major foundations have promoted field building in two ways. First, they support the adoption of common goals and standards through their grant-making choices. This promotes institutional isomorphism across diverse providers, meaning "organizations are increasingly homogeneous within given domains and increasingly organized around rituals of conformity to wider institutions."[31] Diverse providers that receive major foundation grants must conform to the expectations of their funders. A second field-building mechanism is the development of an organizational network. As Bartley explains, field building "is a process of building social networks that tie a variety of organizations (and individuals) to one another—whether by creating new ties, strengthening existing ones, or even creating new intermediary organizations."[32] The ties enforce the relational aspects of the organizational field—the recognition of a peer group of organizations engaged in similar endeavors.

Grant-making strategies of new foundations have promoted common standards and modes of operating for diverse providers. Given that the Gates Foundation is such a large source of funding for diverse providers and other nonprofits, the foundation is able to exert strong pressure on these groups to adopt some common standards.[33] In interviews, grantees confirmed that the Gates Foundation emphasizes particular standards of evaluation, including high school graduation rates and college attendance. According to Norm Fruchter, former director of the community involvement program at the Annenberg Institute for School Reform, the Gates Foundation wanted to see how community organizing "will lead to increases in student graduation rates and college going. [We need to] define links between our organizing and those kinds of outcomes."[34] Grantees often underscore their attention to the specific goals of funders. The 2008 *Annual Report* of New Visions for Public Schools highlights its emphasis on graduation rate and college-going through the small schools it created in New York City. The first two pages of the report have only six sentences printed against a photo backdrop stating: "In 2002, many schools were failing students across the city. On the Kennedy High School Campus only 39% made it to graduation. Today, success is the new standard at Kennedy. New Visions established four small schools within Kennedy High School. In 2008, 80% of those students graduated. 84% of graduates were accepted to college."[35]

Improving high school graduation and college attendance are undoubtedly laudable goals. Yet heightened emphasis on certain goals may compromise or crowd out other goals, particularly when those goals are backed by the world's largest philanthropy. For example, a recent report on the small-school reform in New York City states that 39 percent of four-year graduates from the new, small high schools received the "local" diploma—a diploma based on minimum standards for graduation that the city is phasing out.[36] When students obtain this minimal diploma, it can boost the four-year graduation rate. Yet, perhaps more students would have obtained the more rigorous Regents diploma if four-year graduation rate was not a key evaluative measure. Furthermore, the majority of students in New York City continue to attend large high schools, and "the gains for students at the small schools came at the expense of other students, some of whom were even needier than those who attended the new small schools."[37] Thus, the emphasis on small schools as a vehicle to achieve these goals has consequences for the quality of education districtwide in New York City.

Other new philanthropies, such as the Broad Foundation, also have a reputation for holding grantees to specific evaluation standards in order to receive funding. According to the Broad Foundation Web site: "Through the terms of each grant, we request periodic reports from grantees on their progress toward expected milestones—over the life of a grant. These milestones, or 'metrics', clearly define what we expect of our grantee organizations . . . If there is limited progress made towards meeting these targets, we may terminate an investment early."[38]

Jennifer Drake, chief development officer at LA Alliance, a charter management organization, explained that funding from the Broad Foundation depends on whether LA Alliance schools meet "metrics that [Broad] set . . . [The Broad Foundation's] evaluation determines disbursement of the funds."[39] The LA Alliance is required to report specific data to the Broad Foundation, which the foundation analyzes and interprets to inform grant-making decisions. It is not at all unexpected or new that foundations would want to evaluate the effectiveness of their grant making. Yet by emphasizing "return on investments," foundations like Broad place heightened importance on systematic tracking and evaluation of grantees. For example, the Broad Foundation approach is a sharp contrast to the evaluation of the Annenberg Challenge, which allowed each of the Challenge sites "to assemble their own evaluation teams."[40] Systematic evaluation by foundations places new demands and expectations on grantees; it means that grantees need to assemble adequate data and have personnel who specialize in gathering and analyzing data.

The development of shared goals among a small set of diverse providers could be promoted by individual foundations working with each of their grantees. Yet the formation of a broad network of mutually interacting organizations involving multiple foundations and dozens of diverse providers requires coordination among grant makers. The emergence of a network further reinforces the organizational field by creating an interlocking group of organizations that share information and regard one another as peer institutions. This type of network is unlikely to emerge if different foundations support distinct sets of grantees. By pursuing overlapping grant-making strategies, foundations are more likely promote relationships between grantees. Grantees with the same sets of funders are subject to similar constraints and expectations, and funders may actively promote networking among their grantees.

Using social network analysis, we can observe the development of the diverse provider organizational field. The networks presented here draw on the foundation grant data from the fifteen largest K–12 grant makers in 2000 and 2005 (figures 10.3 and 10.4). The organizations included in the networks received grants from at least two different major funders *and* share at least two funders with another grantee; organizations that received funding from only one major foundation are excluded. The network data were analyzed using UCINET Version 6.216.[41] I used the NetDraw program available in UCINET to create visual representations of each social network.[42] These social network diagrams highlight instances of convergence in grant making—when foundations support the same grantees. In each network, grantees are represented with circles (nodes)—gray nodes indicate grants for diverse providers or other nonprofit entities that offer services to districts and black nodes are all other types of organizations.[43] The size of the node indicates the amount of grant dollars the grantee received; larger nodes represent more money. A line linking any two organizations indicates that those organizations have two or more funders in common. Thicker lines between organizations indicate higher numbers of shared funders.

Figure 10.3 shows the shared funding links drawn from the 2000 grant data.[44] The network is relatively sparse, given that the 2000 grants database includes more than twelve hundred grants. There are four key organizations at the center of the network that share several funders—Harvard

FIGURE 10.3 Foundation grantee network, 2000

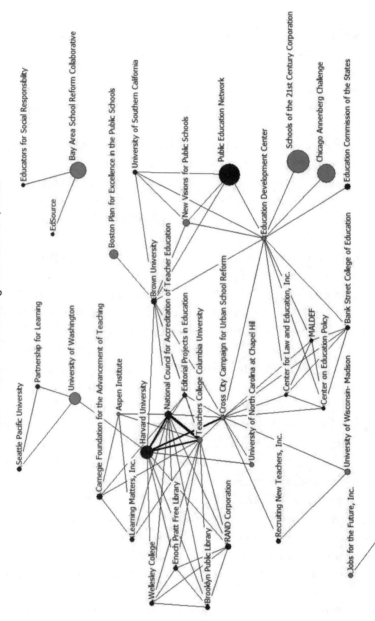

University, Teachers College, the National Council for Accreditation of Teacher Education, and Cross City Campaign for Urban School Reform. The Carnegie Corporation and the Ford Foundation funded all four of these organizations; the Wallace Foundation funded three of them. The network shows a strong focus among grant makers on well-established and highly regarded institutions, such as Harvard University and Teachers College. Also, the network shows that the fairly limited common agenda of grant makers in 2000 was focused on teacher education. In addition to universities, other major grant recipients in 2000 were nonprofit partners in the Annenberg Challenge sites, such as Schools of the 21st Century in Detroit and New Visions for Public Schools in New York City. The Annenberg Challenge organizations are the main grantees that could be classified as diverse providers in 2000; there were relatively few diverse provider organizations receiving substantial foundation funding in 2000.

The picture in 2005 is quite different and provides strong evidence of an emerging field of diverse provider organizations. Figure 10.4 shows the foundation grantee network for 2005.[45] This network is much denser— i.e., there are more cross-cutting links between organizations—than the 2000 network. The network is also more crowded; there are more grantees that share two or more funders in 2005 compared to 2000. The top fifteen K–12 grant makers gave more money in 2005 compared to 2000, but they also gave more of that money in conjunction with other foundations. In 2005, 35 percent of major foundations' grant dollars—more than $230 million in grants—were distributed to grantees that also received funding from other major foundations. In 2000, this type of grant making was only about 21 percent of all major foundation grant making. Thus, in 2000, only about $80 million in grants from major foundations was distributed to grantees that received funds from more than one major foundation.

Furthermore, the gray nodes indicate that diverse provider organizations are more prominent in this network. Although this network points to the emergence of a diverse provider field, it is a somewhat divided field. Among major education grant makers, there are two divergent strategies that draw from overlapping grant-making approaches. One strategy is funding for community-based diverse providers, indicated by the bottom oval. These diverse providers work on the premise that "schools

FIGURE 10.4 Foundation grantee network, 2005

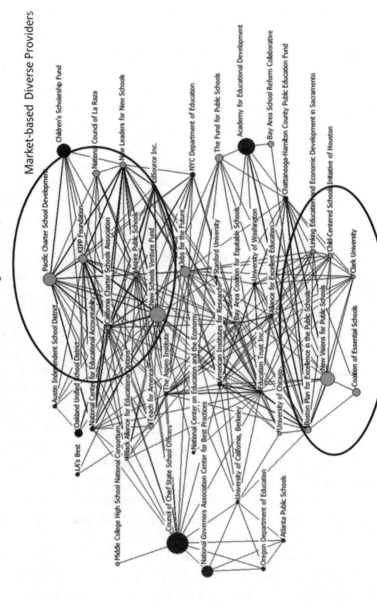

Market-based Diverse Providers

Community-based Diverse Providers

do best when they are organized into networks with others who share their philosophy."[46] Typically, these diverse providers cooperate with public schools and local community organizations to open, operate, or support new schools. The Coalition of Essential Schools and New Visions for Public Schools are examples of this type of organization. Most of the community-based diverse providers receive funding from two or more of the following foundations: the Carnegie Corporation, the Annenberg Foundation, and the Gates Foundation. This grant-making strategy seems to link the older foundations like Carnegie and Annenberg with a newer foundation—the Gates Foundation. Some of these diverse providers, such as New Visions for Public Schools, transitioned from being major recipients of the Annenberg Challenge grants to receiving major grants for small schools from the Gates Foundation.

The other diverse provider grant-making strategy involves market-based diverse providers, indicated by the top oval. These diverse providers include charter management organizations and alternative certification programs such as New Leaders for New Schools. These organizations are based on the premise that "the core problem of American public education is that it is a monopoly and that schools get better only through the injection of competition, parental choice, and other forms of market pressure."[47] Charter management organizations in this group include KIPP and Aspire Public Schools. The main foundations supporting this group of diverse providers are the Broad Foundation, Walton Foundation, and Gates Foundation. In other words, these are self-proclaimed practitioners of "venture philanthropy." The Gates Foundation is the key grant maker that supports both types of diverse providers. Yet the divergent grant-making strategies of these major K–12 grant makers suggest that there are two distinct, but slightly overlapping, fields of diverse providers.

Furthermore, common funding sources are not the only shared tie among diverse providers. Some diverse providers have representatives from the same foundations on their boards of directors, particularly the market-based diverse providers (see table 10.1). Representatives of the Gates Foundation sit on the boards of California Charter Schools Association, EdSource, Jobs for the Future, and New Leaders for New Schools. Thus, the perspective of the foundation is communicated not only through grant making and grantee evaluations, but also through discussions about organization policy

TABLE 10.1   Ties among diverse providers boards of directors

Organization	Foundation affiliations of board members
Alliance for Excellent Education	Ford Foundation
Child-Centered Schools Initiative of Houston	Brown Foundation
California Charter Schools Association	Fisher Fund, Gates Foundation
Children's Scholarship Fund	Broad Foundation, Walton Foundation
EdSource Inc.	Gates Foundation
Jobs for the Future	Gates Foundation
KIPP	Fisher Fund
New Leaders for New Schools	Gates Foundation
Pacific Charter School Development	Broad Foundation, New Schools Venture Fund

Source: Data compiled by author from organization Web sites.

and direction at board meetings. The fact that foundation representation is more prevalent among the market-based providers suggests that foundations and organizational leaders are placing more emphasis on field building among this category of organizations.

Within the diverse-provider organizational field, one organization stands out as a particularly important field builder, occupying an intermediary position between several major foundations and a large cohort of diverse provider grantees. This organization is NSVF, and it is particularly influential in the market-based segment of the field. In the 2005 foundation grantee network, NSVF is the most central organization, meaning that more organizations share two or more funders with NSVF than any other organization in the network. Additionally, NSVF representatives sit on the boards of New Leaders for New Schools and Pacific Charter School Development. These shared relationships help to position NSVF to act as a coordinator in the field. The president and CEO of the Aspen Institute, Walter Isaacson glowingly describes the coordinating role of NSVF in the NSVF ten-year report:

> The central square for this revolution [in education]—the birthplace of its ideas, the meeting place for its generals—has been New Schools

Venture Fund. From the days when Aspire Public Schools and KIPP were just a couple of schools, and no one had heard of a charter management organization, New Schools has helped to guide change that has benefited hundreds of thousands of children.[48]

Whether or not one agrees with Isaacson's claim that NSVF has benefited hundreds of thousands of children, the organization has carved out a crucial role linking funders possessing millions of dollars to diverse providers with aspirations to change public education. As Scott explains, NSVF could be the closest approximation to a business venture capital model applied to education.[49] NSVF takes in revenue from major foundations, including Gates, Broad, and Walton, and distributes the funding through "ventures" focusing on specific strategies such as expansion of charter management organizations or alternative certification programs. Some of the organizations that have received venture funding include: Aspire Public Schools, KIPP DC, New Leaders for New Schools, Pacific Charter School Development, and Teach For America. According to Scott:

> Those interested in funding are encouraged to submit not a grant proposal but a business plan that delineates how the proposed venture will produce measurable outcomes, be scalable, be sustainable, have entrepreneurial leadership, fit with NSVF's investment strategy, and benefit from the fund's investment.[50]

NSVF has enhanced its role as a field builder by holding annual invitation-only summits focused on education reform, developing learning communities for the organizations it supports, and publishing best practices.

In sum, the funding strategies of major foundations in support of diverse providers have converged across several dimensions. First, foundations are focusing their funding on a more limited set of school districts, particularly districts with mayoral or state control. Second, foundations are developing somewhat more consistent standards and evaluation procedures. This places new constraints and expectations on grantees, meaning diverse providers need to develop similar organizational capacities to respond to data and evaluation requests of the funders. Lastly, by 2005, foundations started funding larger numbers of diverse provider organizations and distributing funding to many of the same organizations. There are two slightly divergent sets of diverse providers—community-based and market-based—each supported by a somewhat different group of funders. Nonetheless, a nationally linked field of diverse provider organizations is emerging. Among these organizations, NSVF has occupied a central role as a field builder, particularly among the market-based diverse providers. Given the ongoing work of NSVF and the growing funding support from the Gates Foundation for charter management organizations, it is likely that the market-based diverse providers may eventually dominate the diverse provider field.

CONCLUSION

Foundations have long been criticized for spreading their resources too thin, changing strategies capriciously, and pursuing pet projects. The newest crop of grant makers is trying to show that those are the ways of the past. Major foundations are increasingly concentrating their resources among a select group of school districts and a common set of organizations. Furthermore, they are beginning to develop ties among these organizations by promoting common goals and sitting on organizational boards. What is lost or gained with these new strategies? Perhaps the biggest losses are to smaller nonprofits and independent "mom and pop" charter schools. These organizations are less likely to have the capacity to demonstrate "returns" and scale up investments. If these major foundations now have their pick among charter management organizations operating dozens of schools, it seems less likely that they will support new start-up efforts that have not demonstrated a wider impact. The diverse provider field is likely to become less diverse and more homogeneous even as it gains wider recognition and legitimacy.

As for gains, major funders claim credit for various gains in student achievement and outcomes due to their grants, although these tend to be anecdotal accounts. More rigorous evaluations, such as the evaluation of the Gates Foundation's small-schools initiative by the American Institutes for Research and SRI International, often fail to show significant gains in student achievement.[51] Yet the most significant and lasting impact of these strategies may be political, and it is too early to assess whether it is a gain or a loss. The influence of a small group of large national foundations on education reform has reached a high point. Foundations have helped to set the terms of the national education policy debate by defining which policy strategies are "real" reforms and which actors are "real" reformers. By converging their grant making on a new set of organizations, they have raised the prominence of these groups in relation to traditional stakeholders in education politics. Based on the foundations' selections, "real" reformers are not union leaders or schools of education or school board members; "real" reformers are new nonprofit organizations—Teach For America, KIPP, and New Leaders for New Schools are the exemplars. This simplistic distinction has been fully digested by much of the mainstream media, where celebratory accounts of KIPP and Teach For America abound. More significantly, this distinction has penetrated the appointments and policies of the U.S. Department of Education. The clearest sign of this political achievement was Secretary Duncan's selection of Weiss to lead the Race to the Top program. With this choice, Duncan sought to place a "real" reformer in charge of one of the department's most politically important new programs. Additionally, three other top appointees in the Department of Education previously worked for the Gates Foundation. Duncan has also taken up policy preferences shared by major foundations. Duncan recently stated that if the number of mayors in control of schools did not increase during his term as secretary, he "will have failed."[52] One of the evaluation criteria for states to earn Race to the Top funds is raising their charter school caps. The Broad Foundation's 2009–2010 *Annual Report* glowingly commented on these events:

> The election of President Barack Obama and his appointment of Arne Duncan, former CEO of Chicago Public Schools, as the U.S. secretary of education, marked the pinnacle of hope for our work in education reform. In many ways, we feel the stars have finally aligned. With an agenda that echoes our decade of investments—charter schools, performance pay for teachers, accountability, expanded learning time and national standards—the Obama administration is poised to cultivate and bring to fruition the seeds we and other reformers have planted.[53]

Combined, the converging agendas of major foundations and federal officials could be a powerful force to nationalize education reform. The hyper-local character of education politics and policy has been the norm for much of the nation's history. In the positive sense, increasing nationalization of education reform could indicate a desirable breaking down of bastions of parochialism and facilitate the spread of innovations and best practices. Yet philanthropy has often played a crucial role in building civil society in ways that are too controversial or experimental for public funding. This role would be attenuated if major foundations are steering the national agenda, rather than challenging or critiquing it. Furthermore, if significant private and federal resources begin steering education governance reform in a market-oriented direction with competitive grant making, local districts have little incentive to explore legitimate alternatives. The growing role of national foundations raises worrying questions about whether democratic accountability may be compromised when wealthy private foundations with no direct local stake become players in education policy in communities across the country.

Chapter 10 Appendix

Largest donors to K–12 Education in 2000

1. Bill & Melinda Gates Foundation
2. Annenberg Foundation
3. Walton Family Foundation, Inc.
4. J. A. and Kathryn Albertson Foundation, Inc.
5. Ford Foundation
6. Wallace-Reader's Digest Funds
7. Lilly Endowment, Inc.
8. The Joyce Foundation
9. Ross Family Charitable Foundation
11. Brown Foundation, Inc.
12. Carnegie Corporation of New York
13. William and Flora Hewlett Foundation
14. Skillman Foundation
15. Bank of America Foundation, Inc.
16. W. K. Kellogg Foundation

Largest donors to K–12 Education in 2005

1. Bill & Melinda Gates Foundation
2. Walton Family Foundation, Inc.
3. Lilly Endowment, Inc.
4. Wallace Foundation
5. Annenberg Foundation
6. Broad Foundation
7. Ford Foundation
8. Oberkotter Foundation
9. William and Flora Hewlett Foundation
10. H. N. and Frances C. Berger Foundation
11. Daniels Fund

12. J. A. and Kathryn Albertson Foundation, Inc.
13. Starr Foundation
14. Carnegie Corporation of New York
15. Community Foundation Silicon Valley

Source: Foundation Center, http://foundationcenter.org/findfunders/statistics/gs_subject.html

PART IV

Looking Forward

11

Portfolio Management Models

From the Practitioner's Eyes

Josh Edelman

Since 1991, I have had the privilege of being an educator.* I spent fifteen years teaching and/or being an administrator in private, traditional public, and public charter secondary-school settings. For the past several years, I have strayed into central office leadership, first in Chicago as the executive officer of the Office of New Schools under then-CEO Arne Duncan and now in Washington, D.C., as the deputy chief of the Office of School Innovation with Chancellor Michelle Rhee. What stands out in all my experiences but, especially, from the charter, Chicago Public School, and Washington, D.C., Public School experiences is the importance of entrepreneurialism and talent. Strong, researched-based programs are essential, but *people* aligned with a vision focused on outcomes are the necessary catalyst to create high-quality educational options for our children.

The portfolio management model (PMM) is an extension of my belief system, and I believe it is a model with the potential to have a significant

---

*This chapter was written in collaboration with Katrina Bulkley. However, the substance reflects the ideas of Josh Edelman and thus is written in the first person.

impact on public education today. With President Obama's and Secretary Duncan's emphasis on innovation, their desire to tap into talent from within and outside the traditional system, and their unequivocal results orientation, we as a nation have an opportunity to do special things for students who have often been held back not by their intellect but by the quality of the school environments in which they found themselves.

Part of what is different now from a decade ago is that there is a growing mass of private operators with track records of success. Further, many of these entrepreneurial organizations want to be a piece of the district puzzles where autonomy is offered and accountability is the norm. With school management organizations that want to work within traditional systems and districts open to working with outside operators all aligned on the importance of accountability, there is great potential for success if the conditions are right. The national climate created by President Obama and Secretary Duncan, exemplified by the Race to the Top and i3 competitions, is as good as any we have had to bolster private operators supporting public education.

For PMM to work, though, local contexts have to allow district leaders the flexibility to use accountability as a lever to open and close traditional and operator-led schools based on performance. Most importantly, *talent* matters at the levels of the elected official, superintendent, central office, and, especially, school. In this chapter, by looking at versions of PMM in practice in New York City, Chicago, Philadelphia, and New Orleans and reflecting on the influence of other stakeholders, I will offer instructive lessons to provoke thought and add to the conversation at a policy and practical level about how the model can contribute to systemically improving public education.

MOVING TOWARD A PMM

Leaders considering moving their district toward PMM should consider a number of issues, including overall central office redesign, ways to create and support new schools (including the critical role of school autonomy), and issues of accountability such as data systems and school closure. Across these issues is the need for strong visionary leadership committed to portfolio management and with the authority, will, and skill needed to have an impact on student achievement outcomes. In addition, transparency in processes and decision making is essential at all levels of the PMM system. Finally, those interested in portfolio management need to think carefully about how to identify and enable the human capital necessary to lead successful schools.

Central Office Redesign

What the central office does is critical to creating a climate in which a PMM can be successful. One common strategy for making such changes is through the creation of distinct departments, such as an office of new schools or office of portfolio diversity, to support portfolio management within the broader district structure. Distinct departments may provide a good starting point, but they need the authority and support to be effective. However, they need support from the boundary-spanning and buffering entities described by Honig and DeArmond (chapter 7, this volume). The boundary-spanning role is significantly important when such district personnel are in facilitative roles, often engaging in reactive, firefighting activities on behalf of new schools. Regardless of these reactive efforts by district staff, raising awareness of central office personnel outside the new school unit largely depends on the atmosphere created by the superintendent or CEO. Is the person leading the new school unit high enough, in what is usually a fairly hierarchical organization, to gain respect by title and presence in key meetings? Does the superintendent or CEO provide enough cover to fight internal battles and build capacity department by department? Ideally, each central office department should have a leader who believes in and partners with the new school unit and allocates key point people who can be molded through orientation and training to assist in those areas where PMM support is most necessary. Engendering new school unit respect throughout the central office infrastructure will help buffer schools from bureaucracy by allowing them to be autonomous enterprises only required to comply with processes or complete training aligned with their performance contract language.

The choice of such leaders is important; often, they are people who come from outside the regular district structure, from charter schools or the private sector. Honig and DeArmond raise legitimate concerns about nontraditional leaders going into the "belly of the [central office] beast" without positional authority or previous bureaucratic experience. Such individuals should have specific training, coaching, and support. Similar to the New Leaders for New Schools plan to give principals a coach, why not tee up coaches for such boundary spanners as well?

Overall, districts that take half-steps and don't put the appropriate central office redesign in place, don't fund adequately, don't provide the right amount of autonomy, lack leadership, and have procedural impediments created by policy barriers engender conditions that undermine the chance of good operators to reach legitimate success. While there need to be changes in the overall structure of district central offices, there also needs to be a clear guiding vision that is communicated to everyone in the central office and provides a framework for broadly rethinking people's roles and responsibilities.

Creation and Support of High-Quality Schools

In order to create and support high-quality schools, district leaders and staff need to provide substantial autonomy to school operators as a precondition for improvement, rather than a reward for success. Along with autonomy, there needs to be transparent and rigorous accountability that can lead to school closure if performance targets are not met, and attention to the kinds of human capital essential for school improvement.

Rigorous, thoughtful, and transparent processes for initial authorization and selection of operators, as well as renewal of contracts with operators, are absolutely critical. Sometimes, the broader context can create pressures to authorize or renew, and the stronger and more transparent the processes in these areas, the more able the district will be to resist outside pressures. While authorization and renewal are critical, however, they may be insufficient for developing a portfolio of high-quality schools. While I don't wholly disagree that the goal is to identify operators with the capacity to be successful on their own, I think having a functional central office that is actively involved in the ways that Honig and DeArmond discuss (chapter 7, this volume) is very important. Developing a flexible central office unit is a mind-set shift for many superintendents or CEOs, unless they are committed to PMM substantively, as opposed to seeing it as an isolated approach in which the new school office is isolated and works with operators on its own. Some people see the role of the central office in a PMM as authorizing schools, ensuring compliance, and assessing outcomes or holding schools accountable. As to what happens in the schools in the meantime, that's the sole responsibility of the operator. I believe in some level of guidance for new schools. For example, small operators who only have a single campus, but are successful, may need encouragement and coaching to grow from one to many campuses.

The risk of a laissez-faire approach is that it could, to some extent, set up the system for failure. This is especially true when so few operators really understand and have the capacity to manage schools in the urban marketplace. We, as district leaders and staff, have the responsibility—context by context—to help those entrepreneurs who have demonstrated the potential for success as single or multi-campus operators to solidify their organizations in becoming sustainable and strong for the long term. New Orleans is a testing ground to see what happens with a laissez-faire approach, when true decentralization, market competition, and choice run unfettered. We need to study what is happening in New Orleans carefully to tease out what elements and actions are leading to positive growth for kids and where strategic district support could bolster operator success.

The choice of school operators matters, and a careful selection process tailored to the local context can be important in seeing that the operators selected have what is needed to be successful in certain contexts. In some contexts, the proliferation of charters means authorizers should focus on operators that can show outcome data. Given the glut of still-developing single-campus operators in certain urban markets, a focus on those organizations with track records and a desire to grow means fewer actors to acclimate and introduce over time. Out-of-towners bring resources, national networks, and fewer connections to local officials or influence (see Henig, chapter 2, this volume), which is important for resource-strapped urban districts. Finding the balance between the local and national actors is contextual and a key focus for district leadership within a PMM.

Selecting strong operators, however, is insufficient. A strong portfolio management district needs autonomy with clear parameters for performance and an ongoing evaluation of which autonomies seem to correlate most directly to outcomes. Autonomy acts as an accelerant for talented entrepreneurs who use the flexibility to create more effective and creative models. Can portfolio management occur if the leadership does not believe in granting autonomy? It would be interesting to know whether there are varied levels in the success of portfolio management based on the differences in how a particular district views or employs autonomy. A portfolio management district with autonomy still needs parameters for district expectations of performance (e.g., targets, standards, and so on, what I call the *what*), but the provider has flexibility (or the *how*) for the route to the outcome.

While autonomy is important, the case of New Orleans also hints at some dangers in going too far. The level of autonomy afforded there may make it hard to develop a school system with at least some standardized processes, as opposed to a system of schools so disparate that families don't know how to choose, are unable to access schools as they return to the system, or find themselves starting over when they switch schools because each school's practices and programs are different.

Finally, a transparent performance contract outlining the autonomies received in exchange for accountability is also important. The wording should ensure that the dynamism of the relationship is not hampered by forced compliance in the areas of the *how*, which infringe on the practitioner's space. The focus should be on the desired outcome with as much flexibility as possible for the operator to craft its own path toward success.

Accountability

Accountability through transparent processes for the renewal of contracts and the continuation of relationships with different operators is critical for a PMM district. However, the key question is always *how* this is done. Is it a big-brother, compliance-focused approach with time-consuming processes foisted on operators or a streamlined yet substantive process without a "gotcha" goal, which honors the intentions and efforts of the operator? The end goal of meeting expectations by the law or policy outlined in the performance agreement should be clear, but there should be a spirit of collaboration, not control, coming from the central office within a functional PMM.

In terms of closing schools, leaders must recognize the importance of a clear, transparent process backed by committed district leaders, with a visible distinction between closures due to performance and those due to underenrollment. Leaders also need to to make sure that closures are coupled with options for students that are better than the schools being closed. This is the toughest kind of decision in a PMM and needs to be made carefully and openly because it is so filled with emotion. When turnarounds are possible, they are desirable, because the kids don't need to move to another school. However, this is a very different challenge than opening a new school, and few organizations have demonstrated the willingness to do this. The Academy for Urban School Leadership in Chicago, Mastery Charter Schools in Philadelphia, and Green Dot Public Schools in Los Angeles are a few of the stronger operators with demonstrated potential to turn around schools instead of the district closing those schools.

The role of the community in decisions on school closure needs to be clear. The district must be transparent upfront that there is a substantive and important role for the community. However, it must also say upfront that community input is essential, but that the district, not community groups or individuals, is the final decision maker. Closures are already lightning rods for the community. Closures when students go to poor schools create a flammable situation. Closures can be seen as countermanding parental choice, unless an activist base of parents demands better options. Green Dot has enlisted parents in Los Angeles, and Eva Moskowitz is doing it in New York City at Harlem Success Academy. Duncan and former Chicago Board of Education president, Rufus Williams, often responded to concerned parents who spoke out about their low-performing schools being closed that they should demand better schools and support turnarounds instead of being upset that their low-performing schools were on the chopping block.

In order to have a clear, rigorous process for accountability, districts need to have good data presented so it is accessible to the public. Data need to be used not just to decide whether to close a school or get a different provider, but also to help the central office make midcourse adjustments (e.g., yearly or mid-renewal quality inspections and reviews). The central office must be willing to use the hard data, but also to go beyond when appropriate. Given the PMM's focus on accountability and continuous improvement, an internal data and accountability department that can provide operators and central office leaders with data about performance and ask hard questions about progress is essential. While leading indicators and on-track metrics are key, how to put them in language that the public will understand and buy into is the challenge. How do you go beyond standardized test scores as the only measure? Duncan's focus on value added and growth alongside absolute performance with the reauthorization of the Elementary and Secondary Education Act is an important step in this direction. The impending reauthorization of ESEA could have major implications for districts moving toward portfolio management; the Department of Education has the power to legitimize other indicators of measuring progress beyond absolute thresholds for proficiency.

Human Capital in a PMM

Leaders in a successful PMM must recruit robustly and screen rigorously for talent prior to granting contracts for new schools in a successful PMM. People matter tremendously not only to run great new schools, but also to provide the out-of-box thinking necessary to create innovation. PMM leaders need to think creatively about developing human capital in different ways, such as Joel Klein did when he created the New York City Leadership Academy to prepare leaders for the entrepreneurial work required. The new teacher union contract in Philadelphia provides another important opportunity for improving human capital.

Removing people who don't have the will or skill, while developing those with the will to grow, is essential. Having a robust, multifaceted talent management plan aligned with a clear vision is a key element to the implementation of portfolio management or any attempt at urban educational reform. Although leadership matters at the level of the superintendent, CEO, and central office, it really matters at the operator level if autonomy is the accelerant for producing lasting change. Strong people should be held accountable through appropriate interim or benchmark check-ins. There are serious potential pitfalls if good operators are not the focus. It doesn't take a lot of operator failure to undermine the opportunity for those doing the work well to be able to continue their efforts.

Districts moving toward portfolio management must be mindful of the pace of their growth, given the availability of high-quality human capital. For example, central office leaders in New York City, during the 2007–2008 school year, presupposed that there were enough high-quality principals to adeptly use outside vendor services as they moved toward a model in which all schools needed to choose among the empowerment zone or working with a learning support organization (LSO) or partner support organization (PSO) (see Gyurko and Henig, chapter 4 in this volume). Perhaps between the Leadership Academy pumping out principals with the right skills and mind-sets and more transparent accountability and school inspections, folks thought they could ferret out principals unable to navigate the system or bolster those with potential for strong leadership. Being cognizant of challenges associated with context and the pace of portfolio management implementation is important to achieve benefits from the model.

Given the desire to create market competition for horizontal education support services in most PMM districts, such as private groups competing with district departments to provide central office services at a cost in order to push district efficiency and effectiveness, it would be interesting to explore developments in this area. For example, has New Orleans, a city that has probably seen the most radical change, accomplished more in this regard than other PMM districts? Were there already groups present that could provide these services or did they opportunistically arise to address the need? Are there examples of sectors where such service providers are pushing district departments in a high-quality, competitive fashion?

UNDERSTANDING AND MANAGING THE POLITICS OF A PMM

A successful PMM requires leaders who are effective in the political world. In chapter 2 of this volume, Henig makes the important point that using politics adeptly—versus trying to sidestep it—is necessary because portfolio management is challenging the status quo of the district structure or approach and is predicated on opening and closing schools, which provokes reaction from local actors. The ideas in this book can help policy makers and practitioners think about the development of PMMs, the role of civic and parental engagement in a PMM, and the role of actors outside government (including foundations, management consultants, etc.) in the promotion of PMM ideas.

Development of PMMs

The broader national context has enabled the growth of PMMs. For example, components of NCLB, including contracting out educational services and school management, have made it easier for cities to justify PMM as a legitimate, rather than fringe, approach (see Burch, chapter 9, this volume). The current federal and philanthropic context is one in which both groups support many of the pieces underlying PMMs. Changes in that context, or in the local context of districts taking a lead on the PMM issue, could have a significant impact on sustainability.

A sense of crisis may also create more opportunities for PMM development. While Hurricane Katrina created an immediate crisis in New Orleans, the broader factors (low student performance, fiscal mismanagement, poor facilities, possible state takeover of some schools, a strong state superintendent, a weak local union power base, etc.) created the context in which major changes were made (see Levin, Daschbach, and Perry, chapter 6, this volume).

The system in New York City epitomizes the importance of context and of multiple moving parts coming together. Even though it is imperfect, the system is the best example of PMM in the U.S. urban education landscape for a number of reasons:

- Strong central leaders (Mayor Michael Bloomberg and CEO Joel Klein) who have the authority and the political will and skill to actively support reform

- Strong local sources of talented entrepreneurs and district leaders who are willing to let innovators participate in the system

- Access to substantial public and private monies

Mayoral control has been a common thread in PMM districts and has provided the opportunity for the strong central leadership so critical for PMM development. While not necessary for PMM, mayoral control has proved very useful in many cities. The New Orleans example is one in which the state superintendent, Paul Pastorek, has played a central role. What may be necessary is a local context that allows leaders to create change without needing to navigate challenging political and bureaucratic obstacles.

Although there are national advocates for the kinds of reforms included in PMMs, the statement about the Philadelphia model coming together "not as a result of a grand plan driven by ideology . . . but as a series of policy changes and political adaptations" is accurate for many cities moving in this direction (see Bulkley, Christman, and Gold, chapter 5, this volume). As Henig discusses (chapter 2, this volume), contracting in particular can be done for pragmatic reasons. If a PMM's pragmatism is clear, it will be easier to state the case in terms of student achievement and/or finance upfront so that a basis for action, whether others agree or not, is at least possible. The public will not believe intent until success over time begets belief. Figuring out leading indicators of progress so PMM advocates will be able to point to success and correct course on a city-by-city basis will be essential.

Seeing New York City's unique innovative school base (see Gyurko and Henig, chapter 4 in this volume) and history creates an opportunity to examine the differences in the evolution of PMM from city to city. How important is it to draw from this history? Does having such an example in an urban setting undercut some community pushback on PMM?

Civic and Parental Engagement

Given the statistically significant relationship between organized interests and the scope of contracting (see Henig, chapter 2, this volume), it is critical that PMM districts be cognizant of their context and work proactively with different actors to understand their desires and influence. While community engagement in public education is important, as I discussed earlier, I believe that direct involvement in decision making in a PMM, such as which schools to close or which operators to select for new schools, probably should rest in the central office. However, a clear, transparent process is important not only to ensure good educational decisions, but also to ensure that the community clearly understands central office decisions. While difficult to achieve, a balance between complete central office control and some level of community engagement may offer the best hope for sustainable PMMs.

A lack of sufficient attention to community perceptions can have deleterious consequences. For instance, in Chicago, the pro-charter Civic Committee representing the business community and the Renaissance Schools Fund were actively involved in new school work. Some members of the community perceived that Renaissance 2010 was an anticommunity, anti-union gentrification initiative (see Menefee-Libey, chapter 3, this volume).

Those implementing portfolio management should think carefully about how they can be proactive in involving the community because community groups and members may see portfolio management as undermining the traditional system rather than augmenting it. While community involvement may slow progress in opening and closing schools, it may also create more opportunities to sustain a portfolio approach. Opportunities for innovation and entrepreneurship are valuable, but can also lead traditionalists, unions, and community groups to feel that their voices are minimized in favor of voices from the business community. In this case, scale may work against the possibilities for PMM because opposition can become galvanized, well organized, and build close ties with local and state politicians.

Meaningful civic engagement can provide significant support for portfolio management. New Orleans is an interesting example of such engagement (see Levin, Daschbach, and Perry, chapter 6, this volume). Supportive individual leaders and groups from the faith-based and secular communities can be important partners and messengers. They need to be invested in the work via formal collaborations, opportunities to serve on boards, or informal district or charter networks—all possible mechanisms for retaining them as supporters over the long term.

In New York City, as described by Gyurko and Henig (chapter 4, this volume), many entrepreneurs were invited to participate in the system substantively and given a role in school support organizations (SSO) so that they had an economic stake in its success. This created a large group of advocates across sectors that supported mayoral control and Klein's leadership, as political forces aligned to push back against them. Growing this strong range of supporters underscores the importance of political acumen within a PMM world. As this current chapter underscores, sustainability is difficult, so the SSO effort and keeping public money outside the budget are intentional moves to keep a system going, beyond the individuals involved, since systems need to be structured without being contingent on specific individuals and personal relationships.

Engagement with broader civic organizations is important, but the most immediate constituents for PMMs are the parents. Henig (chapter 2, this volume) discusses the critical issue of parents as "informed" and "quality-conscious education shoppers." How much PMM work is up-front marketing on what it is and is not? Or how much of it is individual school operators adding a more explicit public relations–marketing facet to their work? Defining and enforcing performance is important but rarely done well. Figuring out how to garner trust and support before utilizing accountability frameworks is necessary. We need to know much more about how parents are experiencing these changes, especially in terms of issues of choice. What do parents like or not like? Are the different types of schools with different lotteries confusing to families? The key question to countering the perception that PMM is about anticommunity privatization is how we can bolster parental choice when governmental choice is at the center.

Outside Actors in PMMs

Foundations, consulting firms, and national networks, such as New-Schools Venture Fund (NSVF), have been important influencers and partners in establishing PMMs. Foundations have played a prominent role in the development of PMMs (see Reckhow, chapter 10, this volume). Foundations' focus on a few districts with the right context, on districts with specific political characteristics, and on funding to nonprofits and charters (rather than the district itself) speaks to a desire to use outside providers to shape internal district action. Given the "grantee network" charts in chapter 10, Reckhow seems to suggest that once a group is funded by one foundation, especially if it is Gates, Broad, or Walton, others will come. As in New York, funding was available for Renaissance 2010 in Chicago. Without private monies from national foundations and the Renaissance Schools Fund, the scale of the work could not have happened. The Chicago Public Schools now have more charters and still focus on accountability and the ability to differentiate based on student outcomes, but they may struggle with money and the political context to create new schools versus just managing what is already in place.

Reckhow makes a fair point about the potential influence that funding sources, especially foundations, have on the vision and direction of districts, as well as the uncertainty of their funding long term. This influence of foundations has been particularly critical in New Orleans (see Levin, Daschbach, and Perry, chapter 6, this volume). Superintendent Vallas, charter network leaders, and State Superintendent Pastorek must consider how to continue to invest such stakeholders in the work while developing a contingency plan if funding levels decrease. Certainly, telling a story of vision, outcomes, and action plans is smart public relations meant to keep stakeholders engaged and on board.

The NSVF, which brings together funding from different foundations to support entrepreneurial reforms, has been a very important actor in many portfolio management cities. It is involved in most urban centers with PMM because of its venture capital–like investment in strong charter management organizations (CMOs) or CMO support entities that, in turn, are the basis of portfolio management ventures, for example, Mastery Charter Schools in Philadelphia; the Academy for Urban School Leadership and Chicago International Charter Schools in Chicago; Uncommon Schools, Achievement First, KIPP, and Civic Builders in New York City, and New Schools for New Orleans. A deeper look into its involvement and how it has evolved over time would be worthwhile since it has had as much if not more direct access to urban superintendents and key portfolio management practitioners than more conventional foundations.

McKinsey & Company's involvement in shaping the strategy in New York City and elsewhere has not only established the precedent of working with external consultants, but it has pushed the development of whole educational practices in certain firms. It would be fascinating to chart the growth of the education consulting "shops" of entities such as The Parthenon Group, Boston Consulting Group (BCG), Booz Allen Hamilton, McKinsey, Bain & Company, and the Bridgespan Group because of their roles in the evolution of urban educational systems, in general and specifically, in New York City. Mayoral control has arguably created a whole new industry for external consultants.

WHERE DO WE GO FROM HERE?

While PMM is an exciting idea, it is still emerging. Much still needs to be learned. One critical piece is that of mayoral control. I believe that policy makers (at the federal and state levels) can do more to promote mayoral control. We need to better understand mayoral control and its impact. Is it linked with achievement? Are there ways in which mayors have used control that are particularly promising?

At a grand scale, one potential idea for moving forward with portfolio management is to try a full-scale and thoughtful shift in a pilot city. Is there a city where the conditions exist to attract a superintendent or CEO willing to lead such a venture (e.g., a city with student achievement issues, political will, and levers to attain mayoral or state control, generous per-pupil allotment, etc.)? Would the foundations invest? Would the Department of Education invest through an i3-type application?

Other urban superintendents will look at the example of New York City and see a scale, level of resources, and context that don't match their city and will dismiss what Honig and DeArmond (chapter 7, this volume) mention as necessary. They will fall back on discrete and sometimes sidelined units within a district as enough of a portfolio management approach. Thus, district, state and municipal leaders need to manufacture and track the implementation so that an exemplar offering a road map can be created and disseminated. For example, contexts with more liberal union contracts, like New Haven, or challenging circumstances, like Detroit, that are in process could be targeted for portfolio management experimentation and exploration.

On a smaller scale, Duncan and others could create programs to incentivize human capital creation. For example, how can we train superintendents in portfolio management ideas (e.g., evolving the Broad Superintendents Academy or creating something like New Leaders for New Schools for superintendents)? Also, operators, especially CMOs, need more support to build the talent to do the work at scale.

Better information about portfolio management would also help. The National Alliance for Public Charter Schools and the National Association of Charter School Authorizers have rated state charter laws and authorizing practices. It would be fascinating to track what is operating (successfully or not) and why based on information from states, mayors, elected school boards, district leaders, central office entities, within a portfolio management system. What connects a particular alignment of conditions or structures and outcomes? In addition, rating and comparing portfolio management districts and an agreed-on framework would allow positive scrutiny of efforts.

The right mixture of conditions, visionary leadership, resources, and human capital can make a profound difference in the lives of today's youth.

This particular point in time represents an opportunity in which all the elements of this mixture are coming together, ready to be experimented with. As I said earlier, *people* and *talent matters.* Portfolio management is a system that harnesses autonomy and accountability to allow entrepreneurialism to abound. We need catalytic individuals to set events in motion city by city. Over the past decade, new school work has spawned a generation of leaders willing to take a different path to get different results. Duncan, Klein, and Rhee are only three examples of such urban educational leaders. Who will be next?

12

Where Public Meets Private

Looking Forward

Jeffrey. R. Henig and Katrina E. Bulkley

In a change from the recent past, educational policy these days is debated much more ideologically in national forums than local ones. This is partly due to an evolution in federalism: the relative allocation of decision-making authority across the formal levels of government. No Child Left Behind, enacted under the Bush administration, and Race to the Top, the important initiative of the Obama administration, are key markers of the growing involvement of the federal government in education reform, not just in issues having to do with civil rights and student rights, as had marked federal involvement in the second half of the twentieth century, but increasingly in matters that get close to the core of the educational enterprise, curriculum, teacher qualifications, and the like. Complementing this upward shift in formal federal government involvement has been the growing importance of national nongovernmental venues and groups—foundations, professional associations, think tanks, national advocacy groups, corporate and nonprofit provider groups and their sponsors, and other components of civil society—as forums for setting the educational agenda, debating alternative approaches, and creating constituencies for change.

Compared to the cloistered, parochial, and protective preoccupations that often marked education decision making under the more localized system that previously dominated, this nationalization has opened the discussion to new ideas and created new opportunities for cross-system learning about what does and does not work. Yet it also comes at a cost. National debates can easily become detached from the realities of policy development, implementation, and evolution as they unfold at the "street level," where administrative capacity, economic and demographic context, and political landscape and history can vary tremendously and with important consequences.[1] While battles between unions and school boards can be bitter and intense, local politics is often more pragmatic and differences more amenable to negotiated compromise. Viewed from an orbit of ten thousand feet, broad patterns obscure important surface features, and abstraction and ideology often step into the gap, making for a more polarized discourse in which key issues, like the relationship between the public and private sectors, become either-or battles marked by high intensity but little illumination.[2]

In taking a reading on the portfolio management model (PMM) and the early enthusiasm it is engendering, this volume has considered local experience as well as national forces, concrete cases in addition to abstract theories, and the view from central district offices as well as state capitals and Washington, D.C. What we find is a dynamic and open-ended phenomenon too much in flux and still too embryonic to undergo a summative yea-or-nay appraisal. That does not mean that nothing can be learned and no provisional judgments made. In this final chapter, we highlight four broad themes and offer some thoughts for how to think about the future of the portfolio model and certain risks that citizens and policy makers should keep in mind in the course of deliberations about the future of school reform.

FOUR BROAD THEMES

Design Matters, But Designs Evolve

PMM allows for considerable variation. Districts can make different decisions about numerous program details, including: the *mix among different types of schools* (e.g., charter, contract, district-managed); the overall *extent of autonomy granted* to school-level decision making; which specific *func-*

tions to standardize (common core curriculum? weighted student funding?); favored strategies for *school turnarounds* (e.g., closing, chartering, other forms of reconstitution); form and extent of district *accountability and assessment* (e.g., whether and how to give schools performance grades); the relative reliance on *local versus external providers*; and more. Compared to the other cases in this book, for example, New Orleans is more deeply invested in chartering; New York has done the most in terms of performance grading; Philadelphia has experimented more broadly with private contracting for management of district schools; and Chicago has worked most explicitly to pull different kinds of school management (charters, contract schools, empowered schools) into one overarching policy.

Understanding clearly the nature and extent of variation across these dimensions will require rigorous research that has not yet taken place (see the discussion of a research agenda later in this chapter), but lessons from other policy areas suggest that the devil is often in the details, and we anticipate that that will be the case for PMM as well. Variation in the details, though, exists not just across cities but also within them over time. This is one of the strongest and most consistent findings in this volume, at least for the time being; a portfolio model describes not a fixed policy instrument, but an evolutionary process. That has implications for how we can learn from the existing applications. If performance in one or more of these cities improves, should that be credited to the initial design, an intermediary adaptation, or the regime that exists when the gains come to light? If performance does not rise, or if it even dips, is that the fault of PMM or of the particular application adopted locally? Evaluating mutable policy regimes is always a challenge, and that will certainly be the case in this instance as well.

Variation in details is to be celebrated if it is a genuine function of fitting a policy to local context or of learning and adaptation over time. This volume reminds us, though, that initial choices and subsequent changes can be driven by economic and political factors that may be disconnected from context and local experience. As portfolio models evolve in the first-generation districts, and as they are disseminated into new settings, will they go in the direction of truly "managed" portfolios, or toward the more laissez-faire choice districts described by Levin (see chapter 8, this volume)? The choice between market and democratic accountability is critical and highly contested. PMMs, as explained in the introductory chapter, can be understood as an effort to stake down the overlapping area among differentiation, privatization, and systemic, managed reform. A critical question, as the details unfold, is whether this is solid ground on which to stand, or whether political, ideological, and other forces will drag the movement toward one or another extreme.

Capacity Matters

Part of the motivation behind the portfolio model is the frustration that many feel with perceived inefficiencies, overbureaucratization, mediocre skills, parochialism, and indifference within many traditionally governed school districts. Proponents of vouchers and other forms of more deregulated market models allow themselves to imagine that privatization can serve as a replacement for good governance. But most proponents of the portfolio model have been chastened by the evidence that privatization is not a panacea, either generally or in its particular manifestations in voucher and charter school reform (see Henig, chapter 2, this volume).

The portfolio model is not self-actualizing. Honig and DeArmond, in chapter 7 in this volume, illustrate the many and difficult tasks that central offices must confront in making the switch from their more traditional roles. Theirs is a detailed and empirically based confirmation of the general observation that Van Slyke made after reviewing the evidence about competition and contracting out in other policy areas: to realize the potential benefits, "government must be a smart buyer, a skillful purchasing agent, and a sophisticated inspector of the goods and services it purchases from the private sector."[3]

If portfolio models are to be managed well instead of badly, much will depend on the ability of the government doing the managing to adapt to a new—but still demanding—role. Proponents of the model think this can be done, partly because the tasks themselves may be less demanding in some ways, but mostly because they believe that institution of the model can also open the door to new sources of capacity at all levels of the system, including: more open and broadly based recruitment of talent, tactical contracting with outside providers with proven expertise, and the creation of data and feedback systems that promote continuous learning. While attempts to make this a reality have left their mark on districts, it is still too early to say whether they have succeeded in truly "remaking" the delivery of education in urban districts and the experiences of students in urban schools. Outside organizations that have helped to buttress portfolio models among the early adopters face their own challenges in terms of scaling up.[4] And it is far from clear that the foundation support that has primed the pump by helping to pay for this hired capacity (see Reckhow, chapter 10, this volume) will continue to flow, either to these cities, due to foundations' belief that recipients need eventually to be weaned from dependence on their financing, or to second- and third-wave adapters, which lack the visibility that foundations often prefer and the preexisting administrative capacity of places such as Chicago or New York City.

The availability of the requisite tools is, of course, only half the battle. As has been shown in other reforms, portfolio models also rely on people throughout the system who understand and believe in the idea itself; if high levels of skepticism permeate the system, there seems less opportunity for significant change. Edelman argues forcefully that strong and consistent leadership is critical, and one can easily imagine a city with the structures of a PMM but participants in the system who stay in the comfort zone of compliance-based reform (see chapter 11, this volume). One manifestation of this issue is the challenge that cities seem to wrestle with—and resolve differently—of whether autonomy should be earned or whether it should be provided as a presumed prerequisite to educational gains (and then subject to being pulled back in the case on poor performance).

Civic Capacity

Formal policies and organizational structures depend on a supporting context to generate the resources, cooperation, and continuity they need if they are to have their desired effects. Stone and his colleagues use the term *civic capacity* to describe the interrelationships among various stakeholders—in government, business, and the broad community—that can make it possible to institute meaningful, systemic, and sustained reform.[5] Instituting PMM depends on the availability of civic capacity to build a stable and enduring governing regime. Differences in base-level civic capacity mean that successes in cities like Chicago and New York, which have basically strong stakeholders and traditions of cooperation in collective undertakings, may be more difficult to produce in a city like New Orleans.

Although Katrina sweeping away the old, generally dysfunctional regime accounts for the fact that the city is adopting the model at all, the crisis does not provide the foundation for creating a new supportive regime from scratch, and this may prove more difficult than envisioned. Consideration of governance regimes and civic capacity also suggests that the transfer of the model from first to later generations of adopters may be problematic.

The ability to build strong governing regimes in PMM cities may also be hampered by the shift of attention by parents and community groups from the system to the individual school. In New York City, one could argue that the entire portfolio approach actively encouraged this by delegating some decisions to the school level and inviting (some) parent engagement at that level, but eliminating intermediary institutions (community school districts) and resisting efforts by parents and others to attempt to change or even debate centrally defined policies. Evidence from other cases in this volume also points to this possibility.

It is possible that the portfolio approach can provide the catalyst for the emergence of a new kind of sustaining regime, one that centers more on foundations, new providers, national for-profits and nonprofit groups, mayors, and governors and less on unions, parents, and local school boards, and bureaucracies (Henig, chapter 2, this volume). This is speculative, though, and alternative scenarios are imaginable as well: ones marked by backlash, conflict, and a weakened apparatus for democratic control.

National Influences

Portfolio management is a local option, but this volume has highlighted a number of ways in which it is buoyed by national forces. National government, national foundations, and a growing national network of for-profit and nonprofit providers have helped encourage the adoption of PMM and boosted the resources available to first-round adopters. Whether the PMM spreads and is broadly institutionalized in existing or new cities, or turns into just the latest in a series of faddish but ephemeral reforms may depend on developments in those sectors, including developments that may have little to do directly with how well the model performs.

Not surprisingly, given Secretary of Education Arne Duncan's prior experience in Chicago, the PMM resonates well with the criteria the federal government now appears to be applying in allocating its categorical grant support, including through the Race to the Top competition (RttT) and early plans for the reauthorization of No Child Left Behind. Both Obama and Duncan emphasize pragmatic approaches over ideological purity, making the PMM blend of public management and markets attractive to them for the very same reasons that it is resisted by some of the left ("Say 'no' to privatization") and the right ("Say 'no' to centralized oversight"). The administration has been emphatic in arguing for the expansion of charter schools, but it has been careful to argue against the simple claim that market competition will weed out bad charters without attention to active public oversight and intervention. As Duncan said in his formal remarks delivered to the National Alliance for Public Charter Schools Conference, "The charter movement is putting itself at risk by allowing too many second-rate and third-rate schools to exist. Your goal should be quality, not quantity. Charter authorizers need to do a better job of holding schools accountable—and the charter schools need to support them—loudly and sincerely."[6] Finally, the emphases on measurement as a prime tool for accountability and dramatic interventions in the worst schools, both central to PMM, are among the key criteria the U.S. Department of Education has announced as parts of its RttT rubric for evaluating states and districts as being serious about reform. The federal government's role in sustaining the PMM movement is not limited to the carrots and sticks it offers directly to states and localities, but also through incentives and supports it provides in creating viable markets for the growing private K–12 education sector (see Burch, chapter 9, this volume).

In the near term, then, it seems likely that the federal context will continue to be supportive. But much could depend on electoral cycles and changes that could occur in the White House or Congress. The PMM blend of pragmatism and markets, choice and management has bipartisan appeal, but among Republicans its support is located more in the corporate and traditional wings and not in the more vehemently antigovernment stands currently manifested in the Tea Party Movement. If the latter groups gain in influence, support for PMM-style approaches could wane through two channels. First, pro-states rights and local control contingents have limited toleration for *any* kind of steering from Washington, D.C. Second, where there is support for national leadership, it could get turned back toward the more laissez-faire forms of market choice in which intentional oversight and management are seen as distorting factors rather than critical tools to ensure quality.

Three other national factors could have significant impact on the long-term trajectory for PMMs—the continued support of the philanthropic community, the financial community's assessment of the long-term economic viability of the for-profit education sector, and changes in the broader U.S. economy. Consideration of each of these factors raises complicated issues that make prediction hazardous. We summarize the points briefly here.

The national philanthropic community, as noted throughout this volume, has played a critical role in promoting, legitimizing, and underwriting the start-up of portfolio models. This includes foundations, corporate donors, and so-called nonprofit venture capital philanthropies such as the NewSchools Venture Fund (NSVF). Donors such as these can get the ball rolling, and this might be sufficient if the model ultimately proves able to sustain itself, either because operating costs decline once start-up expenses are digested or by catalyzing public investment. But it remains unclear whether this get-the-ball-rolling strategy will suffice, whether it can be moved serially from place to place, and whether the philanthropic community will lose interest and shift its resources to new priorities. Some of the gung-ho enthusiasm that earlier accompanied the expansion of the for-profit education sector has faded a bit. The rocky and highly visible fortunes of the Edison Project (now EdisonLearning) played a role in this, as has the growing popularity of the nonprofit charter management organization (CMO) sector.

Finally, the financial crisis that came to a head in 2008 exacted a heavy toll on state and local government budgets, leading to significant cuts for public education and the likely loss of thousands of jobs in school districts. The ultimate implications of the economic situation are unclear and likely to vary by location, but in many places the heady talk about expanding investment in public education has been displaced by the imposition of spartan spending regimes. One mark of how fiscal winds can change is found in the way governments are approaching the issue of longer school days, weeks, and years. Proponents of portfolio models occasionally point to extended schooltime as an illustration of the kind of lessons that can come out of the "laboratory of experimentation" that diversification of delivery models can provide. While charter school research has provided empirical support for the notion that more time in school can boost the test score performance of lower-income students, in the current fiscal context states and districts are looking at furlough days, resulting in the contraction of schooltime, rather than wide-scale emulation as might have been hoped. Whether the portfolio model thrives as a cost-saving tool or is put on the back burner because of anticipated transition costs, it is likely that its evolution will be different in a tight budget environment than the early trajectory might lead us to expect.

REASONS FOR CAUTION

The sense of righteous urgency with which some proponents proceed should be moderated. Being powerfully committed to improving public education, especially for the most disadvantaged, *is* the high ground, but in trying to stake an exclusive claim on that position, supporters of portfolio management risk overselling what they can deliver, mistaking reluctance based on an appreciation of complexities for knee-jerk obstructionism, losing opportunities to more systematically test their ideas, and fueling backlash and battles that could undo their reforms regardless of their actual merits. The evidence from contracting out in other policy areas strongly discredits the notion that it is an all-purpose and universal panacea (see Henig, chapter 2, this volume). Contracting with alternative providers can be done well or done poorly. It can work better for achieving some goals than others and differently under circumstances that vary and change. Taking time to deliberate, experiment, and convince others might look like dithering if a clear and proved alternative is at hand. But the alternative is still not clear and certainly not yet proved.

Even the most prominent and highly touted cases—Chicago and New York City—reveal PMM as more a case study in politics and pragmatic adjustment than fidelity to theory and design (Menefee-Libey, chapter 3, this volume; Gyurko and Henig, chapter 4, this volume). That the model has evolved as kinks are worked out in the field should not be taken as a criticism. Pragmatic privatization—the careful and selective use of for-profit and nonprofit groups and processes—can make government more effective in pursuing public goals (see chapter 2). What is problematic is when privatization is used tactically—as a means of recruiting and rewarding political allies—or systemically, as part of a broad effort to undermine the legiti-macy and capacity of government.[7] One possible advantage of the PMM is the fact that its combination of choice and competition with strong public design and accountability makes it less readily incorporated into the sharp ideological clashes, typical of more laissez-faire market-based reforms, where markets and government are posed as polar rivals. Education policy debates at the local level in general tend to be more pragmatic and less ide-ological than those at the national level, too, giving PMMs further room to accommodate adaptation and bargained adjustments than is possible in the hot glare of national policy debates.[8]

The risks are real, though, that local and national politics will unfold in ways that boil away the nuance and contingency, leading proponents to oversell and overreach. Compared to the insider groups that have tended to shape local school district policies in the past, the new contracting re-gimes include a number of actors with at least one foot in broader state and national policy and political networks. Whether out of reformers' sense of mission or more direct organizational or personal stakes, they are likely to distill a more purified narrative about the model in the effort to explain it simply and promote its transplantation to other locales. Three things could go wrong as advocates make these translations.

The first risk is that proponents will *decontextualize* the portfolio model, creating the impression that it is right and appropriate for all or most dis-tricts. Most of the attention to date has focused on cities including Chi-cago and New York City. While the scale of these two districts makes reform always a challenging undertaking, each also has very distinct ad-vantages that other districts do not. Both cities have incubated their port-folio approaches during the administrations of unusually strong mayors with extraordinary formal and informal political resources at their dis-posal. Each has instituted mayoral control of public schools, which places the decision-making levers in the hands of someone elected in general elections where teacher unions do not carry the same weight as they do in traditionally low-turnout elections for school boards. Both cities have strong business and local philanthropic support. And, as showcase cities with national visibility, both also are better candidates than most districts to attract attention and support from nonlocal foundations, like Gates and Broad. Also important, but easily undervalued, each represents a large and attractive market to private for-profit and nonprofit providers. And, at least compared to their counterparts in many other urban areas, each has a school bureaucracy with the core capacity to oversee a contracting regime. Many of these characteristics are consistent with those that Edelman (chapter 11, this volume) argues are important for a potentially successful PMM. And each took the key initiating steps during a period of relative economic growth and fiscal well-being, before the economic collapse of 2008–2009.

Even if time proves the portfolio model to be successful in these two sites, there are good reasons to be wary of presuming the results would be comparable in districts less blessed in terms of infrastructure, resource, and timing. Philadelphia (chapter 5, this volume) and New Orleans (chapter 6, this volume) share some of the advantages of New York City and Chicago. In both places, the state has played a strong role, providing resources and the capacity for an authoritative press ahead despite localized resistance. In the form of Paul Vallas, both literally share leadership with Chicago; if anything, one might assume that Vallas would be more knowledgeable and efficient in his subsequent posts as he has learned from experience and developed stronger national ties. While some portfolio proponents have been quick to label the Chicago and New York City efforts as successes worthy of emulation, observers seem a bit more reticent to weigh in on Philadelphia, where they see creeping recentralization, and New Orleans, where the sheer scale of the challenge, uncertainties about a post-Vallas era, and as yet unresolved questions about a prospective transition from the Recovery School District to a new governance structure leave so much up in the air. It is possible that a PMM will thrive there and in other places—lacking formal mayoral control, lacking strong business support, having to attract attention from foundations and private providers who feel increasingly extended, and operating in a bleaker economic landscape—but the chances of misfire are considerably more pronounced.

The second risk is that the PMM will be portrayed as *self-actualizing*. This is a general problem with urban school reform literature, which tends to underappreciate and understate the many ways in which even the most promising programs require ongoing attention, support, and adjustment. As the descriptions of events in Chicago, New York City, Philadelphia, and New Orleans make clear, there is no clear, straight path leading to portfolio management from a more centralized, top-down delivery model. Leaders in these cities ad-libbed, backtracked, and made things up as they went along. Their zigzag patterns might be due in part to the fact that they were pioneers in the approach. If so, other districts could perhaps learn from their missteps and follow a map that the early innovators had to draw themselves. But much of the zigging and zagging seems less attributable to avoidable missteps than to the unavoidable need to make midcourse corrections based on muddling through. Issues of priority and sequencing, on-the-spot feedback about what is and is not working, reacting as challenges are mounted by opponents, negotiations and compromises required to hold together supporting coalitions: all of these require judgment and balancing, political will, and administrative capacity. Spectator districts may be seduced into thinking that they need only make an up or down decision about *whether* to pursue a PMM approach, without realizing the full burden, diverted attention, and opportunity costs that will be forced on them once the process is put into motion. Those that miscalculate might easily end up making things worse off rather than better.

A third risk is that the institution of a PMM will plant the seeds of its subsequent failures. To succeed, PMM requires that the public-sector actors have the skills and knowledge to stipulate public goals, negotiate fair and enforceable contractual goals, establish and maintain adequate data systems, understand the supply-and-demand conditions, and have the political will and capacity to intervene when providers are failing to meet established terms. Under some conditions, the institution of a portfolio model and the creation of a sustaining contracting regime might alter the political dynamics of the district in ways that leave the public too weak to fulfill its intended responsibilities. There are a number of reasons that these expectations might not be met.

- *Brain drain.* Private providers of education services have incentives to hire away key public-sector personnel. One incentive is to gain access to their inside knowledge about technical aspects of the system. Just as important may be their knowledge of local conditions, history, values, and context. In addition to the information they carry with them, system insiders often can provide political advantages to outside providers, due to their access to local leaders, the local political networks within which they may have ties, and their ability to put a more familiar, local face on provider firms that might otherwise be seen as carpetbaggers. This can contribute to an atrophying of the public sector, however, and make it less able to bargain and intervene strongly in managing its contracts.

- *Proprietary information.* Private providers may exercise claims on specific information, with legal assertions of proprietary rights, intellectual property rights, and the need to protect the privacy of their consumers. As well, if they see one another as competitors, they may not share information that would benefit other providers or districts.

- *Underfunding.* It may be politically difficult to sustain necessary funding for a collective research enterprise at the district level in the face of demands that funds "go to the classrooms." This may be more likely in contracting regimes where groups that favor priorities other than education, including lower taxes, may have more clout than they do in traditional public school regimes that give teacher unions and parents a central role.

- *Providers as interest groups.* Providers may act as interest groups with profit, contracts, and autonomy at stake. They may also use their political clout and central position within an emergent contracting regime to resist demands for information and oversight as representing undue distractions and "overregulation."

WHERE DOES THIS LEAVE US?

The portfolio management approach to urban education is a work in progress. That it shares common elements with service arrangements in other arenas of public policy means that it is neither so new and original as some proponents seem to believe nor so radical and threatening as some critics appear to fear. Contracting with private, or more autonomous public, providers has the potential to increase flexibility, constructive variation, and the infusion of human capital and energies. Yet there are many places at which things may go awry, and it is far from clear that a malfunctioning PMM is preferable to a malfunctioning version of the traditional public school system. There is no reason to pull the plug on existing experiments, but neither is there solid evidence to support the rapid dissemination of PMMs to other places. This is a promising albeit problematic strategy for pragmatic reform. It should be watched closely, and systematic research into its variations and consequences has yet to be done. Designing and interpreting that research will require sensitivity to the critical role of politics and governance in molding the intervention over time, in determining key parameters of implementation and enforcement, and in ensuring—or failing to ensure—that privatized and decentralized delivery remains yoked to public purposes as democratically negotiated.

Issues to Consider for Policy Makers

Like so many of the magic bullets offered as the answer to the challenges of providing high-quality education to all students in large urban districts, the PMM approach is not a panacea. For policy makers considering supporting such ideas in cities already moving in this direction or other cities considering it, we offer some thoughts for consideration. First, issues of capacity in educational reform are always critical, and it is unwise to think that PMM reforms are any different. While some of that capacity may be brought to the system through outside providers and organizations, policy makers should be wary of arguments that capacity in the central office is no longer critical.

Second, accessing external expertise and support can be valuable, but reliance on external support—financial, technical, or political—can prove to be an Achilles' heel. Governors, presidents, and national foundations and provider networks can be fickle allies. Local politics still matters, and if local stakeholders do not buy in to reform efforts, they have the staying power and can draw on local loyalties in mobilizing opposition substantial enough to wound and possibly even unwind the PMM structures, regardless of how well they might be intentioned and designed.

Third, policy makers should be wary of the seductive power appeal of the "big bang" approach, as pursued, for example, in New York City and New Orleans. The big-bang approach tries to get as much in place as possible initially, deliberately displacing old institutions, and favoring building a new reform regime instead of winning over existing stakeholders through incremental implementation and the accumulation of demonstrable success. The big-bang orientation usually is accompanied by rhetoric that suggests speed is a moral imperative and that there already is strong evidence that the new model will work. Yet we've shown that big-bang rhetoric tends to mask muddling through and a zigzag course in which local leaders sometimes make things up as they go along. Recognizing upfront that the path will be slow and that the final arrangements may differ from the initial designs should give local policy makers room to be deliberate and to plan a course that conforms to local values and needs.

Issues to Consider for Research

Cities engaged in PMMs are a ripe arena for future research, especially if this approach continues to gain momentum. However, this is also a challenging area for study, as it is composed of many distinct pieces (operation of schools by outside providers, autonomous schools, charter schools, central office redesign, impact of standards and testing, school closure, etc.), yet, at least in theory, these components are also expected to work in concert. Studying such a reform requires paying attention to both the pieces and the interactions, and recognizing that the "thing" that one is studying is itself evolving in reaction to local, state, and national pressures. Learning about PMMs as a general approach to reform also suggests the need for continued cross-city work, as we have done in this volume. However, the temptation in doing such work can be to seek comparable components across cities as a more manageable task and, in doing so, losing sight of the interactions of the components with one another and with the local context. Research on PMMs needs to attend to at least five levels of analysis within and across cities—the city as a civic unit, the central office, school operators, individual schools, and students—while keeping a close eye on a sixth (the national/state context for reform). The cases in this volume touch on each of these levels, but more in-depth, systematic research is needed.

As the cases in this volume demonstrate, PMMs have implications not just for school practices, but also for the ways in which civic groups, parents, and others engage with—and participate in—discussions and decisions about public education. Research on PMMs needs to attend to these political shifts and ask some difficult questions. Localism has been a powerful force in American educational history, and its legacy has been mixed. At some times and in some places, localism has supported parochial rejection of new ideas, exclusionary practices, and domination by local elites with their own interests in mind.[9] But localism has also been the wellspring of passionate support for public schools and an arena for democratic engagement in shaping an institution that ideally represents communities' best efforts at preparing the generation that will succeed them. Will external promoters of portfolio models shoulder aside local groups limiting democratic engagement? Will providers invoke proprietary rights to shield their activities from effective oversight? Who benefits from PMMs, and who loses? In what ways are PMMs altering the relationship between schools and communities?

At the central office level, the ideas raised by Honig and DeArmond (chapter 7, this volume) and Levin (chapter 8, this volume) provide a critical starting point for research that explores questions such as: How are central offices grappling with both meeting new expectations and moving away from conventional practices in the shift toward a PMM? What does it look like to "manage" a portfolio, are different districts approaching this task in a more "intentional" or a more "laissez-faire" manner, and what are the implications of variations in approaches to management? In what ways are changes in the central office influencing the use of both external and internal research and data in decision making? As Honig and DeArmond demonstrate, attention in such work must focus on both formal structures, policies and procedures, and on informal relationships and collective learning.

Outside and district school operators (whether the district directly, some subunit of the district, or an outside organization) are the most visible manifestation of a PMM, and the units best positioned to have a direct and significant impact on students. While there is a growing body of research on specific kinds of operators (for example, CMOs), more attention to the practices of operators both within and across schools is needed: How are operators working to improve teaching, learning, and leadership? In what ways are operators of multiple schools building broader capacity to support schools? Is there a point at which operators trade off economies of scale for creating bureaucratic practices that mimic those criticized in school districts? While the primary focus on outside organizations in a PMM is on school operators, research must also attend to the other kinds of organizations that are increasingly offering services generally provided by districts or more conventional organizations such as universities. The most visible of these organizations are those that are connected to human capital development—e.g., The New Teachers Project, Teach For America, and New Leaders for New Schools. Edelman argues (chapter 11, this volume) that the availability of high-quality human capital is essential for the potential success of a PMM, so research must consider ways in which districts and others are seeking to develop this particular form of capacity.

At the school level, attention must be paid to critical factors of good education such as: Are there strong leaders who convey a clear vision and an environment supportive of good instruction? Are teachers given the resources, support, and opportunities for ongoing learning that enables them to provide challenging and appropriate instruction that meets the needs of the students? Are resources used effectively and efficiently to support the work of teachers and leaders?

While a challenging task, it is critical to conduct research tracing connections between PMM models in particular cities and changes in a broad set of student outcomes (achievement on tests, but also graduation rates, college attendance and completion rates, and indicators of social outcomes) (see Levin, chapter 8, this volume, for more discussion on outcomes). Because of the considerable variation across cities, it is unlikely that a cross-site "PMM effect" could be identified, but high-quality work on questions of student outcomes could help shine light on the conditions under which PMM approaches have the greatest potential to help students—especially low-income, black, and Latino students who have historically struggled most in large city schools.

And, finally, although the primary focus of research efforts on PMMs will likely be on the issues raised earlier, research must attend to the influence of national and state forces in the development and evolution of this reform. As discussed, the federal government, foundations, and other national organizations are critical actors not only in setting up a context in which PMMs seem a logical direction for change, but in potentially influencing some of the daily practices of those working in central offices, outside organizations, and schools. Research in and across cities must ask questions about these influences and about how such outside influences affect local change.

In this volume, we have sought to both describe some of the critical developments around the PMM idea and raise questions about where this approach will lead public schools and their communities. As PMMs continue to spread and evolve, it is becoming increasingly important that such potentially significant changes in the institutional structure of public education be noted and studied carefully. Without such work, it becomes more likely not that such shifts will not occur, but that they will continue to develop in a piecemeal way that limits opportunities for internal and cross-city learning.

Notes

Chapter 1

1. Paul T. Hill, "Reinventing Public Education," RAND Research Report (Washington, DC: RAND, 1995); in May 2009, the White House announced a goal of "turning around" five thousand of these "failing" schools, with the specific goal of closing and reopening a thousand a year for five consecutive years. See L. Quaid, "Obama Wants to Close 5,000 Failing Schools," Washington Examiner, May 11, 2009, http://www.washingtonexaminer.com/politics/Obama-wants-to-close-5000-failing-schools-44715802.html; L. Steiner, *Tough Decisions: Closing Persistently Low-Performing Schools* (Lincoln, IL: Center on Innovation and Improvement, 2009).

2. National Alliance for Public Charter Schools, "Top 10 Charter Communities by Market Share: Fourth Annual Edition," October 2009, http://www.publiccharters.org/files/publications/MarketShare_P4.pdf.

3. Hill, "Reinventing Public Education"; P. T. Hill, C. Campbell, D. Menefee-Libey, B. Dusseault, M. DeArmond, and B. Gross, "Portfolio School Districts for Big Cities: An Interim Report" (Seattle, WA: Center on Reinventing Public Education, University of Washington, 2009); P. T. Hill and M. B. Celio, *System-changing Reform Ideas: Can They Save City Schools?* (Seattle, WA: The Brookings Institute and the University of Washington, 1997).

4. Hill et al., "Portfolio School Districts for Big Cities," 1.

5. Some advocates of portfolio models have focused on using the approach specifically to improve high schools, in part fueled by the Schools for a New Society initiative funded by the Carnegie Corporation of New York and the Bill & Melinda Gates Foundation. However, the districts we studied applied the ideas to all levels of the educational system. For a review of literature on PMMs at the high school level, see H. P. Maluk and S. A. Evans, *Literature Review: Portfolio of Schools* (Philadelphia: Research for Action, 2008).

6. Hill et al., "Portfolio School Districts for Big Cities."

7. C. Warren and M. Hernandez, "Portfolios of Schools: An Idea Whose Time Has Come. High School Redesign," *Voices in Urban Education* 8 (2005).

8. E. Gold, J. B. Christman, and B. Herold, "Blurring the Boundaries: Private Sector Involvement in Philadelphia Public Schools," *American Journal of Education* 113, no. 7 (2007): 181–212.

9. For an interesting discussion of the role of outside providers in supporting low-performing schools in a different context, see Hess and Squire on diverse providers in Hawaii, F. M. Hess and J. P. Squire, *"Diverse Providers" in Action: School Restructuring in Hawaii* (Washington, DC: American Enterprise Institute, 2009).

10. Hill, "Reinventing Public Education"; Hill and Celio, *System-changing Reform Ideas*.

11. M. Kirst and K. Bulkley, "Mayoral Takeover: The Different Directions Taken in Different Cities," in *A Race Against Time: Responses to the Crisis in Urban Schooling*, eds. J. Cibulka and W. Boyd (Westport, CT: Greenwood/Ablex, 2003).

12. The Carnegie Corporation, long a funder of reform in public education, has also been an active supporter of portfolio management models. See J. Scott, "The Politics of Venture

Philanthropy in Charter School Policy and Advocacy," *Educational Policy* 23, no. 1 (2009): 106–136.

13. S. Reckhow, "Waiting for Bill Gates: Following the Money Trail from Foundations to Urban School Districts (paper presented at the Annual Meeting of the Midwest Political Science Association, 2008), Chicago.

14. D. Tyack, *The One Best System: A History of American Urban Education* (Cambridge, MA: Harvard University Press, 1974), 15.

15. For example, see J. E. Chubb and T. M. Moe, *Politics, Markets, and America's Schools* (Washington, DC: The Brookings Institution, 1990); M. Friedman, *Capitalism and Freedom* (Chicago: University of Chicago Press, 1962).

16. L. S. Hamilton, B. M. Stecher, and K. Yuan, *Standards-based Reform in the United States: History, Research, and Future Directions* (Santa Monica, CA: RAND, 2008); M. Smith and J. O'Day, *Putting the Pieces Together: Systemic School Reform* (New Brunswick, NJ: Consortium for Policy Research in Education, 1991).

17. W. L. Boyd, C. T. Kerchner, and M. Blyth, eds., *The Transformation of Great American School Districts: How Big Cities Are Reshaping Public Education* (Cambridge, MA: Harvard Education Press, 2008); Tyack, *The One Best System*; D. Tyack and L. Cuban, *Tinkering toward Utopia* (Cambridge, MA: Harvard University Press, 1997).

18. Chubb and Moe, *Politics, Markets, and America's Schools*; Friedman, *Capitalism and Freedom*.

19. Gold, Christman, and Herold, "Blurring the Boundaries."

20. P. Burch, *Hidden Markets: The New Education Privatization* (New York: Routledge, 2009); L. M. Rhim, "The Politics of Privatization Practice: An Analysis of State-Initiated Privatization via School Restructuring Statutes in Two Districts," *Educational Policy* 21, no. 1 (2007): 245; C. Richards, M. Sawicky, and R. Shore, *Risky Business: Private Management of Public Schools* (Washington, DC: Economic Policy Institute, 1996).

21. P. T. Hill, L. Pierce, and J. Guthrie, *Reinventing Public Education : How Contracting Can Transform America's Schools (RAND Research Study)* (Chicago: University of Chicago Press, 1997), 66.

22. Rhim, "The Politics of Privatization Practice," 248.

23. Ibid.; Richards, Sawicky, and Shore, *Risky Business*.

24. A. Molnar, G. Miron, and J. Urschel, *Profiles of For-profit Educational Management Organizations: Eleventh Annual Report* (Tempe, AZ: Commercialism in Education Research Unit, 2009).

25. K. E. Bulkley and J. Fisler, "A Decade of Charter Schools: From Theory to Practice," *Educational Policy* 17, no. 3 (2003), 317–342.

26. Center for Education Reform (2010). Charter Connection, http://www.edreform.com/Issues/Charter_Connection/

27. National Alliance for Public Charter Schools, "Top 10 Charter Communities by Market Share."

28. CREDO, *Multiple Choice: Charter School Performance in 16 States* (Stanford, CA: Center for Research on Education Outcomes, 2009); G. Miron and C. Nelson, "Student Achievement in Charter Schools: What We Know and Why We Know So Little," in *Taking Account of Charter Schools: What's Happened and What's Next*, eds. K. E. Bulkley and P. Wohlstetter (New York: Teachers College Press, 2004), 161–175.

29. Education Sector, *Growing Pains: Scaling up the Nation's Best Charter Schools* (Washington, DC: Author, 2009).

30. G. Miron and J. Urschel, *Profiles of Nonprofit Educational Management Organizations: 2008–2009* (Tempe, AZ: Education Policy Research Unit, 2009).

31. The database is available at: http://www.publiccharters.org/charterlaws.

32. A. Duncan, "Turning around the bottom five percent," 2009, http://www2.ed.gov/news/speeches/2009/06/06222009.html

33. National Commission on Excellence in Education, *A Nation at Risk* (Washington, DC: U.S. Government Printing Office, 1983).

34. D. Massell, M. W. Kirst, and M. Hoppe, *Persistence and Change: Standards-based Reform in Nine States* (RR-037) (Philadelphia: Consortium for Policy Research in Education, 1997).

35. Smith and O'Day, *Putting the Pieces Together.*

36. Hamilton, Stecher, and Yuan, *Standards-based Reform in the United States*; W. Clune, "Toward a theory of standards-based reform: The case of nine NSF statewide systemic initiatives," *From the Capital to the Classroom: Standards-based Reform in the States. Yearbook of the National Society for the Study of Education* (Chicago: University of Chicago Press, 2001), 13–38.

37. Hamilton, Stecher, and Yuan, *Standards-based Reform in the United States*; D. Ravitch, *The Death and Life of the Great American School System: How Testing and Choice Are Undermining Education* (New York: Basic Books, 2010).

38. Smith and O'Day, *Putting the Pieces Together.*

39. Hamilton, Stecher, and Yuan, *Standards-based reform in the United States*, 6.

40. C. Smrekar and E. Goldring, *School Choice in Urban America: Magnet Schools and the Pursuit of Equity* (New York: Teachers College Press, 1999).

41. Ibid.

42. For a recent review, see R. Bifulco, C. D. Cobb, and C. Bell, "Can Interdistrict Choice Boost Student Achievement? The Case of Connecticut's Interdistrict Magnet School Program," *Educational Evaluation and Policy Analysis* 31, no. 4 (2009): 323–345.

43. E. Clinchy, "Introduction: The Educationally Challenged American School District," in *Creating New Schools: How Small Schools Are Changing American Education*, ed. E. Clinchy (New York: Teachers College Press, 2000), 1–13.

44. L. Shear, B. Means, K. Mitchell, A. House, T. Gorges, A. Joshi et al., "Contrasting Paths to Small-school Reform: Results of a 5-year Evaluation of the Bill & Melinda Gates Foundation's National High Schools Initiative," *Teachers College Record* 110, no. 9 (2008): 1986–2039.

45. W. D. Stevens and Consortium on Chicago School, *If Small Is Not Enough . . . ? The Characteristics of Successful Small High Schools in Chicago* (Chicago: Consortium on Chicago School Research, 2008).

46. Ravitch, *The Death and Life of the Great American School System*; E. W. Rubelen, "Gates High Schools Get Mixed Reviews in Study," *Education Week*, November 16, 2005, 1, 20; Shear et al., "Contrasting Paths to Small-School Reform"; Stevens and Consortium on Chicago School, *If Small Is Not Enough . . . ?*

47. R. Budde, "Education by Charter," *Phi Delta Kappan* (March 1989): 518–520; A. Shanker, "Restructuring Our Schools," *Peabody Journal of Education* 65, no. 3 (1988): 88–100.

48. C. Lubienski, "Charter School Innovation in Theory and Practice: Autonomy, R&D, and Curricular Conformity," in *Taking Account of Charter Schools* (see note 29), 72–90.

49. A. M. Hightower, M. S. Knapp, J. A. Marsh, and M.W. McLaughlin, eds. *School Districts and Instructional Renewal* (New York: Teachers College Press, 2002); A. K. Rorrer, L. Skrla, and J. J. Scheurich, "Districts as Institutional Actors in Educational Reform," *Educational Administration Quarterly* 44, no. 3 (2008): 307–358.

50. Rorrer, Skrla, and Scheurich, "Districts as Institutional Actors in Educational Reform," 307.

51. K. E. Bulkley, "Bringing the Public into the Private: Changing the Rules of the Game and New Regime Politics in Philadelphia Public Education," *Educational Policy* 21, no. 1 (2007): 155–184; D. Shipps, "Regime Change: Mayoral Takeover of the Chicago Public Schools," in *A Race Against Time: The Crisis in Urban Schooling*, eds. J. G. Cibulka and W. L. Boyd (Westport, CT: Praeger, 2003), 106–128.

Chapter 2

1. F. M. Hess, *Spinning Wheels :The Politics of Urban School Reform* (Washington, DC: Brookings Institution, 1998); D. Tyack and L. Cuban, *Tinkering Toward Utopia: A Century of Public School Reform* (Cambridge, MA: Harvard University Press, 1995).

2. C. D. Hill and D. M. Welsch, "For-profit Versus Not-for-profit Charter Schools: An Examination of Michigan Student Test Scores," *Education Economics* 17, no. 2 (2009): 147–166; P. Hill, C. Campbell, D. Menefee-Libey, B. Dusseault, M. DeArmond, and B. Gross, *Portfolio School Districts for Big Cities: An Interim Report* (Seattle WA: Center on Reinventing Public Education, 2009)

3. M. Friedman, "The Role of Government in Education," in *Economics and the Public Interest,* ed. R. A. Solo (New Brunswick, NJ: Rutgers University Press, 1955); M. Friedman, *Capitalism and Freedom* (Chicago: University of Chicago Press, 1962).

4. J. R. Henig, *Rethinking School Choice: Limits of the Market Metaphor* (Princeton, NJ: Princeton University Press, 1994).

5. J. LeGrand and W. Bartlett, *Quasi-markets and Social Policy.* London: MacMillan, 1993); G. Whitty, "Creating Quasi-markets in Education: A Review of Recent Research on Parental Choice and School Autonomy in Three Countries," *Review of Research in Education* 22 (1997): 3–47; J. R. Henig, "Understanding the Political Conflict over School Choice," in *Getting Choice Right: Ensuring Equity and Efficiency in Education Policy,* eds. J. R. Betts and T. Loveless (Washington DC: Brookings, 2005): 176–209; J. R. Henig and C. E. Stone, "Rethinking School Reform: The Distractions of Dogma and the Potential for a New Politics of Progressive Pragmatism," *American Journal of Education* 114, no. 3 (2008): 191–218.

6. J. R.Henig, *Spin Cycle: How Research Is Used in Policy Debates: The Case of Charter Schools* (New York: Russell Sage Foundation/Century Foundation, 2008).

7. New York City, for example, goes to great expense to collect and report survey data from its more than one million families, but the results figure only marginally in its formula for grading schools. Parent responses are combined with teacher and student (for grades 6–12) responses to reach an overall score for "school environment." School environment, then, is weighted to contribute less than 15% of the overall score, with test levels (30%), student progress (55%), and "extra credit" earned for closing achievement gaps much more substantially driving the results. In addition to the letter grade, since 2008, New York City has incorporated "quality reviews" into its accountability system, based on day-and-a-half-long school site visits by trained assessors. The scoring rubric is organized around five criteria, with an assessor scoring the schools on seven subdimensions of each. Of the 35 elements scored, 3 mention parents. Three of these are grouped under the

criterion of "planning and setting goals," but only 1 of the 3 even suggests that schools should take parents' preferences, values, or ideas into account in setting their own objectives. Childress and Clayton include the rubric as Exhibit 7. See S. Childress and T. C. Clayton, "Focusing on Results at the New York City Department of Education," unpublished manuscript, 2008. Two involve the extent to which the school provides information about its goals and expectations to parents. The one that comes closest to incorporating parent views asks assessors to score school leaders and faculty on the extent to which they "invite and enable parents/caregivers to provide useful information to teachers and the school about the learning needs and capacities of their children." It says nothing about whether the school leaders and faculty attend to or act upon this information, and the wording seems to narrow the information to that which parents have about their own children and does not mention goals or values that might relate to the school's policies or the well-being of the children more collectively.

8. A. O. Hirschman, *Exit, Voice, and Loyalty* (Cambridge, MA: Harvard University Press, 1970).

9. C. A. Bell, "All Choices Created Equal? The Role of Choice Sets in the Selection of Schools," *Peabody Journal of Education* 84, no. 2 (2009); G. Elacqua, M. Schneider, and J. Buckley, "School Choice in Chile: Is It Class or the Classroom?" *Journal of Policy Analysis and Management* 25, no. 3 (2006): 577–601; J. R. Henig, "The Local Dynamics of Choice: Ethnic Preferences and Institutional Responses," in *Who Chooses? Who Loses? Culture, Institutions, and the Unequal Effects of School Choice,* eds. B. Fuller and R. F. Elmore (New York: Teachers College Press, 1996), 95–117; M. Schneider and J. Buckley, "What Do Parents Want from Schools? Evidence from the Internet," *Educational Evaluation and Policy Analysis* 24, no. 2 (2002): 133–144; G. R. Weiher and K. L. Tedin, "Does Choice Lead to Racially Distinctive Schools? Charter Schools and Household Preferences," *Journal of Policy Analysis and Management* 21, no. 1 (2002): 79–92.

10. H. Brown, J. R. Henig, T. T. Holyoke, and N. Lacireno-Paquet, "The Influence of Founder Type on Charter School Structures and Operations," *American Education Journal* 111 (2005): 487–522; Hill and Welsch, "For-profit versus Not-for-profit Charter Schools"; N. Lacireno-Paquet, T. T. Holyoke, J. R. Henig, and M. M. Moser, "Creaming versus Cropping: Charter School Enrollment Practices in Response to Market Incentives," *Educational Evaluation and Policy Analysis* 24, no. 2 (2002): 145–158.

11. P. J. DiMaggio and W. Powell, "The Iron Cage Revisited: Institutional Isomorphism and Collective Rationality in Organizational Fields," *American Sociological Review* 48 (1983): 147–160.

12. D. F. Kettl, *Sharing Power: Public Governance and Private Markets* (Washington, DC: Brookings Institution, 1993), 6.

13. L. J. O'Toole Jr. and K. J. Meier, "Parkinson's Law and the New Public Management? Contracting Determinants and Service-Quality Consequences in Public Education," *Public Administration Review* 64, no. 3 (2004): 342.

14. G. W. Ritter, R. Maranto, and S. Buck, "Harnessing Private Incentives in Public Education," *Review of Public Personnel Administration* 29, no. 3 (2009): 253.

15. P. Burch, *Hidden Markets: The New Education Privatization* (New York: Routledge, 2009).

16. O'Toole Jr.and Meier, "Parkinson's Law and the New Public Management?"

17. B. Kisida, L. I. Jensen, and P. J. Wolf, *The Milwaukee Parental Choice Program: Descriptive Report on Participating Schools* (Fayetteville, AR: School Choice Demonstration Program, University of Arkansas, 2009).

18. R. Maranto, "A Tale of Two Cities: School Privatization in Philadelphia and Chester," *American Journal of Education* 111 (2005): 151–190; M. Orr, "Urban Politics and School Reform: The Case of Baltimore," *Urban Affairs Review* 31 (1996): 314–345.

19. G. Hodge, *Privatization: An International Review of Performance* (Boulder, CO: Westview, 2000); E. S. Savas, *Privatization and Public-Private Partnerships* (New York: Chatham House, 2000).

20. J. D. Donahue, *The Privatization Decision* (New York: Basic Books, 1989); J. Ferris and E. Graddy, "Contracting Out: For What? With Whom?" *Public Administration Review* 46, no. 4 (1986): 332–344.

21. Donahue, *The Privatization Decision.*

22. R. Rothstein, R. Jacobsen, and T. Wilder, *Grading Education: Getting Accountability Right* (New York: Teachers College Press, 2008).

23. K. E. Weick, "Educational Organizations as Loosely Coupled Systems," *Administrative Science Quarterly* 21 (1976): 1–19. Although some suggest that standards-based reform and performance-based accountability are creating a more technically oriented and tightly coupled system in which teachers, for better and worse, lack the discretion to reshape policy behind the closed doors of their classrooms. See S. Davies, L. Quirke, and J. Aurini, "The New Institutionalism Goes to the Market: The Challenge of Rapid Growth in Private K–12 Education," in *The New Institutionalism in Education*, eds. H. D. Meyer and B. Rowan (Albany, NY: SUNY Press, 2006), 103–122; L. A. Huerta and A. Zuckerman, "An Institutional Theory Analysis of Charter Schools: Addressing Institutional Challenges to Scale," *Peabody Journal of Education* 84, no. 3 (2009): 414–431.

24. H. M. Levin, "An Economic Perspective on School Choice," in *Handbook of Research on School Choice*, ed. M. Berends (New York : Routledge, 2009), 19–34; B. A. Weisbrod, "Institutional Form and Institutional Behavior," in *Private Action and the Public Good*, eds. W. W. Powell and E. S. Clemens (New Haven, CT: Yale University Press, 1998), 69–84.

25. A. Gutmann, *Democratic Education* (Princeton, NJ: Princeton University Press, 1987); H. M. Levin, "A Comprehensive Framework for the Evaluation of Educational Vouchers," *Educational Evaluation and Policy Analysis* 24, no. 3 (2002): 159–174.

26. Hodge, *Privatization: An International Review of Performance.*

27. Harry P. Hatry, and Eugene Durman, *Issues in Competitive Contracting for Social Services.* (Falls Church, VA: National Institute of Governmental Purchasing, Inc., 1985).

28. D. M. Van Slyke, "The Mythology of Privatization in Contracting for Social Services," *Public Administration Review* 63, no. 3 (2003): 296.

29. Donahue, *The Privatization Decision.*

30. D. S. Nightingale and N. M. Pindus, *Privatization of Public Services: A Background Paper* (Washington, DC: Urban Institute, 1997).

31. Ferris and Graddy, "Contracting Out: For What? With Whom?"; M. Lieberman, *The Teacher Unions: How They Sabotage Educational Reform and Why* (New York: Encounter Books, 2000); Savas, *Privatization and Public-Private Partnerships.*

32. J. C. Morris, "Government and Market Pathologies of Privatization: The Case of Prison Privatization," *Politics & Policy* 35, no. 2 (2007): 318–341; C. J. Wolf, *Markets or Governments: Choosing Between Imperfect Alternatives*, 2nd ed. (Cambridge, MA: MIT Press, 1993).

33. Morris, "Government and Market Pathologies of Privatization."

34. Savas, *Privatization and Public-Private Partnerships.*

35. Donahue, *The Privatization Decision*; Kettl, *Sharing Power: Public Governance and Private Markets,* 6); D. M. Van Slyke, "Agents or Stewards: Using Theory to Understand the Government-Nonprofit Social Service Contracting Relationship," *Journal of Public Administration Research and Theory* 17 (2006): 157–187.

36. A. Hefetz and M. Warner, "Privatization and Its Reverse: Explaining the Dynamics of the Governmental Contracting Process," *Journal of Public Administration Research and Theory* 14, no. 2 (2004): 171–190.

37. Ibid.

38. Ibid.

39. L. Cohen-Vogel and S. Rutledge, "The Pushes and Pulls of New Localism: School-level Instructional Arrangements, Instructional Resources, and Family-Community Partnerships," in *The New Localism in American Education* (*Yearbook of the National Society for the Study of Education,* vol. 108), eds. R. L. Crowson and E. B. Goldring (New York: Teachers College, 2009): 70–103.

40. C. E. Stone, *Regime Politics : Governing Atlanta, 1946–1988* (Lawrence: University Press of Kansas, 1989).

41. D. Shipps, "Pulling Together: Civic Capacity and Urban School Reform," *American Educational Research Journal* 40, no. 4 (2003): 841–878; C. N. Stone, ed., *Changing Urban Education* (Lawrence: University Press of Kansas, 1998); C. Stone, J. R. Henig, B. D. Jones, and C. Pierranunzi, *Building Civic Capacity: Toward a New Politics of Urban School Reform* (Lawrence: University Press of Kansas, 2001).

42. Stone, Henig, Jones, and Pierranunzi, *Building Civic Capacity*; J. R. Henig, R. C. Hula, M. Orr, and D. S. Pedescleaux, *The Color of School Reform* (Princeton, NJ: Princeton University Press, 1999).

43. T. M. Moe, "Political Control and the Power of the Agent," *Journal of Law, Economics, and Organization* 22, no. 1 (2006): 1–29.

44. K. E. Bulkley, "Bringing the Private into the Public: Changing the Rules of the Game and New Regime Politics in Philadelphia Public Education," *Educational Policy* 21, no. 1 (2007): 155–184.

45. S. Reckhow, "Waiting for Bill Gates: Following the Money Trail from Foundations to Urban School Districts." Paper presented at the Annual Meeting of the Midwest Political Science Association, Chicago, IL, Apr 03, 2008.

46. H. Molotch, "The City as a Growth Machine: Toward a Political Economy of Place," *American Journal of Sociology* 82, no. 2 (1976): 309.

47. P. Burch, *Hidden Markets: The New Education Privatization* (New York: Routledge, 2009); N. Hass, "Scholarly investments," New York Times, December 4, 2009, http://www.nytimes.com/2009/12/06/fashion/06charter.html.

48. C. A. Kelleher and S. W. Yackee, "A Political Consequence of Contracting: Organized Interests and State Agency Decision Making," *Journal of Public Administration Research and Theory* 19, no. 3 (2009): 579–602.

49. Ibid.

50. M. B. Berkman and E. Plutzer, *Ten Thousand Democracies: Politics & Public Opinion in America's School Districts* (Washington, DC: Georgetown University Press, 2005); K. McDermott, *Controlling Public Education: Localism Versus Equity* (Lawrence: University Press of Kansas, 1999).

51. M. DeBonis, "Fund and Games: Inside Michelle Rhee's Official Schedule, *City Paper,* March 5–11, 2009, http://www.washingtoncitypaper.com/articles/36893/fund-and-games.

52. Ibid.

53. P. Hill, et al., *Portfolio School Districts*.

54. E. Gold, E. Simon, M. Cucchiara, C. Mitchell, and M. Riffer, *A Philadelphia Story: Building Civic Capacity for School Reform in a Privatizing System* (Philadelphia: Research for Action, 2007).

55. Ibid.,10.

56. It is certainly true that contracting operations can operate at a subcity level. Indeed, old-style political machines often delegated to ward bosses discretion to parcel out contracts and other forms of patronage without central direction. But this kind of spatially fractionalized contracting regime is anathema to many of those promoting the portfolio management model on the contemporary scene.

57. Hess, *Spinning Wheels*.

Chapter 3

1. A. B. Cholo and T. Dell'Angela, "100 New Schools to Be Created; Charter, Small Sites Envisioned," *Chicago Tribune*, June 23, 2004; T. Dell'Angela and G. Washburn, "Daley Set to Remake Troubled Schools; Shut Them Down, Start Over, He Says," *Chicago Tribune*, June 25, 2004; K. N. Grossman, "Daley Unveils Plan to Shut Some Schools to Copy Success Stories," *Chicago Sun-Times*, June 25, 2004.

2. Education Committee, *Left Behind: Student Achievement in Chicago's Public Schools* (Chicago: Civic Committee of the Commercial Club of Chicago, 2003).

3. D. Hursh, "Assessing No Child Left Behind and the Rise of Neoliberal Education Policies," *American Educational Research Journal*, 44, no. 3 (2007): 493–518; S. Page, "What's New about the New Public Management? Administrative Change in the Human Services," *Public Administration Review* 65, no. 6 (2005): 713–727; L. M. Salomon, "The New Governance and the Tools of Public Action: An Introduction," in *The Tools of Government: A Guide to the New Governance*, ed. L. M. Salomon (New York: Oxford University Press, 2002).

4. For a fuller discussion of "permanent crisis" and its importance in contemporary school reform politics, see C. T. Kerchner, D. J. Menefee-Libey, L S. Mulfinger, and S.E. Clayton, *Learning from L.A.: Institutional Change in American Public Education* (Cambridge, MA: Harvard Education Press, 2008); W. L. Boyd, C. T. Kerchner, and M. Blyth, eds., *The Transformation of Great American School Districts: How Big Cities Are Reshaping Public Education* (Cambridge, MA: Harvard Education Press, 2008).

5. A. Russo, ed., *School Reform in Chicago: Lessons in Policy and Practice* (Cambridge, MA: Harvard Education Press, 2004).

6. Chicago Public Schools, "FY09 Budget Book Online" (Chicago: Chicago Public Schools, 2008), http://www.cps.edu/About_CPS/Financial_information/Documents/FY09_Budget_Book_Online.pdf; Chicago Public Schools, "Stats and Facts" (Chicago: Chicago Public Schools, 2009), http://www.cps.edu/About_CPS/At-a-glance/Pages/Stats_and_facts.aspx.

7. D. Shipps, *School Reform, Corporate Style: Chicago, 1880–2000* (Lawrence: University Press of Kansas, 2006).

8. Associated Press, "Schools in Chicago Are Called the Worst by Education Chief," *New York Times*, November 8, 1987.

9. A. S. Bryk, P. B. Sebring, D. Kerbow, S. Rollow, and J.Q. Easton, *Charting Chicago School Reform: Democratic Localism as a Lever for Change* (Boulder, CO: Westview Press, 1999); Designs for Change, *The Chicago School Reform Act: Highlights of Senate Bill 1840* (Chicago: Designs for Change, 1989); Shipps, *School Reform, Corporate Style*.

10. S. Ryan, A. S. Bryk, G. Lopez, K. P. Williams, K. Hall, and S. Luppescu, *Charting Reform: LSCs—Local Leadership at Work* (Chicago: Consortium on Chicago School Research, 1997).

11. R. F. Elmore, *Restructuring Schools: The Next Generation of Educational Reform* (San Francisco: Jossey-Bass, 1990); J. Hannaway and M. Carnoy, *Decentralization and School Improvement: Can We Fulfill the Promise?* (San Francisco: Jossey-Bass, 1993).

12. Shipps, *School Reform, Corporate Style*, 122–123.

13. Bryk et al., *Charting Chicago School Reform*, 25.

14. Shipps, *School Reform, Corporate Style*.

15. M. Roderick, J. Q. Easton, and P. B. Sebring, "Consortium on Chicago School Research: A New Model for the Role of Research in Supporting Urban School Reform," *Consortium on Chicago School Research*, http://ccsr.uchicago.edu/content/publications.php?pub_id=131.

16. A. S. Bryk, P. B. Sebring, E. M. Allensworth, S. Luppescu, and J.Q. Easton, *Organizing Schools for Improvement* (Chicago: Consortium on Chicago School Research, 2009).

17. Catalyst Chicago, "Reform Timeline: Major Events from 1979 to 2008," http://www.catalyst-chicago.org/guides/index.php?id=104.

18. Bryk et al., *Charting Chicago School Reform*; G. A. Hess, *School Restructuring, Chicago Style* (Newbury Park, CA: Corwin Press, 1991).

19. M. Klonsky, "GOP Clears Field, Daley Runs with the Ball, *Catalyst-Chicago*, September 1995, http://www.catalyst-chicago.org/news/index.php?item=840&cat=23; L. Lenz, "The New Law," *Catalyst-Chicago*, September 1995, http://www.catalyst-chicago.org/news/index.php?item=849&cat=30.

20. L. Lenz, "Missing in Action: The Chicago Teachers Union," in *School Reform in Chicago* (see note 5), 125–132.

21. T. D. Brandhorst, "A View from Pershing Road," in *School Reform in Chicago* (see note 20), 117–124.

22. P. G. Vallas, "Saving Public Schools," *Civic Bulletin*, March 1999, 16, http://www.manhattan-institute.org/html/cb_16.htm.

23. R. J. Lake and L. Rainey, *Chasing the Blues Away: Charter Schools Scale up in Chicago* (Washington, DC: Progressive Policy Institute, 2005), 13.

24. M. M. Breslin, "New School to Instruct Pupils—and Teachers," *Chicago Tribune*, August 7, 2001.

25. Vallas, "Saving Public Schools," para. 17.

26. Kerchner et al., *Learning from L.A.*

27. Ibid. I am indebted to Laura Steen Mulfinger for this insight concerning competing logics of confidence.

28. M. Blake, "The Educator's New Clothes: Everybody Loves Arne Duncan. But Do His Reforms Work?" *Understanding Government*, May 30, 2009, http://understandinggov.org/2009/05/30/the-educators-new-clothes-everybody-loves-arne-duncan-but-do-his-reforms-work/.

29. J. Myers, "District Amps up Autonomy," *Catalyst Chicago*, February 2006, 10–11.

30. Blake, "The Educator's New Clothes."

31. Chicago Public Schools, "Every Child, Every School: An Education Plan for the Chicago Public Schools" (Chicago: Chicago Public Schools, September 2002).

32. M. Kelleher, "Rocky Start for Renaissance," *Catalyst Chicago*, October 2004, 6–9.

33. Chicago High School Redesign Initiative, "About CHSRI," Chicago Public Schools, 2008, http://chsri.info/about.html; R. F. Elmore, A. S. Grossman, and C. King,

Managing the Chicago Public Schools (Public Education Leadership Project case No. PEL-033) (Cambridge, MA: Harvard Graduate School of Education, 2006).

34. P. T. Hill, C. Campbell, D J. Menefee-Libey, B. Dessault, M. DeArmond, and B. Gross, *Portfolio School Districts for Big Cities: An Interim Report* (Seattle, WA: Center for Reinventing Public Education, 2009), 1.

35. Shipps, *School Reform, Corporate Style*, 140.

36. Target Area Development Corporation, *Parent Perceptions vs. Student Realities: The Results of the City Wide Education Organizing Campaign* (Chicago: Target Area Development Corporation, 2009).

37. D. C. Humphrey and P. M. Shields, *High School Reform in Chicago Public Schools: An Overview* (Part One of a Series of Five Reports) (Chicago: Consortium on Chicago School Research, 2009); L. Sartain, R. J. McGhee, L. Cassidy, M. I. Abasi, V. M. Young, S. E. Sporte, and P. M. Shields, *High School Reform in Chicago Public Schools: Autonomous Management and Performance Schools* (Part Four of a Series of Five Reports) (Chicago: Consortium on Chicago School Research, 2009).

38. Autonomous Schools Office, "Growing a Community of Schools: Fostering and Supporting Local Innovation," Chicago Public Schools, May 2009, 1.

39. W. D. Stevens, S. Sporte, S. R. Stoelinga, and A. Bolz, "Lessons from High Performing Small High Schools in Chicago," Consortium on Chicago School Research. 2008, http://ccsr.uchicago.edu/content/publications.php?pub_id=127.

40. C. M. Payne, *So Much Reform, So Little Change: The Persistence of Failure in Urban Schools* (Cambridge, MA: Harvard Education Press, 2008).

41. S. Karp, "Turnaround Schools Keep Most Students," *Catalyst Notebook*, July 30, 2009, http://www.catalyst-chicago.org/notebook/index.php/entry/360/.

42. S. Karp, "Four of Seven Turnarounds See Progress, High Schools Now on Deck," *Catalyst Notebook*, July 13, 2009, http://www.catalyst-chicago.org/notebook/index.php/entry/354/Four_of_seven_turnarounds_see_progress%2C_high_schools-now_on_deck.

43. Kelleher, "Rocky Start for Renaissance."

44. K. N. Grossman, "Board Votes to Close 10 Chicago Schools," *Chicago Sun-Times*, June 24, 2004.

45. Chicago Public Schools, "A General Guide to Turnarounds, Phaseouts, Closings and Consolidations (Chicago: Chicago Public Schools, 2009), http://www.cps.edu/News/Announcements/2009/Pages/schoolclosingguide.aspx.

46. R. Harris and S. Karp, "Dozens of Chicago Schools Eligible for Closure, Turnaround under New Criteria," *Catalyst Notebook*, January 6, 2010, http://www.catalyst-chicago.org/notebook/index.php/entry/493/Dozens_of_Chicago_schools_eligible_for_closure%2C_turnaround_under_new_criteria.

47. M. D. L. de la Torre and J. Gwynne, *When Schools Close: Effects on Displaced Students in Chicago Public Schools* (Chicago: Consortium on Chicago School Research, 2009).

48. E. M. Allensworth and T. Rosenkranz, *Access to Magnet Schools in Chicago* (Chicago: Consortium on Chicago School Research, 2000).

49. Illinois Facilities Fund, *Here and Now 2: Change We Can Measure* (Chicago: Illinois Facilities Fund, 2009); E. Kneebone, T. Logue, S. Cahn, and M. McDunnah, *Here and Now: The Need for Performing Schools in Chicago's Neighborhoods* (Chicago: Illinois Facilities Fund).

50. Chicago Public Schools, "Establish Renaissance Schools," Chicago Public Schools Policy Manual Section 302.7, June 27, 2007, http://policy.cps.k12.il.us/documents/302.7.pdf.

51. M. Joyce, "Social Justice High School: Little Village and Lawndale's Experimental High School, Four Years after the Hunger Strike," *Chicago Weekly*, April 16, 2009, http://chicagoweekly.net/2009/04/16/social-justice-high-school-little-village-and-lawndales-experimental-high-school-four-years-after-the-hunger-strike/; D. Stovall, "Communities Struggle to Make Small Serve All," *Rethinking Schools Online*, Summer 2005, http://www.rethinkingschools.org/archive/19_04/stru194.shtml

52. Hill et al., *Portfolio School Districts for Big Cities*.

53. D. I. Aarons, "Focus on Instruction Turns around Chicago schools," *Education Week*, January 6, 2010, http://www.edweek.org/ew/articles/2010/01/06/16turnaround_ep.h29.html?tkn=MRPFheVzf6NMYOhfiWesmWD%2BHxtYpgg7KZUW& print=1.

54. V. Anderson, "Q & A with Schools CEO Ron Huberman," *Catalyst Notebook*, May 26, 2009, http://www.catalyst-chicago.org/notebook/index.php/entry/325/.

55. L. Forte, "Huberman Outlines Strategies to Improve Chicago Schools," *Catalyst Notebook*, September 3, 2009, http://www.catalyst-chicago.org/notebook/index.php/entry/376.

56. R. Rossi, "Renaissance 2010: Daley Pledges to Continue Replacing Bad Ones with Good," *Chicago Sun-Times*, January 6, 2010.

57. L. Cassidy, D. C. Humphrey, M. E. Weschler, and V. M. Young, *High School Reform in Chicago Public Schools: Renaissance 2010* (Part Three of a Series of Five Reports) (Chicago: Consortium on Chicago School Research, 2009); Humphrey and Shields, *High School Reform in Chicago Public Schools: An Overview*; J. K. Lesnick, I. Sartain, S. E. Sporte, and S. R. Stoelinga, *High School Reform in Chicago Public Schools: A Snapshot of High School Instruction* (Part Five of a Series of Five Reports) (Chicago: Consortium on Chicago School Research, 2009); Sartain et al., *High School Reform in Chicago Public Schools: Autonomous Management and Performance Schools* (Part Four of a Series of Five Reports); S. E. Sporte, M. Correa, H. M. Hart, and M. E. Wechsler, *High School Reform in Chicago Public Schools: Instructional Development Systems* (Part Two of a Series of Five Reports) (Chicago: Consortium on Chicago School Research, 2009); V. M. Young, D. C. Humphrey, H. Wang, K. R. Bosetti, L. Cassidy, M. E. Weschler, E. Rivera et al. *Renaissance Schools Fund-Supported Schools: Early Outcomes, Challenges, and Opportunities* (Chicago: Consortium on Chicago School Research, 2009).

58. Center for Research on Education Outcomes (CREDO), *Charter School Performance in Illinois* (Palo Alto, CA: Stanford University, 2009).

59. K. Booker, B. Gill, R. Zimmer, and T. R. Sass, *Achievement and Attainment in Chicago Charter Schools* (Santa Monica, CA: RAND Corporation, 2009), http://www.rand.org/pubs/technical_reports/TR585-1/

60. M. de la Torre and J. Gwynne, *Changing Schools: A Look at Student Mobility Trends in Chicago Public Schools Since 1995* (Chicago: Consortium on Chicago School Research, 2009), http://ccsr.uchicago.edu/content/publications.php?pub_id=129

61. Education Committee, *Still Left Behind: Student Learning in Chicago's Public Schools* (Chicago: Civic Committee of the Commercial Club of Chicago, 2009), http://www.civiccommittee.org/Still%20Left%20Behind%20v2.pdf/

62. Target Area Development Corporation, *Parent Perceptions vs. Student Realities*.

63. Shipps, *School Reform, Corporate Style*.

64. Boyd et al., *The Transformation of Great American School Districts*.

65. Lenz, "Missing in Action," 130.

66. D. R. Moore, V. Valdez, A. Ragona, and G. Mount, *The Big Picture: School-Initiated*

Reforms, Centrally Initiated Reforms, and Elementary School Achievement in Chicago (1990 to 2005) (Chicago: Designs for Change, 2005).

67. K. Berg, "Implementing Chicago's Plan to Transform Public Housing," *The Changing Face of Metropolitan Chicago* (presented at the Conference on Chicago Research and Public Policy, Chicago, Loyola University of Chicago, 2005).

68. S. Chambers, *Mayors and Schools: Minority Voices and Democratic Tensions in Urban Education* (Philadelphia: Temple University Press, 2006).

69. Parents United for Responsible Education, "8 Major Problems with Renaissance 2010," *PURE Online*, February 2, 2009, http://pureparents.org/index.php?blog/show/ 8_major_problems_with_Renaissance_2010_.

70. S. Karp, "Duncan Says Turnarounds Not to Blame for School Violence," *Catalyst Notebook*, October 7, 2009, http://www.catalyst-chicago.org/notebook/index.php/entry/403/ Duncan_says_turnarounds_not_to_blame_for_school_violence/

71. National Commission on Excellence in Education, *A Nation at Risk: The Imperative for Educational Reform* (Washington, DC: U.S. Department of Education, 1983).

72. J. Hannaway and M. Carnoy, *Decentralization and School Improvement.*

73. C. Peters, "A Neoliberal's Manifesto," *The Washington Monthly*, May–18, 1983; Salomon, "The New Governance and the Tools of Public Action."

74. D. B. Tyack, *The One Best System: A History of American Urban Education* (Cambridge, MA: Harvard University Press, 1974).

75. Hill et al., *Portfolio School Districts for Big Cities.*

76. D. Stone, *Policy Paradox: The Art of Political Decision Making*, 3rd ed. (New York: W.W. Norton, 2001).

77. D. F. Labaree, "Public Goods, Private Goods: The American Struggle over Educational Goals," *American Educational Research Journal* 34, no. 1 (1997): 39–81.

78. W. J. Bushaw and J.A. McNee, "The 41st Annual Phi Delta Kappa/Gallup Poll of the Public's Attitudes Toward the Public Schools," *Phi Delta Kappan* 91, no. 1 (2009): 8–23.

79. K. E. Weick, "Educational Organizations as Loosely Coupled Systems," *Administrative Science Quarterly* 21 (1976): 1–19.

80. Hill et al., *Portfolio School Districts for Big Cities*, 22.

81. Salomon, "The New Governance and the Tools of Public Action."

Chapter 4

1. Various people have read drafts, provided helpful feedback, or were interviewed for this paper. The authors wish to thank: Katrina Bulkley, Michele Cahill, Stacey Childress, John Elwell, Norm Fruchter, Robert Hughes, Henry Levin, Eric Nadelstern, Aaron Pallas, Diane Ravitch, and Claire Sylvan. Notwithstanding their assistance, the paper's omissions, errors, and interpretations are the authors' alone.

2. D. Ravitch, *The Great School Wars* (Baltimore, MD: Johns Hopkins University Press, 1974).

3. A. Goodnough, "A Wider Audience," *New York Times*, April 28, 1999.

4. R. Perez-Pena, "Albany Backs Mayoral Rule over Schools," *New York Times*, June 11, 2002.

5. Klein: "One of the first things I did, even before I think I actually took the job, is I went out to San Diego and met with Alan Bersin, someone that I knew from my time in the Clinton administration, and Tony Alvarado. And I spent the day with the two of them and their teams, talking about the issues. I spent time with Roy Romer, who's also a nontraditional superintendent who's in Los Angeles. I still spend time with these

people with Arne Duncan, in Philadelphia, just recently. I was talking to some other superintendents on a pretty regular basis, and Tom Payzant, whom you mentioned." See J. Klein, Joel Klein interview with Hedrick Smith, transcript, http://www.pbs.org/makingschoolswork/atp/briadcoast/html. Gendar and Saltonstall say, "Klein lost no time yesterday reaching out, calling state Regents such as Merryl Tisch of Manhattan and business leaders like Kathryn Wylde, president of the New York City Partnership, a business coalition." A. Gendar and D. Saltonstall, "Lawyer Picked as Chancellor," *New York Daily News* July 30, 2002.

6. C. N. Stone and J. R. Henig, *Building Civic Capacity: The Politics of Reforming Urban Schools* (Lawrence: University of Kansas Press, 2001).

7. The Commission on School Governance, appointed by the City's Public Advocate, tempered its generally critical review of some aspects of the Bloomberg–Klein regime by observing: "From 2002 to the present, the New York City school system has undergone more change than it has in any similar period in its history . . . Although change is not synonymous with progress, it is a prerequisite for progress. The current governance arrangement has allowed for more of it. The capacity to implement change could be the single most important and measurable advantage of mayoral control when the current governance arrangement is compared to the one that preceded it. Notwithstanding the advantages derived from centralization of power in the hands of a single official, it is necessary to recognize and safeguard against the risks incurred from centralization in a democratic system of government." Commission on School Governance, *Final Report of the Commission on School Governance. Volume I: Findings and Recommendations*, 2008, prepared for Betsy Gotbaum Public Advocate for the City of New York, 7.

8. C. E. Lindblom, "The Science of Muddling Through," *Public Administration Review* 19, no. 2 (1959).

9. Some observers, including New York University professor Joseph Viteritti and education historian Diane Ravitch, doubted if Bloomberg had any plan at all. See J. Traub, "A Lesson in Unintended Consequences," *New York Times*, October 6, 2002.

10. A. Goodnough, "Fixing the Schools," *New York Times*, October 4, 2002.

11. A. Goodnough, "Klein Taking Time to Make His Mark as Schools Chancellor," *New York Times*, November 24, 2002.

12. See Reckhow, chapter 10, this volume, for a deeper analysis of the role that foundations are playing in promoting both mayoral control and the portfolio management model.

13. "Although DOE officials had repeatedly claimed there were public school parents and working classroom teachers in these [Children First] groups," Leonie Haimson reports that a Freedom of Information Act request eventually made it "clear that there were none." L. Haimson, "Children First: A Short History," in *NYC Schools under Bloomberg and Klein: What Parents, Teachers, and Policymakers Need to Know* (New York: Lulu, 2009), 8.

14. Goodnough, "Fixing the Schools"; Goodnough, "Klein Taking Time to Make His Mark as Schools Chancellor"; D. Tyack, *The One Best System* (Cambridge, MA: Harvard University Press, 1974) p. 77.

15. A. Goodnough, "Vision for the Schools: Overview; Mayor Sets Plan for Tight Control over City Schools," *New York Times*, January 16, 2003.

16. This curriculum was optional for 200 top-performing schools.

17. D. M. Herszenhorn, "Class Is in Session: Principal Candidates Report for Summer School," *New York Times* July 8, 2003.

18. Goodnough, "Vision for the Schools."

19. Ibid.
20. D. M. Herszenhorn, "Despite Victory Won by Mayor, School Control Is Not Assured," *New York Times*, April 14, 2003; D. M. Herszenhorn, "Albany Attacks Bloomberg's School Plan," *New York Times*, April 23, 2003.
21. D. M. Herszenhorn, "Mayoral Control Changes the Politics of the Schools," *New York Times*, May 21, 2003.
22. Herszenhorn, "Despite Victory Won by Mayor, School Control Is Not Assured."
23. Over the ensuing years, Klein was repeatedly criticized for ignoring the wishes of parents and educators. As demonstrated in this volume, the absence of stakeholder and community input is a recurring criticism of the portfolio approach as developed in the examined cities. A. Goodnough, "Some Parents Fear Weaker Role in Centralized Schools," *New York Times*, January 17, 2003.
24. D. M. Herszenhorn, "As City Goes Back to School, Bloomberg's Plan Faces Test," *New York Times*, September 4, 2003.
25. D. M. Herszenhorn, "Overhaul Has Led to Chaos, Principals' Union Charges," *New York Times* November 15, 2003.
26. E. Gootman and D. M. Herszenhorn, "Broad Overhaul of City Schools Causing Strains," *New York Times*, January 5, 2004.
27. Ibid.
28. A. Goodnough, "Senior Officials Sent Packing in Overhaul of City's Schools," *New York Times*, January 29, 2003; D. M. Herszenhorn, "Despite Outflow, City Schools Administration Is Said to Remain Solid," *New York Times*.
29. M. Winerip, "The Lost Year: Classes in Crisis; City Retools Special Education But Pupils Slip Through the Cracks," *New York Times*, July 4, 2004.
30. D. M. Herszenhorn, "Teachers' Leader Hurls Criticism at Mayor," *New York Times* December 3, 2004.
31. D. M. Herszenhorn, "Decentralization Foe Now Assails Mayor's Rule," *New York Times* December 15, 2004; D. Ravitch, *The Death and Life of the Great American School System: How Testing and Choice Are Undermining Education* (New York: Basic Books, 2010).
32. Gootman and Herszenhorn, "Broad Overhaul of City Schools Causing Strains."
33. By the late 1990s, the community school districts were stripped of most of their hiring authority, making the charge of patronage potentially moot. Regardless, the association remained strong in the public's mind and the administration made use of this perception to justify its efforts. Traub, "A Lesson in Unintended Consequences."
34. As part of the Children First reforms, schools were required to hire math and literacy coaches and parent coordinators.
35. C. Childress and T. Cheek Clayton, "Focusing on Results at the New York City Department of Education," Public Education Leadership Project at Harvard University, PEL-054, 2008.
36. E. Reisner, M. Rubinstein, M. Johnson, and L. Fabiano, "Evaluation of the New Century High Schools Initiative," Policy Study Associates, Inc. Washington, DC, 2003. Subsequent reports are available at http://www.newvisions.org/our-goal/results.
37. The effort was modeled on even earlier reforms such as the Julia Richmond High School complex of small alternative high schools created during the Annenberg Challenge in the early 1990s.
38. The ten principles were: rigorous instruction; personalized relationships; clear focus and expectations; instructional leadership; school-based professional development and collaboration; meaningful and continuous assessment of student learning; partnerships

with community organizations; family engagement and involvement; student participation and youth development, and effective use of technology and information.

39. The effort New Visions put into establishing these regional offices is another indication that, by all accounts, those working within the school system believed that the centralized, ten-region structure was permanent rather than a temporary transitional structure leading to a system of portfolio management.

40. Center for Education Reform, 2009, http://www.edreform.com/_upload/ranking_chart. pdf.

41. A. Goodnough, "Scope of Loss for Privatizing by Edison Stuns Officials," *New York Times*, April 3, 2001.

42. In a 2010 ranking by the National Alliance for Public Charter Schools of state charter laws, New York placed second nationwide on measures of quality control; http://www. publiccharters.org/charterlaws/state/NY.

43. A. Mindlin, "Requiem for a Much-Beloved School," *New York Times*, July 4, 2004.

44. School Construction Authority, "Children First 2005-2009 Five- Year Capital Plan," 2009 Final report, http://source.nycsca.org/pdf/capitalplan/2009/ClosoutAmendment-09Classic.pdf.

45. Education Sector, *Growing Pains: Scaling Up the Nation's Best Charter Schools* (Washington, DC: Education Sector, 2009).

46. Exemptions were based on state assessment results with some effort to control for student characteristics.

47. A. Goodnough, "City Is Converting Reading and Math to Uniform Course," *New York Times*, January 22, 2003.

48. C. Christenson, C. Johnson, and M. Horn, *Disrupting Class: How Disruptive Innovation Will Change the Way the World Learns* (New York: McGraw Hill, 2008); F. Hess, *The Future of Educational Entrepreneurship: Possibilities for School Reform* (Cambridge, MA: Harvard Education Press, 2008).

49. S. Fliegel, *Miracle in East Harlem: The Fight for Choice in Public Education* (New York: Crown Publishers, 1993); J. R. Henig, *Rethinking School Choice, Limits of the Market Metaphor* (Princeton, NJ: Princeton University Press, 1994).

50. C. Glickman, *Those Who Dared: Five Visionaries Who Changed American Education* (New York: Teachers College Press, 2009).

51. D. M. Herszenhorn, "Schools Chancellor to Give Principals More Autonomy," *New York Times,* January 20, 2006. C. Childress and T. Cheek Clayton, "Focusing on Results at the New York City Department of Education," 2008.

52. The autonomy-for-accountability trade-off was more an abstract promise than a concrete and detailed plan; there was not a clear line drawn between specific indicators of performance and specific consequences, and it remains unclear at this point precisely how the trade-off has been operationalized in practice.

53. Herszenhorn, "Schools Chancellor to Give Principals More Autonomy."

54. D. M. Herszenhorn, "Bucking the Tide of School Reform, A Superintendent Gets Results," *New York Times* December 4, 2006.

55. C. Childress and T. Cheek Clayton, "Focusing on Results at the New York City Department of Education," 2008

56. D. M. Herszenhorn, "City Weighs Bigger Private Role in Managing the Public Schools," *New York Times* October 5, 2006.

57. Ibid.

58. Herszenhorn, "Schools Chancellor to Give Principals More Autonomy.

59. C. Childress and T. Cheek Clayton, "Focusing on Results at the New York City Department of Education," 2008.
60. Klein's accountability efforts are among the most controversial of his administration's many reforms. ARIS was criticized for its cost and unreliability. School letter grades have been challenged, given their reliance on one-year changes in test scores and dependence on questionable state assessments. For a full critique, see Ravitch, *The Death and Life of the Great American School System*. C. Childress and T. Cheek Clayton, "Focusing on Results at the New York City Department of Education," 2008.
61. D. M. Herszenhorn, "Overhaul of Schools Would Let Teachers Rate Principals," *New York Times* January 19, 2007; D. M. Herszenhorn, "Klein Specifies Restructuring of City Schools," *New York Times* April 17, 2007.
62. Herszenhorn, "Klein Specifies Restructuring of City Schools.
63. The city's "marketplace" of school support organizations suggests that a pure autonomy–for-accountability approach might have set too many schools adrift. On-the-ground experience of the Gates-funded intermediaries demonstrated the importance of non-supervisory support. As such, the advisory and capacity-building functions of the school support organizations are a distinguishing component of New York City's approach to portfolio management and perhaps unique to the city, given its robust civic capacity.
64. Available at http://schools.nyc.gov/AboutUs/schools/support/default.htm.
65. School support information available at http://schools.nyc.gov/Accountability/School Reports/ ProgressReports/default.htm
66. D. M. Herszenhorn, "Mayor Repeats Policy: No Cellphones in Schools," *New York Times*, May 6, 2006.
67. J. Bosman, "Cellphone Raid Roils Manhattan School," *New York Times*, June 1, 2007; A. Hartocollis, "Parents to Sue Over Schools' Cellphone Ban," *New York Times*, July 13, 2006; J. Medina, "Court Upholds School Cellphone Ban," *New York Times*, April 22, 2008.
68. E. Green, "City urged superintendents to favor leadership academy principals," September 23, 2009, http:// www.gothamschools.org.
69. A. Phillips, "ATR pool shrinks rapidly as school starts and principals hire," September 10, 2009, http://www.gothamschools.org.
70. Satisfaction survey results available at http://schools.nyc.gov/NR/rdonlyres/A63034F4-40DF-4492-ABEE-30652972BA44/0/pss_2009.pdf; accessed on January 20, 2010.
71. A. Phillips, "Education Officials Rethinking How Schools Get Support, Again," www.gotham schools.org.
72. D. M. Herszenhorn, "In Push for Small Schools, Other Schools Suffer," *New York Times*, January 14, 2005.
73. P. Cramer and E. Green, E. "DOE dropping school closure plan that drew UFT, parent lawsuit," April 2, 2009, www.gothamschools.org; E. Green, "Parents, Weingarten sue DOE, Klein over charter school siting," March 24, 2009, http://www.gothamschools.org.
74. P. Cramer, "Just two F's amid nearly straight A's on 2009 progress reports," September 2, 2009, www.gothamschools.org.
75. S. Otterman, "City to Get Federal Aid to Fix or Close Weak Schools," *New York Times*, January 22, 2010; S. Otterman, "Large High Schools in the City Are Taking Hard Falls," *New York Times*, January 25, 2010; S. Otterman, "Schools' Supporters Fear They Weren't Heard," *New York Times*, January 27, 2010.

76. "Bloomberg's Politics: A Post-Partisan Savior, or Just Another Spoiler?" *Wall Street Journal*, June 21, 2007.

77. A. Bridges, *Morning Glories: Municipal Reform in the Southwest* (Princeton, NJ: Princeton University Press, 1999).

78. M. Crenson, *The Unpolitics of Air Pollution: A Study of Nondecisionmaking in the Cities* (Baltimore, MD: Johns Hopkins University Press, 1971).

79. A. Hartocollis, "Politics Absent as Mayor Picks School Panelists," *New York Times*, July 19, 2002.

80. M. Winerip, "On Education: Fired for Disagreeing, Ex-panelist Fears the Mayor Is Discouraging Advice He Needs to Hear," *New York Times*, March 24, 2004.

81. For example, when Michele Rhee, chancellor in the Washington, D.C., Public Schools, announced the firing of 98 central office employees, Council Chairman Vincent C. Gray (D) asked Rhee for a list of the fired employees and said he was also going to request their evaluations. "What do the evaluations look like?" he asked. "I want to see." V. D. Haynes and S. Moreno, "Workers, Council Question Firings," *Washington Post*, March 9, 2008, http://www.washingtonpost.com/wp-dyn/content/article/2008/03/08/AR2008030802438.html.

82. The lack of checks on the mayor's powers was a major bone of contention during the debate over the extension of mayoral control. In the summer of 2009, when the state legislature extended the mayor's basic authority, it did make some changes intended to address this, including giving the Independent Budget Office a role in reviewing the DOE budget.

83. http://schools.nyc.gov/FundForPublicSchools/AboutUs/PressKits/default.htm.

84. Reminiscent of Robert Moses's infamous construction of the Jones Beach beach house foundation—exhausting all of the allocated state funding in the process—and going back to the state capital time and time again for more funding.

85. J. L. Pressman and A. B. Wildavsky, *Implementation*, 2nd ed. (Berkeley: University of California Press).

86. Bloomberg appears to have been committed to hire a nontraditional superintendent well before he settled on Klein as his pick. A July 14, 2002 article in the *New York Times* speculated the mayor was looking first toward the corporate sector, mentioning Gerald M. Levin, retired AOL Time Warner CEO, and Louis V. Gerstner Jr., the chairman of I.B.M., as people who had been considered. A. Hartocollis, "Schematic for a Schools Chancellor; Seeking Business Circuitry, a Hard Shell and 'Fire in the Belly'," *New York Times*, July 14, 2002. Moreover, given Klein's lack of school administrator credentials, his appointment required a waiver from New York's State Education Department.

87. H. Zelon, "The education business: Teachers missing at the top," *City Limits Weekly*, no. 688, June 1, 2009,http://www.citylimits.org/content/articles/viewarticle.cfm?article_id=3749

88. N. M. Tichy and W. G. Bennis, *Judgment* (New York: Penguin Portfolio Hardcover, 2007).

89. The reasoning being that it would be easier to shift principals and teachers from a high- to low-performing school if both were within the same administrative unit than if such transfers required moving across those units.

90. The later reform phase took this logic further. As one top official explained, the school support networks are a-geographic because if you map out district to perfectly match political boundaries "all you get is patronage."

91. http://www.nycleadershipacademy.org/aspiringprincipals/app_overview.

92. D. Rogers, *110 Livingston Street: Politics and Bureaucracy in the New York City Schools* (New York: Random House, 1968).

93. M. L. Needleman and C. E. Needleman, *Guerrillas in the Bureaucracy: The Community Planning Experiment in the United States* (New York: John Wiley & Sons, 1974).

94. One of the ten regional superintendents, and former superintendent of Community School District 15, who succeeded Deputy Chancellor for Instruction Diana Lam.

95. A key figure in the early District 4 adoption of public school choice, who became an early and often adviser to Klein and whose organization was subsequently engaged as one of the school support organizations.

96. "*New York Times* New York City Poll, Apr. 16-21, 2004," http://www.nytimes.com/packages/html/politics/20040423_poll/20040423_poll_results.pdf

97. In addition to the mayor, the law, which had twice been supported by public referenda, applied to the public advocate, comptroller, borough presidents, and council members. M. Barbaro and T. Arango, "Bloomberg Said to Test a Term-limit Reversal," *New York Times*, August 22, 2008.

98. In a televised interview with Hedrick Smith, Klein reflected on the outcome of the San Diego reform agenda of Alan Bersin. Bersin was someone Klein admired; someone he had taken pains to visit even before he formally took office. But Bersin subsequently was ousted before the initiatives he was pursuing had a chance to take root. "It's a tragedy," Klein observed, "that a man of that talent and quality, who has done some of the most serious and important, transformative work in education fundamentally got beat by the politics of it." Asked by Smith, "How many years does it take to really get traction on the kinds of problems you and I have been talking about for the last hour, and you've been working on for the last many months?" Klein replied, "A decade. I think, in a decade you can actually restructure the system, create new incentives, new rewards; find a dynamic, new approach to labor-management relations. . . . One of the things that I thought was brilliant about what Michael Bloomberg did when he secured mayoral control right at the outset—he had no illusions about what it takes to transform a system like this—but he knew that under mayoral control we would have a mayor and a chancellor together for two terms at a minimum: eight years." J. Klein, Interview with Hedrick Smith, transcript, http://www.pbs.org/makingschoolswork/atp/broadcast.html.

99. S. Chan, "Bloomberg Says He Wants a Third Term as Mayor," *New York Times*, October 2, 2008.

100. This ad campaign predated the mayor's announcement that he would seek a third term, and was more directly tied to the issue of extending the mayoral control governance structure than to extending the Bloomberg–Klein administration itself, although in retrospect, it seems likely that the mayor and some of his supporters may have had the latter also in mind (and anecdotal reports suggested that, at the time, Joel Klein believed that even if term limits ended Bloomberg's tenure, there was a good chance that Klein might be asked to continue as chancellor by whomever succeeded him in office.

101. The details of the mayoral control battle will be outlined in a forthcoming report commissioned by the Donors Education Collaborative and prepared by Research for Action.

102. E. E. Schattschneider, *Politics, Pressure and the Tariff* (New York: Prentice Hall, 1935).

103. J. Soss and S. F. Schram, "A Public Transformed? Welfare Reform as Policy Feedback," *American Political Science Review* 101 (200&):111–127.

104. To the extent that this is a tactical premise, we're not fully convinced that it is an accurate one. The implicit assumption seems to be that schools will be effective political

constituencies that can mobilize to defend the resources and autonomy they've been granted. But much of the Bloomberg–Klein approach has entailed the deliberate detachment of schools from their geographically based constituencies, and it is not clear that principals—themselves largely detached from parent and community-based networks—would have much leverage to resist recentralization efforts, should a strong new regime attempt to pull back the reins.

105. M. Barbaro, "Criticism of Bloomberg over Nonprofits' Support," *New York Times* October 19, 2008; M. Barbaro and D. W. Chen, "Bloomberg Enlists His Charities in Bid to Stay," *New York Times*, October 17, 2008; B. Fertig, "Should the mayor control NYC schools?" WNYC Radio, March 18, 2008.

106. Ibid. Reverend Calvin Butts of the Abyssinian Baptist Church is a third board member. According to one report, Good Shepherd and Abyssian between them have received about $400 million in city contracts over the past decade.

107. C. Campanile, "Gates' $4 Million Lesson," *New York Post*, August 17, 2009.

108. For instance, Explore Charter Schools; Girls Preparatory Charter Schools; Harlem RBI.

109. Michael Bloomberg is listed as giving $700,000 on its 2008 990 form, http://www.learningleaders.org/about/mission_and_impact.

110. In May 2008, the Office of School and Youth Development requested and had approved a retroactive, no-bid $391,660 contract for TASC to continue after-school programs previously funded by 21st Century Grants and as "special legislative projects." See http://schools.nyc.gov/Offices/DCP/GeneralInformation/ExceptiontoCompetitive Bidding /CommitteeonContracts/Default.htm.

111. Public Eyes on Public Schools, P.B. (2009). Retrieved from http://ednotesonline.blog spot.com/2009/04/nearly-one-third-of-grassroots.html.

Chapter 5

1. This research was supported with lead funding from the William Penn Foundation and related grants from Carnegie Corporation of New York, The Samuel S. Fels Fund, the Edward Hazen Foundation, the Charles Stewart Mott Foundation, The Pew Charitable Trusts, The Philadelphia Foundation, the Spencer Foundation, Surdna Foundation, and others. The opinions expressed in this research are those of the authors and do not necessarily reflect the views of funders.

2. In this case, the DPM reform is "market-based" because of its use of contracting, not because of increases in family or student choice. W. L. Boyd, J. B. Christman, and E. Useem, "Radical Privatization in Philadelphia: School Leaders as Policy Entrepreneurs," in *The Transformation of Great American School Districts: How Big Cities Are Reshaping Public Education*, eds. W. L. Boyd, C. T. Kerchner, and M. Blyth (Cambridge, MA: Harvard Education Press, 2008), 2.

3. P. T. Hill, L. Pierce, and J. Guthrie, *Reinventing Public Education : How Contracting Can Transform America's Schools (RAND Research Study)* (Chicago: University of Chicago Press, 1997); C. Warren and M. Hernandez, *Portfolio of Schools: An Idea Whose Time Has Come* (Providence, RI: Annenberg Institute for School Reform, 2005).

4. Interview conducted in 2006, as cited in J. B. Christman, E. Gold, and B. Herold, *Privatization "Philly Style": What Can Be Learned from Philadelphia's Diverse Provider Model of School Management?* Updated edition, June (Research Brief) (Philadelphia: Research for Action, 2006).

5. Ibid.

6. E. Useem, J. B. Christman, and W. L. Boyd, "The Role of District-level Leadership in Making Radical Reform Work: Philadelphia's Education Reform under the State Takeover, 2001–2006" (working paper; Philadelphia: Laboratory for Student Success, Temple University, 2006).

7. T. Corcoran and J. B. Christman, *The Limits and Contradictions of Systemic Reform: The Philadelphia Story* (Philadelphia: Consortium for Policy Research in Education, 2002).

8. Boyd, Christman, and Useem, "Radical Privatization in Philadelphia."

9 Christman, Gold, and Herold, *Privatization "Philly Style."*

10. At the end of the 2002–2003 school year, the contract with Chancellor Beacon Academies was terminated by the district.

11. E. Useem, R. Offenberg, and E. Farley, *Closing the Teacher Quality Gap in Philadelphia: New Hope and Old Hurdles* (Philadelphia: Research for Action, 2007).

12. K. E. Bulkley and E. Travers, "Variations on a Theme: The Shift from Distinction to Commonality in Philadelphia's Diverse Provider Model" (Paper presented at the Annual Meeting of the American Educational Research Association, San Diego, CA, April 15, 2009); J. B. Christman, R. C. Neild, K. E. Bulkley, S. Blanc, C. Mitchell, R. Liu, et al., *Making the Most of Interim Assessment Data: Lessons from Philadelphia's Managed Instruction System* (Philadelphia: Research for Action, 2009); E. Gold, J. B. Christman, and B. Herold, "Blurring the Boundaries: Private Sector Involvement in Philadelphia Public Schools," *American Journal of Education* 113, no. 7 (2007): 181–212.

13. Quoted in Christman, Gold, and Herold, *Privatization "Philly Style,"* 14.

14. Corcoran and Christman, *The Limits and Contradictions of Systemic Reform.*

15. K.E. Bulkley, "Bringing the Public into the Private: Changing the Rules of the Game and New Regime Politics in Philadelphia Public Education," *Educational Policy,* 21, no. 1 (2007): 155-184; Corcoran and Christman, *The Limits and Contradictions of Systemic Reform.*

16. B. Gill, R. Zimmer, J. B. Christman, and S. Blanc, *State Takeover, School Restructuring, Private Management, and Student Achievement in Philadelphia* (Santa Monica, CA: RAND Corporation, 2007).

17. R. Zimmer, S. Blanc, B. Gill, and J. B. Christman, *Evaluating the Performance of Philadelphia's Charter Schools* (Santa Monica, CA: RAND Education, 2008).

18. Christman, Gold, and Herold, *Privatization "Philly Style."*

19. Along with the small schools, a growing number of charter schools with high school grades began to change the high school landscape. Many of the "large" neighborhood high schools began to depopulate, and they themselves became "medium" (700—1,500 students) size.

20. Christman, Gold, and Herold, *Privatization "Philly Style."*

21. K. E. Bulkley, L. M. Mundell, and M. Riffer, *Contracting Out Schools: The First Year of the Philadelphia Diverse Provider Model* (Research Brief) (Philadelphia: Research for Action, 2004).

22. As quoted in ibid., 5.

23. Hill, Pierce, and Guthrie, *Reinventing Public Education*; Warren and Hernandez, *Portfolio of Schools*

24. S. Blanc and E. Simon, "Public Education in Philadelphia: The Crucial Need for Civic Capacity in a Privatized Environment," *Phi Delta Kappan* 88, no. 7 (2007): 503–506.

25. Christman, Gold, and Herold, *Privatization "Philly Style."*

26. Ibid.

27. See, for example, B. Gill, R. Zimmer, J. B. Christman, and S. Blanc, *State Takeover, School Restructuring, Private Management, and Student Achievement in Philadelphia* (Santa Monica, CA: RAND Corporation, 2007).
28. Ibid.
29. P. E. Peterson and M. M. Chingos, "For-profit and Nonprofit Management in Philadelphia Schools," *Education Next* 2 (2009): 64–70.
30. Christman, Neild, Bulkley, Blanc, Mitchell, Liu, et al., *Making the Most of Interim Assessment Data.*
31. Boyd, Christman, and Useem, "Radical Privatization in Philadelphia."
32. C. B. Zogby, "Glass-half-empty Analysis Misses the Point," *Philadelphia Inquirer*, February 23, 2007; Boyd, Christman, and Useem, "Radical Privatization in Philadelphia."
33. D. Mezzacappa, "Vallas Leaves a Changed District, Again in Tumult," *Philadelphia Public School Notebook*, 14, no. 4 (2007): http://www.thenotebook.org/summer-2007/07119/vallas-leaves-changed-district-again-tumult; P. Socolar, "District Negotiates to Modify EMO Model at 28 Schools," *Philadelphia Public School Notebook* 17, no. 2 (2009): http://www.thenotebook.org/fall-2009/091825/district-negotiates-modify-emo-model-28-schools
34. Zimmer, Blanc, Gill, and Christman, *Evaluating the Performance of Philadelphia's Charter Schools.*
35. T.A. Hartmann, R. J. Reumann-Moore, S.A. Evans, C. Haxton, H.P. Maluk, R.C. Neild. "Going Small: Progress and Challenges of Philadelphia's Small High Schools." (Philadelphia: Research for Action, 2009)
36. M. Cucchiara, "From Center Stage to the Sidelines: Community Organizations and the State Takeover of Philadelphia Schools" (Unpublished paper, Research for Action, 2003); M. Cucchiara, E. Gold, E. and E. Simon, "Contracts, Choice, and Customer Service: Marketization and Public Engagement in Education," in press, *Teachers College Record.*
37. E. Gold, M. Cucchiara, E. Simon, and M. Riffer, *Time to Engage? Civic Participation in Philadelphia's School Reform* (Research Brief) (Philadelphia: Research for Action, 2005).
38. E. Gold, E. Simon, M. Cucchiara, C. Mitchell, and M. Riffer, *A Philadelphia Story: Building Civic Capacity for School Reform in a Privatizing System* (Philadelphia: Research for Action, 2007).
39. Mezzacappa, "Vallas Leaves a Changed District, Again in Tumult."
40. Ackerman's language about a "system of great schools" echoes language used earlier by Joel Klein in New York City.
41. K. A. Graham, "Unusual Trio Visit Phila. Schools," *Philadelphia Inquirer*, September 29, 2009.
42. K. A. Graham and M. Woodall, "14 Phila. Schools Eligible for Improvement Program," *Philadelphia Inquirer*, January 28, 2010.
43. D. Mezzacappa, "Teacher Contract Is signed; 'Real Work Begins Now,'" *Public School Notebook*, February 2010.
44. School District of Philadelphia, *Imagine 2014: Building a System of Great Schools* (Philadelphia: Author, 2009).
45. S. Snyder, "Philadelphia Teachers Approve Contract," *Philadelphia Inquirer*, January 21, 2010.
46. D. Mezzacappa, "AFT President: New Contract a Breakthrough," Dale Mezzacappa's Blog, January 23, 2010.

47. A. Hefetz and M. Warner, "Privatization and Its Reverse: Explaining the Dynamics of the Governmental Contracting Process," *Journal of Public Administration Research and Theory* 14, no. 2 (2004): 171–190.

48. School District of Philadelphia, *Review of EMO Performance Data 2002–2008* (Philadelphia: Author, 2009).

49. Interview with Ben Rayer, Sept. 2009.

50. D. Tales, "Plan Would Limit Charter Schools' Independence," *Philadelphia Daily News*, September 11, 2009.

51. K. A. Graham, "Charter School Suspends Two Administrators," *Philadelphia Inquirer*, April 18, 2008.

52. M. Woodall, "Mastery Charter Schools Aim to Transform Education," *Philadelphia Inquirer*, October 1, 2009.

53. The number of students served is based on information provided by the district's Office of Accountability in March 2010.

54. Christman, Gold, and Herold, *Privatization "Philly Style"*; Gold, Christman, and Herold, "Blurring the Boundaries."

55. Bulkley and Travers, "Variations on a Theme"; Gold, Christman, and Herold, "Blurring the Boundaries."

56. E. D. Sclar, *You Don't Always Get What You Pay for: The Economics of Privatization* (Cornell, NY: Cornell University Press, 2001).

57. M. Minow, "Public and Private Partnerships: Accounting for the New Religion," *Harvard Law Review* (2003): 1229–1270; Ibid.

58. Blanc and Simon, "Public Education in Philadelphia"; Cucchiara, Gold, and Simon, "Contracts, Choice, and Customer Service"; Gold, Cucchiara, Simon, and Riffer, *Time to Engage?*

59. Research for Action is a Philadelphia-based research organization that has conducted a number of studies of the impact of the state take-over on the Philadelphia School District. Two of the authors of this study, Jolley Christman and Eva Gold, were the founders of RFA. The remaining author has done her research in Philadelphia in conjunction with RFA.

60. Blanc and Simon, "Public Education in Philadelphia;" Cucchiara, Gold, and Simon, "Contracts, Choice, and Customer Service;" Gold, Cucchiara, Simon, and Riffer, *Time to Engage?*

61. Blanc and Simon, "Public Education in Philadelphia," 506.

62. Gold, Simon, Cucchiara, Mitchell, and Riffer, *A Philadelphia Story*.

63. Gold, Christman, and Herold, "Blurring the Boundaries."

64. K. E. Bulkley, "Educational Performance and Charter School Authorizers: The Accountability Bind," *Education Policy Analysis Archives* 9, no. 37 (2001), http://epaa.asu.edu/epaa/v9n37.html.

65. C. N. Stone, J. R. Henig, B. D. Jones, and C. Perannunzi, *Building Civic Capacity: The Politics of Reforming Urban Schools* (Lawrence: University of Kansas Press, 2001).

66. Bulkley, "Bringing the Public into the Private."

67. Ibid.

68. Cucchiara, Gold, and Simon, "Contracts, Choice, and Customer Service"; Gold, Simon, Cucchiara, Mitchell, and Riffer, *A Philadelphia Story*.

69. Gold, Christman, and Herold, "Blurring the Boundaries," 17.

70. Minow, "Public and Private Partnerships."

Chapter 6
1. This chapter is adapted from a paper prepared under the Project on Governance of Choice School Districts, Teachers College, Columbia University, funded by the Ford Foundation.
2. K. McCarthy, D. J. Peterson, N. Sastry, and M. Pollard, *The Repopulation of New Orleans after Hurricane Katrina* (New Orleans: Rand Gulf States Policy Institute, 2006).
3. Louisiana Department of Education, *School Facilities Master Plan for Orleans Parish, Blueprint*, August 2008, http://www.rsdla.net/InfoGlance/Rebuilding_schools/SFMPOP.aspx.
4. Louisiana Department of Education, *Students, Assessment, and Accountability*, 2006, http://www.louisianaschools.net/lde/saa/2273.html.
5. Louisiana Department of Education, *Education Finance: FY 2004–2005 Resource Allocation*, 2005, http://www.doe.state.la.us/lde/uploads/11790.xls; http://www.doe.state.la.us/lde/uploads/11785.xls.
6. Cowen Institute for Public Education Initiatives, *State of Public Education in New Orleans* (New Orleans: Cowen Institute, 2009).
7. BESE is the administrative policy-making body for elementary-secondary schools. Eight elected members from the eight BESE districts serve on the board along with three members-at-large appointed by the governor. Schools with a Louisiana School Performance score below 60 are considered academically unsuccessful. SPS is a composite of indicators on attendance, assessment, dropout data, and graduation rates, depending on grades served.
8. For a good overall summary of development since Katrina, see Cowen Institute for Public Education Initiatives, *State of Public Education in New Orleans, 2010*.
9. A. Rasheed, ed., *New Orleans Parents' Guide to Public Schools*, 1st ed. (New Orleans: New Schools for New Orleans, Summer 2007).
10. For example, see D. Simon, "More New Orleans Schools to Convert to Charter Status," *Times Picayune*, December 22, 2008, http://www.nola.com/news/index.ssf/2008/12/more_schools_to_join_new_orlea.html; K. G. Newmark and V. De Rugg, "Hope after Katrina," *Education Next* 6, no. 4 (2006): 13–21.
11. Bring New Orleans Back Commission Education Committee, "Rebuilding and Transforming: A Plan for Improving Public Education in New Orleans," 2006, p. 25, http://www.bringneworleansback.org/.
12. Since the release of this report, KIPP has been awarded several charters and would fit into the system as another network of charter schools.
13. Middle School Advocates now operates as FirstLine Schools.
14. Recovery School District Advisory Committee (RSDAC), Louisiana Department of Education, "Committee Presentation: Transfer of Schools," 2006, http://www.louisianaschools.net/lde/uploads/8632.ppt.
15. For details, see P. Devlin, "School Voucher Future Is Uncertain in Louisiana," *Times Picayune*, September 5, 2009, http://www.nola.com/education/index.ssf/2009/09/school_vouchers_future_is_unce.html.
16. R. Sims and A. Ball, *2008 Quality of Life Study: Orleans and Jefferson Parishes*, (New Orleans: University of New Orleans Survey Research Center, 2008).
17. 2009–2010 academic year.
18. BESE has authorized thirty-nine Type 5 charter schools in New Orleans.
19. Cowen Institute for Public Education Initiatives, *State of Public Education in New Orleans, 2010*.

20. For the cost figures, see S. Stokes, Recovery School District Increases Per-pupil Spending," *Times Picayune*, March 2, 2008, http://www.nola.com/news/index.ssf/2008/03/recovery_school_district_incre.html. The magnitudes of differences from different sources suggest that these should be used only as rough guides. We are not familiar with any well-defined expenditure studies with audited numbers. A more comprehensive and detailed analysis is found in Cowen Institute reports, but they still lack an overall picture on spending because of the complexity of multiple sources and purposes and the many different types of schools and school authorities. Cowen Institute for Public Education Initiatives, *State of Public Education in New Orleans*, 2009, 2010.

21. The first recommendation of a similar Cowen Institute report is the call for greater transparency in financial matters. See M. Schwam-Baird and L. Mogg, "Is Educational Reform in New Orleans Working? A Few Facts Swimming in a Sea of Unknowns" (Cowen Institute for Public Education Initiatives, presentation at conference at Loyola University, October 16, 2009, http://coweninstituteforpubliceducation.cmail2.com/T/ViewEmail/y/D955B96BFA39E464/1D8DDEA65D3E1928C9C291422E3DE149; Cowen Institute for Public Education Initiatives, *Public Education in New Orleans: A Financial Analysis* (New Orleans: Cowen Institute, 2009).

22. The most comprehensive comparison of costs is Cowen Institute for Public Education Initiatives, *State of Public Education in New Orleans,* 2010, 15–21.

23. Ibid., 27.

24. In January 2010, the State of Louisiana announced that it would raise the academically unacceptable SPS from 60 to 75 between 2010 and 2012, so current schools with a score below 75 will be challenged in the future. See http://www.doe.louisiana.gov/lde/comm/pressrelease.aspx?PR=1376; Cowen Institute for Public Education Initiatives, *Public Education in New Orleans: A Financial Analysis*.

25. The detailed perspective of the teacher union is best presented in United Teachers of New Orleans, Louisiana Federation of Teachers, and American Federation of Teachers, *"National Model" or Flawed Approach: The Post-Katrina New Orleans Public Schools* (New Orleans: United Teachers of New Orleans, 2006).

26. A. Rasheed, ed., *New Orleans Parents' Guide to Public Schools*, 1st ed. (New Orleans: New Schools for New Orleans, Summer 2007).

27. Save Our Schools New Orleans Louisiana, "What We Do," http://www.sosnola.org/sosnola-home/WhatWeDo.asp.

28. G. Filosa, "School Leaders Assail Move to Charters," *Times Picayune*, June 25, 2006.

29. Average 2008–2009 SPS for RSD-operated schools were 44. Charter schools in New Orleans had an average SPS of 79.5. OPSB-operated schools had an average SPS of 98.5, but these are mainly comprised of a few selective magnet schools. Louisiana Department of Education, "2008–2009 Baseline School Performance Scores," 2009, http://www.louisianaschools.net/lde/uploads/2009_SPS/2009_SPS_(ALPHA).xlsx; Cowen Institute for Public Education Initiatives, *State of Public Education in New Orleans,* 2010, 27.

30. Cowen Institute for Public Education Initiatives, *State of Public Education in New Orleans*, 2009, 9.

31. L. Darling Hammond, D. J. Holzman, S. J. Gatlin, and J. V. Heilig, "Does Teacher Education Matter? Evidence about Teacher Certification, Teach for America & Teacher Effectiveness," *Educational Policy Analysis Archives*13, no. 42 (2005), http://epaa.asu.edu/epaa/v13n42/.

32. M. Raymond, S. H. Fletcher, and J. Luque, *Teach for America: An Evaluation of Teacher Differences and Student Outcomes in Houston, Texas* (Stanford, CA: Hoover Institution, Center for Research on Educational Outcomes [CREDO], 2001).

33. T. Baquet, "Paul Vallas to Stick with New Orleans Recovery School District Another Year," *Times Picayune*, October 29, 2008, http://www.nola.com/news/index. ssf/2008/10/vallas_to_stick_with_no_recove.html.

34. Belfield and Levin found that competition among schools was associated with a modest improvement in student achievement across a large number of studies, although the costs of increasing competition were not accounted for. C. Belfield and H. M. Levin, "The Effects of Competition Between Schools on Educational Outcomes: A Review for the U.S." *Review of Educational Research* 72, no. 2 (2002): 279–341.

35. B. Thevenot, "Pastorek: State Likely to Run New Orleans Public Schools for Years," *Times Picayune*, August 28, 2009, http://www.nola.com/education/index.ssf/2009/08/pastorek_state_likely_to_run_n.html.

36. Rasheed, *New Orleans Parents' Guide.*

Chapter 7

1. M. Berends, S. J. Bodilly, and S. N. Kirby, "The Future of Whole School Designs: Conclusions, Observations, and Policy Implications," in *Facing the Challenges of Whole School Reform: New American Schools After A Decade*, ed. M. Berends, S. J. Bodilly, and S. N. Kirby, 142-154. Santa Monica: Rand Education, 2002; S. C. Purkey and M. S. Smith, "School Reform: The District Policy Implications of the Effective Schools Literature," *The Elementary School Journal* 85, no. 3 (1985): 353-389.

2. M. I. Honig, "No Small Thing: School District Central Office Bureaucracies and the Implementation of New Small Schools Initiatives," *American Educational Research Journal* 46, no. 2 (2009): 387–422.

3. M. I. Honig, "Building Policy from Practice: Central Office Administrators' Roles and Capacity in Collaborative Education Policy Implementation," *Educational Administration Quarterly* 39, no. 3 (2003): 292–338; Honig, "No Small Thing."

4. Chicago Public Schools, "New Schools," 2009, https://www.cps.edu/About_CPS/Departments/Pages/OfficeofNewSchools.aspx, para. 1.

5. School District of Philadelphia, *Imagine 2014: Building a System of Great Schools* (Philadelphia: School District of Philadelphia, 2009), 43.

6. New York City Board of Education, *Children First: A Bold, Common-sense Plan to Create Great Schools for All New York City Children* (New York: New York City Department of Education, 2008).

7. School Distirct of Philadelphia, *Imagine 2014*, 41.

8. Ibid.

9. New York City Board of Education, "Rewards and Consequences," 2009, http://schools.nyc.gov/Accountability/RewardsandConsequences/default.htm, para. 3.

10. P. T. Hill, C. Campbell, D. Menefee-Libey, B. Dusseault, M. DeArmond, and B. Gross *Portfolio School Districts for Big Cities: An Interim Report* (Seattle: Center on Reinventing Public Education, 2009).

11. Menefee-Libey, chapter 3, this volume.

12. Chicago Public Schools, *CEO Huberman Announces Initiative Aimed at Ensuring Integrity of CPS Data* (Chicago: Chicago Public Schools, 2009).

13. T. Daly, D. Keeling, R. Grainger, and A. Grundies, *Mutual Benefits: New York City's Shift to Mutual Consent in Teacher Hiring* (New York: The New Teacher Project, 2008).

14. J. I. Klein, "Reactions from an Urban School Superintendent," in *Creating a New Teaching Profession*, eds. D. Goldhaber and J. Hannaway (Washington, DC: The Urban Institute Press, 2009), 259–273.

15. Daly et al., *Mutual Benefits*; J. Levin, J. Mulher, and J. Schunck, *Unintended Consequences: The Case for Reforming the Staffing Rules in Urban Teachers Union Contracts* (New York: The New Teacher Project, 2005); J. Levin and M. Quinn, *Missed Opportunities: How We Keep High-Quality Teachers out of Urban Classrooms* (New York: The New Teacher Project, 2003).

16. E. Sanchez, D. Kline, and E. Laird, *Data-Driven Districts: Building the Culture and Capacity to Improve Student Achievement* (Washington, DC: Data Quality Campaign, 2009).

17. Honig, "Building Policy from Practice"; M. I. Honig, "District Central Office-Community Partnerships: From Contracts to Collaboration to Control," in *Educational Administration, Policy, and Reform: Research and Measurement*, eds. W. K. Hoy and C. G. Miskel (Greenwich, CT: Information Age Publishing, 2004), 59–90; M. I. Honig, "Street-level Bureaucracy Revisited: Frontline District Central Office Administrators as Boundary Spanners in Education Policy Implementation," *Educational Evaluation and Policy Analysis* 28, no. 4 (2006): 357–383; Honig, "No Small Thing"; J. P. Spillane, "A Cognitive Perspective on the Role of the Local Educational Agency in Implementing Instructional Policy: Accounting for Local Variability," *Educational Administration Quarterly* 34, no. 31 (1998): 31–57; J. P. Spillane, "State Policy and the Non-monolithic Nature of the Local School District: Organizational and Professional Considerations," *American Educational Research Journal* 35, no. 1 (1998): 33–63; J. P. Spillane and K. A. Callahan, "Implementing State Standards for Science Education: What District Policy Makers Make of the Hoopla," *Journal of Research in Science Teaching* 37, no. 5 (2000): 401–425; J. P. Spillane and C. L. Thompson, "Reconstructing Conceptions of Local Capacity: The Local Education Agency's Capacity for Ambitious Instructional Reform," *Educational Evaluation and Policy Analysis* 19, no. 2 (1997): 185–203.

18. B. A. Bimber, *School Decentralization: Lessons from the Study of Bureaucracy* (Santa Monica, CA: RAND Corporation, 1993); B. A. Bimber, *The Decentralization Mirage: Comparing Decision-making Arrangements in Four High Schools* (Santa Monica, CA: RAND Corporation, 1993); B. Malen, R. T. Ogawa, and J. Kranz, "What Do We Know about School-based Management? A Case Study of the Literature—A Call for Research," in *Choice and Control in American Education, Volume 2: The Practice of Choice, Decentralization, and School Restructuring*, eds. W. H. Clune and J. F. Witte (London: The Falmer Press, 1990), 289–342.

19. For example, see Honig, "Building Policy from Practice"; Honig, "District Central Office-Community Partnerships"; M. I. Honig, "The New Middle Management: Intermediary Organizations in Education Policy Implementation," *Educational Evaluation and Policy Analysis* 26, no. 1 (2004): 65–87; M. I. Honig, "Where's the 'Up' in Bottom-up Reform?" *Educational Policy* 18, no. 4 (2004): 527–561; Honig, "Street-level Bureaucracy Revisited"; Honig, "No Small Thing."

20. Honig, "Building Policy from Practice"; Honig, "Where's the 'Up' in Bottom-up Reform?"; J. Swinnerton, "Brokers and Boundary Crossers in an Urban School District: Understanding Central-Office Coaches as Instructional Leaders," *Journal of School Leadership* 17 (2007): 195–221.

21. Honig, "Building Policy from Practice"; Honig, "No Small Thing."

22. Ibid.

23. Honig, "Building Policy from Practice,"

24. Ibid.; M. I. Honig "District Central Offices as Learning Organizations: How Sociocultural and Organizational Learning Theories Elaborate District Central Office Administrators' Participation in Teaching and Learning Improvement Efforts," *American Journal of Education* 114 (2008): 627-664; Honig, "No Small Thing."

25. Honig, "No Small Thing."

26. Ibid.

27. Ibid.

28. Honig, "Where's the 'Up' in Bottom up?"; Honig, "Street-level Bureaucracy Revisited."

29. A. Goodnough, "Senior Officials Sent Packing in Overhaul of City's Schools," *New York Times*, January 29, 2003.

30. Hill et al, "Portfolio School Districts for Big Cities"

31. For an elaboration on this paradox, see Honig, "Street-level Bureaucracy Revisited."

32. For an elaboration on what such a systemwide central office reform effort could look like, see M. I. Honig, M. A. Copland, L. Rainey, J. A. Lorton, and M. Newton, *Central Office Transformation for District-wide Teaching and Learning Improvement* (Seattle: Center for the Study of Teaching and Policy, 2010).

33. R. D. Behn and P. A. Kant, "Strategies for Avoiding the Pitfalls of Performance Contracting," *Public Productivity & Management Review* 22, no. 4 (1999): 470–489; R. Dehoog Hoogland and L. M. Salamon, "Purchase-of-Service Contracting," in *The Tools of Government: A Guide to the New Governance*, ed. L. M. Salamon (New York: Oxford University Press, 2002), 319–339.

34. The idea that productive district relationships with external organizations are often partnerships, rather than product-exchanges, echoes findings from public management research on social service performance contracting. As Behn and Kant argue, "Creating an arms-length market relationship with a vendor makes little sense," when there is no market to regulate the price and quality, as if the case with most social services. Behn and Kant, "Strategies for Avoiding the Pitfalls of Performance Contracting," 482.

35. J. Supovitz, "Melding Internal and External Support for School Improvement: How the District Role Changes When Working Closely with External Instructional Support Providers," *Peabody Journal of Education* 83 (2008): 459–489.

36. Ibid., 473.

37. Honig, "No Small Thing."

38. M. Honig and G. S. Ikemoto, "Adaptive Assistance for Learning Improvement Efforts: The Case of the Institute for Learning," *Peabody Journal of Education* 83 (2008): 328–363.

39. K. E. Bulkley, L. Mundell, and M. Riffer, *Contracting out Schools: The First Year of the Philadelphia Diverse Provider Model* (Philadelphia: Research for Action, 2004); C. Coburn, S. Bae, and E. O. Turner, "Authority, Status, and the Dynamics of Insider-Outsider Partnerships at the District Level," *Peabody Journal of Education* 83 (2008): 364–399; L. M. Rhim, *Restructuring Schools in Chester Upland, Pennsylvania: An Analysis of State Restructuring Efforts* (Denver: Education Commission of the States, 2005).

40. Bulkley, Mundell, and Riffer, *Contracting out Schools*.

41. Rhim, *Restructuring Schools in Chester Upland, Pennsylvania*.

42. For example, see J. G.March, *A Primer on Decision Making* (New York: The Free Press, 1994); J. G. March and J. Olsen *Rediscovering Institutions* (New York: The Free Press, 1989).

43. Honig, "Street-level Bureaucracy Revisited"; Honig, "No Small Thing."
44. M. I. Honig and C. Coburn, "Evidence-based Decision Making in School District Central Offices: Toward a Policy and Research Agenda," *Educational Policy* 22, no. 4 (2008): 578–608; Honig et al., Central Office Transformation for District-wide Teaching and Learning Improvement.
45. M. M. Kennedy, *Working Knowledge and Other Essays* (Cambridge, MA: Huron Institute, 1982).
46. Ibid.
47. Honig and Coburn, "Evidence-based Decision Making in School District Central Offices."
48. C. Coburn, J. Toure, and M. Yamashita, "Evidence, Interpretation, and Persuasion: Instructional Decision Making at the District Central Office," *Teachers College Record* 11, no. 4 (2009): 1115–1161.
49. J. P. Spillane, B. J. Reiser, and T. Reimer, "Policy Implementation and Cognition: Reframing and Refocusing Implementation Research," *Review of Educational Research* 72, no. 3 (2002): 387–431.
50. C. Coburn and J. Talbert, "Conceptions of Evidence Use in School Districts: Mapping the Terrain," *American Journal of Education* 112, no. 4 (2006): 469–495; Honig and Coburn, "Evidence-based Decision Making in School District Central Offices."
51. Spillane, Reiser, and Reimer, "Policy Implementation and Cognition."
52. Spillane and Thompson, "Reconstructing Conceptions of Local Capacity: The Local Education Agency's Capacity for Ambitious Instructional Reform."
53. M. de la Torre and J. Gwynne, *When Schools Close: Effects on Displaced Students in Chicago Public Schools* (Chicago: Consortium on Chicago School Research at the University of Chicago, 2009); V. Dempsey and G. W. Noblit, "Cultural Ignorance and School Desegregation: Reconstructing a Silenced Narrative," *Educational Policy* 7, no. 3 (1993): 318–339; A. Galletta and J. Ayala, "Erasure and Survival: Creating a Future and Managing a Past in a Restructuring High School," *Teachers College Record* 110, no. 9 (2008): 1959–1985; J. K. Rice and B. Malen, "The Human Costs of Education Reform: The Case of School Reconstitution," *Educational Administration Quarterly*, 39, no. 5 (2003): 635–666.
54. PURE, "CPS 'Hearing' Tomorrow on Carpenter Building Giveaway," 2009, http://pure-parents.org/index.php?blog/show/Carpenter_bldg_to_Ogden, para. 1.
55. A. Russo, "What Happened at the Protest," 2009, http://www.catalyst-chicago.org/RUSSO/index.php/entry/1545/What_Happened_At_The_Protest; C. Sadovi, "Parents Attack Plan to Close 6 Schools—District Leaders Cite Low Enrollment," *Chicago Tribune*, January 11, 2009, NewsBank online database (Access World News).
56. A. Chavez, "Union Sues LAUSD over Charter Schools," *San Fernando Valley Sun*, December 23, 2009; R. Kaye, "Breaking up LAUSD—50 Schools at a Time," *City Watch* 7, no. 69 (August 28, 2009).
57. J. Medina, "N.Y. Senate Renews Mayor's Power to Run Schools," *New York Times*, August 6, 2009.
58. S. Otterman, "Big Schools Fall Hard in City Plan," *New York Times*, January 26, 2010; S. Otterman, "Boos and Personal Attacks as City Panel Prepares to Vote on School," *New York Times*, January 27, 2010.
59. Otterman, "Big Schools Fall Hard in City Plan."
60. C. Rotella, "Class Warrior: Arne Duncan's Bit to Shake up Schools," *The New Yorker*, February 1, 2010, 27.

61. De la Torre and Gwynne, *When Schools Close.*
62. W. L. Boyd and D. R. Wheaton, "Conflict Management in Declining School Districts," *Peabody Journal of Education* 60, no. 2 (1983): 25–36; K. E. Bulkley, "Educational Performance and Charter School Authorizers: The Accountability Bind," *Education Policy Analysis Archives,* 9, no. 37 (2001), http://epaa.asu.edu/epaa/v9n37.html; B. C. Hassel and M. Batdorff, *High-Stakes: Findings from a National Study of Life-or-Death Decisions by Charter School Authorizers* (Chapel Hill, NC: Public Impact, 2004); F. M. Hess, "Whaddya Mean You Want to Close My School?: The Politics of Regulatory Accountability in Charter Schooling," *Education and Urban Society* 33, no. 2 (2001): 141–156.
63. B. Malen, "Revisiting Policy Implementation as a Political Phenomenon," in *New Directions in Education Policy Implementation,* ed. M. I. Honig (Albany: State University of New York Press, 2006), 83–104.
64. J. Kowal and B. C. Hassel, "Closing Trouble Schools" (NCSRP working paper; Seattle, WA: Center on Reinventing Public Education, 2008); Boyd and Wheaton, "Conflict Management in Declining School Districts."
65. Kowal and Hassel, "Closing Trouble Schools."
66. Honig et al., *Central Office Transformation for District-wide Teaching and Learning Improvement.*

Chapter 8

1. P.T. Hill, L. Pierce, and J. Guthrie, *Reinventing Public Education: How Contracting Can Transform America's Schools* (Chicago: University of Chicago Press, 1997).
2. Schwartz documented the decentralization of schools in Edmonton, Alberta, and in a small school district in Florida that comprises six charter schools. H. Schwartz, "The Endurance of Centralized Governance Systems in An Age of School District Decentralization" (Study prepared for the Ford Foundation Project on Choice District Governance; National Center for the Study of Privatization in Education, Teachers College: Columbia University,2009).
3. K. McCarthy, D. J. Peterson, N. Sastry, and M. Pollard, *The Repopulation of New Orleans After Hurricane Katrina* (New Orleans: Rand Gulf States Policy Institute, 2006).
4. The data in this section are taken from the excellent summary of New Schools for New Orleans. New Schools for New Orleans, *A Brief Overview of Public Education in New Orleans, 1995–2009* (New Orleans: New Schools for New Orleans, 2009).
5. For example, see D. Simon, "More New Orleans Schools to Convert to Charter Status," *Times Picayune,* December 22, 2008, http://www.nola.com/news/index.ssf/2008/12/more_schools_to_join_new_orlea.html; K. G. Newmark and V. De Rugg, "Hope After Katrina," *Education Next* 6, no. 4 (2006): 13–21.
6. Although an earlier version of this paper focused on a "pure choice" district of charter schools, this chapter takes into consideration some of the important challenges associated with managing a portfolio of suppliers.
7. R. Haveman and B. Wolfe, "Schooling and Economic Well-Being: The Role of Nonmarket Effects," *Journal of Human Resources* 19, no. 3 (1984): 377–407; D. M. Cutler and A. Lleras-Muney, "Education and Health: Evaluating Theories and Evidence," in, *Making America Healthier: Social and Economic Policy as Health Policy,* eds. R. F. Schoeni, J. S. House, G. A. Kaplan, and H. Pollack (New York: Russell Sage Foundation, 2008), 29–60.
8. A. Guttman, *Democratic Education* (Princeton, NJ: Princeton University Press, 1987); J. Dewey, *Education and Democracy* (New York: Macmillan, 1916).

9. "Philosophical and Normative Issues in Educational Finance," theme issue, *Education Finance and Policy* 3, no. 4 (2008); J. Rawls, *A Theory of Justice* (Cambridge, MA: Harvard University Press, 1971); R. Rothstein, *Class and Schools: Using Social, Economic and Educational Reform to Close the Achievement Gap* (Washington, DC: Economic Policy Institute, 2004).

10. B. Barber, *A Passion for Democracy* (Princeton, NJ: Princeton University Press, 2000), chaps. 16–17; Dewey, *Education and Democracy*; J. Goodlad, *In Praise of Education* (New York: Teachers College Press, 1997); Guttman, *Democratic Education*.

11. A. Hirschman, *Exit, Voice, and Loyalty* (Cambridge, MA: Harvard University Press, 1970).

12. M. Friedman, "The Role of the State in Education," *Capitalism and Freedom* (Chicago: University of Chicago Press, 1962), chap. 5.

13. M. Schneider, P. Teske, and M. Marschall, *Choosing Schools: Consumer Choice and the Quality of American Schools* (Princeton, NJ: Princeton University Press, 2000).

14. H. M. Levin, "Educational Vouchers: Effectiveness, Choice, and Costs," *Journal of Policy Analysis and Management* 17, no. 3 (1998): 373–392; J. Scott, ed., *School Choice and Diversity: What the Evidence Says* (New York: Teachers College Press, 2005).

15. For example, this is implied by Friedman in his famous article that introduces educational vouchers though recognizing the need for schools to provide an education imbued with democratic values. Friedman, "The Role of the State in Education."

16. Barber, *A Passion for Democracy*, chaps. 16–17; Dewey, *Education and Democracy*; Goodlad, *In Praise of Education*; Guttman, *Democratic Education*.

17. W. Duncombe and J. Yinger, "How Much More Does a Disadvantaged Student Cost?" *Economics of Education Review* 24, no.5 (2005): 513–532.

18. M. G. Springer, ed., *Performance Incentives: Their Growing Impact on American K–12 Education* (Washington, DC: Brookings Institution Press, 2009).

19. Friedman, *Capitalism and Freedom*, chap. 5.

20. Schneider, Teske, and Marschall, *Choosing Schools*.

21. H. M. Levin, "A Comprehensive Framework for Evaluating Educational Vouchers," *Educational Evaluation and Policy Analyis* 24, no. 3 (2002):170–171.

22. He also suggests that the basic voucher be of modest size, increasing incentives for families who can afford to pay more to do so and restricting the funding of education for those who must depend on the basic voucher. Friedman, *Capitalism and Freedom*, chap. 5.

23. For example, Levin and Driver found that costs in the $1,000-a-pupil range for each transported student were highly likely over a decade ago. A casual check with one charter school network in New Orleans found that this amount was probably too modest for accepting students citywide. H. M. Levin and C. Driver, "Costs of an Educational Voucher System," *Education Economics* 5, no. 3 (1997): 265–283.

24. Virtually any textbook on microeconomics devotes considerable attention to the determinants of costs and economies of scale. See, for example, D. Besanko and R. Braeutigam, *Microeconomics*, 3rd ed. (New York: John Wiley, 2008), 274–277.

25. Transaction costs were first addressed, although not by that name, in the classic article by Ronald Coase. R. Coase, "The Nature of the Firm," *Economica* 4, no. 16 (1937): 386–405. However, their fuller treatment is usually attributed to Williamson. O. Williamson, *Markets and Hierarchies: An Analysis and Antitrust Implications* (New York: The Free Press, 1975. For an application of the concept to relations between legislative versus executive branches of government where there is separation of powers, see D. Epstein and S. O'Halloran, *Delegating Powers* (New York: Cambridge University Press, 1999). A concise and illuminating application of transaction costs to organization theory is found

in O. Williamson, "Transaction Cost Economics and Organization Theory," in *Organization Theory*, ed. O. Williamson (New York: Oxford University Press, 1995), 207–256.

26. Besanko and Braeutigam, *Microeconomics*, 657–675.

27. Friedman, *Capitalism and Freedom*, 86.

28. Friedman, *Capitalism and Freedom*, chap. 5.

29. A. Krueger and M. Lindahl, "Education for Growth: Why and for Whom?" *Journal of Economic Literature* 39, no. 4 (2001): 1101–1136.

30. E. Moretti, "Human Capital Externalities in Cities (NBER Working Paper No. W9641; Cambridge, MA: National Bureau of Economic Research, 2003); W. McMahon, "Recent Advances in Measuring the Social and Individual Benefits of Education," *International Journal of Educational Research* 27, no. 6 (1997): 449–501.

31. Cutler and Lleras-Muney, "Education and Health"; Krueger and Lindahl, "Education for Growth: Why and for Whom?"

32. E. Glaeser and R. Saks, "Corruption in America," *Journal of Public Economics* 90, no. 6–7 (2006): 1053–1072.

33. T. Parry, "Achieving Balance in Decentralization: A Case Study of Educational Decentralization in Chile," *World Development* 25, no. 2 (1997): 211–225.

34. V. Vandenberghe, "Combining Market and Bureaucratic Control in Education: An answer to market and bureaucratic failure?" *Comparative Education* 35, no. 3 (1999): 271–282.

35. Levin and Driver address these issues. Levin and Driver, "Costs of an Educational Voucher System."

36. The tension between school choice and Public Law 94-142 is also found more generally with charter schools. See J. B. Cullen and S. G. Rivkin, "The Role of Special Education in School Choice," in *The Economics of School Choice*, ed. C. M. Hoxby (Chicago: University of Chicago Press, 2003), 67–106; and L. M. Rhim, E. M. Ahearn, C. M. Lange, and M. J. McLaughlin, "Balancing Disparate Vision: An Analysis of Special Education in Charter Schools," in *Taking Account of Charter Schools*, eds. K. E. Bulkley and P. Wohlstetter (New York: Teachers College Press), 142–159.

37. D. M. Van Slyke, "The Mythology of Privatization in Contracting for Social Services," *Public Administration Review* 63, no. 3 (2003): 296.

38. M. de la Torre and J. Gwynne, *When Schools Close: Effects on Displaced Students in Chicago Public Schools* (Chicago: Consortium on Chicago School Research, 2009).

39. P. T. Hill, C. Campbell, D. Menefee-Libey, B. Dusseault, M. DeArmond, and B. Gross, *Portfolio School Districts for Big Cities: An Interim Report* (Seattle: Center on Reinventing Education, 2009).

Chapter 9

1. N. Epstein, "Introduction: Who Should Be in Charge of Our Schools? in *Who's in Charge Here?* ed. N. Epstein (Denver: Education Commission of the States, 2004), 1–6; J. E. Ryan, "The Tenth Amendment and Other Paper Tigers: The Legal Boundaries of Education Governance," in Epstein, *Who's in Charge Here?*, 42–74.

2. See, http://www2.ed.gov/policy/gen/leg/recovery/factsheet/idea.html.

3. A. C. Porter and M. S. Polikoff, "The Time for National Content Standards," *Education Week*, June 11, 2009, http://www.edweek.org/ew/articles/2009/06/11/35porter.h28.html ?tkn=RTTFJl4KyyPn2mDv7JNaBQzRVZm6ifwcYhoL&print=1.

4. My arguments on the changing nature of K–12 school improvement industry draws from a larger study of K–12 education contracting in the United States. The purpose of

the study was to begin to explore how public education is being transformed below the radar by new forms of privatization. In this work, I traced both the patterns and the hidden effects of the expanding role of for-profit firms in the daily operations of schools and districts. I examined the growth of large and small firms that sell technology, curriculum, tests, management expertise, and tutoring services to public school districts and thus fund their own growth with public dollars. The study was conducted over a one-and-a-half year period (from December 2006–June 2008). For more detail on the design of the study and its methods, see P. Burch, *Hidden Markets: The New Education Privatization* (London: Routledge Falmer, 2009).

5. Ibid.
6. P. Starr, "The Meaning of Privatization," *Yale Law and Policy Review* 6 (1988): 6-41.
7. Thanks to Jeff Henig for helping me think about the disconnect between NCLB's theory and language or choice and its emphasis on public management and contracting arrangements.
8. M. Hill and P. Hupe, *Implementing Public Policy* (London: SAGE Publications, 2002).
9. M. W. McLaughlin, "Learning from Experience: Lessons from Policy Implementation," *Educational Evaluation and Policy Analysis* 9, no. 2 (1987): 171–178.
10. P. J. DiMaggio and W. W. Powell, "The Iron Cage Revisited: Institutional Isomorphism and Collective Rationality in Organizational Fields," *American Sociological Review* 48, no. 2 (1983): 147–160.
11. W. R. Scott, *Institutions and Organizations*, 2nd ed. (Thousand Oaks, CA: Sage, 2001).
12. J. R. Henig, *Rethinking School Choice: Limits of the Market Metaphor* (Princeton, NJ: Princeton University Press, 1995).
13. L. M. McDonnell, "No Child Left Behind and the Federal Role in Education: Evolution or Revolution?" *Peabody Journal of Education* 80, no. 2 (2005): 19–38.
14. Ibid.
15. P. Burch, "The New Educational Privatization: Educational Contracting in the Era of High Stakes Accountability," *Teachers College Record* 88, no. 2 (2006): 129–135; Burch, *Hidden Markets.*
16. M. Stein and E. Bassett, Staying Ahead of the Curve: A Value Chain Analysis of the K-12 Assessment Market. Boston: Eduventures Inc, 2004
17. Burch, "The New Educational Privatization."
18. Education Industry Association, "Overview of the Education Industry Association," n.d., http://www.educationindustry.org/tier.asp.
19. Textbook publishers such as Houghton Mifflin and McGraw-Hill were slow to see this change. Test publishers such as Princeton Review have been slowly moving in this direction.
20. Burch, *Hidden Markets.*
21. A. Molnar, *School Commericalism: From Democratic Ideal to Market Commodity.* New York: Routledge, 2005.
22. Edison Inc., *10-K* (New York: Author, September 9, 2003).
23. Ibid.
24. Chief executive officer, personal communication, June 30, 2006.
25. Chief executive officer, personal communication, June 28, 2006.
26. President George W. Bush discussing supplemental educational services available under the No Child Left Behind Act, October 5, 2006.
27. Burch, *Hidden Markets.*

28. K12, *Annual Report S-1/A* (Herndon, VA: Author, July 2007).
29. Firms' dependence on federal policy in defining business strategy continues under the Obama administration. In a 2010 SEC filing, Princeton Review stated to its shareholders,

> Public school funding is heavily dependent on support from federal, state and local governments and is sensitive to government budgets. In addition, the government appropriations process is often slow and unpredictable. Funding difficulties also could cause schools to be more resistant to price increases in our products, compared to other businesses that might be better able to pass on price increases to their customers.
>
> The SES market depends on federal, state, city and school district politics, all of which are in constant flux. In 2009 we experienced greater variability in school districts' willingness to fully utilize funds allocated to SES programs, as well as greater competition from individual school districts that developed and offered internally developed SES programs. In addition, there is increased uncertainty about the future of NCLB and the concept of adequate yearly performance as a means of allocating Title I funding. As a result, we are carefully monitoring developments in the SES regulatory framework, and we will continue to evaluate the extent of our participation in this business. *Princeton Review.* 2009. December 3 10K New York. Author.
>
> Other firms, while noting broadly downturn in U.S. economy, remain optimistic about federal monies as a secure source of revenue, and reference the Obama administration's support for charter schools and ARRA stimulus funds.

30. The Race to the Top initiatives were in development at the time of publication, with first round of grants being awarded to states. The Obama administration also had just released a blueprint for the reauthorization of ESEA that significantly revised the parent choice options.
31. U.S. Department of Education, *No Child Left Behind: A Desktop Reference, 2002* (Washington, DC: Office of Elementary and Secondary Education, 2002), http://www.ed.gov/admins/lead/account/nclbreference/reference.pdf.
32. It can be argued that the pairing of choice with stronger managerial incentives is completely consistent with the principle of neoliberal thinking—or the idea that achieving social aims, including equity-oriented goals, requires government entities to operate more like a market. However, I have come to see some of this lumping of quasi-market strategies in education as obscuring a distinction between "democratic" purposes (informed citizenry, schools that are responsive to less organized interests) and market-oriented reforms that position parents primarily as consumers of others designs.
33. Burch, *Hidden Markets.*
34. At the time of writing, the choice provisions of NCLB were still intact but their future unclear.

Chapter 10

1. http://www.ed.gov/news/pressreleases/2009/05/05192009c.html.
2. http://www.newschools.org/about/news/press-releases/summit-2009-awards.
3. The adjective *diverse* applies to the collection of organizations and the heterogeneity they add to the range of organizations active in providing public education services; they

may or may not be diverse internally. Diverse providers may operate in districts that are not actively managing portfolios of schools, but portfolio management districts almost always rely on diverse providers to a substantial extent.

4. T. Bartley, "How Foundations Shape Social Movements: The Construction of an Organizational Field and the Rise of Forest Certification," *Social Problems* 54, no. 3 (2007): 231.

5. M. D. Millot, "Leveraging the Market to Scale up School Improvement Programs: A Fee-for-Service Primer for Foundations and Nonprofits," in *Expanding the Reach of Education Reforms: Perspectives from Leaders in the Scale-up of Educational Interventions*, eds. T. K. Glennan, S. J. Bodilly, J. R. Galegher, and K. A. Kerr (Santa Monica, CA: RAND Corporation, 2004), 610.

6. P. J. DiMaggio and W. W. Powell, "The Iron Cage Revisited: Institutional Isomorphism and Collective Rationality in Organizational Fields," in *The New Institutionalism in Organizational Analysis*, eds. W. W. Powell and P. J. DiMaggio (Chicago: University of Chicago Press, 1991), 63-82.

7. Bartley, "How Foundations Shape Social Movements," 233.

8. All of the foundations' Form 990-PFs were downloaded at: http://www.eri-nonprofit-salaries.com.

9. For one of the top fifteen grant makers in 2000, the Ross Family Charitable Foundation, I was unable to locate a tax return (nor could I find any records of the foundation's grants on the Internet). Thus, I was unable to gather data on these grants, and the 2000 database includes fourteen of the fifteen largest grant makers.

10. I located this information for all but twenty-five grants in the 2005 dataset and for all but twenty-nine grants in the 2000 dataset.

11. S. P. Borgatti, M. G. Everett, and L. C. Freeman, *UCINET for Windows: Software for Social Network Analysis* (Harvard, MA: Analytic Technologies, 2002).

12. In 2000, grantees in Seattle received more funding from the Gates Foundation than any other district—nearly 18 percent of all K–12 grants distributed by Gates that year. In 2005, the Gates Foundation distributed 99 percent of its K–12 grants outside its home city, indicating a serious shift toward national ambitions.

13. http://www.newvisions.org/schools/nchs/index.asp.

14. http://www.urbanassembly.org/ourschools.html.

15. http://www.replications.org/schools.htm; http://www.studentachievement.org/home/schoolpartners_partnerschools_ny.html; http://www.nycoutwardbound.org/schools/visit.html.

16. S. Reckhow, "Waiting for Bill Gates: Following the Money Trail from Foundations to Urban School Districts" (presented at the Annual Meeting of the Midwest Political Science Association, Chicago, April 3-6, 2008).

17. Broad Foundation, *Annual Report*, 2008, 11.

18. Broad Foundation, *Annual Report*, 2009–2010, 9.

19. Interview with author, February 9, 2009.

20. Personal correspondence, July 7, 2008.

21. Interview with author, May 16, 2008.

22. J. Rubin, "L.A. Charter Schools Are Investment Grade to Broad," *Los Angeles Times*, May 24, 2007.

23. Bill & Melinda Gates Foundation, IRS Form 990-PF, 2005.

24. Bill & Melinda Gates Foundation, IRS Form 990-PF, 2005.

25. Foundations can make tax-exempt grants to for-profits if two conditions are met: "First, the grant funds must be used only to further the charitable activities of the grantee. Secondly, the foundation must exercise expenditure responsibility" ("Legal Basics: What Every Foundation Leader Should Know." Council on Foundations, 2007, p. 7); http://www.cof.org/files/Documents/Education_Collaborations/Handout1.pdf

26. B. Cervone, "When Reach Exceeds Grasp: Taking the Annenberg Challenge to Scale," in *Reconnecting Education and Foundations*, eds. R. Bacchetti and T. Ehrlich (San Francisco: Jossey-Bass, 2007), 147.

27. Ibid., 159.

28. Millot, "Leveraging the Market to Scale up School Improvement Programs," 608.

29. J. Scott, "The Politics of Venture Philanthropy in Charter School Policy and Advocacy," *Educational Policy* 23, no. 1 (2009): 116.

30. http://www.broadeducation.org/asset/1042-dkspeech_at_dems_for_ed%20reform.pdf.

31. DiMaggio and Powell, "The Iron Cage Revisited," 68.

32. Bartley, "How Foundations Shape Social Movements," 233.

33. See DiMaggio and Powell, "The Iron Cage Revisited"; Bartley, "How Foundations Shape Social Movements."

34. Interview with author, September 19, 2008.

35. http://www.newvisions.org/sites/default/files/publications/AnnualReport2008.pdf.

36. C. Hemphill, K. Nauer, H. Zelon, and T. Jacobs, *The New Marketplace: How Small School Reforms and School Choice Have Reshaped New York City's High Schools* (New York: The Center for New York City Affairs at the New School, 2009).

37. Ibid., 2.

38. http://www.broadeducation.org/about/faq.html#research.

39. Interview with author, March 9, 2009.

40. Cervone, "When Reach Exceeds Grasp," 153.

41. Borgatti, Everett, and Freeman, *UCINET for Windows*.

42. S. P. Borgatti, *NetDraw: Graph Visualization Software* (Harvard, MA: Analytic Technologies, 2002).

43. The coding of diverse provider organizations was based on two things. First, organizations that operate schools or provide specific services in school districts as their main function were coded as diverse providers. Second, other organizations and institutions that have broader functions, such as universities, were coded as diverse providers if they received a grant to provide specific services to school districts.

44. Grantees that received less than $100,000 in grants were excluded from this network.

45. Grantees that received less than $1 million in grants were excluded from this network.

46. N. Hoffman and R. Schwartz, "Foundations and School Reform: Bridging the Cultural Divide," in *Reconnecting Education and Foundations* (see note 25), 116.

47. Ibid., 115.

48. http://www.newschools.org/files/10YearReport.pdf.

49. Scott, "The Politics of Venture Philanthropy in Charter School Policy and Advocacy," 123.

50. Ibid., 123.

51. http://www.gatesfoundation.org/learning/Documents/Year4EvaluationAIRSRI.pdf.

52. http://blogs.edweek.org/edweek/campaign-k-12/2009/03/arne_duncan_advocates_mayoral.html

53. Broad Foundation, *Annual Report*, 2009–2010, 5.

Chapter 12

1. M. Lipsky, *Street Level Bureaucracy* (New York: Russsell Sage Foundation, 1983).
2. J. R. Henig and C. E. Stone, "Rethinking School Reform: The Distractions of Dogma and the Potential for a New Politics of Progressive Pragmatism," *American Journal of Education* 114, no. 3 (2008): 191–218.
3. D. M. Van Slyke, "The Mythology of Privatization in Contracting for Social Services," *Public Administration Review* 63, no. 3 (2003): 296–315.
4. J. Smith, C. Farrell, P. Wohlstetter, and M. Nayfack, "Mapping the Landscape of Charter Management Organizations" (paper presented at the 2009 Annual Meeting of the American Educational Research Association, San Diego, CA, and the 2009 National Charter Schools Conference, Washington, D.C., 2009).
5. C. N. Stone, J. R. Henig, B. D. Jones, and C. Perannunzi, *Building Civic Capacity: The Politics of Reforming Urban Schools* (Lawrence: University of Kansas Press, 2001).
6. A. Duncan, "Turning Around the Bottom Five Percent" (Secretary Arne Duncan's Remarks at the National Alliance for Public Charter Schools Conference, June 22, 2009, Washington, D.C.
7. H. Feigenbaum, J. R. Henig, and C. Hamnett, *Shrinking the State: The Political Underpinnings of Privatization* (Cambridge, UK: Cambridge University Press, 1998); J. R. Henig, "Understanding the Political Conflict over School Choice," in *How School Choice Affects Students and Families Who Do Not Choose*, eds. J. R. Betts and T. Loveless (Washington, DC: Brookings, 2005).
8. Henig and Stone, "Rethinking School Reform."
9. J. L. Hochschild, *The New American Dilemma: Liberal Democracy and School Desegregation* (New Haven, CT: Yale University Press, 1984); K. McDermott, *Controlling Public Education: Localism Versus Equity* (Lawrence: University Press of Kansas, 1999).

About the Editors

Katrina E. Bulkley is an associate professor of educational leadership at Montclair State University in New Jersey. Bulkley holds an MA in political science from the University of North Carolina at Chapel Hill and a PhD in administration and policy analysis from the Stanford University School of Education. She is the coeditor, with Priscilla Wohlstetter, of *Taking Account of Charter Schools: What's Happened and What's Next?* (Teachers College Press, 2004) and, with Lance Fusarelli, of "The Politics of Privatization in Education: The 2007 Yearbook of the Politics of Education Association," which was published as a special double issue of *Educational Policy.*

Jeffrey R. Henig is a professor of political science and education at Teachers College, Columbia University and a professor of political science at Columbia University. He earned his PhD in political science at Northwestern University in 1978. His most recent book, *Spin Cycle: How Research is Used in Policy Debates; The Case of Charter Schools* (Russell Sage Foundation/Century Foundation, 2008), won the 2010 American Educational Research Association "Outstanding Book" award.

Henry M. Levin is the William Heard Kilpatrick Professor of Economics and Education at Teachers College and the David Jacks Professor of Higher Education and Economics, Emeritus, at Stanford University. He is also the director of the National Center for the Study of Privatization in Education (NCSPE) and codirector of the Center for Benefit Cost Studies in Education (CBCSE), both at Teachers College. Levin has published extensively in the area of the economics of education and educational policy.

About the Contributors

Patricia Burch is a professor of public policy and education at the University of Southern California. She holds an MA in sociology and a PhD in education from Stanford University. She has written and lectured extensively on equity issues in contemporary education reform and K–12 education policy. She is the author of *Hidden Markets: The New Education Privatization* (Routledge Falmer Press, 2008).

Jolley Bruce Christman, PhD, is a founder and senior research fellow emeritus of Research for Action. Most recently, her research has focused on the topics of instructional communities, school leadership, organizational learning, and privatization in public education. Another important focus of her work has been on the use of research to inform policy and practice. She has worked extensively with teachers, principals, parents, students, and other public school activists to incorporate research and reflection into their efforts to improve urban public schools. She is a lecturer at the University of Pennsylvania's Graduate School of Education where she teaches qualitative research methods.

Joseph Daschbach is chief operations officer at Lagniappe Academies of New Orleans, a charter school opening in Fall 2010. In addition to his work with Lagniappe Academies, Dsachbach is currently working on his EdD in leadership, policy, and politics in the Education Leadership Department at Teachers College, Columbia University. A former teacher in both the New Orleans and New York City public school systems, Daschbach is interested in school governance reforms, particularly school choice and decentralization, including privatization. His dissertation uses the public school system in New Orleans as a case study to examine the impact of different political governance and organizational management structures on a variety of school-level indicators.

Michael DeArmond is a researcher at the Center on Reinventing Public Education and a doctoral student in educational leadership and policy studies at the University of Washington. His research interests include human resource management reforms and teacher policy. His recent publications include "Zooming in and Zooming Out: Rethinking School District Human Resources" with Kathryn Shaw and Patrick Wright in *Creating a New Teaching Profession* (Urban Institute Press, 2009) and "Is It Better to Be Good or Lucky? Decentralized Teacher Selection in 10 Elementary Schools" with Betheny Gross and Dan Goldhaber in *Education Administration Quarterly*. DeArmond holds an MPA in social policy and education from the University of Washington and a BA in history from Brown University. Prior to working as a researcher, he was a middle school history teacher.

Josh Edelman is the deputy chief of School Innovation (OSI) for the Washington, D.C., public schools. OSI oversees efforts to support and empower fifty-nine public schools through the infusion of unique programmatic elements targeting student investment and achievement. Previously, Edelman was the executive officer of the Office of New Schools (ONS) at Chicago Public Schools, which worked to recruit, develop, and support new schools and, ultimately, hold them accountable for high-performance measures. Edelman has also held various leadership positions at The SEED Foundation, first on the board of directors, then as principal of The SEED School, a public charter boarding school in Washington, D.C. Edelman is also a seasoned educator; after teaching at Milton Academy in Massachusetts, he taught social studies for seven years at Menlo-Atherton High School in Atherton, California, where he was also the founder and executive director for Realizing Intellect through Self-Empowerment (RISE), a youth development program targeted at African American youth. Edelman has a BA in American history from Harvard University, an MA in education from Stanford University, and a second master's degree in educational administration with administrative credential—also from Stanford University. He has received fellowships from the Mellon Foundation and Echoing Green and has served on the Boards of The SEED Foundation, the Center for the Future of Teaching and Learning, and was a MENtor for Real Men Read in Chicago.

Eva Gold, PhD, is a founder and senior research fellow at Research for Action. She has served as primary investigator for numerous local and national studies examining the dynamics between schools and communities, with a special focus on the role of community and youth organizing in school reform. She has published on the topics of privatization of public education, civic capacity in a privatizing school district, and on systemic barriers to the improvement of ninth grade in Philadelphia and the transition to high school. She is a lecturer at the Graduate School of Education at the University of Pennsylvania, where she leads a seminar for dissertation students on data collection, analysis, and writing.

Jonathan Gyurko is a cofounder of and vice president for policy and strategic planning at Leeds Global Partners, a new firm providing education advisory and implementation services in Abu Dhabi. From 2000 to 2010, he led school reform efforts in New York City, where he served in high-level positions at the New York City Department of Education and the United Federation of Teachers. Gyurko was a Morehead Scholar at the University of North Carolina at Chapel Hill and holds a MPA from Columbia University's School of International and Public Affairs. He is completing a PhD in politics and education from Teachers College, where he is also an adjunct instructor. He began his career as a teacher in South Africa.

Meredith I. Honig is associate professor of education policy and leadership at the University of Washington in Seattle where she is also a senior fellow at the Center for Educational Leadership, and an adjunct associate professor of public affairs. Her research and teaching focus on policy implementation, decision making, and organizational change in urban school systems. For the past fifteen years, she has studied how urban school district central office administrators participate in the implementation of ambitious educational improvement strategies, including school-community partnership initiatives, new small autonomous schools policies, and efforts to improve teaching and learning districtwide.

David Menefee-Libey is professor and chair of the Politics Department at Pomona College. He is coauthor of *Learning from LA: Institutional Change in American Public Education* (Harvard Education Press, 2008), and lead author of "The Persistence of Ideas in Los Angeles Public School Reform," a chapter in *The Transformation of Great American School Districts* (Harvard Education Press, 2008). Menefee-Libey received his PhD in political science from the University of Chicago. Before joining the Pomona faculty in 1989, he worked for the Community Renewal Society in Chicago, was a research fellow at the Brookings Institution, and did research on education policy in the Washington, D.C., office of the RAND Corporation.

Andre Perry, PhD, is associate dean of the University of New Orleans College of Education and Human Development and chief executive officer of the Capital One-University of New Orleans Charter School Network. As chief executive of UNO's charter school network, Perry is responsible for leading a pre-Kindergarten through high school educational network and fulfilling its mission of providing access and placements in community colleges and the University of New Orleans. He also serves as an advocate for quality public education, leading UNO's mission to rebuild its surrounding neighborhoods. Perry is charged with advancing the working partnership between UNO's faculty and charter school teachers, as well developing community partnerships with businesses, non-profit organizations, universities, schools, and neighborhood organizations. Perry earned his PhD in education policy and leadership, with an emphasis in higher education, from the University of Maryland. He holds a bachelor's degree from Allegheny College. His research and teaching interests are college access and retention, immigrant educational rights, and philosophy and history of education.

Sarah Reckhow is an assistant professor in the Department of Political Science at Michigan State University. She received her PhD in political science from the University of California, Berkeley. Her research focuses on urban politics, education policy, policy reform, and racial and ethnic politics. She is currently completing a book manuscript on the role of major foundations, such as the Gates Foundation, in urban school reform. Reckhow taught in the Baltimore City Public School System as a Teach for America corps member.

Index